THE MERTON ANNUAL

Studies in Culture, Spirituality, and Social Concerns

Volume 9   1996

Edited by

George A. Kilcourse, Jr.

A Liturgical Press Book

THE LITURGICAL PRESS
Collegeville, Minnesota

1   2   3   4   5   6   7   8   9

The Merton Annual

Volume 9	1996

REVIEWS

A Review Symposium of
Run to the Mountain: The Story of a Vocation
Edited by Patrick Hart, O.C.S.O.

Introduction

News of a More Complex
Merton Industry

George A. Kilcourse, Jr.

*"And while Joyceans are busily revealing Joyce to us, we must soberly
take account of the fact that they are also distorting and concealing him."*
Thomas Merton, "News of the Joyce Industry"[1]

It was the summer of 1968 and Patricia Welsh, reference librarian at Bellarmine College (for whom I worked as a student assistant), alerted me that Thomas Merton was dropping by that afternoon. She wanted to introduce me to him when he arrived to identify some correspondence being archived in the fledgling "Thomas Merton Room" collection. Like many Bellarmine students in those days, I knew that this monk from the Bardstown monastery was a famous writer. In my junior year of high school, Fr. C. J. Wagner had assigned *The Seven Storey Mountain* for our honors English course. (He also had coerced this same class to arrive at school half-an-hour early one semester so that he could read Shakespeare's tragedies to a captive audience— another formidable act of persuasion and a memorable indulgence on the part of a thespian wannabe.) I had already witnessed several "Merton sightings" during my three years at the college: once Merton in full Trappist habit had in tow a tall, elegantly dressed businessman, whom I later learned was his New Directions publisher, J. Laughlin; on another occasion Merton sailed through the library offices attired in

1. *The Literary Essays of Thomas Merton,* ed. Patrick Hart (New York: New Directions, 1981) 13.

Roman collar and black suit, and wearing a big yellow panama hat. Word usually spread among students in the Philosophy and English departments that he was on campus or had been observed with the dean, Franciscan Fr. John T. Loftus, or Msgr. Alfred F. Horrigan, the president. That was an era when Bellarmine College unashamedly claimed the Catholic ethos and insisted that it be reflected throughout the curriculum and campus life with an authentic and creative post-Vatican II élan. Merton enjoyed and encouraged that congenial habitat, even to the point of once directing a faculty retreat at the abbey.

Having been advised of the exact hour to hover around the library's audio-visual department adjacent to The Merton Room, I loitered for a few minutes until Ms. Welsh brought Thomas Merton for the introductions. He smiled pleasantly and shook my hand, and then he handed me a scrawled list of books and voiced a request that I retrieve them from the stacks. As I walked to the card catalog I realized that the volumes were all works either of or about James Joyce. Having fortunately found the books on the second-floor shelves, I returned to hand them to Merton just at the moment when another librarian arrived awkwardly with ice cream treats for the staff. Betty Delius, the director of the library, quickly whispered to offer hers to Merton— memory still sees the pool of melted, untouched chocolate sundae on the table after he left!

Two impressions of Merton's presence linger. First, the glimpse of his crystal, light blue eyes. He smiled easily and his eyes were clear and awake. There is a rare color photograph of Merton with his mentor, Dan Walsh, at Walsh's ordination in 1967, a happy day for both, and only that photograph comes close to recapturing for me the hue and spirit of those light blue eyes. The second impression also concerns a physical observation, the fact that Merton was so *ordinary*, not even noticeably tall. He was wearing his monastery denim work clothes, looking like every other Nelson County farmer. One might have expected a towering, seven-story high colossus when you met the "famous" Thomas Merton. Not so.

Anecdotal events about Merton punctuated my work with Ms. Welsh (after her marriage, Mrs. Oliver) during those final two collegiate years. There was the morning when she opened a letter from the Abbey of Gethsemani sent by a conscientious monk who had retrieved from the wastebasket a poem that Merton had typed off-the-cuff and then crumpled and tossed away. Together we read the hilarious mock rendition of Joyce Kilmer's "Trees," which Merton had transformed into "CHEE$E" by "Joyce Killer Diller." Then, in the summer of 1969, just after I had graduated, Ms. Delius asked me to assist with inventorying the avalanche of boxed Merton materials being sent from the monastery in the months after Merton's death. Unfolding the typescripts and manuscripts tucked into manila envelopes made me aware of both the energy and the hurried, primitive "filing system" that Merton had used. I sorted and catalogued peace writings and monastic essays. Notebooks were identified and recorded. Letters were placed in stacks and chronologically arranged, the then-unfamiliar names unreeling before my eyes: Wu, Allchin, Leclercq, Giroux, Von Balthasar, Van Doren, Levertov, Parra, Ahern, and on and on.

The autumn of 1969 brought me to New York City and graduate studies in theology at Fordham University. On occasion, someone who knew I was from Kentucky would remark about Merton's monastery being near Louisville, and I would be reminded of my brief encounter with "Father Louis." Since I was disciplining myself with the fervor and methodic work habits of a new graduate student, I spent much of my time in the Duane Library at Fordham. The holdings of the periodical room afforded me interludes to indulge in reading something besides Old Testament studies and historical reconstructions of the Modernist crisis. One October afternoon I distinctly remember paging through *The Sewanee Review* and being bolted by an article in the summer issue that had been on the shelves only a few weeks: "News of the Joyce Industry" by Thomas Merton. Yes, the books I had retrieved for Merton from Bellarmine's shelves had provided the raw materials for one of his final essays before the journey to Asia.

Months later in December 1969 I attended one of the country's first conferences on Merton after his death, this one at Fordham's Lincoln Center campus. I recall it was jointly sponsored by *Renascence*, the Catholic literary journal. Dom Damasus Winzen of Our Savior Monastery spoke with wisdom about Merton as a transcultural monk. And I listened spellbound as an erudite and witty Jesuit from Fordham's English faculty, Fr. John D. Boyd, delivered a seminal paper on Christian patterns in Merton's poetry. It began to dawn upon me that I was about to find in Father Boyd a genial mentor and the compass for my own doctoral dissertation on Thomas Merton.

The essay "News of the Joyce Industry" has repeatedly reoriented my own study of Merton for obvious personal reasons, but also for more important interpretive reasons. It is timely to recall the latter because of the particular essays in this volume of *The Merton*

Annual and because of the recent and ongoing publication of Merton's own journals. Let me offer an integrative reflection upon: (1) the new complexity in Merton scholarship; (2) insights from Merton's essay on Joyce; and (3) an introductory note to the excellent essays comprising this ninth volume of *The Merton Annual.*

I

Twenty-seven years after Merton's death, Abbot Timothy Kelly, O.C.S.O., of Gethsemani, once a novice under Merton, was finally invited to participate in an interview about his former novice master and confrere. It was only during the course of our conversation published here as "'The Great Honesty': Remembering Thomas Merton" that the fuller importance of Merton's genius in providing for the publication of his journals became apparent to me. It is easy to appreciate Merton's sensitivity in restricting the journals for twenty-five years after his death because of the candor and frankness with which he frequently makes mention of relationships with persons, many of whom would still have been living during this intervening quarter of a century. Abbot Timothy, however, puts it well in the interview: "I wonder if his voluminous writing isn't part of his own effort to keep from becoming a myth." The abbot rightly recommends that "every jot and tittle" and "the whole work" of Merton be published to give us access to "his very human, in the best sense of the word, person."

Let me offer but two small examples of the importance of ongoing research with and publication of the Merton sources. In his Joyce essay, Merton reminds readers that in the wake of distorting and concealing interpretations of the Irish author, "One can come back to [the works of Joyce] freely again."[2] Advice to be vigilantly heeded in the Merton industry.

In 1973 my research at Columbia University's Butler Library gave me access to Thomas Merton's letters to Mark Van Doren. They spanned some thirty years of correspondence beginning in 1939. A one-page 1939 handwritten letter headed with a typescript of the short poem "Song for Our Lady of Cobre" was sent from the mountains near Santiago while Merton was traveling in Cuba.[3] It is a fascinating dis-

---

2. Ibid., 21.
3. One vexing fact is the failure to publish this early version of "Song for Our Lady of Cobre" in the Merton letters to Mark Van Doren. See *The Road to Joy,*

covery because this original version of the thirteen-line poem uses two verbs that are later changed in the published poem. I surmise that Van Doren, who was awarded the Pulitzer Prize for poetry in 1940, suggested the changes and his former student agreed to revise accordingly.

In the same trove of Merton letters in the Van Doren files at Columbia, I discovered a 1964 letter to Bob Lax. The 1978 published version in *A Catch of Anti-Letters* failed to include the second page of the letter that adds three short paragraphs.[4] Even though Merton only playfully mocks the upcoming presidential election and goads Lax about Barry Goldwater's prospects, this oversight in the published edition of Merton-Lax letters gives a scholar pause. What other "jot and tittle" may have been missed?

What strikes me about these two examples is the matter of the "text" itself and what scholars refer to as a *critical edition* of an author's canon. Patrick O'Connell's discovery of additional Merton notebooks at St. Bonaventure's (reported in Patrick Hart's essay in this volume, where he reflects on the project of editing the Merton journals) dramatically makes this point. While this new material has been included in the paperback edition of *Run to the Mountain*,[5] it raises the kinds of questions that William H. Shannon poses in his contribution to *The*

---

selected and edited by Robert E. Daggy (New York: Farrar, Straus & Giroux, 1989) 7. The two variations from the published version go unremarked and are therefore lost to the reader. This points to a recurrent flaw in the five volumes of selected Merton letters: the principle of exclusion is neither clear nor apparent. Daggy touches momentarily on the matter when he states in the introduction to volume 2: "Some portions of letters have been omitted where material was of slight interest or repetitious" (xiii). Of "slight interest" to whom? I discovered a gem of a paragraph on Duns Scotus excised from a Mark Van Doren letter; see my *Ace of Freedoms: Thomas Merton's Christ* (Notre Dame, Ind.: University of Notre Dame Press, 1993) 242–3, n. 26. The omnipresent marks of ellipsis throughout the letters create an enormous research problem for Merton scholars. This is compounded by the fact that other letters are omitted entirely. Another example is the arbitrary omission from the October 31, 1964, letter from Merton to Robert Lax (discussed in the next paragraph of this introduction).

4. *A Catch of Anti-Letters* (Kansas City, Mo.: Sheed Andrews and McMeel, 1978). The new, 1994 edition of this volume does correct this oversight.

5. *Run to the Mountain*, ed. Patrick Hart (San Francisco: HarperCollins, 1996), appendix, 473–83. Another example of rewriting is Merton's notebook transformed into *Woods, Shore, and Desert*; see Michael Mott, *The Seven Mountains of Thomas Merton* (Boston: Houghton Mifflin, 1984) 521–2.

Merton Annual Symposium Review assessing the first of the Merton journals: "Were the journals, as we now have them, completely spontaneous, that is to say, just as he wrote them on the spur of the moment, without any emendation?" Shannon's conjecture that Merton indeed changed, corrected, added to, or even rewrote and polished material transferred from a smaller notebook into the larger ledger-type books he used for journals points to the complexity of establishing the original first-draft texts.

Biographer Michael Mott has built a compelling case throughout his superbly researched biography that Merton could be his own harshest critic. In *The Seven Mountains of Thomas Merton* his most persuasive example of the monk's elaborate reworking of material focuses upon the famous vision at Fourth and Walnut Streets in Louisville. Mott's careful textual analysis of both the original journals and the later, refined passage in *Conjectures of a Guilty Bystander* led him to conclude that "'The Vision in Louisville' has not worn well as writing." He goes on to identify "part of the problem" with Merton's seeing the crowds in Louisville "through his reading of the Third of Thomas Traherne's *Centuries:* 'There is no way of telling people that they are all walking around shining like the sun.'" Mott reminds us that it would be five years after the 1958 vision before Merton received a copy of Traherne's work. He quotes Merton's own complaint on September 20, 1965, about the tedious task of editing the journals for publication as *Conjectures:* "A lot of rewriting. For instance rewrote an experience of March 18, 1958 (entry of March 19) in light of a very good meditation on Saturday afternoon. Developed and changed. A lot of telescoping etc. In a word, transforming a Journal into 'meditations' or 'Pensées.'"[6]

Mott has quoted from an entry in Merton's journal for October 2, 1967, a passage that has significant bearing on this issue. Merton recorded a visit to The Merton Room at Bellarmine, that "bloody cuckoo's nest" as he called it; Mott juxtaposes this space with "the hermitage, the 'casa'" and lets Merton speak for himself:

> Merton Room again—ambiguity of an open door that is closed. Of a cell where I don't really live. Where my papers live. Where my papers are more than I am. I myself am opened and closed. Where I reveal most I hide most. There is still something I have not said: but what it is I don't know, and maybe I have to say it by not saying it. Wordplay won't do it, or *will* do it=Geography of Lograire.

6. Mott, *The Seven Mountains of Thomas Merton,* 312.

Writing this is most fun for me now, because in it I think I have finally got away from self-consciousness and introversion. It may be my final liberation from all diaries. Maybe that is my one remaining task.[7]

One colleague commented to me after his reading of *Run to the Mountain*, "Merton comes off as a real 'whiner' in this first journal." Perhaps that is the flip side of seeing his spiritual "struggle," the word so many reviewers and commentators have used to epitomize these journals. Nonetheless, Merton's desire for "my final liberation from all diaries" gives us pause as we receive this series of newly published journals.

A final note about the "texts" themselves. Patrick Hart points out that the publisher, HarperSanFrancisco, dictated that the "trade edition" would have a minimum of footnotes. I share with him and others a disappointment that readers are handicapped by this decision. There is, after all, some reasonable *midpoint* between such a trade edition and what the publisher is quoted as calling "a German doctoral dissertation with more footnotes than text." One would expect that the prestigious publishing event of the Merton journals would have equipped the editors with a stronger negotiating stance on this score, as well as on others.

II

The ongoing Merton industry needs to remind itself that an "examination of conscience" exercise resides in Merton's Joyce essay, "News of the Joyce Industry." It is a non-debatable fact of life that there is a "Merton Industry." So what caveats and resolutions can we garner and apply from his own critique of Joyce studies? Let me offer a handful, punctuated with excerpts from Merton himself.

(1) *"Others may be deterred from reading Joyce, convinced . . . that he is the exclusive property of humorless gnostics and mandarins."*[8]

A significant part of Merton's canon will remain the legitimate object of academic specialists and monastic scholars. But this in no way limits the popular appeal or interest in his work. It points to a different kind of interest and concern with Merton's writings and their

7. Ibid., 500.
8. "News of the Joyce Industry," *The Literary Essays of Thomas Merton*, 12.

place in American culture and spirituality. The key word in the quotation, above, is "exclusive." To that end, the editors of the Merton journals have assisted readers in gaining fuller access to his canon. However, we do need to brace ourselves for the inevitable new mountain of commentary and interpretations of the journals; some of it will inevitably be of poor quality and of little use in assisting readers as a Baedeker, or guidebook. One hopes for Merton studies to produce equivalents to Anthony Burgess' study of Joyce, described by Merton as "a readable book that makes Joyce more accessible to nonspecialists."[9] What may prove difficult for Merton enthusiasts is the sheer quantity of material in the seven projected volumes of journals. While they multiply the evidence of Merton's gifts as a writer, they also increase the amount of hitherto unpublished turgid prose he was capable of producing. To say nothing of disenchanting some readers with earlier, less polished versions of events such as the Fourth and Walnut vision.

(2) *"The mature critic recognizes that, in a work of such richness and complexity as Joyce's, one must not try to pin everything down, categorize, label, define, explain, classify, and prescribe. The art of Joyce is always rich in suggestion and in open possibilities, in delicate tensions, contrasts, unresolved problems that are meant to be left in the air, questions and polarities that are not meant to be reduced to definitive certainties. The stasis of the Joycean aesthetic is not a full stop in inertia, an end of living contradictions, but a delicate balance between them."*[10]

An axiom of Merton studies states that virtually everything he wrote holds an autobiographical dimension. If so, then few if any passages in Merton's writing could rival the hermeneutical key he offers here for interpreting his own work by way of analogy to Joyce's. There is an echo of Merton's new voice heard in the preface to *Conjectures of a Guilty Bystander:* "I do not have clear answers to current questions. I do have questions, and, as a matter of fact, I think a man is known better by his questions than by his answers."[11] Perhaps here we find an intersection with the first quotation because Merton recommends the comic characters in Joyce as comic "precisely because they insist on judging and solving, on giving absolute and definitive answers to

9. Ibid., 14.
10. Ibid., 14–15.
11. *Conjectures of a Guilty Bystander* (Garden City, N.Y.: Doubleday, 1966) 5.

questions that must remain more or less open if our lives are to preserve a living and human measure."[12] The abundant ironies in Merton's writing, particularly in his later poetry, are strongly influenced by this admiration of Joyce's work and Merton readers do well to regard his cue.

(3) *"Now the main problem of the Joyce industry is that it tends to reward scholars for ignoring and destroying this delicate balance. . . . The job to be done is not one of qualitative judgment but of quantitative accumulation. You pile up a mountain of evidence and set your chosen theme on top of it in splendid isolation. You select a small part of Joyce, remove it from its context, sterilize it, sedulously cleanse it from every trace of living and dynamic relationship with other organic parts of the whole."*[13]

The question of a complex identity comes into play in every domain of Merton studies. His multifaceted personality (monk, poet, social critic, ecumenist, mystic, sapiential theologian) demands an appreciation of each of these interrelated parts. John Howard Griffin first alerted us to the phrase "a hidden wholeness," from the poem "Hagia Sophia," as *the* metaphor for Merton's own complexity. For this very reason, an interdisciplinary approach proves the natural method for interpreting Merton's work. The importance of context plays an important role because whether a Merton quotation belongs in 1941, 1959, or 1967 can make all the difference; as can the fact of whether he utters a statement in his journals, a letter, an essay, a poem, or a book review. The key words in this excerpt from the Joyce essay are "dynamic" and "organic." Lacking those dimensions, interpretations of Merton risk what he lamented as fabricated, "artificial relationships" in Joyce studies, which "stand Joyce on his head." With sarcasm and scolding, Merton concluded, "Evidently the academic eye finds him more intriguing in that position."[14]

(4) *"Certainly Joyce was full of conflicts. He never fully recovered from the traumatic wounds of his childhood and adolescence. . . . The conscience of James Joyce . . . was the conscience of a European of the post-Victorian era, of a man in a sophisticated, complex, self-contradictory culture about to fall apart in World War I."*[15]

12. "News of the Joyce Industry," 15.
13. Ibid.
14. Ibid.
15. Ibid., 18

The careful research and interpretations of David D. Cooper's *Thomas Merton's Art of Denial* and Robert E. Daggy's pair of essays on Merton's childhood traumas[16] following his mother's death and his father, Owen's, extramarital affairs are ample evidence that Joyce and Gethsemani Abbey's famous monk held more in common than literary talents. But the latter half of this quotation reminds us of the complexity of the era in which Merton himself lived. He personified the Western world's spiritual quester in the wake of World War II horrors. And he lived to see the Neo-Orthodox systems of modernity (including the deliberations of the Second Vatican Council) begin to shift into a moment tentatively dubbed "post-modern." But Merton's roots were European, formed in the lycées and boarding schools of France and England. He eventually claimed American citizenship but embraced a wider citizenship in solidarity with the voices and sufferings of the Third World and of America's own racist-spawned ghettoes. As a cultural critic, Thomas Merton confronted us with the sins and emptiness of our North American pseudo-culture that gave us "mass man" and technology. Like Joyce, Merton was indeed "sophisticated and complex," attempting to serve as midwife to a future of creative, spiritual wakefulness.

(5) *"The year 1968 has seen the somewhat elaborate publication in book form of a Joyce notebook . . . under the title* Giacomo Joyce. *. . . It is a collection of prose epiphanies, mere essentials and jotted 'quiddities' of experience that are nowhere elaborated, nowhere developed. As such they have a kind of freshness and contemporaneousness which make the publication more than timely."*[17]

The further complexity of the Merton industry resides in his own "working notebooks." Mention is occasionally made of their eventual publication. However, if questions have been raised about the satisfactory nature of a "trade edition" of the journals, even more serious reservations remain for the project of publishing the cryptic, abbreviated, and erudite glosses in Merton's notebooks. In many in-

16. David D. Cooper, *Thomas Merton's Art of Denial* (Athens: University of Georgia Press, 1989); Robert E. Daggy, "Birthday Theology: A Reflection on Thomas Merton and the Bermuda Menage," *The Kentucky Review* 7 (1987) 62–89; and "Question and Revelation: Thomas Merton's Recovery of the Ground of Birth," *Your Heart Is My Hermitage*, papers presented at The Southampton Conference of the Thomas Merton Society at LSU College, May 1996 (London: The Thomas Merton Society of Great Britain and Ireland, 1996) 60–76.

17. "News of the Joyce Industry," 21.

stances he uses the right-hand page to note excerpts and the left-hand page to record his own reflections or queries; on occasion there are even original drafts of poems or journal entries. It will be fascinating to juxtapose these notebooks with both Merton's letters and his journals. So we will undoubtedly reach another new plateau of Merton studies when they are published, hopefully in a university press edition as they would warrant, replete with the requisite footnotes. Again, turning to Joyce, we find a hint of the same "treasure hunt"[18] Merton attributes to the author of *Ulysses* and *Finnegan's Wake:* "I submit that [the notebook's] importance is not to be measured simply by its few pages or by the fact that Joyce threw it aside. . . . It is an essential item in the Joyce canon and something that every interested reader of Joyce will surely enjoy."[19] *Continuabitur.*

III

Essays in this year's *The Merton Annual* exemplify how scholarly research can make Merton more accessible to a wider readership. Not only do the authors return to the sources and carefully analyze Merton's development, but they also situate their study in the contexts that contribute a more intelligent appreciation of Merton's *spiritual* journey. Thomas Merton's *He Is Risen,* originally published in 1975 by Argus Communications (and now out of print), provides readers with original Merton material. Margaret O'Brien Steinfels assesses the impact of *Gaudium et spes* some thirty years after Vatican Council II; Merton's own enthusiasm for this text was dramatically evident in his multifaceted initiatives in dialogue with the modern world. Lawrence S. Cunningham's "Harvesting New Fruits: Merton's 'Message to Poets,'" the springboard address to the 1995 meeting of the International Thomas Merton Society, appeals to this same instinct. He directs us to advance from Merton's own text in order "to engage some broader issues . . . at the heart of Merton's larger, more significant pertinence for us now thirty years distant from his original writing."

Christopher Burnham unravels the process of revisions in two Merton texts, the "Prisoner's Base" first sub-chapter of *The Seven Storey Mountain* and "Rain and the Rhinoceros." The result is a clarification of Merton's rhetorical purpose. It also reveals Merton's practice of the

18. Ibid., 12.
19. Ibid., 22.

editing process as the way he "writes his way back to experience" and self-discovery. Burnham's reconstruction of drafts of "Rain and the Rhinoceros" brilliantly interprets the shifts in Merton's own spiritual self. The reader will discover in this essay new insights about the seemingly insignificant Coleman stove and lantern at the hermitage, as well as Merton's emergence as social critic. Paul Pearson's study of Merton's autobiographical early novels complements Burnham's method of textual criticism. Pearson presents a persuasive case for the centrality of autobiography in these works, quite in contrast to the more intentionally autobiographical *The Seven Storey Mountain.* He discovers Merton "telling the story of his life" in these surviving texts of novels and elevates them to autobiographical status parallel to the journals and poetry.

Another context is provided by Ross Labrie's fine assessment of Merton's romanticism, and the influence and resonance with Emerson, Whitman, Thoreau, and Hart Crane. He analyzes how Merton's early inclination to romanticism is "crimped" by his desire to center himself in the Church, but reasserts itself in the final decade, replete with a social consciousness gravitating toward "political anarchy" and his overtures to Asian religion, resistant to rational approaches. Labrie's essay proves the importance of carefully contextualizing Merton.

Adding to these essays that evidence the writer's struggle as an exercise in self-discovery is Thomas Del Prete's investigation of Merton as a teacher of collegians at Columbia University and St. Bonaventure's. Del Prete has pioneered research on Merton's person-centered philosophy as the foundation for his pedagogy. The themes of autobiography and the truth illuminated by experience radiate from his careful reconstruction of Merton-the-teacher, coaxing his writing students to "trust their own personal experience." He rounds out this essay with excerpts from Merton's lectures to novices at Gethsemani, where the emphasis was not on information but education as an introduction to the artistic way of "seeing and responding to beauty in life."

A pair of essays completes this year's volume by directing attention to Merton's engagement with broader issues. Dennis Patrick O'Hara widens a horizon by speculating how Merton's awareness of the dawning ecological consciousness in his own time signals sources in his spirituality that we might well employ today. By paralleling the reflections of Thomas Berry with Merton's own emphasis upon creation (rooted in patristic and Franciscan sources) and christology, this essay draws readers to consider the contribution of contemplatives to the new spiritual arena of Eco-Theology. Under collective authorship, a trio of ethicists under the leadership of Glen Stassen pursues one of Merton's most ardent interests in their Abbey Center for the Study of Ethics conference report on "Just Peacemaking Theory." The initiatives they propose and the new perspective they introduce to discourse about peacemaking will be a novel, constructive approach to many readers. Duane K. Friesen's essay is appended to this report as a significant contribution to the same conference. In the fall of 1996 a follow-up conference convened at the Carter Center in Atlanta for further study of just peacemaking theory.

Two essays address Merton's writings on Asian spirituality. Robert Faricy provides a new hermeneutic for reading *Zen and the Birds of Appetite*. John Wu, Jr. offers an illuminating, careful interpretation of Merton's attention to Confucian rites.

Not to forget the monastic voices, two monks (who were also friends of Merton) contribute to our *Annual* with a note on the publication of the journals and an interview. Patrick Hart describes and reflects upon the project of publishing Merton's journals from his vantage as general editor of the series and editor of the first volume, *Run to the Mountain*. He also reconstructs his journey to Patmos to consult with Bob Lax about transcriptions of the St. Bonaventure's journals, and discusses the discovery of "The Fitzgerald File" at St. Bonaventure's, which contained additional entries that have now been appended to the paperback edition of *Run to the Mountain*. We reproduce the missing texts along with Hart's article. Abbot Timothy Kelly of Gethsemani responded affirmatively to my invitation for an interview and Kimberly Baker (who edited the interview) and I enjoyed a delightful afternoon in his office at the abbey. He both reminisced and looked forward while reflecting about his former novice master and brother monk. Now in his third decade as abbot at the Kentucky monastery, Abbot Timothy offers a unique perspective to readers about the person he remembers and reveres for "the great honesty" he humbly gave us.

Rounding out these pages is the annual bibliographical review-essay for 1995, written this year by Michael Downey. In addition to the regular book review section of the *Annual* there is also a Review Symposium on *Run to the Mountain*, both ably coordinated by Victor A. Kramer.

I owe a special debt of gratitude to Stefana Dan, a M.Div. student at the Southern Baptist Theological Seminary, for her genial assistance in proof-reading these pages you are about to read. And to Marquita Breit, Technical Services Librarian at Bellarmine College, for once again compiling our useful Index.

He Is Risen

Thomas Merton

"He has risen, he is not here . . . he is going before you to
Galilee" (Mark 16:6-7).

Christ is risen. Christ lives. Christ is the Lord of the living and
the dead. He is the Lord of history.

Christ is the Lord of a history that moves. He not only holds the
beginning and the end in his hands, but he is in history with us, walking ahead of us to where we are going. He is not always in the same
place.

The cult of the Holy Sepulchre is Christian only in so far as it is
the cult of the place where Christ is no longer found. But such a cult
can be valid only on one condition: that we are willing to move on, to
follow him to where we are not yet, to seek him where he goes before
us—"to Galilee."

So we are called not only to believe that Christ once rose from
the dead, thereby proving that he was God; we are called to *experience*
the Resurrection in our own lives by entering into this dynamic movement, by following Christ who lives in us. This life, this dynamism, is
expressed by the power of love and of encounter: Christ lives in us if
we love one another. And our love for one another means involvement
in one another's history.

Christ lives in us and leads us, through mutual encounter and
commitment, into a new future which we build together for one another. That future is called the Kingdom of God. The Kingdom is already established; the Kingdom is a present reality. But there is still
work to be done. Christ calls us to work together in building his
Kingdom. We cooperate with him in bringing it to perfection.

Such is the timeless message of the Church not only on Easter
Sunday but on every day of the year and every year until the world's

1

end. The dynamism of the Easter mystery is at the heart of the Christian faith. It is the life of the Church. The Resurrection is not a doctrine we try to prove or a problem we argue about: it is the life and action of Christ himself in us by his Holy Spirit.

A Christian bases his entire life on these truths. His entire life is changed by the presence and the action of the Risen Christ.

He knows he has encountered the Risen Christ, as Paul encountered him on the road to Damascus. Such an encounter does not have to be dramatic, but it has to be personal and real. Baptism is, of course, the seal and sign of this encounter.

But Baptism must be lived out in subsequent encounters with Christ: in the Eucharist, in the other sacraments, in reading and hearing the word of God, and in realizing that the word is preached to us personally. True encounter with Christ in the word of God awakens something in the depth of our being, something we did not know was there.

True encounter with Christ liberates something in us, a power we did not know we had, a hope, a capacity for life, a resilience, an ability to bounce back when we thought we were completely defeated, a capacity to grow and change, a power of creative transformation.

For the Christian there is no defeat, because Christ is risen and lives in us, and Christ has overcome all that seeks to destroy us or to block our human and spiritual growth.

In the Easter sequence the Church sings of the duel of death and life in our heart. This is a bitter, desperate fight, the combat of life and death in us, the battle of human despair against Christian hope.

The risen life is not easy; it is also a dying life. The presence of the Resurrection in our lives means the presence of the Cross, for we do not rise with Christ unless we also first die with him. It is by the Cross that we enter the dynamism of creative transformation, the dynamism of resurrection and renewal, the dynamism of love.

The teaching of St. Paul is centered entirely on the Resurrection. How many Christians really understand what St. Paul is talking about when he tells us that we have "died to the Law" in order to rise with Christ? How many Christians dare to believe that he who is risen with Christ enjoys the liberty of the sons of God and is not bound by the restrictions and taboos of human prejudice?

To be risen with Christ means not only that one has *a choice* and that one *may* live by a higher law—the law of grace and love—but that one *must* do so.

The first obligation of the Christian is to maintain his freedom from all superstitions, all blind taboos and religious formalities, indeed from all empty forms of legalism.

Read the Epistle to the Galatians again some time. Read it in light of the Church's summons to complete renewal.

The Christian must have the courage to follow Christ. The Christian who is risen in Christ must dare to be like Christ: he must dare to follow conscience even in unpopular causes. He must, if necessary, be able to disagree with the majority and make decisions that he knows to be according to the Gospel and teaching of Christ, even when others do not understand why he is acting this way.

"The followers of Christ are called by God not according to their accomplishments, but according to his own purpose and grace."* This statement effectively disposes of a Christian inferiority complex which makes people think that because they never have amounted to anything in the eyes of others, they can never amount to anything in the eyes of God. Here again we see another aspect of St. Paul's teaching on freedom.

Too many Christians are not free because they submit to the domination of other people's ideas. They submit passively to the opinions of the crowd. For self-protection they hide in the crowd, and run along with the crowd—even when it turns into a lynch mob. They are afraid of the aloneness, the moral nakedness, which they would feel apart from the crowd.

But the Christian in whom Christ is risen dares to think and act differently from the crowd. He has ideas of his own, not because he is arrogant, but because he has the humility to stand alone and pay attention to the purpose and the grace of God, which are often quite contrary to the purposes and the plans of an established human power structure.

If we have risen with Christ then we must dare to stand by him in the loneliness of his Passion, when the entire establishment, both religious and civil, turned against him as a modern state would turn against a dangerous radical. In fact, there *were* "dangerous radicals" among the Apostles.

Simon the Zealot was a member of the extreme left wing of Jewish politics, a would-be freedom fighter against Roman imperial rule.

---

*Vatican Council II, "Constitution on the Church," n. 40.

If we study the trial and execution of Jesus we find that he was condemned on the charge that he was a revolutionary, a subversive radical, fighting for the overthrow of legitimate government.

This was not true in the political sense. Jesus stood entirely outside of all Jewish politics, because his Kingdom was not of this world. But his actions could be twisted to look like political revolutionism. And yet he was a "freedom fighter" in a different way. His death and resurrection were the culminating battle in his fight to liberate us from all forms of tyranny, all forms of domination by anything or anyone except the Spirit, the Law of Love, the "purpose and grace" of God.

When we understand these things, we can understand what lies behind St. Paul's words in praise of the freedom which comes only in the Cross and Resurrection of Christ: "When Christ freed us," said Paul, "he meant us to remain free. Stand firm, therefore, and do not submit again to the yoke of slavery."

This is in the Epistle to the Galatians (5:1), where Paul rebukes the Christian converts for still thinking that certain legal observances were necessary for them: as if they could not be saved without being circumcised. The Galatian converts were tempted to something that we might describe today as religious overkill. They wanted to make absolutely sure that everything was completely taken care of.

So they not only adopted the Christian faith but all the ritual practices of Judaism as well. Thus, if Christianity turned out to be not good enough, they would still be covered by Jewish observance!

This spirit of overkill is characteristic of the Christian who is afraid to be simply a Christian in the world of our time. He is not content with faith in the Risen Christ, not content with the grace and love of Christ: he wants the comfort and justification of being on the side of wealth and power. In some cases, Christianity becomes literally the religion of overkill: the religion in which you prove your fidelity to Christ by your willingness to destroy his enemies ten times over. In order to do this you have to conveniently forget all those disturbing statements in the New Testament about the love of enemies!

St. Paul says, "The whole of the Law is summarized in a single command: Love your neighbor as yourself. . . . If you are guided by the Spirit you will be in no danger of yielding to self-indulgence, since self-indulgence is the opposite of the Spirit" (Galatians 5:14-16). He goes on to outline the hard line of self-denial which is inseparable from the Cross of Christ.

We have been called to share in the Resurrection of Christ not because we have fulfilled all the laws of God and man, not because we are religious heroes, but because we are suffering and struggling human beings, sinners fighting for our lives, prisoners fighting for freedom, rebels taking up spiritual weapons against the powers that degrade and insult our human dignity.

If we had been able to win the battle for freedom without his help, Christ would not have come to fight for us and with us. But he has come to gather us around him in the battle for freedom. The fact that we have been wounded in the fight, or the fact that we may have spent most of the time, so far, running away from the battle makes no difference now. He is with us. He is risen.

The Gospel account of the Resurrection in Mark is very suggestive. Not only is the Resurrection the key and center of the Christian life, but our Easter experience often follows the pattern of the experience of the Apostles and other witnesses of the Resurrection. The experience of the holy women at the tomb gives us a typical example of the dynamics of Christian faith.

We often forget that in all accounts of the Resurrection, the witnesses started out with the unshakable conviction that Christ was dead. The women going to the tomb thought of Jesus as dead and gone.

They had only one thing in mind: to embalm his body. But there was a problem. The tomb was sealed with a stone too heavy for them to move. They did not know how they would find someone who would roll away the stone for them so they could come to his dead body.

Now this is a kind of psychological pattern for the way we too often act in our Christian lives. Though we may still "say" with our lips that Christ is risen, we secretly believe him, in practice, to be dead. And we believe that there is a massive stone blocking the way and keeping us from getting to his dead body. Our Christian religion too often becomes simply the cult of the dead body of Christ compounded with anguish and desperation over the problem of moving the immovable stone that keeps us from reaching him.

This is no joke. This is what actually happens to the Christian religion when it ceases to be a really living faith and becomes a mere legalistic and ritualistic formality. Such Christianity is no longer life in the Risen Christ but a formal cult of the dead Christ considered not as the Light and Savior of the world but as a kind of divine "thing," an extremely holy object, a theological relic.

This is the result of substituting something else for the Living Presence and Light of Christ in our lives. Instead of the unspeakable, invisible, yet terribly near and powerful presence of the Living Lord, we set up a structure of pious images and abstract concepts until Christ becomes a shadow. At last he becomes a corpse-like figure of wax. Yet people go to extraordinary lengths to venerate this inert object, to embalm it with all kinds of perfumes, and to make up fantastic tales about what it can do to make you rich and happy by its powerful magic.

We must never let our religious ideas, customs, rituals, and conventions become more real to us than the Risen Christ. We must learn, with St. Paul, that all these religious accessories are worthless if they get in the way of our faith in Jesus Christ, or prevent us from loving our brother in Christ. Paul looked back on the days when he had been a faultless observer of religious law, and confessed that all this piety was *meaningless*. He rejected it as worthless. He wanted one thing only. Here are his words:

> I believe nothing can happen that will outweigh the supreme advantage of knowing Christ Jesus my Lord. For him I have accepted the loss of everything as so much rubbish, if only I can have Christ and be given a place in him. I am no longer trying for perfection by my own efforts . . . but I want only the perfection that comes from faith in Christ. . . . All I want to know is Christ in the power of his Resurrection and to share his sufferings by reproducing the pattern of his death (Philippians 3:8-11).

When the holy women arrived at the tomb, they found the stone was rolled away. But the fact that the stone was rolled away made little difference, since the body of Jesus was not there anyway. The Lord had risen. So too with us. We create obscure religious problems for ourselves, trying desperately to break through to a dead Christ behind a tombstone. Such problems are absurd. Even if we could roll away the stone, we would not find his body *because he is not dead.*

He is not an inert object, not a lifeless thing, not a piece of property, not a super-religious heirloom: HE IS NOT THERE, HE IS RISEN.

The Christian life, Christian worship, Christian community, the Eucharist, all these have been obscured by a limited ritualistic piety that insists on treating the Risen Lord as if he were a dead body, a holy object, not Spirit, and Life, and Son of the Living God.

Today let us come with faith to the banquet of the Lamb, the Risen Savior, to the Bread of Life that is not the food of the dead but the true and Risen Body of Christ. He who encounters the Risen Christ in the banquet of his Body and Blood will live forever!

Come, People of God, Christ our Passover is sacrificed, and in sharing his banquet we pass with him from death to life! He has risen . . . he is going before us into his Kingdom! Alleluia!

Merton Lecture, Columbia University, November 15, 1995

Margaret O'Brien Steinfels

Gathering in this domed space reminds us of the perennial human effort to create a sacred space, a space set apart in the midst of human work and human folly. The great dome that rises above us both contains and expresses the longings of men and women for a sign of the transcendent, of the divine. The roundedness of its height and its expanse looms above us as the undercroft of heaven beyond which human hearts have risen for millennia in the hope of glimpsing some larger purpose for the human travail and human triumph that can be found just outside those back doors.

Many religious traditions gather under this dome with different purposes, different prayers, different beliefs. But who could doubt that every eye is drawn upward with the same hope and the same yearnings.

Thirty years ago when *Gaudium et spes* (Pastoral Constitution on the Church in the Modern World) was promulgated that was not so. Oh, Catholics may have gathered here for Mass—down in the red room if I remember correctly. But then our differences were far greater than they are today—not only with the Episcopalians for whom this chapel was once consecrated, but the Lutherans, and certainly Buddhists and Hindus. Our differences are still considerable, but in this space it is our common yearnings that shine forth.

The Second Vatican Council was for Catholics the moment when we stopped concentrating on what divided us from other Christian bodies, from Judaism and other faith traditions, from the world outside our doors, and began looking at what united us with the whole human community. Many of the documents of Vatican II lent force to that reorientation. This fall we celebrate not only the thirtieth anniversary of *Gaudium et spes,* about which I want to speak tonight, but *Nostra aetate* (Declaration on Relations with Non-Christian Religions) and *Dignitatis humanae* (Declaration on Religious Liberty).

There may have been other documents that had a more immediate, clear, and direct impact on the life of the church itself: the constitutions on revelation, liturgy, and the church, for example. But in a fashion more diffuse—in fact, in a fashion that suffused everything that the council did—none was more important than *Gaudium et spes.* For many of the great minds that have reflected on the Second Vatican Council, *Gaudium et spes* is the text that summed up what was particular and distinctive about Vatican II, the pivot on which the conciliar enterprise turned and the lens through which we should read all the conciliar texts.

Thirty years after the council, one finds among Catholics, and sometimes non-Catholics too, a certain distress. Among the more traditional it is expressed as a keen sense of loss at what is gone; among the more progressive, a keen sense of disappointment that more has not been achieved. As we all know and experience, there is more than a little disorientation in the whole Church, along with worthy disagreements and silly squabbling. Robert Lauder succinctly captures that sense in a short essay recently published in *Commonweal* in which he remembers his ordination thirty years ago, just before the final session of the council (October 20, 1995): "Much that was firm was shaken, much that was crystal clear became cloudy, and much that was deemed immutable changed."

Gaudium et spes has not escaped the resulting mood of complaint; in fact, for some it is the main cause of complaint. It has been accused of being naively optimistic. It has opened the Church itself to the insidious and corrosive influences of democracy and populism. In some quarters of the Church, it has been brushed aside as a period piece, largely superseded by the more recent statements and encyclicals of John Paul II (even though themes and phrases from it appear prominently in the pope's address to the United Nations earlier this fall).

Yet I think that if we are to shake off the malaise, the polarization, the ecclesiastical gridlock that often seems to afflict the people of God today, *Gaudium et spes* remains the restorative, the balance, the compass, and the inspiration that the Catholic Church, indeed the whole Christian Church, needs.

The subject of *Gaudium et spes,* we should remember, was not the Church in the world, a subject as old as St. Paul and on which the classical treatment, at least for me, remains H. Richard Niebuhr's *Christ and Culture.* No, *Gaudium et spes* addressed the "church in the world today" or, even better, the "church in the modern world."

It was the Church's relationship with modernity that *Gaudium et spes* reconsidered. It attempted to nurture a conversation where there had been a blanket refusal to be on speaking terms at all. Thirty years have taught us that this conversation is not easy to sustain, that it demands skills in listening, precision in speaking, and an integrity in both maintaining and renewing our identity—all skills that we seem not to have yet sufficiently developed.

"Siege mentality" is by now such a well-worn way of describing the Church's stance toward the world in the nineteenth century and first half of the twentieth that we forget how literally true it was. The emblematic gesture took place in 1870. Pope Pius IX declared himself a prisoner in the Vatican as a protest at the seizure of the papal states by the newly united state of Italy. This was the culmination of the papacy's long struggle against the Enlightenment, the French Revolution, the spread of liberalism, nationalism, and democracy. Six years earlier, in 1864, Pius had condemned all of this in the Syllabus of Errors, along with Bible societies, the separation of Church and state, freedom of the press, freedom of religion, all summed up in the denial that "the Roman pontiff can and ought to reconcile himself and reach agreement with progress, liberalism and modern civilization."

This condemnation, unfortunate as it was, was not unprovoked. Hurricane John Paul II is very fresh in our memories, and all the recent attention and affection heaped upon him by hundreds of thousands of the faithful and by the world's political leaders should not bring us to forget that the nineteenth century began with Napoleon actually humiliating and imprisoning not one, but two successive popes. The toll that the century took on the Church can be seen in this: it was a century that began with the political power imprisoning the pope and ended with the pope imprisoning himself.

That image of the prisoner in the Vatican conveys another deep and ironic truth. The Church was at war with modernity. Yet in the very act of waging that war the Church itself became a very modern institution. Father Joseph Komonchak has pointed this out in a brilliant and too little known essay: in opposing the rise of centralized states and highly articulated bureaucracies, the church itself took on, as never before, the character of a centralized government and highly articulated bureaucracy. To the new popular loyalties, mass organizations, and encompassing ideologies, the church raised its own parallel structure of popular devotions, organizations of everything from Catholic farmers to Catholic trade unions and Catholic political parties, and an apologetics of Catholicism that with implacable logic and fervent exclusion of every doubt or smidgen of mystery matched the militant tracts of positivists, Darwinians, and socialists.

In other words, even while the Catholic Church was aggressively refusing to be at home in the modern world, the structures and mentality of the modern world were making themselves very much at home in the Church. It is a situation that we still live with, and it should be a warning to us never to pretend that too sharp a line can be drawn between the Church and the social-cultural-political soup in which it swims. In fact, *Gaudium et spes* contains some very instructive language on this point. In paragraph 40, which opens chapter 4, we read: "The church at once a visible organization and a spiritual community, travels the same journey as all mankind and shares the same earthly lot with the world. . . . That the earthly and the heavenly city penetrate one another is a fact open only to the eyes of faith."

The idea of a sharp separation between believers and the world in which they live may be approximately possible for a small sect of "come-outers," as the Pilgrims were originally called. It is not a very credible stance for a Church of a billion people, which baptizes infants before they can declare themselves, embraces sinners before they can confess themselves, excommunicates only in exceptional cases, and leaves it to God to separate the wheat from the chaff.

It was to this outward breach and unacknowledged embrace between the Church and modernity that *Gaudium et spes* finally spoke in 1965. I want tonight to look at the impact of *Gaudium et spes* over the last thirty years, to consider the criticisms raised against it, and to make the case for its continuing relevance. But first, in the course of an anniversary year, it is not inappropriate to spend a few minutes looking at what it said, a little *explication de texte à la Steinfels.*

Gaudium et spes begins:

> The joy and hope, the grief and anguish of the men [and women] of our time, especially those who are poor or afflicted in any way, are the joy and hope, the grief and anguish of the followers of Christ as well. Nothing that is genuinely human fails to find an echo in their hearts.

In 1965 these were astonishing words; those who heard them and saw their full import could not fail to have been moved by them. They set loose a new dynamic, one of dialogue and engagement. This first paragraph signaled a profound shift in the Church's understanding of itself and its relation to the world. And it ends with the sentence: "Christians cherish a feeling of deep solidarity with the human race and its history."

I suppose that can sound banal, even laughable: Yes, of course, Christians live in this world, are part of this human race; for better, and not infrequently worse, we have made this history along with everyone else. Like everyone else, this is the only world that Christians have. We do not inhabit a world apart from others. So said *Gaudium et spes* as it began to dismantle a reified other world in which at least some Catholics thought they lived.

That sentence—"Christians cherish a feeling of deep solidarity with the human race and its history"—admits two things: a sense of historical consciousness and a commitment to human solidarity—not of a history through which the Church passes unaffected by events, not a world of two humanities, Catholic and non-Catholic, but of one. We all live in the same world, a world that the second paragraph describes "as the theatre of human history, bearing the marks of its travail, its triumphs and failures," but also a world that the Christian knows in faith "has been created and . . . sustained by the love of its maker, which has been freed from the slavery of sin by Christ."

The contrast between the seen and the unseen is drawn, not in some gnostic way, but in a straightforward language, acknowledging the world as it sees and understands itself. The very same world, the council wants to say, can also be known and more fully understood through the revealed word of God and through Christian understanding of creation, the incarnation, and the saving acts of Jesus.

This turn outward, this change of focus also requires a change of heart, of affect; there is a change in ideas and a change in language and tone. There is a surprising warmth and emotional resonance in *Gaudium et spes*. It does not condemn in the rhetoric of Pius IX or instruct in cool scholastic propositions; rather, as paragraph 3 says, "it longs to set forth the way it understands the presence and function of the Church in the world of today," which is "to carry on the work of Christ under the guidance of the Holy Spirit," the work of "Christ who came into the world to bear witness to the truth, to save and not to judge, to serve and not to be served." Those words bespeak a meekness that the Church had rarely used of itself; words addressed more-over not only to the world, but to the church its very self, words whose standards are not earthly power or worldly ambition, but the example of Christ.

Following this preface, the introduction (4–10) describes and analyzes the Church's responsibility for "reading the signs of the times and of interpreting them in the light of the Gospel." Repeated through-out the introduction is a major theme of the whole document and of the council, and certainly an important sign of the times: that of change and its consequences; of human progress and of scientific advances that benefit humankind and yet turn upon us and confront us with new dilemmas and conundrums. Change affects the individual and society in ways that are often unanticipated. Changes come about so rapidly, one upon the other, that the very foundations of social and cul-tural life are shaken and fractured, what sociologists and philosophers now call the reflexivity of the modern world.

There is a synergistic effect in these changes, the whole begins adding up to more than the sum of its parts; in fact, *Gaudium et spes* was speaking of the whole achievement and dilemma of moderniza-tion. If the Church was late in acknowledging modernization, that has not been a barrier to its understanding not only its benefits, but the darker elements of modernity as well.

At the center of these challenges stands the human person, de-scribed in paragraph 9 as "an individual and as a member of society who craves a life that is full, autonomous, and worthy of his/her na-ture as a human being; he/she longs to harness for his/her own wel-fare the immense resources of the modern world." But this is not, you can be sure, Candide being profiled here. There is self-consciousness and the power of thought to turn back upon itself; individualization brings with it the erosion of community; and with the growing capac-ity to control human destiny comes fear of annihilation. *Gaudium et spes* describes this paradox of modernity as the "dichotomy of a world that is at once powerful and weak, capable of doing what is noble and what is base, disposed to freedom and slavery, progress and decline, brotherhood and hatred."

Even religion is not immune from the effects of modernity. In paragraph 7 *Gaudium et spes* acknowledges that magical world views which sometimes support religious belief are passing away at the same time that people are demanding a more personal sense of the divine. The Church, it says, has a responsibility to speak of that which is not apparent, what is hidden; to pay attention to the human condition in its modern manifestation; to say that religion has meaning in everyday life and to say it in a way that can be apprehended. And finally, to say it "with a loving awareness of humanity in its actual condition and a loving sense of responsibility to it." Religion and a spiritual life are not just the province of clergy and religious, but of everyone. Fiats, mystification, obscurantism can no longer serve as props to religious authority.

The Church that wrote *Gaudium et spes* was not only turning from a monological to a dialogical stance toward the world, it was (we were) beginning a dialogue with its own people (with ourselves), all of us, the whole Church. And it is perhaps this dialogue more than any other that frustrates and vexes us today.

What was the world with whom this dialogue has taken place like?

In 1965, the council ended and the spirit of Vatican II began. *Gaudium et spes* appeared in the United States at a time of great hope and optimism. There were certainly clouds on the horizon—urban rioting in 1964, Watts in 1965. The cold war was sealed in concrete by the building of the Berlin Wall; there was continuing and apparently irremediable isolation of Eastern Europe; international relations were fixed around the cold war's bipolar goals. Ever increasing militarization of the world's economies was threatening the promise of development and democracy in newly decolonized nations of Africa and Asia. Certainly many problems had to be faced. It may be hard to believe now, but in 1965 most Americans believed that the economic and political framework for the struggles against racism, poverty, hunger, and tyranny were in place, that the war on poverty, affirmative action, and Great Society programs could remedy problems at home. The Soviets could be beaten without selling our souls; development in far-off lands could be helped through the efforts of American college students organized into a Peace Corps. The prospects seemed good for steady progress without intractable conflict. In 1965, *Gaudium et spes* was read by American Catholics with eagerness and enthusiasm.

This optimism dissipated under a long string of unanticipated turns in the story; I will get back to those in a moment.

I want to first pick up another strand that *Gaudium et spes* helped weave in the history of our time, for what it said and encouraged had an enormous if sometimes delayed impact around the world. Think of Eastern Europe, where the most amazing and unexpected events of 1989 and 1990 took place. Attention has focused on leaders, military might, political staying power, and strategy. But among the most important actors were the people of Central Europe themselves; especially in Poland and Czechoslovakia, where brave groups pressed back, in a nonviolent way, the constrictions of Soviet power. The key idea here is summed up in Poland's labor union movement, solidarity, a phrase from *Gaudium et spes*. It is also a phrase raised as a *cri de coeur* in Czechoslovakia post-1968, and whose velvet revolution was built on the commitment of the "solidarity of the shaken" (in Jan Patocka's evocative phrase).

Both a civil and religious understanding of human dignity and human rights is implicit in this sense of human solidarity; it recognizes the innate value of each and every person and the communal ground upon which those human rights must be established, acknowledged, observed.

The international human rights movement has varied origins: in the work of Pawel Wlodkowic at the fifteenth-century Council of Constance (as the pope reminded the UN), and certainly in the values of the Enlightenment and of liberal political thought. But at Vatican II, in *Gaudium et spes*, and in subsequent papal and episcopal documents, many of them from our own bishops, the Church has supported and augmented a view of human rights largely, though not wholly, compatible with the secular one. As a result, all around the world—in El Salvador, Chile, Brazil, and the Philippines—we have seen over the last three decades Catholic communities living out the meaning of human dignity and claiming their human rights against political and economic tyranny—sometimes suffering martyrdom. In lands where Catholics are a minority—in South Africa, especially—solidarity with the majority helped to bring down tyranny in a nonviolent struggle. And now often in fragile but promising ways, all of these countries are becoming democratic societies committed to human dignity and human rights. What would Pius IX say?

In the United States, the consistent ethic of life—another form of the Church's embrace of human rights—recognizes the dignity of every individual from the unborn to the dying, from the immigrant to the prisoner on death row, and acknowledges that those rights can only be protected in communities, can only have meaning in solidarity with the poor and the vulnerable.

But as all of this was going on, the world was passing through a very different period, sometimes termed in shorthand "the Sixties."

The struggle in the Third World about which I just spoke, from Latin America to South Africa, gave rise to liberation theologies, some of which stressed conflict and political-cultural insurgency. In the United States and Western Europe, there were the beginnings of the counterculture whose attacks on authority came to permeate American society and American campuses in the late sixties and early seventies. This counterculture challenged virtually all authorities, traditions, and established institutions, all the while accelerating the secularization well underway in Europe. The two places, Poland and Ireland, which, for different reasons, were exceptions to that secularization, are today struggling to be churches in societies confronting and being confronted by modernity belatedly and often with a vengeance.

These events, part and parcel of the last thirty years, have left another legacy of *Gaudium et spes:* the legacy of its critics.

They come from both left and right. From the liberationist left came the view that modernity was a much nastier, more exploitative, more intractable place than that proposed by the liberal and reformist agenda, which they read in *Gaudium et spes.* In particular, the Marxist-influenced exponents of this criticism argued that *Gaudium et spes* did not acknowledge the possibility that there were fundamentally different views of the world, depending on one's position in society, that is, from the bottom or from the top, and that these class conflicts could not be bridged by anything but struggle, possibly even armed struggle.

This liberationist left was not against dialogue but favored a very selective dialogue, limited largely to those forces that saw modernity in the same highly ambivalent fashion as they. Some of this critique remains unanswered today. But some of it simply missed the subtlety and complexity in *Gaudium et spes*'s own view of modernity. Ironically enough, this critique was most seriously undermined by its own naiveté and lack of ambivalence about the utopian project of revolutionary socialism in which it vested so much hope, in Cuba, Nicaragua, and other places, especially in Central and Latin America.

From the right, the challenge to *Gaudium et spes* took several forms. The first was simply an extension of the pre-conciliar attitude toward modernity. Some conservatives in the curia and elsewhere viewed the council as something like a massive failure of nerve and dialogue, a prelude to surrender.

In the late sixties and early seventies, however, this outlook won new recruits, shell-shocked by the cultural revolution in society and its influence in the Church, or disappointed that secularization had accelerated in Western Europe, especially in Germany, France, and the Netherlands, which had been wellsprings of the council.

Like the left, the right concluded that the modern environment was far more hostile to Christianity and the Church than they thought *Gaudium et spes* recognized. From this world there was less to learn and more to fear, hence sympathy with it was less justified and dialogue with it much riskier. Once again emphasis shifted not just to the threat that the modern world posed to humanity in all its fullness—a theme certainly sounded in *Gaudium et spes*—but to a threat very specifically aimed at the integrity of the Church.

In practical terms, this viewpoint has produced attempts to restore the tightly bounded Church of the preconciliar period. If this approach succeeds at all in today's very different historical circumstances, it is hard to see how the outcome will be any different than what it was in preconciliar Western Europe: the decline of religious practice among masses of people, the isolation of the Church from the mainsprings of culture, and the weakening of the Church's ability, as in the era of fascism and Nazism, to resist the most ominous currents of history.

Yet another, more sophisticated variation on this critique of *Gaudium et spes* has emerged, one that makes ample use of the concept of "postmodernity." Postmodernity, of course, can be a very flexible, even vaporous notion. In this case, it means the extreme relativism that undermines all of the major post-Enlightenment challenges to religious faith, including scientific materialism, historicism, Darwinism, Marxism, Freudianism, and belief in progress.

In this analysis, modernity's challenge to the Church had been vanquished, largely by modernity's own self-destruction. Postmodernity, in its jumble of fragmented experience without any direction, and in its questioning of all stable meanings, has initiated a reign of moral decadence and intellectual chaos against which the Church stands as the primary, if not even the lone, rescuer.

Conservative critics use postmodernity less as a reason to reject *Gaudium et spes* than to ignore it. It is rendered irrelevant by its concern with a world that has reputedly metamorphosed, and attention is redirected to more recent writings, primarily those of the current Pope in which the culture of death has figured so prominently.

The postmodernity analysis, though often stimulating and sometimes infuriating, is also exaggerated. Virtually no one, except a few inhabitants of Soho and some literature departments, really live in postmodernity, and I am not sure about them when they are on the subway. But apart from that, the postmodernity analysis risks being just a fancy wrapper on yet another denunciation of today's Dark Ages, a curious characterization, since Catholic conservatives do not believe that the Dark Ages of yore were really dark ages. Their view is that postmodernity is so devoid of substance that the Church need not converse with it. Postmodernists here tonight will, of course, see that this stance is itself postmodern: Catholic Christianity becomes another lifestyle in the postmodern bazaar; reading the Bible our way becomes perfectly okay in a world where you can read texts in virtually any way.

The rejection or marginalizing of *Gaudium et spes* that has emerged from the right has led to a concerted strategy promoting what I have elsewhere and at length called the Countercultural Temptation.

In the last decade, the cry that the Church must be counter-cultural has become a familiar part of the Church's vocabulary. Like the term prophetic—an adjective with far deeper roots in our tradition—the word countercultural is easily abused. In fact, sometimes it seems that countercultural has become to conservatives what prophetic has been to the Church's left, a phrase that covers a multitude of sins.

This language entered official Catholic circles through Cardinal Ratzinger, who borrowed it from those militant students of the sixties that I spoke about before. The head of the Holy Office, a former academic, clashed with leftist German students. Like all intellectuals he knows how effective it is to steal the thunder of one's adversary by stealing their words. But even back in the sixties the term counter-cultural lent itself to oversimplification and self-congratulation, sometimes even delusions about how far from the culture one actually stood in announcing oneself countercultural.

Of course, the idea of being countercultural expresses some truth. The Church must stand against the powers and principalities. But a major accomplishment of the Catholic tradition—reasserted at Vatican II and in *Gaudium et spes*—has been to produce and to hold distinctions that avoid the language of dichotomy and dualism, to use language that says both/and rather than either/or.

In the present case, "countercultural" raises several problems for the Church, problems that undermine the spirit of *Gaudium et spes*.

First of all, our culture—in the United States more than anywhere else—is not monolithic; a fact of life for all of us who live on the west side where Thai bagels are served with bacon and eggs. Being countercultural in a middle-class or affluent Westchester parish is far different than being countercultural on the streets of Harlem.

There is no one culture. And there is no one way to be counter-cultural. In thinking we are bravely speaking out against what we label "The Culture," we need to be sure that we are not confusing conformity with courage, holding positions comfortably in harmony with our own social, political, and intellectual surroundings. In this neighborhood, affirming the human dignity of homosexuals, however important, is not a very countercultural thing to do—not nearly as countercultural as affirming the permanence of marriage. In many other neighborhoods reality runs in the opposite direction. It is easy to wield the language of countercultural as a slogan against someone else's culture.

A second problem with this appeal to be countercultural is that it is essentially negative, tempting us to overvalue condemnation and confrontation. It naturally surfaces and promotes people who are denunciatory and rigid, people so convinced of their views—so right about what is wrong—that they see no need to persuade others of their views, to recast their argument so that others can grasp it, to empathize with their opponents sufficiently to see the obstacles that bar understanding and perhaps some agreement. The countercultural encourages a tendency to say: We do not have to make the case for our Christian convictions by dialogue and persuasion.

There are several dangers in this strategy. The most obvious is the danger to truth. Our culture is far from universally corrupt. It harbors much that is good, much that reflects our Christian heritage, and much that stems from other sources but gives us new corrective insights into God's revelation in Jesus. To ignore this not only distorts reality, it can give us a vested interest, an unattractive tinge of satisfaction, in our culture's deepest troubles.

Then there is the danger of this outlook taking opposition and criticism as a barometer of the Church's rightness and greatness. We all know there have been more than a few moments in Catholic history when criticism and hostility were earned not by the Church's greatness but by its pettiness, its narrowness, and the betrayal of its own true mission. Just because people hate the Church does not mean we are doing what Jesus told us to do.

Finally, the great danger is to turn our backs on the dialogic stance the Church took in *Gaudium et spes*—a stance that recognized not only that the Church has something to teach modern culture, but that it has something to learn as well. One of the ironies of the current moment is that Catholics have become more adept in listening, re-specting, and carrying on that dialogue with other Christian bodies, with the Jewish community, and with the world outside our doors, than among ourselves.

For we have not done badly at being a Church in the modern world, in reading the signs of the times in the highways and byways and learning to respond as followers of Jesus should. It is only when the world has crossed our own threshold, when the signs of the times appear within our own precincts, that so many revert to a monologue. One of the characteristic polarizing positions in the Church today is precisely that so many are ready to teach a lesson while so few are will-ing to listen and to learn. The Pope, cardinals, and bishops certainly do this; but they do not have a monopoly on the franchise. Prioresses wag their finger at the hierarchy. Theologians issue novel teachings, for ex-ample, just last weekend, on the discipleship of equals. Even editors long to hurl anathemas. It is in the Church itself where the dialogic stance of *Gaudium et spes* is most needed and least practiced.

Listening to the words of John Paul II at the United Nations, how many of you, like me, longed to have these words pronounced to Catholics around the world from the balcony overlooking St. Peter's Square?

> We must overcome our fear of the future. But we will not be able to overcome it completely unless we do so together. The "answer" to that fear is neither coercion nor repression, nor the imposition of one social "model" on the entire world. The answer to the fear which darkens [our] existence . . . is the common effort to build the civilization of love, founded on the universal values of peace, solidarity, justice, and liberty. And the "soul" of the civilization of love is the culture of freedom; the freedom of nations, lived in self-giving solidarity and responsibility.

That is the spirit of Vatican II and of *Gaudium et spes;* and now we, the Church, must learn from it.

Harvesting New Fruits:
Merton's "Message to Poets"

Lawrence S. Cunningham

In the late spring of 1963 the Argentinean poet Miguel Grinberg, who today honors us with his presence, invited Thomas Merton to a meeting of poets that was to be held in Mexico City the following February. In June of the same year Merton wrote to Grinberg explaining that he could not come. That correspondence resulted in a later published article on nine questions Grinberg put to Merton, as well as a correspondence that continued through 1966, and a "Message to Poets," which Merton sent to the conference to be read *in absentia*.[1]

It is that latter document that I wish to use as the locus of my remarks to this distinguished meeting of the International Thomas Merton Society. This talk is billed as a "springboard" lecture by which, I think, the purpose is to get people to reflect on various points and observations that the speaker proposes.

I will think of this address as a springboard in one other sense, which is to say, to advance from the text of Merton's message to engage some broader issues that I think to be at the heart of Merton's larger, more significant pertinence for us now thirty years after his original writing.

This strategy is not, I think, unfair to Merton's text. After all, he wrote his message for an underfunded, rather spontaneous conference

---

1. The correspondence is published in Thomas Merton, *The Courage for Truth*, ed. Christine Bochen (New York: Farrar, Straus & Giroux, 1993) 195–204. "Message to Poets" is in *The Literary Essays of Thomas Merton*, ed. Patrick Hart (New York: New Directions, 1981) 371–4. It was also published in Thomas Merton, *Raids on the Unspeakable* (New York: State Mutual Book & Periodical Series, 1994).

organized without the usual support from foundations, government granting agencies, or financial "angels." Indeed, the editor of Merton's literary essays notes in the prefatory remarks to the message that one Peruvian poet sold her piano in order to finance her trip to the conference. The occasion of the conference in Mexico was, for Merton, a kind of springboard that permitted him to say some things that were in his heart and on his mind.

That kind of informal, hidden, and, dare I say, eremitical kind of affair in Mexico would have much appeal to Merton. Whatever other charisma Merton may have been given by the Spirit, organization, tight planning, and financial acumen were not among them. That the meeting was in Mexico would have also appealed to him since his eyes and his heart had been focused south of the border for nearly a decade prior to the Mexico meeting.[2] It is for that reason that I am emboldened to offer some mildly disorganized and somewhat loosely planned theses about what was in this poetic manifesto. I offer, then, not an exegesis of the text but some reflections inspired by it.

Poets, of course, are makers, as the very etymology of the word poet suggests (from the Greek verb "to make"). I understand the word poet here in the most generous sense of everyone who responds to the world by making it his or her own through the construct of response, which is by listening and saying. Not to be a poet, in this sense, is not to be human.

What does the poet make? I suggest, as our concurrent sessions tell us, that we can say that the poet makes at least four things.

Poets Are Makers of a New Language

If there is one thing that explains why Merton was—and is—so phenomenally powerful to the generation that first read him and to those who still read him, it is because he was able to express the most primordial realities of religious faith and transcendental meaning in a new and compellingly fresh fashion. Ironically enough, his capacity to help himself (and us) to see religious faith anew grew from the very old practice of monastic *lectio,* which I will call here *sapiential reading.*

By sapiential I mean nothing more elaborate than the practice of careful reading with an openness to the wisdom that may come from

2. Even earlier if one takes seriously his love for Cuba registered in *The Secular Journal.*

words pregnant with meaning. In the context of the Bible the person of faith, of course, expects God to speak through the text at many levels, but it is more than the Bible to which I refer here. I mean something like that sense of communication that can come in depth when one person meets another through the text: heart and mind speaking to heart and mind.

It may seem paradoxical coming from a professional theologian, but what helped Merton write so compellingly was his own modest reading in what passed for standard theology in his day. He read the "standard" textbooks in scholastic theology as part of his training for the priesthood, but he had no passion for that kind of theology. From his earliest monastic training he drew from the old tradition of monastic theology, which encouraged this deep faith in the revelatory power of words, especially the Scriptures.

Close students of Merton will agree with him that the one time he attempted a scholastic analysis of spirituality (in *The Ascent to Truth*) he and his critics both agreed that the attempt was a failure. He candidly admitted as much in the preface to the French translation of the book where he realized that, from the perspective of seven passed years, he should have written a different kind of work concerned less with scholasticism, "which is not the true intellectual climate of the monk."[3]

Conversely, Merton, from his earliest monastic days, attempted to draw on resources to push beyond text to naked meaning. In an early letter to the Carthusian Dom Porion, he said, rather disingenuously, that the only thing that he was writing (this was 1952) were "maxims." Merton would write out a compressed Latin saying and give it to his monastic students with the request that they "think about the words, enter into them, and give me something of their own in return."[4] These lapidary texts still ring true.[5] With them Merton intended to add some short meditations and produce, as he says, a truly monastic

3. The complete preface is in Thomas Merton, *"Honorable Reader": Reflections On My Work,* ed. Robert E. Daggy (New York: Crossroad, 1989) 27–28. I have unburdened myself on the way(s) we might call Merton a theologian in "Thomas Merton as Theologian: An Appreciation," *Kentucky Review* 7:2 (1987) 90–97.

4. Thomas Merton, *The School of Charity: The Letters of Thomas Merton on Religious Renewal and Spiritual Direction,* ed. Patrick Hart (New York: Farrar, Straus & Giroux, 1990) 34.

5. One beautiful example: *fons vitae silentium in corde noctis* ("silence, in the heart of the night, is a fountain of life").

book. Through a process of transformation, this exercise became a manuscript called "Thirty-Seven Meditations," which in turn, after refinement, would be published as one of Merton's most nourishing books: *Thoughts in Solitude*.

The motivation and strategy behind this particular exercise is to be discovered in the classic text *Ladder of Monks* by the medieval Carthusian Guigo II: that exercise in sapiential reading by which a reader moved from reading to meditation to the response of prayer and, finally, to contemplation. For Guigo the language of Scripture was a source of nourishment but the word(s) had to be assimilated by the reader (Guigo uses the images of eating and nourishment) as that reader encountered the text and the text, in turn, encountered the reader.[6]

My deepest conviction about Merton is that his whole life was an attempt to create a vocabulary worthy of expressing those things which most deeply affected him, whether it was a prophetic stand against the world or speaking about the fundamental experience of God in prayer.

That desire to search for the deepest meaning of language haunted him as a young person in his admiration for the verbal excavations of James Joyce,[7] to his early monastic life when he mastered both the technique and necessity of *lectio*, to his later years when he attempted to construct verbal landscapes in works like *Cables to the Ace*. He set out the challenge of language most starkly in a few lines that bear repeating:

> If you write for God you will reach many men and bring them joy.
> If you write for men—you may make some money and you may give someone a little joy and you may make a noise in the world for a little while.

6. Guigo addresses God by using the image of "breaking the bread" of Scripture: "the more I see You, the more I long to see You, no more from without in the rind of the letter, but within, in the letter's hidden meaning" (*The Ladder of Monks and Twelve Meditations* [Kalamazoo, Mich.: Cistercian Publications, 1981] 73). Merton alluded to Guigo in his letter to Dom Porion.

7. The 1939–41 journals (recently edited by Patrick Hart) written before he went into the monastery are filled with *catenae* of words that were either new to him or caught his eye in his reading of everything from billboard notices to literary texts in various languages.

If you write only for yourself you can read what you yourself have written and after ten minutes you will be so disgusted
you will wish you were dead.[8]

The first message from the messenger is a question: How do we
find the words today that, in the welter of words, provide joy to a
world which drowns in a vocabulary of death? How do we push language to affirm the God who is the foundation of all and everyone and
not alienate those who thirst for a "good word" and receive plummy
platitudes or poisonous clichés? This does not necessarily involve a
new vocabulary, although it can also mean that. It most emphatically
means giving new currency and a new edge to words as simple as
"bread" or "love" or "I'm home." It also means that we must be alert
to language that poisons or deadens our sense of what is real.

Here is one hint: you do *not* repeat the language of Thomas
Merton; you take the challenge he presents and go out to discover language afresh. As the Zen master, cited by Bonnie Thurston at our last
ITMS meeting, would have it: look at the direction and not at the finger that points the way.

Makers of Personal Conviction

In his message Merton speaks of "interior personal convictions
'in the Spirit.'"[9] At the root of conviction (like the cognate word "convince") is the twofold movement of shedding what is false in order to
embrace what is true. When a felon is convicted in court it means that
the truth of who he or she is and the consequences of that discovery
are discovered.

In that sense conviction is very much like what the gospel calls
metanoia—that change by which we leave off one way of life in order
to embrace another. *Metanoia* (conversion) is widely used in the New
Testament both in the mouth of Jesus and in the vocabulary of the
primitive church.[10]

I do not intend to develop a theology of *metanoia* here, but I do
want to make one point crucial for this paper: in the New Testament

8. Thomas Merton, *New Seeds of Contemplation* (New York: New Directions,
1961) 111.

9. Merton, "Message to Poets," 372.

10. One can find an exhaustive analysis in Kittel, *Theological Dictionary of the
New Testament* (Grand Rapids, Mich.: Eerdmans, 1985) *sub voce.*

metanoia is demanded in response to a call articulated in language; one hears a word and one responds or does not respond. This is true for Jesus, who announces the kingdom of God and asks for conversion, just as it is for the early apostles, who proclaim the Good News and demand a response. Kierkegaard said that what distinguished the genius from the apostle is that the apostle announces the truth and that the warrant for the announcement is that it *is* the truth.

Merton was a monk and the monk is the one who is commanded to hear the word. Benedict begins his rule: "Listen, my child!"[11] Listen to what? Instruction *(praecepta)*. How? By inclining the ear of the heart. Furthermore, this "hearing" is not a once and for all proposition. Indeed, as Benedict makes clear, it is a hearing in a school (schola).[12] In that sense, at least, one could call the monastic life an education in listening.

It would not be too far off the mark to describe the procession of Merton's published journals—from *The Sign of Jonas* to the posthumous *Asian Journal*— as landmarks of hearing that mark the continuation of the way first begun as he undertook his new life described in *The Seven Storey Mountain.*

We should not overly schematize his life's journey, but it does seem clear that Merton's life was a series of convictions—those turnings from error into truth which led him, he believed, by faith to the truth who said "I am the Way, the Truth, and the Life." Such convictions come to us in illuminating moments that are never free from pain.

Spiritual listening is a pluriform exercise. It could be the ecstatic moment of listening to the awe-ful mystery of God in the bell tower of Gethsemani in 1952 or listening to the presence of the people at the corner of Fourth and Walnut, just as it could be listening to cries of the murdered children in Alabama or the silences of the hermitage or the wisdom found in the sound of turning prayer wheels or the flutterings of prayer flags of an exiled Tibetan community in Northern India.

---

11. Prologue to the *Rule of Benedict*. The earlier *Rule of the Master* (Kalamazoo, Mich.: Cistercian Publications, 1977) expresses the same sentiment but in a far more prolix fashion: "You who are reading, first of all, and you who are listening to me speak, dismiss now other thoughts and realize that I am speaking to you and through my words God is instructing you."

12. Benedict calls a monastery "a school of the Lord's Service" at the end of the prologue of his *Rule*. The *Rule of the Master* uses *schola* as a synonym for the monastery.

Everyone has a particular ear, but the voice that gives us conviction is one even if that voice speaks in many different words. To be a person of conviction "in the Spirit" demands a rootedness in life; indeed, Merton says that the solidarity of poets (i.e., of makers) is rooted in life and not "artificial systems." If one listens to the world and then speaks back to it there is a primordial trust—a conviction—that one is on unshakeable ground; indeed, one is on the way to the conviction of truth.

Merton was so convinced of that fact that he could as a young monk lament that he and so many others lacked the burning integrity of such unmonastic figures as D. H. Lawrence just as he could, in his later years, note the convictions of a Pasternak or a Camus or a Dalai Lama or a D. T. Suzuki. He could discern their path because he also was a traveler who was listening and hastening to the source of what he heard.

Here is a second hint: One cannot make another's convictions one's own, but everyone is challenged to become a listener for the truth in order to make the change (conversion) from error to truth. That truth (which many call God) is beyond human comprehension, but is the ultimate source of conviction if only we can decipher the language we hear. And that language, Merton would slyly add, is to be found in silence. Think of these words from Merton's "Hagia Sophia":

> There is in all things an inexhaustible sweetness and purity
> A silence which is the fount of action and joy.
> It rises up in wordless gentleness and flows out to me from the unseen roots of all created being
> Welcoming me tenderly
> saluting me with indescribable tenderness.

Makers of Extraordinary Possibilities

The phrase "extraordinary possibilities" seems so grandiose that it may be worthwhile to unpack it a bit. Extraordinary is not the opposite of ordinary; it is the enhancement or the thickening of the ordinary. The poet, after all, sees ordinary things but in a manner that makes them new and fresh. Cézanne saw more than apples in his luminescent still lifes, just as Emily Dickinson saw death in carriages when her Amherst contemporaries saw only vehicles.

Merton had that kind of "eye." One need not exegete his poetry or gloss his prose to see that. One need only thumb through his published photographs. His pictures of people tended to be snapshots of no great merit, but when he was left alone at his hermitage with the leisure to look—ah, well, then we see the ordinary take on a Hopkinesque depth of the "dearest, freshness, deep down things." If one wishes to understand Merton the contemplative, one could well begin to look attentively at those tree stumps, roots, paint buckets, chairs, mottled leaves, and bare autumn limbs that caught his eye. Both the ordinary facticity of nature and the detritus of human culture take on a new thickness that speaks of that *Grund* which the mystic says is at the root of all.

Closely connected to the capacity to see the ordinary as beyond (as "extra") is the conviction of possibility. Possibility carries with it the promise of the not-yet-explored, of the alternative density of what impinges on us in our ordinary journey. To see possibility is to be able to hope in the face of the implacable presence of the seemingly impermeable hereness and the ordinariness of the present moment.

Anyone who hopes, especially if one has drunk deep of the doctrine of monastic hope, sees both the danger of the future and the redemption of the future. The monk is a watcher (as Merton beautifully describes it in the "Fire Watch" sermon).[13] From the vantage point of the watchtower he may see—Merton saw!—the SAC bombers with their atomic eggs, hear the cries of burned children in Birmingham, the napalm in Vietnam. Those sights signaled possibilities of apocalyptic scenarios. Merton, however, also saw people who struggled against violence. He saw the rustle of SOPHIA in the writings of Pasternak and in the protests of Camus. He saw evil and the good behind it in Flannery O'Connor. He found Zen wisdom in the Desert Fathers and Mothers. He found Cistercian purity and simplicity in the Shakers. He saw possibilities and alternatives in the poets, hippies, and others who lived at the margin.

Whoever hopes, which is to say, whoever can live with the possibility of extraordinary possibilities, is, in a deep sense, a person of prayer. The eminent Oxford theologian John Macquarrie has made the point brilliantly:

> Prayer is *passionate* thinking. . . . Such a thinking is not content to learn what is, but considers what ought to be. . . . Such a thinking is intermingled with painful longing and desire as it catches

---

13. One could explore in some depth Merton's concept of the "watcher"—a term so deeply embedded in prophetic literature.

the vision of what might be and longs for its realization. . . . This passionate thinking, that is, open to feeling the world as well as knowing it, is at least the threshold of prayer. To think of the world with longing for its perfection is a step towards praying for the coming of the kingdom; to think of the world with rejoicing for all that is good is inarticulately to hallow His name. . . . Wherever there is passionate thinking as described above there is something that has an affinity with prayer.[14]

Merton would not use quite the same terms as Macquarrie. As one who struggled against overconceptualized theories of "mental" prayer all of his life, "thinking" would not be the first verb that would come to his mind.[15] Nonetheless, what Macquarrie attempts to articulate is very close both to the sophianic model that undergirds the "General Dance" at the end of *New Seeds of Contemplation* and the more austere sense of contemplation reflected in the essays posthumously published in *Contemplation in a World of Action*.

Poets Create Beyond All Objects

To prepare to reflect on this final part of the paper I sat down and reread Merton's "Message to Poets." I saw something there that I had not seen before and it struck me with the force of intuition. This message is not about poetry and it is not about poets; it is about the *community* of poets. Some gathered in Mexico and another single poet in Nelson County, Kentucky, but all bound together beyond place, appearance, race, nationality, and their poetry both read and unread. Thus, Merton speaks of the solidarity of poets who are "all monks," "standing together," "united," "Children of the Unknown," "Dervishes in the water of life," etc. It is human community and not the poem as "artifact" that binds.

Merton lived in an enclosed contemplative community for twenty-seven years. One could create a fever chart of his attitude toward that community consisting of spikes and valleys: the monastic community was a *paradisus claustralis*, a "foretaste of heaven," or even,

---

14. John Macquarrie, *Paths in Spirituality*, 2nd ed. (Harrisburg, Pa.: Morehouse, 1992) 26.

15. He would have liked, however, Macquarrie's further reflections on "compassionate" thinking where Macquarrie borrows heavily from the Buddhist tradition. Macquarrie, *Paths in Spirituality*, 27ff.

"the center of America." But, when the old fogs of what Cassian calls *accedie* struck him, the monastery was parodied as an all-American, go-getting cheese factory housing neurotics and pseudo-contemplatives. Indeed, as one who has lived with his journals over the past few years, I think it fair to say that the spikes and valleys could be charted on an almost weekly basis. It much depended on what he was reading, how loud the tractors were rumbling, and whether he and the abbot were talking about this or that.

Apart from the ordinary travails of living as a solitary by disposition in a community to which he had been bound by vows, Merton was thinking about something far more ambitious: how to live in the hidden fastness of rural Kentucky while simultaneously living compassionately with those persons who were fellow searchers and pilgrims on the contemplative way. In point of fact, Merton discovered a way of community that suited his own needs, which was the way of the heart.

Let me illustrate what I mean by reference to a short introduction that Merton wrote in 1960 for the first volume of his *Obras Completas*,[16] which had been published in Buenos Aires. When Merton wrote this introduction he already had a long and intimate acquaintance with a number of Latin American intellectuals and a passionate interest in the southern hemisphere, fueled largely from his deep friendship with Ernesto Cardenal, who had been his novice in the 1950s. Merton wrote that he had attempted to join in his life a deep appreciation for Latin American culture by his prayerful encounter with its poets and artists, novices and mystics. He then concluded:

> I cannot be a partial American and I cannot be, which is even sadder, a partial Catholic. For me Catholicism is not confined to one culture, one nation, one age, one race. . . . My Catholicism is all the world and all ages. It dates from the beginning of the world. The first man was the image of Christ and contained Christ, even as he was created, as saviour in his heart.[17]

That is a profound statement in its own right and a powerful description of Merton's vocation as monk/writer/poet. First of all, it moves a description of Catholicism away from being a mere denomi-

---

16. There were no follow up volumes, although other works than those in this first volume were translated into Spanish.

17. This introduction may be found in Merton, *"Honorable Reader,"* 41.

national tag toward a larger, more theological conception of what Catholicity at its deepest really means: the capacity to hold in tension the particular and the universal; the openness necessary to see the largest picture while remaining faithful to whom one is and where one stands in this life. To be a true Catholic means to be able to reconcile the particular with the universal; to keep in balance the *coincidentia oppositorum*.[18] Adam, Merton says in the above quote, was one person, but Adam's life held the promise of all life: we are all of Adam's race.

This was not merely an aside in Merton's understanding of his Catholicism. He expressed himself of this same sentiment to many others in his personal correspondence. To Czeslaw Milosz: "I cannot be a Catholic unless it is made quite clear that I am a Jew and a Moslem, unless I am execrated as a Buddhist, and denounced for having undermined all that this comfortable and social catholicism stands for."[19] To Lawrence Ferlinghetti he wrote that the "you gotta go to confession" routine was not what he meant by drawing on Catholic roots, but "fidelity to conscience, or to the inner voice, or to the Holy Spirit: but it involves a lot of struggle and no supineness and you probably won't get much encouragement from anybody."[20]

This was not a recipe for syncretism or for indifference but for the deepening of one's attentiveness to the Holy Spirit starting from where one was intellectually and existentially.

Merton wanted to do something like that in his intellectual and contemplative life. Indeed, his experiment in actually living that way not only provides a key for understanding his many interests, but is also a template for seeing how he attempted to integrate the seemingly contrary poles of his desires (e.g., solitude/community; activism/contemplation; writing/asceticism; etc.).

Think of the instances in Merton's life that demonstrate his desire for a Catholic union to be achieved within his own person:

- His desire to unite Eastern and Western Christian thought by his own reverential readings in the Orthodox tradition.

- His desire to reach out to the novelist Boris Pasternak because of his conviction that he detected Sophianic themes in *Doctor Zhivago*.

18. For this concept of Catholicity see the brilliant theological meditation of Avery Dulles, *The Catholicity of the Church* (Oxford: Clarendon, 1983).

19. Letter of 18 Jan. 1962 in Merton, *The Courage for Truth*, 79.

20. Letter of 2 Aug. 1961 in ibid., 269.

- His desire that Ecuador's Jaime Andrade sculpt a Madonna and Child of the Andes so that his novices could see a fuller picture of Christ in the Americas.

- His love for Suzuki, who deepened his understanding of Cistercian simplicity and discipline through the eyes of Zen (and how that eye, trained in Zen, could look so lovingly at Shakertown and understand its aesthetics perfectly).

- His deep conviction, expressed in his prefaces to Japanese translations of his work, that he desired his life to be simultaneously a *no* to violence, degradation, and inhumanity while being a simultaneous *yes* to all that was good and human and beautiful and decent.

- His intention to go to the Tibetans in Northern India not as a guru, but as a pilgrim and a learner.

- His belief that a life-long look back to the deepest strains of the monastic life could help him to understand the ascetic writer of Algeria, Albert Camus, as well as the Native Americans of his own continent.

- His vocation to be a contemplative who could live in direct compassion with the world he loved and the people who loved him.

And how did he do this? First of all by practical (and sometimes impractical) strategies: writing to people; organizing a "little journal" timed to self-destruct after four issues, small retreats, and gatherings; sending off mimeographed letters to friends; sharing books, articles, and ideas; obeying inner impulses to strike up a correspondence.

Secondly, and paradoxically, by deeper strategies: living in silence, walking in the woods, saying his psalms, sitting quietly—all of the things monks ought to do.

And finally, by obeying the old monastic dictum of listening to the most profound silence there is—the great silence at the heart of things; by being a watcher of the times and of the presence of Sophia in a redeemed world; by being hospitable to ideas, people, movements.

Are all those old monastic themes not present in his message to poets?

Where are those poets today? Only God knows. Who from the conference remembers Merton's words? It is difficult to say. It is not important. The "Message to Poets" is a temporal artifact, an occasional thing, a souvenir of a past now long gone from us.

Here is what is important: Decades after he wrote his message we are here as part of a web of people who are academics and activists, poets and artists, people who want to listen and watch and learn. At least partially, we find inspiration in the life and work of a person who believed it worthwhile to write to poets in Mexico, flower children in the Bay Area, Nobel Laureates, and prelates precisely to expand new communities of fellow seekers. His language was flexible enough to speak to these audiences either singly or as groups, just as his books today are read by a range of people whose arc would move from the devout to the quizzical.

And this because authentic spirituality for Merton was never a matter of "chatting" about God or of punishing oneself or of fleeing from the thickness of life. Contemplation for Merton was the "deep resonance in the inner center of our spirit in which our very life loses its separate voice and re-sounds with the majesty and mercy of the Hidden and Loving One."[21]

That, in brief, is what I have learned from reading and living with the "Message to Poets." I can summarize what I have been driving at by re-calling two stories from traditions that Merton loved:

"Abbot Bessarion, dying said: The monk should be all eye like the Cherubim and Seraphim."[22]

"A pilgrim asked the Buddha: 'Are you a god or a magician?' The Buddha said: 'I am neither god nor magician.' 'What are you?' The Buddha said: 'I am awake.'"

21. Merton, *New Seeds of Contemplation*, 3.

22. In Merton's translation in *The Wisdom of the Desert* (New York: New Directions, 1960) 49.

Merton and the American Romantics

Ross Labrie

Early in 1976 I received a letter from Merton's friend and fellow poet, Robert Lax, in which Lax recalled some of the poets of whose work Merton was especially fond (see appendix to this article). What caught my interest was Merton's preference for poets like Wallace Stevens and Hart Crane, both of whom were twentieth-century poets writing, thematically at least, in the tradition of the American romantics of the nineteenth century. Other American Romantic poets were also to be the subject of Merton's admiration from time to time, as was William Everson (Brother Antoninus), whose writing Merton recommended to Czeslaw Milosz.[1] Similarly, in a letter to William Carlos Williams in 1961, Merton spoke warmly about the poetry of Allen Ginsberg, particularly about *Kaddish,* which Merton characterized as "great and living poetry and certainly religious in its concerns."[2] This linking of poetry and religion recalls Merton's remark in *The Seven Storey Mountain* that his reading of the great English romantic poet Blake had led him into the Catholic Church.[3] The ease with which Merton drew alternately on romantic and religious sources can be seen in an early reference in *The Sign of Jonas* in which he likened the writings of St. John of the Cross and of Thoreau in helping him to see the importance of separating "reality from illusion."[4]

While critics like Michael Mott and Michael Higgins have discussed Blake's role in Merton's fundamental outlook as a writer, and

---

1. Thomas Merton, *The Courage for Truth: The Letters of Thomas Merton to Writers,* ed. Christine M. Bochen (New York: Farrar, Straus & Giroux, 1993) 70.
2. Ibid., 290.
3. Thomas Merton, *The Seven Storey Mountain* (New York: Harcourt, Brace, 1948) 88.
4. Thomas Merton, *The Sign of Jonas* (New York: Harcourt, Brace, 1953) 317.

while Dennis McInerny has initiated the inquiry into Merton's debt to the American romantics,[5] much has yet to be added to both sorts of analyses. In the 1993 collection of letters by Merton to other writers edited by Christine Bochen, for example, Merton indicates the depth of the influence of the great American romantics of the nineteenth century upon him. Writing to Henry Miller in 1962 he declared that Thoreau was "one of the only reasons" why he became an American citizen, and he was pleased that Miller had compared him to American transcendentalists like Emerson and Thoreau, adding that he would try to be worthy of the comparison.[6] Although in the same letter Merton conceded that he was not nearly as familiar with Emerson as he was with Thoreau, he indicated that he liked what he had read by Emerson.

Merton's debt to Thoreau is inestimable—not only in terms of Thoreau's thought but even stylistically as Michael Mott has suggested.[7] The connection between Merton and Thoreau is all the more convincing when one recalls that both writers sought a balance between the active and contemplative, and specifically between social protest and spiritual and aesthetic contemplation. Not only did Merton characterize Thoreau's gift to America as "incomparable" in *Conjectures of a Guilty Bystander*,[8] but the whole course of his life would in significant respects parallel that of Thoreau, especially when he moved into a woodland hermitage in the 1960s. Indeed, he confided wryly in 1967 in the evocative essay "Day of a Stranger" that he had been accused of "living in the woods like Thoreau instead of living in the desert like St. John the Baptist,"[9] an accusation he did not deny. What he did instead was to redefine the spiritual life so that it resembled a paradigm that Emerson and Thoreau might well have embraced: "Up here in the woods is seen the New Testament: that is to say, the wind comes through the trees and you breathe it."[10] In this

---

5. See Dennis McInerny, "Thomas Merton and the Tradition of American Critical Romanticism," *The Message of Thomas Merton*, ed. Patrick Hart (Kalamazoo, Mich.: Cistercian Publications, 1981) 166–91.

6. Merton, *Courage for Truth*, 277.

7. Michael Mott, *The Seven Mountains of Thomas Merton* (Boston: Houghton-Mifflin, 1984) 268.

8. Thomas Merton, *Conjectures of a Guilty Bystander* (Garden City, N.Y.: Doubleday, 1966) 227.

9. Thomas Merton, "Day of a Stranger," *Hudson Review* 20:2 (summer 1967) 211–8.

10. Ibid., 214.

passage Merton rejects the association of spirituality with guilt, and instead bends his thoughts on the subject in the direction of simplicity and cosmic unity, both of which were emphasized by Emerson and Thoreau. Merton's continuous urging of the need to simplify recalls similar sage advice by Thoreau throughout *Walden*. In *Raids on the Unspeakable* Merton wrote that "only he who has the simplest and most natural needs can be considered to be without needs, since the only needs he has are real ones."[11] In *The Sign of Jonas* Merton underlined the passage in *Walden* in which Thoreau recalled that he had gone to live in the woods in order to confront the "essential facts of life."[12]

The greatest threat to cosmic unity perceived by Emerson, Thoreau, and Merton was the intellect in its rational operations. In *Walden* Thoreau had described the rational intellect as a cleaver, a coarse and intrusive instrument that "discerns and rifts its way into the secret of things."[13] Merton's romanticism can be seen in his evolving resistance to a predominantly rational approach to religion, which he increasingly came to think of in an intuitive and mystical rather than in a systematic and theological manner. In *Conjectures of a Guilty Bystander*, for example, Merton confided that at moments he experienced a "flash of Zen" in the "midst of the Church," but that such experiences were often foreshortened by "reasoning too much about everything."[14]

From Merton's mystical and romantic perspective all that existed was part of the dance of life, as he visualized it, echoing Yeats, in the incandescent ending of *New Seeds of Contemplation*. Similarly, in a letter to Marco Pallis in 1965 Merton argued that the division between the natural and supernatural in religion was "misleading and unsatisfactory."[15] The letter signaled a turnaround for Merton from an earlier letter to Aldous Huxley in 1958 in which he contended that Huxley ought to have distinguished "experience which is essentially *aesthetic*

11. Thomas Merton, *Raids on the Unspeakable* (New York: New Directions, 1966) 23.

12. Merton, *Sign of Jonas*, 316.

13. Henry David Thoreau, *Walden and Civil Disobedience*, ed. Owen Thomas (New York: Norton, 1966) 66.

14. Merton, *Conjectures of a Guilty Bystander*, 136.

15. Thomas Merton, *The Hidden Ground of Love: The Letters of Thomas Merton on Religious Experience and Social Concerns*, ed. William Shannon (New York: Farrar, Straus & Giroux, 1985) 470.

and natural from that which was *mystical and supernatural.*"[16] While Merton's initial romanticism, which predated his entry into the monastery, was somewhat crimped during the 1940s and early 1950s by his desire to center himself on the Church, as he grew older his romanticism reasserted itself, especially in the post-Vatican II liberalism of the 1960s.

Merton's wariness about the limitations of rationalism are ubiquitous in his writings, but he is most convincing when he places rationalism within the fertile context of the sort of unified perception sought by all romantic writers. An instance is the poem "O Sweet Irrational Worship," in *Emblems of a Season of Fury:*

> By ceasing to question the sun,
> I have become light. . . .
> I am earth, earth
> All these lighted things
> Grow from my heart.[17]

Merton's identification with the natural elements and his submerging of his intellect recall Emerson's celebrated essay on "Nature" in which the writer describes himself as a "transparent eyeball" in which the "currents of the Universal Being" circulated through him and in which he felt "part or particle of God."[18] Similarly, Thoreau in an equally famous passage describes his head in an ecstatic moment as an "organ for burrowing" through which he would "mine" his way through the low hills around him.[19] Like the monistic Emerson and Thoreau, Merton strove ceaselessly for unity both in perception and feeling, bristling at the apparently artificial borders of systematic thought—as when he noted in a letter to Czeslaw Milosz that the doctrine of the immortality of the soul was not "fully and really Christian" since it was the "whole person" who was immortal.[20]

As with American romantic writers of both the nineteenth and twentieth centuries Merton proclaimed the priestly role of the poet and of the creative artist, writing to the Latin-American poet Nicanor

16. Ibid., 437.
17. Thomas Merton, "O Sweet Irrational Worship," *Emblems of a Season of Fury,* in *The Collected Poems of Thomas Merton* (New York: New Directions, 1977) 344.
18. Ralph Waldo Emerson, *Collected Works of Ralph Waldo Emerson* (Cambridge, Mass.: Harvard University Press, 1971) 1:10.
19. Thoreau, *Walden,* 66.
20. Merton, *Courage for Truth,* 76.

Parra in 1965, for example, that contemporary artists tended to fulfill many of the functions that were once the "monopoly of monks."[21] Similarly, in the essay "Answers on Art and Freedom" in *Raids on the Unspeakable* Merton argued that the modern artist had inherited the combined functions of "hermit, pilgrim, prophet, priest, shaman, sorcerer, soothsayer, alchemist and bonze."[22] Here, one hears echoes of Whitman's proclamation in *Democratic Vistas* that the "priest departs, the divine literatus comes,"[23] as well as of Wallace Stevens' well-known pronouncement that the poet was the "priest of the invisible," the "intermediary between people and the world in which they live."[24] This belief about the artist has become so deeply ingrained in contemporary aesthetics that many might not perceive its roots in American romanticism. One cannot imagine eighteenth-century writers like Swift, Pope, or the American poet, Philip Freneau, however, affirming such an idea.

As with other romantic writers Merton embraced the primitivism of romantic thought, which was characteristically linked to nature and to the corollary that society, and cities in particular, were corruptions of the primal beauty of the world.[25] Romantic primitivism can also be observed, as it can in Whitman, in Merton's celebration of the child, the human embodiment of primitivism. The most famous example of this symbolism of the child in Whitman is in the long poem "Out of the Cradle Endlessly Rocking." While Merton's use of the child as a symbol of romantic primitivism can no doubt be traced back to Blake, it is likely that he was also familiar with Whitman's use of this motif. There is an admiring reference to Whitman, for example, in *The Geography of Lograire*,[26] and in introducing the poetry of Ruben Dario, Merton noted the mood of "fraternal love" in Whitman's poetry.[27] In an essay on the American poet Louis Zukofsky, Merton describes

21. Ibid., 212.

22. Merton, *Raids on the Unspeakable*, 173.

23. Walt Whitman, Democratic Vistas, *The Portable Walt Witman*, ed. Mark Van Doren (New York: Viking, 1973) 321.

24. Wallace Stevens, *Opus Posthumous*, rev. ed. (New York: Knopf, 1989) 195, 189.

25. C. Hugh Holman, *A Handbook to Literature*, 6th ed. (New York: Macmillan, 1992) 374.

26. Thomas Merton, *The Geography of Lograire*, in *The Collected Poems of Thomas Merton*, 582.

27. Thomas Merton, *The Literary Essays of Thomas Merton* (New York: New Directions, 1981) 306.

the speech of the child as "paradise speech."[28] This romantic motif was christianized when Merton, in speaking of Karl Barth, declared that though Barth had matured into a great Protestant theologian, Christ had remained a "child" in him.[29]

The most memorable poem in *Emblems for a Season of Fury* is "Grace's House," which focuses on the sublimity and primacy of the child's vision. The occasion for the poem was Merton's receiving a child's drawing of her house. Her name, Grace, along with the pristine sketch, had a suggestive effect on Merton's imagination:

> Where all the grass lives
> And all the animals are aware!
> The huge sun, bigger than the house
> Stands and streams with life in the east
> While in the west a thunder cloud
> Moves away forever.[30]

"Alas," the speaker notes, looking at the drawing, there was "no road to Grace's house."[31] Merton's romantic primitivism can be seen in his desire to recover, here on earth, the consciousness of the unity that had been "shattered by the 'knowledge of good and evil,'" as he put it in *Zen and the Birds of Appetite.*[32] Reconciling his adherence to both romanticism and Catholicism, Merton declared in the preface to an Argentinean edition of his writings that his faith dated from the "beginning of the world," when the first human being emerged in the "image of Christ."[33]

In common with the American romantics of the nineteenth century, Merton affirmed the supremacy of the imagination over reason in generating an experience of transcendental awareness. In *Bread in the Wilderness* he identified the imagination with an ability to perceive that which is spiritual.[34] Furthermore, in an essay entitled "Poetry and

28. Ibid., 130.

29. Merton, *Conjectures of a Guilty Bystander*, 4.

30. Thomas Merton, "Grace's House," *Emblems of a Season of Fury*, in *The Collected Poems of Thomas Merton*, 331.

31. Ibid.

32. Thomas Merton, *Zen and the Birds of Appetite* (New York: New Directions, 1968) 117.

33. Thomas Merton, *Honorable Reader*, ed. Robert Daggy (New York: Crossroad, 1989) 41.

34. Thomas Merton, *Bread in the Wilderness* (New York: New Directions, 1953) 30.

Contemplation: A Reappraisal," he associated the recovery of paradise and a renewed contact with God with the exercise of human creativity.[35] In writing about the poetry of Zukofsky, Merton noted that all "valid" poetry, that which generated "imaginative life," was a kind of "recovery of paradise."[36] Similarly, in discussing the writings of Boris Pasternak, and in particular his character, Zhivago, Merton identified the artist, specifically, as one who can evoke the primal experience of paradise: "It is as artist, symbolist, and prophet that Zhivago stands most radically in opposition to Soviet society. He himself is a man of Eden, of Paradise. He is Adam, and therefore also, in some sense, Christ."[37] All of the elements of Merton's hybrid Christian romanticism are present in this passage, notably the romantic insistence on the spiritual transcendence offered by the imagination and the heightened value of human nature made possible by the death and resurrection of Christ.

For Merton, as for the American romantics, no human eloquence, particularly of a rational kind, could rival the eloquence of nature itself. In "Rain and the Rhinoceros," one of Merton's most memorable essays, the sound of the rain is described as "wonderful, unintelligible, perfectly innocent speech," and is contrasted with the "noises of cities, of people," of the "greed of machinery that does not sleep."[38] In a sense not only is society rejected here, but the language used by society as well. For this reason the poet represents an alternative to the debased language of the group, an attempt to begin over again, to seek the voice of the primal, that which still bears the imprint of the divine hand.

Although Merton argued in his M.A. thesis on Blake that Blake, unlike Wordsworth, did not idolize nature,[39] there is a tendency in Merton's writings to perceive the natural order as morally superior to the social order, and in this respect Merton is closer to Emerson, Thoreau, and Whitman than he is to Blake. When Czeslaw Milosz chided Merton for his uncritical approval of nature in a letter written in 1960, Merton was forced to admit that "nature and I are very good friends, and console one another for the infamy of the human race and

35. Merton, *The Literary Essays*, 345.
36. Ibid., 128.
37. Ibid., 47.
38. Merton, *Raids on the Unspeakable*, 10.
39. Merton, *The Literary Essays*, 426.

its civilization."[40] Merton was not altogether consistent in his behavior toward nature, though. One remembers that in the evocative, impressionistic natural setting of "Day of a Stranger" he recounts having killed a copperhead snake, presumably as luminous an example of natural order as any other.

More than Emerson and Whitman, Thoreau had dwelt on the predatory aspects of nature. The most obvious example is the grisly battle of the ants scene in Walden.[41] In a dramatic scene in *The Sign of Jonas* Merton focused directly on these harsher aspects of nature. Having settled down after being frightened by an eagle, a flock of starlings is described moving about on the ground, singing. Suddenly, a hawk swoops down, flying "straight into the middle of the starlings" just as they were getting off the ground. Rising into the air, Merton writes, there was a slight scuffle on the ground as the hawk got his "talons into the one bird he had nailed."[42] Merton ponders the scene: "It was a terrible and yet beautiful thing, that lightning flight, straight as an arrow, that killed the slowest starling."[43] Merton does not overlook the violence of the scene, but shows the hawk in the field "like a king," taking his time in eating: "I tried to pray, afterward," Merton confides. "But the hawk was eating the bird." It is clear that Merton was not so much repelled as awed, feeling finally that the hawk should be studied by "saints and contemplatives; because he knows his business."[44] Although the episode might have spurred troubled thoughts about the creator of a Darwinian universe, there is no sign of such reflections. Merton accepts the mystery of nature, is as stirred by its beauty as by its power, and piously leaves the answer of its inner riddle to God. Furthermore, though attracted to nature, he portrays nature as ultimately doomed. Consequently, the resourceful pilgrim will want to pass through nature, to some other place, so as to look not only at nature but through it. Otherwise, Merton's symbolic episode implies, one will suffer the fate of the starlings.

Characteristically in Merton's writings, nature serves as an agent of transcendental experience, as can be observed in a scene in *Conjectures of a Guilty Bystander* in which he found himself absorbed by a bowl of flowers in a monastery chapel:

40. Merton, *Courage for Truth*, 65.
41. Thoreau, *Walden*, 152–4.
42. Merton, *Sign of Jonas*, 274.
43. Ibid., 275.
44. Ibid.

Beauty of sunlight falling on a tall vase of red and white carnations and green leaves on the altar of the novitiate chapel. The light and dark. The darkness of the fresh, crinkled flower: light, warm and red, all around the darkness. The flower is the same color as blood, but it is in no sense whatever "as red as blood." Not at all! It is as red as a carnation. Only that.

This flower, this light, this moment, this silence: Dominus est. Eternity. He passes. He remains. We pass. In and out. He passes. We remain. We are nothing. We are everything. He is in us. He is gone from us. He is not here. We are here in Him.[45]

Resisting the impulse to turn the flowers into symbol, Merton holds fast to them as reservoirs of the beauty of creation, and in so doing comes fortuitously into contact with their creator and equally fortuitously experiences a temporary release from time. Here, though, the moment of transcendence is linked with an orthodox Catholic theology instead of the pantheism that permeated the writings of Emerson, Thoreau, and Whitman.

Nature placed Merton in touch with the creative hand of God. He wrote in his beautiful essay "Hagia Sophia" that there is in all things

inexhaustible sweetness and purity, a silence that is a fount of action and joy. It rises up in wordless gentleness and flows out to me from the unseen roots of all created being, welcoming me tenderly, saluting me with indescribable humility. This is at once my own being, my own nature, and the Gift of my Creator's Thought and Art within me.[46]

As with the American transcendentalists of the nineteenth century Merton's thought proceeds by means of a number of intuitive equations. This is because the transcendentalists derived their thinking in part from Kant, who posited the legitimacy of certain kinds of a priori perceptions.[47] Thus, in Merton's writings the city and society, for example, are perceived as an estranged wildness that contrasts with the sacred wildness of creation. The contrast can be easily seen in the

---

45. Merton, *Conjectures of a Guilty Bystander*, 131.

46. Thomas Merton, "Hagia Sophia," *Emblems of a Season of Fury*, in *The Collected Poems of Thomas Merton*, 363.

47. James D. Hart, *The Oxford Companion to American Literature*, 5th ed. (New York: Oxford UP, 1983) 770.

poem "The City After Noon," from that splendid volume of poems *The Tears of the Blind Lions:*

> What if the wild confinement were empty
> And the lunatic pigeons were once again sane! . . .
>
> What if the wild contentment were full
> And there were nothing left in the world
> But fields, water and sun
> And space went on forever to eternity, without a rim?
>
> What if the wild confinement were empty
> And the sheriffs were free to go home![48]

Here, Merton pictures a tortured and perverse wildness generated by society, a bleak and unnecessary substitution for the natural wildness that would free the spirit.

Thus, Eden is sometimes portrayed by Merton not as a garden but as a naturally wild place, as in the poem "Dry Places" from *The Tears of the Blind Lions:*

> For we cannot forget the legend of the world's childhood
> Or the track to the dogwood valley
> And Adam our Father's old grass farm
> Wherein they gave the animals names
> And knew Christ was promised first without scars
> When all God's larks called to Him
> In this wild orchard.[49]

While there is a certain tension in the poem between the idea of Eden as a "farm" and a "wild orchard," it is clear that the latter represents the closest proximity to God. Furthermore, one cannot help but notice the depth of Merton's optimism, again more typical of the American romantics than of Blake, in which the desolation of the fall is instantly extinguished by the prediction of the coming of Christ.

Therefore, the way forward, spiritually, in Merton, is also the way back, toward the source, as the twentieth-century American romantic poet Robert Frost put it. Nature, the backward leaning soul,

---

48. Thomas Merton, "The City after Noon," *The Tears of the Blind Lions,* in *The Collected Poems of Thomas Merton,* 213–4.

49. Thomas Merton, "Dry Places," *The Tears of the Blind Lions,* in *The Collected Poems of Thomas Merton,* 217.

and God are pitted against a futuristically oriented society and technology, and typically (in a romantic writer) the soul peeks out at night when it is not overwhelmed by the active day, which eclipses the imagination—the soul's route of survival. The poem "Nocturne" in *The Strange Islands* is illustrative. In that poem, we are told: "Night has a sea which quenches the machine" and which tracks "all countries where the soul has gone." In the darkness the simplified light of the moon conveys a wisdom that "sails from God."[50] The night and moon symbols recall Whitman's use of such imagery in "Out of the Cradle Endlessly Rocking," as well as Thoreau's vision of eternity in *Walden* as a night sky that is "pebbly with stars."[51]

Merton's ecstatic consciousness of the immanence of the divine was not, strictly speaking, pantheistic since he attributed his own conversion to Catholicism to the realization of the presence of God as a distinct being in *"this present life,* in the world and in myself," as he put it, adding that his task as a Christian was to live in "full and vital awareness of this ground of my being and of the world's being."[52] At the same time, reflecting the hybrid nature of his thought as Christian and romantic, Merton affirmed his being a *"part of nature,"* though a "special" part, that which is "conscious of God."[53] This ontological view was continuous with, though not identical with, Merton's more theologically conventional observation that for those who believe in the incarnation there should be no one on earth in whom we are not prepared to see, "in mystery, the presence of Christ."[54] Indeed, typically in Merton's writings, particularly in the first half of his career, this view of the role of Christ, a perfectly orthodox one, was grafted almost invisibly onto the residual romanticism that he took with him into the monastery.

Merton's interest in the primal matter of creation attracted him to the unconscious, the spontaneous, and the instinctive. Thoreau showed a similar interest in submerging his intellect and imagining his head as the largely physical and instinctive head of a burrowing animal.[55] Guided by his religious training, however, Merton did not look

50. Ibid., 230.
51. Thoreau, *Walden*, 66.
52. Merton, *Conjectures of a Guilty Bystander*, 292–3.
53. Ibid., 268.
54. Thomas Merton, *New Seeds of Contemplation* (New York: New Directions, 1961) 296.
55. Thoreau, *Walden*, 66.

uncritically at the unconscious, but went so far as to urge the eradication of the "unconscious roots of sin" by exposing the darker side of the unconscious.[56] Similarly, in "A Letter to Pablo Antonio Cuadra Concerning Giants," included in *Emblems of a Season of Fury*, Merton described his age as one in which political leaders and technocrats had acted out "bad dreams" in which external form was given to the "phantasms of man's unconscious."[57] Merton exhorted his readers to take command of the "mechanisms of natural instinct" instead of being swept away "blindly" by these subconscious forces.[58] Merton's wariness concerning the unconscious stemmed from what he perceived as threats to the freedom and sovereignty of human beings. Rather than confront the apparent contradiction between examples of his romantically optimistic and more pessimistic, theological readings of nature, Merton held to the center, upholding the need for human beings to celebrate the beauty and transcendental power of the unconscious while cautioning against the dangers of its more threatening undertow.

What distinguished nineteenth-century American romanticism from English romanticism was its strong social dimension. Members of the Transcendental Club, as is well known, launched the social experiment of Brook Farm, an experiment that was dramatized in Hawthorne's novel *The Blithedale Romance*. Moreover, the American and romantic belief in the primacy of the individual gave rise in Thoreau's case to civil disobedience. "The only obligation which I have a right to assume," Thoreau wrote, "is to do at any time what I think right," adding that any person more "right than his neighbors" constituted a "majority of one."[59] Like Thoreau, Orestes Brownson, and other American transcendentalists of the 1840s, Merton's romanticism took on not only a contemplative but also a social form.

Rooted in the consciousness of the supremacy of the individual soul, romantic writers tend to be anarchists politically. The reason is that romanticism affirmed the privileged status of individual consciousness over collective authority. At one point Thoreau scornfully described the state as "half-witted," afraid to confront a "man's sense,

56. Merton, *Conjectures of a Guilty Bystander*, 98.

57. Thomas Merton, "A Letter to Pablo Antonio Cuadra Concerning Giants," *Emblems of a Season of Fury*, in *The Collected Poems of Thomas Merton*, 374.

58. Merton, *Conjectures of a Guilty Bystander*, 107.

59. Thoreau, *Walden*, 225, 232.

intellectual or moral, but only his body, his senses."[60] Going even further, he contended that there would never be a "free and enlightened State" until the state came to recognize the individual as a "higher and independent power, from which its own power and authority are derived."[61] Moreover, there was a strong agrarian strain in the American transcendentalists, which also forms part of Merton's thought. There were also specifically Catholic influences on the development of Merton's social ideas. In addition, for example, to the influence of Dorothy Day and Catherine Doherty upon Merton, in the early 1960s Daniel Berrigan played an important role in the development of Merton's social thought. This influence was consistent with that of the American transcendentalists in some important respects. Day and Berrigan supported civil disobedience while Day and Doherty were agrarians.

Rather like Thoreau, Merton saw the artist politically as a necessary anarchist. In "Answers on Art and Freedom" Merton maintained that society ironically benefits when the artist "liberates himself from its coercive or seductive pressures," adding that the contemporary artist would likely only "find himself" if he were a "nonconformist and a rebel."[62] Moreover, rather like Thoreau, in "A Letter to Pablo Antonio Cuadra Concerning Giants" Merton measured the weight of the individual against the bureaucratic and technocratic state and found the state to be of thinner substance. The size of the state and corporate machinery, Merton argued, does not mean that it possesses "metaphysical solidity."[63] As a solitary Merton told Czeslaw Milosz in 1965 that he had no intention of joining movements even in the case of causes he supported,[64] reinforcing his earlier statement to Milosz that even as a Catholic he was a "complete lone wolf."[65] Similarly, in a striking remark in a letter to Henry Miller in 1962, Merton noted that in an oppressive, bureaucratic period the individual was the "only power that is left."[66]

As with Thoreau, Merton grounded his anarchism not only in a belief in the primacy of the individual but in a conviction that the

60. Ibid., 236.
61. Ibid., 243.
62. Merton, *Raids on the Unspeakable*, 172.
63. Merton, "A Letter to Pablo Antonio Cuadra Concerning Giants," 373–4.
64. Merton, *Courage for Truth*, 84.
65. Ibid., 60.
66. Ibid., 278.

promise of the American republic had been betrayed. Indeed, in an essay on William Melvin Kelley he characterized Thoreau, like himself, as a "hermit and a prophet of nonviolence" who believed that the American Revolution had "either misfired or had never really taken place."[67] Echoing these sentiments in a letter to William Carlos Williams in 1961, Merton described the period in which he was living as one of "infidelity to the original American grace."[68]

Merton contrasted his hermitage life, which he called "cool," with the "hot" life lived by those in community—including those in the monastery near him. Again, like Thoreau and Whitman, he associated society, including his own monastery, with a peremptory rationalism that involved the need to clarify, endlessly clarify, experience, as he put it in "Day of a Stranger."[69] Regarding the tyranny of reason, Merton's views resemble not only Blake's, but those of Whitman at the end of "Song of Myself":

> Do I contradict myself?
> Very well then I contradict myself,
> (I am large, I contain multitudes.)[70]

The rebelliousness of Merton's late poems, *Cables to the Ace* and *The Geography of Lograire,* can be explained in part by his anarchic platform as an artist. In particular, the pervasive irony of these poems, both thematic and linguistic, was part of a stratagem that he had announced to Milosz in 1959 for the artist to be a "complete piece of systematic irony" in the midst of the "totalitarian life—or the capitalist one. And even the official religious one."[71] The depth of Merton's revolt against the state and against institutionalism is indicated in another part of the letter to Milosz in which Merton observed caustically that we all have "our little game with Caesar, the little Father who is no longer human and who therefore *ought* to be cheated, in the name of humanity." Reflecting his view as both Christian and romantic, Merton argued in *Conjectures of a Guilty Bystander* that the order imposed on individuals by society bore no apparent relation to their "real needs as persons," while that order at the same time summoned them

67. Merton, *The Literary Essays,* 169.
68. Merton, *Courage for Truth,* 269.
69. Merton, "Day of a Stranger," 213.
70. Whitman, "Democratic Vistas," 96.
71. Merton, *Courage for Truth,* 64.

through legislation to cooperate in the work of "their own alien-ation."[72]

Merton's argument against technology was integral with his objection to social oppressiveness, and in this respect he again lines up with Thoreau and to some extent with Hart Crane, whose great poem about the Brooklyn bridge was, according to Robert Lax (see appendix), a favorite of Merton's. Crane's anxious ambivalence about American technology issued from his fear that the imaginative genius that made great technology possible also and incidentally enslaved those who used it. As Thoreau had aphoristically put the matter in *Walden* a century earlier: "We do not ride on the railroad; it rides upon us."[73] The passage was one that Merton commented on directly in "Rain and the Rhinoceros," observing that whereas Thoreau had sat in his cabin criticizing the railways, Merton sat in his, wondering ironically about a world that "has, well, progressed."[74]

In "Day of a Stranger," looking up at the bomb bay of an SAC plane flying over his woods, Merton wrote angrily that he did not consider this "technological mother" with its nuclear "egg" to be the "friend of anything I believe in."[75] Set implacably against the burden of modern technocracy was the artist with his or her view of the value of that which technology overlooks: "If one does not understand the usefulness of the useless and the uselessness of the useful," Merton cautioned in "Rain and the Rhinoceros," one cannot understand art. And a country that does not understand art, he added, was a country of "slaves and robots."[76]

A poem that dramatically conveys the cluster of values surrounding Merton's antipathy to technology is "Gloss on the Sin of Ixion" in *Emblems of a Season of Fury.* Ixion, the Thessalonian king in Greek mythology who was bound to a wheel of fire because he tried to seduce the goddess Hera (Merton uses her Roman name, Juno), is projected by Merton as a symbol of the sort of grasping ambition that he associated with modern technocracies:

> Our world too must steam and flame.
> Ours must spin. Effort will break

72. Merton, *Conjectures of a Guilty Bystander,* 232.
73. Thoreau, *Walden,* 62.
74. Merton, *Raids on the Unspeakable,* 12.
75. Merton, "Day of a Stranger," 211.
76. Merton, *Raids on the Unspeakable,* 21.

A bank. Work will run
(Wheels within wheels)
Monopolies.[77]

The assault by contemporary societies is upon "sacred man," that is, human beings in their created, primal state, traces of which still inhere in their beings as individuals.

In Merton's imagination the rulers of technocracy are inevitably the wagers of war, represented in the poem by the "Giant mechanical boys," the centaur monsters who were the offspring of Ixion:

Heavy-set brothers of mess and fight,
Smoky bulldozers!
Wheeling cities burn!
Glass monsters break
Open faces, lit with high money.[78]

The monsters bred by greed and sustained by the political and economic infrastructure entrenched in contemporary Western society are provocatively linked by Merton with a ruthless sexual drive to seize and rape the earth for profit, an analogue to the desire by Ixion to rape the sacred:

"Go hug dear mother profit in the dark, Possess earth,
"Possess money!"
Yet he missed.
He spilled.[79]

The ejaculation of semen into the void symbolizes the ultimately doomed and sterile result of the ravishing of human beings and of the earth by the perverse social powers that surround them.

The poem concludes with a vision of a fiery war:

Up now comes
Out of earth and hell
Giant war Ixion
Rolling and fighting on the red wheel.[80]

---

77. Thomas Merton, "Gloss on the Sin of Ixion," *Emblems of a Season of Fury,* in *The Collected Poems of Thomas Merton,* 313.

78. Ibid., 314.

79. Ibid.

80. Ibid., 315.

The symbols of materialism, debased sexuality, war, and technocracy are all fused in the poem through the underlying assumption that all represent a radical drive for a power that begins in competitiveness and ends in destruction. Beneath this symbolic equation lay Merton's belief, shared certainly by Thoreau, that institutions were incapable of love, that one of the characteristics of a collectivity, as Merton put it in "Rain and the Rhinoceros," involved rejecting certain classes of people in order to strengthen its own self-awareness. Conversely, the "solitary" person cannot survive unless he is capable of "loving everyone."[81] Merton's prophetic categories are intended to represent not simply actual societies and individuals, but rather ways of living. Paradoxically, he discerns societies as tending toward the sorts of classification that exclude and herd those within them in contrast to those solitary individuals who live as persons in open, sympathetic union with the life within and around them rather than enduring the sorts of collective lives of quiet desperation spoken of, for example, by Thoreau in *Walden*.[82]

Merton's romanticism turned him in the direction of Asian religion, as had occurred in the case of the transcendentalists of the nineteenth century. Like Emerson and Thoreau, Merton was attracted to Asian religions, especially Buddhism, because of their transrational inclusiveness. On one occasion Merton described Zen Buddhism glowingly as the awareness of pure being "beyond subject and object," an awareness that thus circumvented the Western "dualistic division between matter and spirit."[83] Set aside was the relentless search for articulated meaning. Merton illustrated this sort of awareness in "Day of a Stranger" in an impromptu, whimsical sermon to the birds:

> "Esteemed friends, birds of noble lineage, I have no message to you except this: be what you are: be birds. Thus you will be your own sermon to yourselves!"
> Reply: "Even this is one sermon too many!"[84]

Merton was greatly attracted to Asian religious thought, particularly in his later writings, especially for its emphasis upon consciousness. He regarded Christianity as focused upon action, particularly salvific

81. Merton, *Raids on the Unspeakable,* 22.
82. Thoreau, *Walden,* 5.
83. Thomas Merton, *The Zen Revival* (London: Buddhist Society, 1971) 5.
84. Merton, "Day of a Stranger," 216.

action, and in contrast he thought Buddhism much more developed as a religion in its understanding of religious experience than other major religions. In *Mystics and Zen Masters* Merton celebrated the capacity of "pure consciousness" of a romantic and monistic kind in accepting things fully, in complete oneness with them, looking "out of them" as though fulfilling the role of consciousness "not for itself only but *for them also.*"[85]

The Asian Journal, which appeared following Merton's death in Thailand, reveals a romantic and mystical consciousness in full flower, centering as it does on the ecstasy of transcendental awareness. The breakthrough in consciousness that Merton achieved at Polonnaruwa in Ceylon affected him with as much surprise as exhilaration. The huge stone Buddhas, one seated and the other reclining, both symbolized and made possible the sort of transcendental relationship with the world around him that his studies of Eastern religions had been preparing him for. The quiet smiles of the Buddhas were filled with "every possibility, questioning nothing, knowing everything, rejecting nothing, the peace not of emotional resignation but of Madhyamika, of sunyata, that has seen through every question without trying to discredit anyone or anything—*without refutation.*"[86] The passage recalls the celebratory open-endedness of the poetic visions of Emerson and Whitman, who were unencumbered by any tendency toward exclusivity.

The relationship between Merton's romantic/Zen vision in *The Asian Journal* and his Christianity is difficult to ascertain since his focus is on Asian religion. One is tempted to see this journal as Merton's ecumenical reconstruction of his religion, at least in its contemplative dimensions, so that it articulated the unity of vision toward which his romanticism had always predisposed him. This does not mean that Merton was thinking of abandoning his vocation, as Emerson had abandoned Unitarianism because of what he regarded as its narrowness. Rather, Merton now perceived his vocation in a new and larger spiritual context in which he felt himself able, by relying on other religious traditions, to expand the experience and meaning of his own— even though he had also been troubled by the thought of Christian sectarianism, as can be seen in his later reservations about *The Seven*

85. Merton, *Mystics and Zen Masters,* 233.
86. Thomas Merton, *The Asian Journal of Thomas Merton,* ed. Naomi Burton, Patrick Hart, and James Laughlin (New York: New Directions, 1973) 233.

Storey Mountain. Through a consciousness immersed in both Christian and romantic mysticism, Merton drew attention to our spiritual roots as human beings, evoking feelings of unity in readers who, like himself, had sought to have the experience of God.

Appendix to "Merton and the Romantics":
Letter written in 1976 from Robert Lax to Ross Labrie

Dear Ross Labrie,

Your letter jumped out of a bunch of others (mostly Christmas cards) today & said: answer me!

1) pound & eliot certainly meant a lot to merton; he admired early williams imagist poems, too; hart crane, too; & not impossibly, cummings. wallace stevens, too. (& h d). feel on surest ground with williams, crane & stevens. might well have liked whitman (at least never said he didn't). can't remember a word about poe's poetry (doubt that p's kind of rhythm would have appealed) but think he'd read and like the narrative of arthur gordon pym (& the other stories). i think of all these hart crane & the bridge (but his other poems too, & west indian ones) were closest to being real enthusiasms.

other american enthusiasms, though not from poem-books: new orleans kansas city chicago & new york: louis armstrong, bessie smith, joe turner, meade lux lewis, albert ammons, teddy wilson, baby dodds, cripple clarence lofton, bunk johnson, kid ory, count basie, duke ellington: blues lyrics, too; good morning blues (for example) a real favorite; bix biederbe cke, j c higginbottom, pee wee russell, fats waller, billie holiday: all people & artists he really liked and went out of his way to hear//// movies a big influence, too: mark bros charlie chaplin marjorie dumont, w c fields allison skipworth, j carrol naish (nash?) , oscar homolka (hitchcock, too) rene claire(a nous l liberte a real favorite, fred astaire; marched himself off to see edw g robinson in brother orchid when none of the rest of us wld go; may have liked lupino lane; did like wheeler & woolsy, laurel & hardy, j edgarx kennedy, harry langdon, buster keaton & hedy lamarrr likedaldous huxley, hemingway & evelyn waugh jack oakie, too. (but not don ameche who wanted to play t merton in a movie version of 7 storey mt).

of british contemporaries he liked: auden, spender, c day lewis, louis macniece (george barker, too, i think; especially for poem called 'no other tiger walked that way that night') dylan thomas was a major enthusiasm, so, i think was auden; & early spender lots of spanish & south americans, too: jimenez; octavio paz; jorge de lime; (alfonso?) pessoa, (& of course) ernesto cardenal. & you mentioned lorca (a real enthusiasm)

classical britons: shakespear, marlowe, donne, suckling, chaucer, spenser,too; crashaw (*big* enthusiasm)herbert, too southey, sir philip sydney; blake (huge enthusiasm) hopkins (great, too) nashe, john lyly, webster; abraham golding, too (all these really meant lots to him) so did all good french poets: rimbaud & apollinaire, gerard de nervals & moreclassi cal ones, racine (for example); x not lamartine; cocteau as novelist & cinematographer; picasso james joyce, a huge enthusiasm. st john perse a big one too st john of the cross: (& teresa of avila) still others. xxxx rabelais, too (big); and chinese novels, like *monkey* liked-kerouac, ginsberg & ferlingheti, too

it might be eaiser to name the five authors he *didn't* like, but i can't think of who they'd have been. malthus, adam smith, jeremy bentham, and, just possibly, john stuart mill.

role of anti-poetry: don't know. st jason: not a clue, at least from memory.

best wishes to you, & best to patrick hart.

sincerely,

Bob Lax

Out of the Shadows:
Merton's Rhetoric of Revelation

Christopher C. Burnham

Thomas Merton's history as a thinker and writer follows a progression from the absolutism of conservative Catholic theology, in his case intensified by the asceticism of his Trappist formation and practice, to an autonomy grown from ongoing conflicts with his community and his study of world religions. His journey culminates in the radical social and political writing of his late career. The various roles he played map his development. As a convert, he transforms from the cynical dandy of his university days to the pious convert and postulant of the 1948 *The Seven Storey Mountain.* In 1951, he begins serving as master of scholastics, introducing innovations to help form the monastic conscience of the young men who came to Gethsemani, often following Merton's own example. By 1957, he is beginning to evolve into the autonomous self of the late controversies over mysticism, radical social action, and the hermitage (Mott, 304–6). This progression is evident in the substance of Merton's writing, as well as in his composing practices.

These claims are based on comparisons of Merton's published texts with the various drafts and personal journal sources through which he arrived at them. The key to this argument is the degree to which Merton begins writing under a shadow of influence, either theological or monastic, but then, through revision, writes his way back to his own authentic experience.

Merton first learned revision under the direction of Robert Giroux, his editor for *The Seven Storey Mountain.* Giroux helped Merton clarify his rhetorical purpose and construct an effective ethos. Later Merton became his own best editor. This can be illustrated by tracing the development of the essay "Rain and the Rhinoceros" through several surviving draft versions, its original publication in *Holiday,* and a subsequent revision for the anthology *Raids on the Unspeakable.* In these revisions, Merton works through veiled allusions and personal allegory to clarify and then begin to act upon his abhorrence of American militarism and the war in Vietnam.

Giroux and Revising *The Seven Storey Mountain*

Before turning to "Rain and the Rhinoceros," let us examine draft materials and the published version of *The Seven Storey Mountain.* Here we see the positive influence of Robert Giroux, the editor charged with helping Merton turn *The Seven Storey Mountain* from an inaccessible theological tract into an autobiography that is still read as a touchstone of the spiritual malaise and moral struggle of post-World War II America.

Giroux was largely responsible for moving Merton back from the pietistic, nearly medieval rhetorical stance of the manuscript of *The Seven Storey Mountain* toward a more direct and accessible account of his personal experience. Specifically, Giroux helped Merton out from under the self-imposed domination of his superiors, Merton's original audience. With this audience the original version of *The Seven Storey Mountain* read more like a theological treatise than an autobiography. Giroux helped Merton conceive a new audience and rhetorical purpose, thereby allowing him to project a sympathetic and accessible ethos, or rhetorical self. Theological treatise becomes historical and personal narrative, and Merton transforms his ethos to that of a representative soul abandoning the spiritually wasted post-war secular world in order to seek both temporal and eternal peace at Gethsemani. Many believe Giroux's influence was responsible for the popularity of the book. Close examination of the manuscript validates this belief.

The book that we read as *The Seven Storey Mountain* is significantly different from Merton's original draft. The draft referenced Catholic themes such as grace and contained elaborate theological arguments to such a degree that Naomi Burton Stone, Merton's agent and long-time friend, wondered whether the book would be accessible to a general audience (Mott, 231). Once the book was accepted for publication, Robert Giroux was assigned editorial responsibility. His task was to help Merton transform a theology-dominated apologia written under the influence of his Trappist formation into a widely accessible autobiography. Giroux directed Merton away from theological argument written for an audience of insiders, his superiors, toward personal narrative that presents Merton as a representative man, struggling against and ultimately rejecting his contemporary secular world for Gethsemani's stable sacred tradition.

From a rhetorical perspective, Giroux's task was two-fold. First, he needed to demonstrate to Merton that his original rhetorical purpose—writing an apologia in the great tradition of Augustine—so limited the audience that only those who already knew what he knew and believed as he believed could read and understand the book. As a corollary, Giroux had to convince Merton to shift from argument to narrative. This shift would allow more readers to identify with him as a representative modern man working through contemporary spiritual alienation. Once readers could identify with Merton, then they could be moved by the account of his transformation and conversion.

Giroux's second but related task involved tempering Merton's ethos. Ethos is the self-image a writer creates through language, tone, and style. When not engaged in the pietism of high theological argument with its technical and elevated language and style, Merton used wit and bitter sarcasm, generally directed at himself, thereby creating the ethos of a clever, if jejune, "wise guy." This wise-guy stance, reminiscent of Merton's satires at Columbia, was off-putting, working against both the original argumentative purpose and the new narrative purpose.

Close examination of the layers of composition and revision in the drafts shows how Merton, under the direction of Giroux, wrote his way out from under the domination of authorities. They further illustrate how Merton creates an accessible and sympathetic ethos. The first subchapter of *The Seven Storey Mountain*, "1. Prisoner's Base," provides an example. I will be comparing Merton's original typed draft (hereafter cited as typed draft), which includes very few corrections in his own handwriting; an intermediate version (hereafter cited as edited draft), which includes editorial and typesetting marks including cross outs, bracketing, and corrections in Giroux's handwriting; and the final published version. Both draft manuscripts are held in the Merton Collection of the Rare Book and Manuscript Library of the Columbia University Library.

In Merton's typed draft, the first subsection runs for eight pages and includes thirty paragraphs. In the edited draft, this same section is reduced to two pages including only ten paragraphs. The published version covers less than one and one-half pages and includes eight paragraphs. Obviously, Giroux and Merton did a great deal of condensing.

My analysis, however, concentrates on what was eliminated in order to condense. Most of the work occurred between the original typed draft and the edited draft, and the differences are suggestive. The typed draft began with a discourse on the soul, an argument shaped in theological terms and depending on specialized vocabulary. The discourse constitutes twenty of the thirty paragraphs of the subsection. It establishes a strong sense of self-contempt rooted in Merton's belief in his own and humankind's debased nature. The theme invokes the doctrine of original sin and includes an apostrophe to God:

> You Who, in Eden, has offered me the heaven of Your infinite liberty and peace, I despised, preferring instability and slavery, loving changing and uncertain goods. I forsook Your immense and unutterable reality, which is Pure Act, without any imperfection or unfulfillment, and gave away participation in XXXX the unending playing of the Three Persons in the Essence of One Infinite Love, in exchange for a thousand petty and complicated XXXXXXXX appetites and cravings, hatred and XX envies, uncertainties and doubts, trying to draw contingent things into the empty center of my own godless being as if to convince myself that I was the XXXXXX kernel of the universe, I was the end of all creation, and not you (typed draft, 2; here and throughout "X" indicates crossouts and emendations that are unreadable: the number of X's approximates the number of characters crossed out).

The literary apostrophe invokes conventional theological themes and language. The specific use of instability suggests an audience of superiors who recognize such use as a direct reference to the vow of stability, one of the several vows Merton professed as a monk of Gethsemani. Only after three paragraphs of such theological discourse does Merton allow a concrete reference to geography, events, or people. He notes his birth, offers impressionistic descriptions of his mother and father, and invokes scenes of World War I. Subsequently, both the edited draft and published version begin with these concrete references.

These concrete references run from paragraph seven through sixteen of the original thirty paragraphs of the subsection. Then, barely one-half way through the first subsection, the discourse on the soul recommences, running from paragraph seventeen through twenty-nine. Merton offers a long sermonic exposition on the three potential destinies of the soul. He mentions limbo, where the pagans Confucius and Aristotle reside, and the hell reserved for those who reject the Christian God. He provides an extensive catalog of sins, including traditional moral aberrations, such as simony, as well as contemporary atrocities, including Nazism (typed draft, 6). He describes the third and final "true destiny . . . to become One Spirit with God, and participators in Divine Nature" (typed draft, 7). In this argument Merton also reveals his theological source by quoting Duns Scotus (typed draft, 8).

Merton ends the subsection with thinly veiled personal references to one,

> born with too much wit, and too much understanding . . . [who] knows everything, he will not bother to look for the answer to anything: all his questions will be merely rhetorical, and their purpose will be merely to advertise his own wisdom and acuteness (typed draft, 8).

> There is hope, however, that these egoists will "find out XXXXXX XXXX, by experience, the fact of their own ignorance and stupidity and nothingness.
> "Because then their questions XXXXXXXXXXX may, perhaps, turn into XXXX prayers, and there will be some chance of their XXXXXXXXXXXXXX receiving an answer" (typed draft, 8).

In addition to the theological argument that would be of interest only to an audience of superiors and other informed Catholics, the typed draft also includes examples of the sarcastic wise-guy stance of the Merton of "too much wit" noted above. Merton portrays existence in limbo in the following terms: "Yet at best, I suppose people like Confucius and Aristotle enjoy an eternity that is about equivalent to a Sunday afternoon at the beach, indefinitely extended, and with grit in all the sandwiches" (typed draft, [5]; page is not numbered but comes between 4 and 6). The humor here turns to sarcasm demonstrating a less-than-charitable attitude in Merton.

He speculates on his destiny if he had not converted:

> I might have ended up in an eternity little worse than a bad dream, separated from God, but enjoying the tedious conversations of a lot of pious philosophers and protestant XXXXX ministers and all the ladies who, under Queen Victoria and since, have XXXXX expired in the suburbs of London without ever having seriously offended God and without ever having loved Him or any one else either (typed draft, [5]).

Here Merton makes his point at the expense of others, ministers and ladies, whom he had come to loathe during his public school and Cambridge days. Such excess may have raised a smile in critics who snidely remark the vacuousness of proper British culture, as Merton frequently did in his satires. But the style also alienates readers who do not hold similar views, especially Americans for whom the criticism of Queen Victoria would make little sense. When Merton does grant himself permission to adventure away from conventional theology in the original typed draft, he engages in stylistic excess and uncharitable commentary that compromises, even defeats, his rhetorical purpose and calls into question the ethical worthiness of the man about to narrate his conversion.

The edited draft produced by revision under the direction of Giroux demonstrates changes in substance and style. These changes document a shift of rhetorical purpose from theological argument with satiric commentary to historical and personal narrative. As noted earlier, Merton condenses eight pages to two. Gone are Dun Scotus and most of the theological argument. Gone is the apostrophe to God and the sermonizing stance it represents. References to Merton's and humankind's debased nature and consequent self-loathing are greatly tempered. The ten paragraphs that remain are all built around concrete historical and personal events. The discourse on the soul's destinies and the catalog of sins is condensed into a one-paragraph portrayal of a world "that was the picture of hell" (edited draft, 1). In the revision, Merton does not indulge himself in generalized theological assertion. Concrete references to historical events in a troubled world at war abound: "Not many hundreds of miles away from the house where I was born, they were picking up the dead men that rotted in the rainy ditches among the dead horses and the ruined XXXXXXXX seventy-fives, in a forest of trees without branches along the river Marne" (edited draft, 1).

Merton carries one significant image from the original typed draft to the edited draft, a reference to "crooked mirrors at Coney Island." He retains this image from the original draft seemingly as an accommodation to an American audience that is, given Merton's revised rhetorical purpose, now his primary audience. In the typed draft, the image comes after Merton's references to the nearby war in Marne and Champagnes: "Too many of us had souls that showed God's image, yes, but XXXX distorted and without likeness, after the manner of the crooked mirrors they have on Coney Island" (typed draft, 2). In the edited draft, the image is used to end the now one-paragraph-long discourse on the soul. Merton starts with general references to his contemporary world, and then builds a generalization about the relation between God and humankind: "It was a XXXXXX world of idolaters, trying to draw all things into their emptiness the way God draws them back into His own fullness: little starved souls, made in the image of God and then twisted out of shape XXXXXXXXXXXXXX like the things you see in those crooked mirrors at Long Island" (edited draft, 1).

Two specific changes deserve note. First, this sentence includes one of the only two uses of "soul" to survive from this section of the original typed draft. The other comes in a paragraph about his mother. Both uses of soul, however, are excised in the published version. Originally serving as a central theme in the argument of the original, soul appears but does not serve as a central theme in the edited draft, and disappears entirely in the published version of the first subsection, "1. Prisoner's Base." The revisions done under the direction of Giroux show Merton abandoning the formal theological concerns and obsessions instilled in him through his conversion and monastic training.

The second change involves Merton's transforming the image from a nonpersonal one—"in the manner" (typed draft, 2)—to a direct personal address to the reader—"like the ones *you see*" (edited draft, 1; emphasis added). The change is an invitation to American readers to participate directly in the text. Further, this direct reference to American culture is treated without sarcasm or humor, allowing American readers to identify with Merton, rather than alienating them as his earlier wise-guy ethos had. These references to Coney Island mirrors do not survive in the published version, perhaps because they are not anchored to a specific historical event or to Merton's personal experience. Giroux convinced Merton that only material with specific and concrete reference could continue in the book.

Nevertheless, the change between original and edited draft demonstrates a key element of Giroux's positive influence on Merton. They show how Merton has established a new rhetorical purpose for *The Seven Storey Mountain.* His purpose now is to present his life and conversion as a concrete and accessible model for those interested in spiritual renewal. And they show how Merton carefully crafts a new ethos to earn the sympathy of his readers. The new "representative man" ethos encourages positive identification between writer and reader, thereby allowing Merton to accomplish his new rhetorical purpose.

Between the edited draft revision and the final published version there are few changes. In addition to excising the references to soul noted earlier, one change deserves note. Merton eliminates a paragraph-long description of his mother's religious attitudes. The excision represents a softening, clearly in the spirit of charity.

The preceding paragraphs present his father in a very sympathetic light: "His vision was religious and clean, and therefore his paintings were without decoration or XXXXXX superfluous comment, since a religious man respects the power of God's creation to XXXX XXXXX bear witness for itself.

"My father was a very good artist. His name was Owen Merton" (edited draft, 2).

Then comes the paragraph on his mother. "My mother was not quite like that." The rest of the paragraph portrays her as "mathematical," and "abstract and idealistic," trying "to get everything else to take the stamp of that idea" (edited draft, 2). She imposed a "Doric neatness that haunted the depths of her soul" (edited draft, 2). Even these brief references provide considerable fuel for exploring the relationship between Merton and his mother. But these are not the point of the book. Excising these references moves the narrative forward, avoiding a distraction. They also make Merton's ethos more sympathetic and accessible.

In sum, the revisions of the first subsection of *The Seven Storey Mountain*, "1. Prisoner's Base," show the strong and positive influence of an editor helping Merton to move beyond his immediate influences and to abandon the sarcasm that, though central to his secular writing, disrupted his spiritual autobiography. These revisions, however, do not tell the whole story of the writing of *The Seven Storey Mountain*, nor do they show the development of Merton as an autonomous thinker and writer. Comparing another set of drafts, journals, and published texts will detail the mature Merton's evolution toward an autonomous, actualized self.

"Rain and the Rhinoceros"

In "Rain and the Rhinoceros" we see Merton acting as an autonomous self. Thinking more and more independently, he focuses his analysis upon his own monastic experience, judges his current practice unsatisfactory, and acts to change it. In both figurative and literal terms, the revisions of "Rain and the Rhinoceros" show

Merton rejecting the comfort and protection of the community, and, along with that comfort, the conformity communal life demands. He seeks a vital but more risky alternative: "vulnerability and death" in the process of discovering his "inner self." Rather than a denial, however, the changes represent "an act and affirmation of solitude" (15; unless noted otherwise, page references are to *Raids on the Unspeakable*). As a consequence, Merton becomes the entirely responsible author of his actions. The revisions also show an ironic consequence of Merton's autonomy: the solitude that ostensibly should complete Merton's withdrawal from the world causes him to re-engage the world by working against injustice, militarism, and war through the radical social and political writing of the last part of his career.

"Rain and the Rhinoceros" originally appeared in *Holiday* in May 1965. Merton's journals indicate he was drafting the essay through the late fall of 1964; he notes completing the manuscript on December 20 of that year. He later submitted a revision, the publication draft, to *Holiday* on January 31, 1965. My analysis is based on comparisons of the original typed draft, including Merton's extensive handwritten changes, the publication typed draft sent to *Holiday* with only a few changes, and the published version. The manuscripts are held in the collection of the Thomas Merton Studies Center at Bellarmine College in Louisville, Kentucky.

The original typed draft represents the transition from early to finished draft. The changes are significant; nine pages grow to thirteen. The title changes from "The Long Night's Festival" to "Rain: Or Ionesco Is Nearer than You Think," and finally to "Rain and the Rhinoceros." These changes reflect a shift in emphasis from poetic reflection to personal and social critique. A similar shift is also evident in Merton's substantive revisions. Yet another version appears in *Raids on the Unspeakable*, an anthology of Merton essays published by New Directions in August 1966. At that time, Merton adds a new ending, a revision that is central in my argument. In sum, almost two years pass between original drafting, the appearance in *Holiday*, and publication in the anthology. That time marks a major period of growth for Merton in spiritual, psychological, and literary matters.

In "Rain and the Rhinoceros," Merton reflects on the anguish of existence in a material culture disconnected entirely from nature and spirit. The reflection begins in the din created by a hard rain falling on the flat roof of his hermitage. Merton is absorbed in the noise. The rain suspends time and activity, creating a festival, opening up space to examine the everyday.

Through the essay, Merton argues that solitude allows the individual to penetrate material and social illusions, to discover the self-alienation of constantly escalating but insatiable needs created by collective material culture, and to transcend these illusions by reconnecting with God through the Spirit. This progression follows the model of Christ's temptation and triumph in the desert. Merton explores a sequence of antitheses. The natural and spiritual oppose the technical and material. Woods and desert stand against the city. The solitary contrasts the social collective. These culminate in a defense of the useless and meaningless, antipathies of the collective that undermine secular materialism through passive resistance. Not to contribute is to subvert. To withdraw is to confront. This is Merton's cultural critique.

Merton invokes sources as various as Philoxenos, a sixth-century Syrian hermit, Thoreau in *Walden,* and Ionesco and the theatre of the absurd. Coleman white gas appliances play a major symbolic role representing a technological means of finding meaning in having "fun." The box of the Coleman lamp advertises its purpose: *"Stretches days to give more hours of fun"* (13).

The festival stops only once during this all-night-through-late-the-next-afternoon deluge when Merton's concentration is broken: "At three-thirty A.M. the SAC plane goes over, red lights winking low under the clouds, skimming the wooded summits of the south side of the valley, loaded with strong medicine. Very strong. Strong enough to burn up all these woods and stretch our hours of fun into eternities" (14). The interruption creates an urgent sense of the world beyond the hermitage, establishing a suggestive relation between the solitary and the worldly that Merton takes a long time working out, both in the essay and his life.

Close analysis of the text in progress shows how Merton changes his ethos, his manner of presenting himself through writing, from a hermit to a social critic attacking mainstream American material culture. Merton's authority, however, does not reside in his superior moral stature as monk. Rather, it originates in his own experience of alienation from the collective. This alienation is signaled in his desire to move to the hermitage. "Rain and the Rhinoceros" and its revisions contain a personal allegory, the internal drama of Merton's self-realization. The drama is not complete until Merton himself recognizes that the ultimate end of solitude will be action—radical protest.

"Rain and the Rhinoceros," according to *Holiday*'s headnote to the essay, "reveals the value of solitude" (8). In the process, Merton offers a radical critique of contemporary American culture. The essay begins with a sense of urgency. "Let me say this before rain becomes a utility that they can plan and distribute for money" (9). The culture of commerce and the city has sufficient power and will to declare anything useful so it can be traded. Merton feels compelled to take this fleeting opportunity to celebrate the rain's "gratuity and meaninglessness" (9). He begins his critique here: culture creates individuals in its own image and for its own ends; the individual works obsessively to be useful and productive in order to satisfy an unending series of needs that exist merely to perpetuate the culture.

Here Merton begins to introduce elements of conflict between him and his community, subtly initiating the private allegory. By the third paragraph he has established his separation from the community: "I came up from the monastery last night, sloshing through the cornfield, said Vespers, and put some oatmeal on the Coleman stove for supper" (9).

The Coleman stove plays a key role in Merton's internal drama. It represents a vehicle of separation from the community and, further, defiance of his superiors. As noted in Mott's biography (359–60), the Coleman appliances were major sources of concern among Merton's censors. Merton had only recently received permission to spend time in the hermitage. Permission was predicated on Merton accepting the hermitage as temporary and experimental. Merton's explicit references to the stove indicate defiance, as if he no longer accepted the original plan and had moved to the hermitage permanently.

He intimates the personal significance of the Coleman appliances: "Coleman's philosophy is printed on the cardboard box which I have (guiltily) not shellacked as I was supposed to, and which I have tossed in the woodshed behind the hickory chunks" (13). This comment seems casual, almost humorous, but it represents defiance significant in inverse relation to its tone. The lantern box was to be shellacked in order to preserve it. Preserving the box reinforces the experimental nature of the hermitage project. In theory, if either Merton or his superiors wanted, the experiment could be called to an end and the appliances packed back in their boxes and stored for some other use. Merton, however, does not shellack and preserve the box; rather, he registers a protest by throwing the box into the woodshed among hickory blocks and other kindling.

While the censors are concerned about the message that might be sent by the references to the Coleman appliances, specifically that Merton has moved to the hermitage and is taking his meals alone, Merton himself is equally concerned that that message be sent. He is withdrawing from his community. He is finding his own way. Merton makes the Coleman appliances symbolic of the collective and its potential negative influences, either the cultural or monastic collective. And cleverly he makes these references so crucial to the essay that they could not be easily excised even if the censors so demanded.

The Coleman stove plays a concrete role in Merton's evolving epiphany concerning the nature of solitude. "It [the oatmeal] boiled over while I was listening to the rain and toasting a piece of bread at the log fire. The night became very dark" (9). With this conventional mystical allusion to the dark night comes a paradoxical realization about the rain and the nature of silence and solitude:

> The rain surrounded the whole cabin with its enormous virginal myth, a whole world of meaning, of secrecy, of silence, of rumor. Think of it: all that speech pouring down, selling nothing, judging nobody, drenching the thick mulch of the dead leaves, soaking the trees, filling the gullies and crannies of the woods with water, washing out the places where men have stripped the hillside! What a thing it is to sit absolutely alone, in the forest at night, cherished by this wonderful, unintelligible, perfectly innocent speech (9–10).

In fact, the dark night's epiphany depends on the interruption provided by the Coleman stove boiling over. Merton moves back and forth from the technological to the natural (stove to rain), from distraction to concentration (stove boiling over to the rain's silence), ultimately to the meditation-stopping sound of the SAC bomber overhead. He establishes a pattern of disruption, yet solitude and its insights come through the silence created by the rain's "perfectly innocent speech" (10). Merton leaves the monastery to achieve solitude, but this solitude contains speech, the antithesis of silence, except that it is purposeless, "selling nothing, judging nobody."

Within the context of Merton's experiment with solitude, the rain's speech accomplishes a great deal. He notes the rain drenches the "mulch of dead leaves" and washes out "places where men have stripped the hillside." In this rain of immanence and transformation, a cleansing sacramental rain, Merton symbolically washes himself of the guilt of separation from community. In a sense he is arguing his case against the community and his superiors. He goes to the hermitage to perfect his solitude. He finds the transforming speech of the rain, discovered in the dark night, made real to him only after being distracted by the crackling noise of the oatmeal boiling over on the Coleman stove. Through this paradoxical process, Merton has finally found his place. And he will take advantage of the opportunity it provides: "It will talk as long as it wants, this rain. As long as it talks I am going to listen" (10).

All this occurs in the essay's first four paragraphs. My analysis points to the embedded personal drama of "Rain and the Rhinoceros" and its paradoxical conclusion. Understanding the significance of the Coleman appliance references within the hermitage experiment, we understand that Merton's ethical and moral authority do not originate in his public role of monk and spiritual writer, but from his own personal experience of ongoing conflict with his community and superiors. This struggle maps the same move toward autonomy that he recommends for the victims of the collective. In addition, the paradoxical relations between solitude, distraction, and insight anticipate Merton's ultimate realization of the moral and ethical imperative to reengage the world through radical protest.

Two revisions in the drafts of "Rain and the Rhinoceros" best exemplify Merton's move toward autonomy. Taken together they underscore the paradox through which solitude brings epiphany and reengagement, the real lessons of the Coleman appliances, Philoxenos, and Ionesco worked out by Merton at the hermitage.

The first revision involves excising a paragraph from the original marked typed draft. This paragraph defended Ionesco's stance as a Platonic gadfly whose purpose is not "giving the audience 'something positive' to take away with them" (21) but only to raise questions and thus call attention to the absurdity of society. Ionesco's plays raise questions, but, because these questions concern the collectivity, which is itself illusory and absurd, they are meaningless. Answering the questions makes one a participant: "To constitute oneself as the single-handed opponent to the rest of the collectivity is to accept the collective fiction at its own face, to set it up as a windmill and exhaust oneself fighting it" (original typed draft, 8). Through the rest of the paragraph Merton offers more support for Ionesco's choice to withdraw and not answer the questions. Any answer is futile.

But Merton ends the paragraph with an ambiguous image affirming the adolescent and irresponsible posture of acting like a child "throwing your ice cream on the floor and screaming until you get spanked" (original typed draft, 8). In the original version Merton defends Ionesco, who assumes the egocentric and morally compromised posture of identifying problems but refusing to become implicated by considering solutions. In this early draft, Merton is defending his own as yet unresolved role as monk and solitary. He too identifies problems in the struggle against the collectivity to personhood, but he will not implicate himself. His solution resembles the adolescent response of the absurdist, but in a different context. He does not throw his ice cream on the floor, but, as narrated in *The Seven Storey Mountain*, he rejects the world and withdraws to the cloister.

That Merton has grown beyond this adolescent response is clear in the revision of this section. In the final version, Merton allows Ionesco to present his own defense. Ionesco denies that he is raising questions but refusing to be implicated or to assume responsibility by suggesting solutions. Merton references another Ionesco work—not a new work that Merton recently discovered but material he had already been using while writing "Rain and the Rhinoceros"—that "portrays the absurdity of a logically consistent individualism which, in fact, is a self-isolation by pseudo-logic of proliferating needs and possessions" (10). Merton argues that since Ionesco has previously theorized existential anxiety and absurdity, the *Rhinoceros* is an application of this theory. He notes that "Ionesco protested that the New York production of *Rhinoceros* as a farce was a complete misunderstanding of his intention. It is a play not merely against *conformism* but about *totalitarianism*" (20). Ionesco, then, is opposing communism, which is, for Merton, one of the demons of contemporary politics.

Later, Merton quotes Ionesco himself in response to the charge that he offers no answers:

> "They (the spectators) leave in a void—and that was my intention. It is the business of the *free man* to pull himself out of the void by his own power and not by the power of other people!" In this Ionesco comes very close to Zen and Christian eremitism (21, emphasis added).

Merton defends Ionesco for not moralizing or providing answers; the individual must create and assume responsibility for answering these questions. This is the lesson Merton is learning through his own experience moving to the hermitage.

In defending Ionesco, however, Merton fails to turn the critique directly against himself. He remains complacent, satisfied to find his own answer by withdrawing to the desert after the model of Philoxenos. He invokes Philoxenos' exhortation to go to the desert to discover Christ: "I will make you true rich men who have need of nothing" (23). Merton accommodates this Christ-like ideal to his *Holiday* audience: "Obviously we will always have *some* needs. But only he who has the simplest and most natural needs can be considered without needs, since the only needs he has are the real ones, and the real ones are not hard to fulfill, if one is a *free man!*" (23, emphasis added).

Merton, by nature of his withdrawal to solitude, has constituted himself a free man, so his reflection is complete. The rain stops. He praises the transforming power of the rain with a resurrection image: "A dandelion, long out of season, has pushed itself into bloom between the smashed leaves of last summer's day lilies" (23). He again invokes the useless noise of the rain, "There is nothing I would rather hear, not because it is better than other noises, but because it is the voice of the present moment, the present festival" (23).

So ends the version of "Rain and the Rhinoceros" that appeared in *Holiday*. In that context it is a satisfying and appropriate ending. Merton's goal was to convince an audience steeped in collective material culture of the value and efficacy of solitude in the festival of the present. Given the struggle documented in *A Vow of Conversation*, Merton's edited and published journals from the period, however, he has committed the same ethical error he earlier first accepted and then challenged in Ionesco, the error of irresponsible withdrawal, of refusing to implicate himself in the problem.

The distance and disinterestedness that critics perceived in Ionesco parallel the complacency and equivocation of Merton listening to the rain in the hermitage, withdrawn, inner directed, Buddha-like, lost in contemplating his own existence. This is the ending Merton sent to *Holiday*, but it is not the ultimate ending of "Rain and the Rhinoceros." Something happens to him between the publication in *Holiday* and the version anthologized in *Raids on the Unspeakable*. Merton adds a coda with a reference to ongoing disturbances in the monastery and at Fort Knox, the military reservation. It signals his realization that he himself is implicated in the world's anguish.

"Rain and the Rhinoceros" appears as the first essay in *Raids on the Unspeakable*, an anthology Merton published with New Directions, a press renowned for its radical aesthetics and politics. In "Prologue: The Author's Advice to His Book," Merton comments that this volume signals a change in him, a change that has been met by resistance by his community and superiors. As a consequence this book needs "special advice" because it too may be met with resistance and hostility. Merton explains that the book is

> unusual. It's your poetic temperament. I would hardly call you devout, though I have found you meditating in your own way (not often in Church). But you must remember that most of your brothers went to the seminary, and you will be expected to be like a seminarian yourself. This, I fear, is where you will get into trouble (1).

In reality, the book had been to seminary, just as the others had, but this book and Merton had gone beyond, all the way to the hermitage, where it learned to "be not so much concerned with ethical principles and traditional answers to traditional questions, for many men have decided no longer to ask themselves these questions" (2). The interest now is in "difficult insights at a moment of human crisis. Such insights can hardly be either comforting or well-defined: they are obscure and ironic" (2). The book addresses "the critical challenge of the hour, that of dehumanization . . . [dealing] with it as you could, with poetry and irony rather than tragic declamation and confessional formulas" (3).

Few could miss the reference to his earlier writing, especially *The Seven Storey Mountain* with its declamations and confessions. Now, however, Merton risks going beyond the safety of formulas to assert an autonomous world view. He must because both he and the world are experiencing a moral and ethical standoff, "a theological point of no return, a climax of finality in refusal, in equivocation, in disorder, in absurdity, which can be broken open again to truth only by miracle, the coming of God" (4).

The essays anthologized in *Raids on the Unspeakable* deal with controversies that had not been traditional concerns of cloistered Christian monks. They range from nuclear arms and militarism through racism and third-world revolutions to Sufi mysticism. "Rain and the Rhinoceros" functions as a perfect introduction to the volume.

And though already published, Merton makes a change in the essay, a significant gesture in light of the risk-taking promised in the prologue.

The *Holiday* version ended with a celebration of the present festival. Now comes a new ending: "Yet even here the earth shakes. Over at Fort Knox the Rhinoceros is having fun" (23). Merton recognizes that he cannot escape the world, even as he tries to perfect his solitude at the hermitage. The reference to the earth-shaking missiles and guns at Fort Knox is illuminated in *A Vow of Conversation*, Merton's edited journals from 1964–65.

Numerous entries document Merton's struggle toward the solitude of the hermitage and his responses, from ecstasy to severe self-criticism, during his initial time there. What he discovers is that solitude does not come from his presence in a particular place; rather, it comes through a painful process much like Christ's experience in the desert referenced in "Rain and the Rhinoceros." The journal reveals several stages of conflict and resolution. His commentaries against his community range from harsh critique to melancholic reflection.

On November 24, 1964, he remarks on another SAC bomber flyover that distracted him during the consecration at the conventual Mass. He continues by reflecting on a full day at the hermitage and the contrast between his vital hermitage life and the numbing life of the community:

> Only here do I feel that my life is fully human. And only what is authentically human is fit to be offered to God. There is no question in my mind that the artificiality of life in the community is in its own small way, something quite deadly (saved by the fact that the artificiality of life in the 'world' is totally monstrous and irrational) (103).

The latter point is the explicit argument of "Rain and the Rhinoceros." The critique of the monastic community, however, shows the more significant struggle through which he creates an ethos to legitimize his social commentary. A later entry compares "the power, the energy of truth" (111) released in solitude to the dulling conformity of life in community. The comment invokes a melancholy: "It seems to me though that these streams [of energy and truth] do not get to run for me in the community and that I simply go along in the heavy, secure, confused neutrality of the community, though perhaps for others the springs are running" (111). Throughout this period the journal records the conflict between individual and community, often in the same language—community is referred to as "collectivity"—that constitutes his critique of mainstream American culture in "Rain and the Rhinoceros."

The journal includes numerous references to SAC bomber flyovers and to the distracting din of the guns and missiles firing at Fort Knox. The journal documents Merton's growing objections to the war in Southeast Asia specifically and to America's militarism in general. The noise of the guns at Fort Knox results from training exercises preparing conscripted young men to be sent to Asia to fight the war that Merton is coming more and more to abhor. Bombers fly over and exploding shells and missiles shake Gethsemani's earth, distracting Merton from the concentration he seeks in solitude. The noise, first noted as a nuisance, becomes an obsession. Just as in "Rain and the Rhinoceros," this distraction brings an epiphany:

> The guns were pounding at Fort Knox while I was making my afternoon meditation, and I thought that, after all, this is no mere distraction. I am *here* because they are *there;* indeed, I am *supposed* to hear them! They form a part of an ever renewed decision and commitment on my part, for peace. But what peace? (117).

The final question refers to a growing tension between the inner personal peace he seeks through solitude and peace in a world shattered by guns and encircled by bombers carrying nuclear weapons.

The entry becomes more and more complex as Merton is pulled between the silent and prayerful goal of solitude and the need to turn back to the world to seek justice, a tension Merton ultimately surrenders "to the mysterious and sovereign intention of the Lord, the Master whom I have come here to serve" (117). The entry stops short of committing Merton to radical anti-war and social protest, but his subsequent life and writings indicate the direction he chose.

The journal, however, documents Merton's own awareness of the growing tension in his life. His final commitment to God's sovereign intentions, however, is not mediated by the security and confident trust in convention represented by the community, nor by trust in and obedience to his superiors, as promised in his monastic vows, but only in his own growing awareness, self-knowledge, and inexhaustible questioning, questioning that creates a burden on and discord in Merton's heart. He cannot turn away from these questions any more than he can ignore worldly explosions: "Yet even here the earth shakes. Over at Fort Knox the Rhinoceros is having fun" (23).

Having moved out of the shadows of literary and theological influence, Merton no longer uses conventional rhetoric to affirm traditional theology; now, as an autonomous self, he allows revelation to act directly on him. As we trace this process through his revisions, we witness Merton's rhetoric of self-discovery and actualization.

(In addition to the appreciation offered to Dr. Robert Daggy and the Thomas Merton Studies Center and the Rare Books Collection of the Columbia University Library for access to the manuscripts used in this essay, I must also thank New Mexico State University's College of Arts and Sciences for grants supporting my travel and research. I also acknowledge the help of Professor Kevin McIlvoy and the students in my fall 1995 Nonfiction Prose Graduate Workshop who read and responded to various drafts of this material.)

Works Cited

Merton, Thomas. *Raids on the Unspeakable*. New York: New Directions, 1966.
_____. "Rain and the Rhinoceros." *Holiday* 37 (May 1965) 8–16.
_____. *The Seven Storey Mountain*. New York: Harcourt Brace Jovanovich, 1948.
_____. *A Vow of Conversation*. New York: Farrar, Straus, and Giroux, 1988.
Mott, Michael. *The Seven Mountains of Thomas Merton*. Boston: Houghton Mifflin Company, 1984.

Thomas Merton in Search of His Heart: The Autobiographical Impulse of Merton's Bonaventure Novels

by Paul M. Pearson

"I am still trying to find out: and that is why I write."
"How will you find out by writing?"
"I will keep putting things down until they become clear."
"And if they do not become clear?"
"I will have a hundred books, full of symbols, full of everything I ever knew or ever saw or ever thought."[1]

These words of Thomas Merton, first published in 1969, provide a vital key to his enormous literary output. They point to his continual questioning and search for the truth, both his own personal truth, the truth of his life, as well as truth for the whole of humanity—two paths to truth Merton saw as inseparable. But that dialogue, published in 1969, was written at St. Bonaventure's in June 1941 and comes from Merton's autobiographical novel *My Argument with the Gestapo*. They are prophetic words for the rest of Merton's life and show the intensity of his self-awareness and his self-knowledge from the very earliest days of his writing career.

In the years following Merton's baptism, immediately prior to his entry into the Abbey of Our Lady of Gethsemani in December 1941, his literary output steadily increased; however, except for some book reviews and a few poems, little was published at that time. Merton spent the summer of 1939 and part of the summer of 1940 at Olean in

---

1. Thomas Merton, *My Argument with the Gestapo: A Macaronic Journal* (New York: New Directions, 1975) 52–53.

the cottage of Lax's brother-in-law, Benji Marcus, with Bob Lax and Ed Rice. The three friends spent the summer of 1939 writing novels, and Merton tells us his novel "grew longer and longer and longer and eventually it was about five hundred pages long, and was called first *Straits of Dover* and then *The Night Before the Battle*, and then *The Labyrinth*."[2] The following year Merton wrote *The Man in the Sycamore Tree*, and in 1941, while teaching at St. Bonaventure's, he completed *My Argument with the Gestapo*. He tried without success to get *The Labyrinth*, *The Man in the Sycamore Tree*, and *My Argument with the Gestapo* published at that time. On his entry to Gethsemani he carefully preserved *My Argument with the Gestapo* and sent it to Mark Van Doren, but believed he destroyed the other novels. Merton was mistaken, however, and in recent years a fragment of both *The Straits of Dover* and *The Man in the Sycamore Tree* have come to light, as well as the greater part of *The Labyrinth*.[3]

Merton describes these works as novels, saying of *The Labyrinth* that it was partly autobiographical, covering some of the ground later covered by *The Seven Storey Mountain*. He also says he mixed up "a lot of imaginary characters"[4] with his own story, a technique he also used in *My Argument with the Gestapo*. Naomi Burton Stone, to whom Merton submitted these novels, also remembers them as autobiographical, describing *The Man in the Sycamore Tree* as strongly autobiographical and *My Argument with the Gestapo* as containing "many scenes from his boyhood."[5]

The autobiographical novel is a definite literary form[6] and has been used by numerous writers including Lawrence and Joyce, both of whom Merton was reading at this period of his life. In an autobiographical novel characters are frequently "put into situations which

---

2. Thomas Merton, *The Seven Storey Mountain* (London: Sheldon Press, 1975) 240.

3. A near-complete copy of *The Labyrinth* was found, according to Michael Mott, in a folder with the erroneous title "Journal of My Escape from the Nazis" in pencil on the cover, and a number of pages from *The Straits of Dover* and *The Man in the Sycamore Tree* were found among papers Merton gave to Father Richard Fitzgerald at St. Bonaventure's before Merton left for Gethsemani. Michael Mott, *The Seven Mountains of Thomas Merton* (London: Sheldon Press, 1986) 126–7.

4. Merton, *The Seven Storey Mountain*, 241.

5. Merton, *My Argument with the Gestapo*, 15.

6. Roy Pascal, *Design and Truth in Autobiography* (London: Routledge & Kegan Paul Ltd., 1960). See in particular ch. 11.

can be called extreme" and "in which the posited potentialities of the character have the utmost room to develop"[7]—one could think here of Merton's return to London and France in *My Argument with the Gestapo* as an illustration of this. The autobiographical novel allows the writer to discover something of their "infinite range," whereas autobiography proper "tends towards practical wisdom" recounting the way in which the author has "come to terms with reality" and found a way to "the realised self"[8]; it can reveal "in a person what in life may be hidden and only latent"[9] and point to what the author "feels is his potential reality."[10] A novel is "complete in itself while the autobiography always reaches forward"[11] to the writer. Finally, the literary form of the autobiographical novel is more suitable to a younger writer, since a younger one would be unlikely to have the perspective necessary to write what Pascal has called a "significant autobiography."[12]

The section of *The Straits of Dover* that has been found can hardly be described as an autobiographical novel—it is much more straightforward autobiography than novel. In it Merton describes Oakham and its surroundings and some elements of his life there. There are also a few pages describing his life at Cambridge, and he makes some references to his grandfather and Aunt Maud. Similarly *The Labyrinth*, which Merton points out in *The Seven Storey Mountain* is developed from *The Straits of Dover*,[13] is largely autobiographical, although it contains three sections that would fit better into the classification of the novel.[14] *The Labyrinth* begins with Merton returning to England from New York and goes on to describe life at Oakham, his visit to Cambridge to take the entrance exam, his European trip after his eighteenth birthday, including his visit to Rome, his first year at

---

7. Ibid., 176.
8. Ibid., 178.
9. Ibid., 176.
10. Ibid., 178.
11. Ibid., 164.
12. Ibid., 178.
13. Merton, *The Seven Storey Mountain*, 240.
14. Thomas Merton, *The Labyrinth* [unpublished manuscript], Thomas Merton Studies Center, Bellarmine College, Louisville, Kentucky. (Merton's original page-numbering is missing from many pages, so page numbers referred to here are those added at some later point and run through the whole manuscript.) These novel sections are pp. 15–25 about Terence Park, pp. 98–106 describing Jato in Marseilles, and pp. 119–44 entitled "The Memoirs of a Prince of the Blood."

Cambridge and "the party in the middle of the night," his return to New York, and his early months back there. Mott has suggested Merton developed some sections from *The Labyrinth* in writing *The Seven Storey Mountain*, and in writing *The Sign of Jonas* in 1948 Merton describes *The Seven Storey Mountain* as "the book I couldn't make a go of ten years ago"[15]—obviously a reference to *The Labyrinth*.

Only the opening part of *The Man in the Sycamore Tree* has been preserved and, of all these unpublished works, this is the closest to an autobiographical novel. Naomi Burton Stone described it as "a wild and wonderful story, often extremely funny,"[16] while at the same time acknowledging its "strong autobiographical streak." Unlike *The Straits of Dover* and *The Labyrinth*, Merton no longer speaks using the first person singular; instead, he very thinly disguises himself as one of the novel's characters—Jim Mariner. The character is obviously Merton: he writes stories and poems, is working on an M.A. on Blake, reads Gilson and Maritain, is melancholy, very pious, greatly troubled by the news from Europe, and is attracted to the priestly life.

My Argument with the Gestapo, written shortly after Merton's Easter visit to Gethsemani, is the only complete example of these novels and the only one to be published. Originally called *Journal of My Escape from the Nazis*, it frequently reads more like a journal than a novel.[17] In addition to containing many scenes from Merton's boyhood, it also reflects his questioning and the dilemmas he was facing at the time he wrote it.[18]

15. Thomas Merton, *The Sign of Jonas* (London: Hollis & Carter, 1953) 107. Merton makes a similar remark in a letter of October 1948 to Father Raymond Flanagan describing *The Seven Storey Mountain* as "definitely the book God has been wanting me to get off my chest all these years. I was already trying it ten years ago." Thomas Merton, *Witness to Freedom: Letters in Times of Crisis*, ed. William H. Shannon (New York: Farrar, Straus, Giroux, 1994) 236.

16. Merton, *My Argument with the Gestapo*, 13.

17. A point made by Anthony Padovano in his book *The Human Journey, Thomas Merton: Symbol of a Century* (Garden City, N.Y.: Image Books/A Division of Doubleday & Company, 1984) 10. In a letter of November 1941 to Mark Van Doren Merton himself calls it a journal saying "the book is confusing anyway, except as a Journal, which is what it is." Thomas Merton, *The Road to Joy: Letters to New and Old Friends*, ed. Robert E. Daggy (New York: Farrar, Straus, Giroux, 1989) 12.

18. A number of drafts of *My Argument with the Gestapo* exist and the major difference between them and the version published in 1969 is that they contain two sections of material omitted from the published version. First, a section is omitted from p. 133 of the published version in which Merton discusses in further detail

Recalling *My Argument with the Gestapo* in *The Seven Storey Mountain*, Merton wrote of it that it was "the kind of book that I liked to write." He found it satisfying as "it fulfilled a kind of psychological necessity that had been pent up in me all through the last stages of the war because of my sense of identification, by guilt, with what was going on in England. . . . It was something I needed to write."[19] Returning to look at the book in 1951, for the first time in ten years, Merton found it a "very inhibited book"[20] and suggested it gave a false solution to the question of his relationship with the world. But Merton was never able to abandon this book and occasionally raised the question of publishing it with his literary agent. In 1968 Merton describes *My Argument with the Gestapo* as "a book I am pleased with. . . . There is good writing and it comes from the center where I have really experienced myself and my life."[21] He tells Naomi that "it reads well, just as well as it ever did."[22] By the end of Merton's life he seemed keener on *My Argument* than he is on *The Seven Storey Mountain*, suggesting the author of the latter was dead not once, but many times[23]—an attitude very different from his 1968 comments on *My Argument*. A possible reason for his attitude change could be that, in the end, *My Argument with the Gestapo* is truer to Merton than his best-selling autobiography. *My Argument* and these other novel fragments provide a balance, to some extent, to *The Seven Storey Mountain*, where Merton, in the early fervor

---

Charlie Chaplin films, which he describes as "big, important events of my life." He concluded the omitted section by saying, "A list of Charlie Chaplin's pictures and the places where I saw them is like the outline for the story of my life." (Merton's reference to the places where he saw these films in this quote is important as it points to the way in which an autobiography can be laid out by significant landmarks in the autobiographer's life, thus a possible structure for an autobiography is one that traces "the significant geography of a life." See Irwin J. Montaldo, "Toward the Only Real City in America: Paradise and Utopia in the Autobiography of Thomas Merton" [MA thesis, Emory University, 1974] 11.) Second, the unpublished version contains a couple of extra pages at the end in which Merton speaks to his completed book and sends it on its way. These two sections are to be found in a first typescript draft of *Journal of My Escape from the Nazis*, with undated author's corrections, held at the Merton Studies Center, and in a version contained in vol. 3 of Merton's *Collected Essays*, also held at the Studies Center.

19. Merton, *The Seven Storey Mountain*, 336.
20. Merton, *The Sign of Jonas*, 313.
21. Mott, *The Seven Mountains of Thomas Merton*, 513.
22. Merton, *Witness to Freedom*, 150.
23. Merton, *The Sign of Jonas*, 320.

of his monastic life, presents both his life and the world in black and white terms. In Merton's pre-monastic novels he does not see things in such clear-cut terms but, as he says in *My Argument*, "I am all the time trying to answer both you and myself. I am all the time trying to make out the answer, as I go on living."[24] He is continuing to search for answers, unlike in *The Seven Storey Mountain* where he presents Gethsemani as the answer. In *My Argument* Merton was also struggling to "rediscover his own past in some meaningful continuity with his present circumstances,"[25] working through his own difficulties and doubts at a crucial time of decision for him so that his preoccupations in Europe are "those of the actual Merton at that time in America":[26]

> If you want to identify me, [if I want to identify myself] ask me not where I live, or what I like to eat, or how I comb my hair, but ask me what I think I am living for, in detail, and ask me what I think is keeping me from living fully for the thing I want to live for.[27]

These are the very questions Merton was asking himself in the summer of 1941 after his first visit to Gethsemani.

In all four of these novels Merton explores his own inner truth, attempting to make sense of his story, and, in writing it for publication, attempting to make that story known to others. Over the course of Merton's early work from *The Straits of Dover* to *The Seven Storey Mountain* a sense of direction develops. Robert Giroux felt that *The Straits of Dover* "got nowhere"[28] and in *The Labyrinth* there is much rushing about but "no clear purpose to the rushing."[29] In *My Argument with the Gestapo* Padovano has suggested there is "paralysis at the heart of the novel despite the frenzy on the surface,"[30] but Merton is beginning to ask the right questions. In his unpublished ending to *My Argument*

24. Merton, *My Argument with the Gestapo*, 161.

25. David D. Cooper, *Thomas Merton's Art of Denial: The Evolution of a Radical Humanist* (Athens: University of Georgia Press, 1989) 281.

26. George Woodcock, *Thomas Merton, Monk and Poet: A Critical Study* (Edinburgh: Canongate, 1978) 33.

27. Merton, *My Argument with the Gestapo*, 160–1.

28. William H. Shannon, *Silent Lamp: The Thomas Merton Story* (New York: Crossroad, 1992) 17.

29. Mott, *The Seven Mountains of Thomas Merton*, 126.

30. Padovano, *The Human Journey*, 13. In *The Sign of Jonas*, 313, Merton describes this problem with the book as follows: "A situation presents itself and the stream of the book—which after all has a stream—stops and forms a lake. It is sometimes quite a bright lake. But I can do nothing with it."

with the Gestapo Merton gives a definite impression that he is coming close to an answer as "we are girded with white chords, (being secret monks) that we may remember Ariadne's subtle string that solved the maze's mathematic."[31] In *The Seven Storey Mountain* the impression Merton gives is that he has quite clearly found the answer he was searching for equating Gethsemani with the paradise of Dante's *Divine Comedy*. His epilogue, though, does sow further questions, and such questions will be more central to the remainder of Merton's life and work than any answers he may appear to have found in *The Seven Storey Mountain*. This movement in Merton's life from his dissipated early life to the rigid order and narrowness of life in the monastery and then, in later years, returning to a much broader vision of himself and the world, but rooted in the relationship he developed with Christ in his early days at Gethsemani, is like the shape of an hourglass.[32]

The picture of Merton that appears through his pre-monastic novels is fascinating and provides a balance to the picture presented in *The Seven Storey Mountain*. Three aspects of that picture are worth examining in detail so as to illustrate both the intensity of Merton's self-awareness and his self-knowledge from the earliest days of his writing career, as well as the balance Merton's pre-monastic novels provide to his autobiography. First, the connections found between Merton's writing of this period and his later work; second, his own attitude toward his time in Europe, especially England and Cambridge; and, finally, returning to examine the autobiographical nature of these novels.

A Fine Consistency: Early Novels and Late Monastic Writings

Anthony Padovano wrote in *The Human Journey* that "one of the unexpected aspects of the life of Merton is his consistency."[33] He illus-

---

31. Merton, *Collected Essays*, 294–6.

32. David Mack Haynie, "Mysticism as the Basis for Religious Pluralism in the Thought of Thomas Merton" (Th.D. diss., Southwestern Baptist Theological Seminary, 1977). Haynie describes Merton's spiritual pilgrimage as one of "unity emerging from diversity that developed in an hourglass shape. Merton moved downward in a spiraling motion through the diversities of his pre-monastic years to Gethsemani, where his unity with God in Christ was achieved. This movement in his life represented the center of the hourglass." From this unity "Merton's spiritual pilgrimage after 1951 became an outward and expanding spiraling motion into the other half of the hourglass as he sought to encompass and unify all things in and through himself in Christ by love," 55.

33. Padovano, *The Human Journey*, 14.

trated this comment by comparing *My Argument with the Gestapo* with *Cables to the Ace* and *The Geography of Lograire*, drawing attention to the many elements his early novel had in common with his final anti-poetry: they are all autobiographical, concerned with the decay of civilization, present the author on a journey on which he never finds a home, and illustrate his passion for non-violence.[34]

The comparison Padovano makes can be extended. In Merton's unpublished novels there are many themes that will crop up consistently for the rest of his life: the importance of place and geography, feelings of exile, questions concerning nationality, the place of adverts, plague imagery and the use and misuse of language, along with the themes suggested by Padovano. An interesting example of this is Merton's use, for the very first time, of the phrase "something I had been looking for"[35] in *The Labyrinth*. This and similar phrases are phrases he would use a number of times in his life at major critical points, emphasizing the importance of the events he is relating.[36] William Shannon has described such phrases as "a Merton signature for moments of profound experience."[37]

Another important element pointing to the consistency of Merton's life is his early attraction toward solitude. In *The Straits of Dover* Merton describes frequent times at Oakham where he spent time on his own,[38] describing how he would go to Brooke Hill and "walk, or sit, up there for hours, not waiting for anything or looking for anything or expecting anything, but simply looking out over the wide valley, and watching the changes of the light across the hills, and

34. Naomi Burton Stone in her introduction to *My Argument with the Gestapo*, 14, stressed this point and suggested Merton's novel expressed "his lifelong convictions about the futility of war and its brutalizing effects" on humanity.

35. On p. 52 of Merton's typescript of *The Labyrinth* he has added this phrase at some later stage by hand. The following page contains a similar phrase: "something that I was looking for."

36. The most well-known example of his use of this phrase is recorded in *The Asian Journal of Thomas Merton* days before his death after his visit to the carved images of the Buddha at Polonnaruwa. In his journal for December 4, 1968, Merton writes, "I know and have seen what I was obscurely looking for." Thomas Merton, *The Asian Journal of Thomas Merton,* ed. Naomi Burton and others (London: Sheldon Press, 1974) 236.

37. Shannon, *Silent Lamp,* 278.

38. Thomas Merton, *The Straits of Dover* [unpublished manuscript], Thomas Merton Studies Center, Bellarmine College, Louisville, Kentucky. 7, 14–16.

watching the changes of the sky,"[39] noting "I must have had the reputation of rather a solitary fellow."[40]

Merton's Attitude toward Europe

In Merton's pre-Gethsemani novels his attitude toward Europe, especially England, is quite different from the picture he gives in *The Seven Storey Mountain*. In his autobiography he associates his time in England with hell, with Cambridge being the lowest circle of the inferno and remaining for many years the one really bad place in Merton's geography. Gradually, especially in *Conjectures of a Guilty Bystander*, Merton comes to terms with his time in Europe and begins to recall good times that had, in the black and white approach of *The Seven Storey Mountain*, been forgotten or ignored.

Merton's picture of his time in England is quite different in his novel fragments. In *My Argument with the Gestapo*, in an attempt to reconcile his past with his present circumstances in 1941, Merton returns to England and France. In 1940 Merton had written of his concern about the bombing of London, "where I once lived, where there are so many people that were my friends in school, and people that I loved."[41] In *My Argument with the Gestapo* he returns to England for "the reasons Dante made his"[42] journey, recognizing in far more compassionate terms than in *The Seven Storey Mountain* that "because you loved too much, in your childishness, the things the world adored, Christ's Crucifixion flowered in London."[43] In *My Argument with the Gestapo* Merton does not return to Cambridge, although he discusses it with a soldier who concludes, after Merton compares his memory of it to "the waiting rooms of dentists,"[44] that Merton "doesn't like Cambridge."[45]

In writing about London in *My Argument with the Gestapo* Merton presents two views of it corresponding to Blake's poems of innocence

---

39. Ibid., 15.

40. Ibid., 16. This last phrase has been crossed out in the manuscript but is still legible.

41. Mott, *The Seven Mountains of Thomas Merton*, 165. Taken from an entry in Merton's St. Bonaventure Journal dated October 27, 1940.

42. Merton, *My Argument with the Gestapo*, 137.

43. Ibid., 138.

44. Ibid., 107.

45. Ibid., 112.

and experience. One is "a city of angels"[46] and in the other "the masks fall off the houses, and the streets become liars and the squares become thieves and the buildings become murderers."[47] For Merton, "the first city vanished when I walked the streets of the second at night."[48] In *My Argument with the Gestapo* Merton's attitude toward Tom Bennett— Uncle Rafe as he is called in that novel—is quite different. Merton acknowledges some of his debt to Bennett by saying that if he made a list of the things he learned from Bennett it "would be very long"[49] and "only from my father did I learn what would make a longer list than that of the things I first heard of from Uncle Rafe."[50] Finally, he recalls a drunken attempt at apologizing for everything before he left London.[51] Merton's attitude to the Bennetts here is more sympathetic than in *The Seven Storey Mountain* and more in line with a letter he wrote to Iris Bennett in 1966.[52]

Although Merton avoided visiting Cambridge in *My Argument with the Gestapo,* he does not avoid it in *The Straits of Dover* and *The Labyrinth.* In *The Straits of Dover* he writes of his expectations of Cambridge as the place where "I was almost sure that I would find exactly what I wanted."[53] In *The Labyrinth* Merton expands on those expectations of what Cambridge meant:

> . . . almost everything you expected from life. It meant finding out what everything meant, . . . wearing good clothes, . . . talking to interesting people, famous people; finding out about the things that a civilised person had to know: wines and foods and particular kinds of tobaccos. . . . I would drive cars, and row, and ride and hunt; I would write and dance and sing and paint; I would act, I would box and fence; I would go shooting, I would sail, . . . but most important of all I would also run into the queen of all women.[54]

46. Ibid., 33.

47. Ibid., 34.

48. Ibid., 35.

49. Ibid., 143.

50. Ibid., 143–4.

51. Ibid., 148.

52. In Merton's letter to Iris Bennett in 1966 he spoke of "the immense debt I owed to Tom and which, all appearances to the contrary, I have never forgotten. And the debt I owe you, too." Merton, *The Road to Joy,* 77.

53. Merton, *The Straits of Dover,* 21.

54. Merton, *The Labyrinth,* 30.

Similarly, on his visit to Cambridge for the entrance exam, Merton describes himself and his friends as excited, awed, and happy.[55] References such as these are not to be found in *The Seven Storey Mountain,* with its use of the metaphor of hell to describe Merton's youth. The happier times, which certainly existed and which Merton would later in his life acknowledge,[56] have been overlooked.

The chapter of *The Labyrinth* entitled "The Party in the Middle of the Night"[57] is more negative about Merton's time at Cambridge, describing it as the nadir of his sun. However, the following spring Merton can still describe something of the beauty of Cambridge: "The grass sparkled with its own moisture, in the pale, stronger-growing sun. . . . I had always known Cambridge would look like this in the spring. It was very beautiful; everywhere was very beautiful in the spring." He adds—very mildly when compared to his dislike of Cambridge in *The Seven Storey Mountain*—"but here I still couldn't be sure I liked it."[58]

In *The Labyrinth,* by the time Merton left England in the autumn, his view of Cambridge was that he "had not made peace" with it and "actively hated the place."[59] His other memories of England and France are quite different and a contrast to the equivalent passage in *The Seven Storey Mountain.*[60] Merton felt it was heartrending leaving "all the places I have ever most liked, the places I have grown up in." He writes of "places where I have been most happy" saying, "leaving

---

55. Ibid., 32.

56. See, for example, Thomas Merton, *Conjectures of a Guilty Bystander* (London: Burns & Oates, 1968) 168–9.

57. Merton, *The Labyrinth,* 65.

58. Ibid., 75.

59. Ibid., 85.

60. Merton, *The Seven Storey Mountain,* 128ff. There is a discrepancy between Merton's account of leaving England in his autobiography and in *The Labyrinth.* At the end of Merton's first year at Cambridge he went to America for the summer and sailed from Tilbury. When he left England for good in November 1934, he sailed from Southampton. In *The Labyrinth* Merton's description of England is centered around passing through the Straits of Dover after having sailed from Tilbury. This could suggest that his account of sailing from England in *The Labyrinth* is an account of his trip at the end of his first year at Cambridge, but a careful reading of the text reveals quite clearly that Merton sees this voyage as his "going away for good" from England with all his possessions, and that if he ever came back it would be "with a different passport and a new nationality" and as "a completely different person." Merton, *The Labyrinth,* 87.

it behind is like leaving behind my whole life"[61] and, feeling tears in his eyes, Merton has to bite his lip to keep them back.[62] As Merton leaves England in *The Labyrinth* his memories are closer to passages he would later write in *Conjectures of a Guilty Bystander* than to his description of England in *The Seven Storey Mountain*, including in both *The Labyrinth* and *Conjectures* lists of places important to his personal geography.

A similar comparison can be made between Merton's accounts of his 1933 trip to Rome in *The Labyrinth* and *The Seven Storey Mountain*. In *The Labyrinth* he describes it as "the same good city," adding "I was very happy."[63] In *The Seven Storey Mountain* he says, "I was miserable."[64] The episode in *The Seven Storey Mountain* where Merton describes a vision of his dead father is described in *The Labyrinth* as despondency "because I was simply lonely . . . and had no one to talk to";[65] it makes no mention at all of his father.[66] Hawkins suggests that the anticlimax in Merton's narrative after his visit to Rome as recorded in *The Seven Storey Mountain* indicates that "nothing whatsoever really happened to Merton in the Roman hotel room,"[67] which suggests that his account in *The Labyrinth* is possibly closer to his original experience.

Merton's attitude to his earlier life seen in his unpublished novels is more consistent with his later memories of that life as he grew to maturity at Gethsemani than with the account he gives in *The Seven Storey Mountain*. This difference does not undermine Merton's autobiography, as the truth expected from an autobiography is different from that expected from a biography, which is concerned with facts and the reconstruction of a life. The concern of an autobiography is not with the events recalled, but with the person those events have formed, "more

61. Merton, *The Labyrinth*, 84.
62. Ibid., 86.
63. Ibid., 48.
64. Merton, *The Seven Storey Mountain*, 106.
65. Merton, *The Labyrinth*, 60.
66. William Shannon has suggested that in *The Seven Storey Mountain* the eighteen-year-old school boy is being judged with great severity by the thirty-one-year-old monk who is "projecting onto the younger man the moral lapses that would occur later that year at Clare College, Cambridge." Shannon, *Silent Lamp*, 70.
67. Anne Olivia Hawkins, *Archetypes of Conversion: The Autobiographies of Augustine, Bunyan, and Merton* (Cranbury, N.J.: Associated University Presses, 1985) 145.

the revelation of the present situation than the uncovering of the past."[68] Thus in *The Seven Storey Mountain* Merton gives the reader his experience from the standpoint he has reached. When Merton distorts the truth the distortions can be "as revealing as the truth."[69] Thus Merton's presentation of his time in Europe in his autobiography serves to contrast his metaphor of hell, descriptive of his life at that stage, with his later metaphor of Gethsemani as paradise. By emphasizing his embrace of life at Gethsemani in opposition to the life he believed he had renounced and left behind, Merton clearly demonstrates the standpoint he has adopted. Likewise his account of the vision of his father in Rome adds to the story of his conversion and the important place he attributed to his father in both his life and his conversion.

Essentially Autobiography

Merton's pre-Gethsemani novels are all, to varying degrees, autobiographical and, as with Merton's autobiography and the journals he prepared for publication, their titles are metaphors for the experience he is describing in them. *The Straits of Dover*, also a title for a chapter of *The Labyrinth*, refers to a point that was the central crossroads for Merton up until 1934—a geographical and psychological juncture.[70] *The Labyrinth* is descriptive of the mixed up nature of Merton's life, "a maze with no way out for either author or reader."[71] Its title suggests a very different understanding of his life than the one he had when he wrote *The Seven Storey Mountain*. *The Labyrinth* suggests that his view of his life when he wrote that book was of a rather confusing maze, a contrast to the metaphor of *The Seven Storey Mountain*, as James McNerney has remarked: "Where 'Labyrinth' conveys a futile meandering, the other evokes Dante's ascent to Paradise. It is a journey with a destination."[72]

68. Pascal, *Design and Truth in Autobiography*, 11.

69. Ibid., 62.

70. In writing of the Straits of Dover as a crossroads "between all the places I have lived in" Merton goes on to add, in a section that has been crossed out but is still legible, that there were only two important places in his life not reached by this crossroad—New York and Bermuda, recalling Bermuda as an important place in his life without any mention of its importance to him. Merton, *The Labyrinth*, 84.

71. Mott, *The Seven Mountains of Thomas Merton*, 126.

72. James R. McNerney, "Merton and the Desert Experience," *Review for Religious* 43 (1984) 601.

The title of *The Man in the Sycamore Tree* refers to the gospel account of Zacchaeus,[73] the tax-collector, who climbed up into a sycamore tree so he could see Jesus more clearly. Merton's title here reflects his own growing determination to follow the will of God for him and to turn away, like Zacchaeus, from his sins. The name of the character who is obviously Merton is also relevant—Mariner, a name that picks up on Merton's interest in the sea and travel and, more specifically now, his journey to God. In one of Merton's early Gethsemani poems, "The Landfall," a poem describing his discovery of Gethsemani in terms of a voyage, Merton uses the name Mariner saying:

O Mariner, what is the name of this uncharted Land?
On these clean shores shall stand what sinless voyager,
What angel breathe the music of this atmosphere?[74]

Merton's use of a capital M in Mariner implies he is using the word as a proper noun, as opposed to using it to simply describe a seaman.

Merton's autobiographical purpose in *My Argument with the Gestapo*—a book that Mott has suggested should be renamed *My Argument with England,* as the Gestapo are incidental to the story—can be seen both in Merton's title for the book as well as in the quote from Donne that he uses as an epigraph for the book:

I sacrifice this Iland unto thee,
And all whom I lov'd there, and who lov'd mee;
When I have put our seas twixt them and mee
Put thou thy sea betwixt my sinnes and thee.[75]

A fitting epigraph as Merton attempted to reconcile himself with his time in England and France, but not with his sins—a reconciliation not evident in *The Seven Storey Mountain,* but which would surface in Merton's later autobiographical works.

My Argument with the Gestapo, along with the fragments that remain of Merton's other pre-Gethsemani novels, contains varying amounts of autobiographical material and indicates the centrality of

73. Luke 19:1-10.
74. Thomas Merton, *The Collected Poems of Thomas Merton* (London: Sheldon Press, 1978) 190.
75. John Donne, "A Hymne to Christ, at the Author's last going into Germany," *The Divine Poems,* ed. John Hayward (Middlesex: Penguin Books, 1973) 175. Used by Merton as an epigraph to *My Argument with the Gestapo.*

autobiography to Merton's work. His concern with telling the story of his life was not a one-off concern in obedience to his abbot[76] but, as his later works show—especially his journals and poetry, and in fact all his works—it is a key to Thomas Merton, especially to Merton as a writer. Merton's pre-Gethsemani novels very clearly show us this autobiographical impulse present in his writings prior to his entry into Gethsemani. The recent discovery of a number of items of juvenilia by Doctor Robert Daggy and myself, which date from 1929–1931 and contain some highly autobiographical sections in the form of a novel, show an even earlier manifestation of Merton's autobiographical impulse.[77]

76. Although Merton claimed his work was written in obedience to his abbot, Chrysogonus Waddell has pointed out that Merton very early on "took the initiative in choosing his subject matter" which was then "immediately confirmed by the sympathetic Abbot." Chrysogonus Waddell, "Merton and the Tiger Lily," *The Merton Annual*, vol. 2 (New York: AMS Press, 1989) 59–84. In support of this Waddell has quoted in full an important memorandum Merton gave to Dom Frederic in 1946, intended for the Order's General Chapter. In it Merton outlines various books he was hoping to write in the coming years, including the suggestion of a biography of a Gethsemani monk, who was obviously, from the brief description Merton gives, himself. Merton describes his proposal of a biography as "the biography or rather history of the conversion and the Cistercian vocation of a monk of Gethsemani. Born in Europe the son of an artist, this monk passed through the abyss of Communism in the university life of our times before being led to the cloister by the merciful grace of Jesus," 84.

77. These manuscripts were discovered in the possession of Frank Merton Trier, a first cousin of Merton with whom he spent some of his school holidays up until the summer of 1930 when it was decided he would spend his future holidays with his godfather, Tom Bennett. There manuscripts were discovered on December 13, 1993, by Dr. Robert E. Daggy and the present writer. The style of the author's handwriting and the content of the stories, along with Mr. Trier's testimony, verified the authenticity of these manuscripts. Currently these manuscripts remain in the possession of Mr. Trier with photocopies held on file at the Merton Center at Bellarmine College.

One of these manuscripts, *The Haunted Castle*, obviously imitating the Winnie the Pooh stories, is "profusely illustrated in pen and ink" (Merton, *The Seven Storey Mountain*, 52). This is the earliest of these manuscripts and dates back to Merton's Christmas holiday in 1929, which he spent with relatives at Western Cottage, Windsor. See Thomas Merton, "The Haunted Castle," *The Merton Seasonal* 19 (winter 1994) 7–10. Another manuscript, *Ravenswell*, an adventure story filling an exercise book of 158 pages, was written in just twelve days. Another fragment of a story in this collection, *The Black Sheep*, is about life at Oakham. It has a distinctly autobiographical flavor to it, making it difficult to believe that the boy Merton is

In *The Sign of Jonas* Merton had written, "Every book I write is a mirror of my own character and conscience,"[78] a statement that applied to 1949 when he wrote it but which could also be applied anachronistically to much earlier writings and prophetically to much later writings. The whole story of Merton's life was one of a "movement from experience to the inner word and from the inner word"[79] to its expression in the written word. Merton, as William Shannon has pointed out, "was so deeply preoccupied with what was going on in his own heart that he could not write about anything else,"[80] so that by the time of his death he was still "putting things down until they became clear," filling many books with "everything [he] ever knew or ever saw or ever thought."[81]

---

describing in the story is anyone other than himself. The story contains detailed descriptions of Oakham and life at the school based on Merton's own experience.

78. Merton, *The Sign of Jonas*, 160.
79. Shannon, *Silent Lamp*, 41.
80. Ibid., 19.
81. Merton, *My Argument with the Gestapo*, 53.

"The Whole World . . . Has Appeared as a Transparent Manifestation of the Love of God": Portents of Merton as Eco-Theologian

Dennis Patrick O'Hara

When Thomas Merton reflected on the role of the contemplative, he concluded that "a contemplative will . . . concern himself* with the same problems as other people, but he will try to get to the spiritual and metaphysical roots of these problems."[1] Furthermore, Merton insisted, the contemplative will situate him- or herself within the challenges of history accompanied by the "Lord of History" who "weeps into the fire."[2]

Using these comments as a catalyst, this essay speculates how Merton might have engaged the present ecological crisis. In formulating such a speculation, the article begins by recalling how Merton was becoming increasingly alert to ecological issues prior to his death. It then explores Merton's understanding of God's relationship with creation and how that relationship affects the goodness and sacredness of the created world. Finally, Merton's christology is reviewed, with a particular focus on how that christology lends itself to an eco-theological perspective. In each of these discussions, it is suggested how Merton's theological reflections parallel those of contemporary eco-theologians,

*While remarking Merton's lack of inclusive language at the time of his writing, the author has chosen not to amend the exclusive language in quotations of Merton's work cited throughout this essay.

1. Thomas Merton, *Faith and Violence* (Notre Dame, Ind.: University of Notre Dame Press, 1968) 147.
2. Thomas Merton, *Cables to the Ace* (New York: New Directions, 1968) 55.

and it is demonstrated how eco-theologians have applied this theology to the issues of today's ecological crisis. Such parallels suggest how Merton himself might have examined both the "spiritual and metaphysical roots" and the presence of the "Lord of History" in today's ecological challenge. In suggesting that the foundations of their convictions are similar, it is not impertinent to propose that, were he alive today, Merton would share at least the general tenor of these eco-theologians' views. In particular, the parallels between the theological reflections of Thomas Merton and the eco-theologian Thomas Berry are examined.

Like Merton, Berry has spent a good deal of his life being formed through solitude and mystical reflection. He entered the Passionist Order of preachers in 1933, seeking a contemplative existence that "would provide the time and context for meaningful reflection."[3] That reflection was nourished by Berry's keen interest in the literature of the Church Fathers and the Far East. The latter interest eventually culminated in Berry's producing many articles and two texts on Eastern religions and spirituality.

Thomas Berry was ordained a Roman Catholic priest in 1942, the year that Merton received the habit of a choir-monk novice. His academic studies made him acutely aware of the role that religion played in the shaping of cultures. Partly as a consequence of this, he felt drawn to write about the issues confronting contemporary humanity, particularly the impact of modern technologies and economic systems upon society and the planet, a critical perspective that was also explored by Merton. Preferring to deal with the experiences of life rather than the abstractions of theory, Berry's interest in more recent years has been especially focused on the impact of the ecological crisis on the future of the planet, particularly its human dimension.

Berry's writing resembles Merton's because he tends to provide a historical narrative rather than a metaphysical synthesis. Like Merton, he favors the narrative style of Augustine rather than the deductive reasoning of Aquinas, and is more mystic than theologian.[4] Because he

---

3. Mary Evelyn Tucker, "Thomas Berry: A Brief Biography," *Religion and Intellectual Life* 5:4 (1988) 109. It is worth noting that at the time that Berry entered the Passionist Order, the community led what might be described as a semi-monastic life, spending half the year in prayer, study, and reflection within their monastery, and half the year "on the road" preaching to the faithful.

4. Recall Merton's comment in *The Seven Storey Mountain:* "My bent was not so much towards the intellectual, dialectical, speculative character of Thomism, as

often employs rhetorical and poetic language to exhort his readers and to comment upon empirical data, Berry has sometimes been accused of being unduly optimistic and superficial. Such a critique is an unfortunate confusion of style with content—a serious error when applied to either Berry or Merton.

Introduction

Contemplative Life and the Crises of the World

In *Seeds of Destruction* Merton argued that contemplative life cannot be a withdrawal from the crises of the world because to do so would make the bystander an accomplice in the structures that foster these critical situations.[5] Thus, he felt compelled to speak to the issues of his day. The importance of actively engaging the issues of the secular world was also recognized in the Roman Catholic Church's document *Gaudium et spes,* The Pastoral Constitution on the Church in the Modern World. Merton, writing in *Contemplation in a World of Action,* felt that *Gaudium et spes* signaled a shift in the Church's predominant belief that the world was an evil place in which all values must be fixed and preserved by the Church in order that humanity might be saved from its base instincts. "Christian society . . . [had] conceived itself as a world-denying society in the midst of the world. A pilgrim society on the way to another world." In rejecting this view, Merton observed that

> the fact that the Church of the Second Vatican Council has finally admitted that the old immobilism will no longer serve is a bit too overdue to be regarded as a monumental triumph. The Constitution on the Church in the Modern World is salted with phrases which suggest that the fathers were, at least some of them, fully aware of this.[6]

---

towards the spiritual, mystical, voluntaristic and practical way of St. Augustine." Thomas Merton, *The Seven Storey Mountain* (New York: Harcourt, Brace, 1948) 220–1. See also Anne Marie Dalton, "Thomas Berry: Context and Contribution," *ARC* 22 (1994) 22.

5. George Kilcourse, *Ace of Freedoms: Thomas Merton's Christ* (Notre Dame, Ind.: University of Notre Dame Press, 1993) 118.

6. Thomas Merton, "Contemplation in a World of Action," *Thomas Merton: Spiritual Master,* ed. Lawrence S. Cunningham (New York: Paulist Press, 1992) 378–81.

In the words of one of Merton's theological interpreters, "Thomas Merton felt vindicated. His own instincts, his reverence for nature and creation, had already been leading him to this openness and dialogue with the world."[7]

It was not surprising, then, that in the mid-sixties Merton would have developed an interest in ecological issues since this was an area of emerging concern in society. Nor is it surprising that his wide ranging correspondence would include a letter to Rachel Carson, who in 1962 wrote *Silent Spring,* the landmark text on the modern ecological crisis.[8]

Merton's Awareness of the Ecological Crisis

On January 12, 1963, Thomas Merton wrote to Rachel Carson, telling her that he had been reading her "fine, exact, and persuasive book . . . carefully and with great concern." In that letter, he speculates that the same irresponsibility which permits humanity to "scorn the smallest values" also permits nations "to use our titanic power in a way that threatens not only civilization but life itself."[9] The sickness that fosters such irresponsibility and a preoccupation with the acquisition of material wealth underlies society's "despair in the midst of 'plenty'"—a despair that results in "indiscriminate, irresponsible destructiveness, hatred of life, carried on in the name of life itself. In order to 'survive' we instinctively destroy that on which our survival depends."[10]

Merton concludes the letter with further praise of Carson's work and with this admission about his own misguided efforts in the course of work done as the abbey forester: "I love the nature that is all around me here. And I regret my own follies with DDT, which I have now totally renounced."[11]

Ken Butigan argues that as Merton's focus turned increasingly to issues of survival in the 1960s, he became keenly aware of the plight of the planet. "Merton indicated that . . . we must learn *from nature*

7. Kilcourse, *Ace of Freedoms,* 129.

8. Rachel Carson, *Silent Spring* (Cambridge, Mass.: Riverside Press, 1962).

9. Thomas Merton, *Witness to Freedom: Letters in Times of Crisis,* ed. William Shannon (New York: Farrar, Straus & Giroux, 1994) 70.

10. Ibid., 71.

11. Ibid., 72.

how to participate in the replenishing of the world."[12] Butigan retrieves an image described by Merton in *Conjectures of a Guilty Bystander* in which the environment reconstitutes and rehabilitates itself at night, following the ravages it has sustained during the day at the hands of humanity. "We must, Merton holds, learn to become partners *with* the natural world in the healing *of* the natural world."[13]

But mere survival was not a sufficient reason for Merton to be interested in the plight of the planet. His appreciation of life included a greater *raison d'être*, a larger cosmological vision. His letter to Carson also reveals the reasons for his ecological interest, as well as the theological foundations for this perspective. A quotation from that letter catalogues these views:

> [Because of original sin], man has built into himself a tendency to destroy and negate himself when everything is at its best. . . . The whole world itself, to religious thinkers, has always appeared as a transparent manifestation of the love of God, as a "paradise" of His wisdom, manifested in all His creatures, down to the tiniest, and in the most wonderful interrelationship between them. . . . Man is at once a part of nature and he transcends it. . . . He must make use of nature wisely . . . ultimately relating both himself and visible nature to the invisible—in my terms, to the Creator, in any case, to the source and exemplar of all being and all life. . . . But man has lost his "sight." . . . It is in thinking that he sees . . . that he has lost his wisdom and his cosmic perspective.[14]

With this explanation in hand, it is possible to begin an exploration of the theological foundations that underpin Merton's perspective of the natural world, and concurrently to consider how his views correspond to those of contemporary eco-theologians.

Creation

God Is the "source and exemplar of all being and all life"

Merton held that all of reality shared a common source of being—the One, the "invisible, transcendent and infinitely abundant

12. Ken Butigan, "Thomas Merton's Vision of the Natural World," *Cry of the Environment: Rebuilding the Christian Creation Tradition*, ed. Philip N. Joranson and Ken Butigan (Santa Fe, N.M.: Bear & Co., 1984) 344. (Butigan's emphasis.)

13. Ibid. Butigan citing Thomas Merton, *Conjectures of a Guilty Bystander* (Garden City, N.Y.: Doubleday, 1966) 122–3.

14. Merton, *Witness to Freedom*, 71.

Source. . . . [The] reality of the created being [is] a reality that is from God and belongs to God and reflects God."[15] In fact, Merton notes, "The Christian life is a return to the Father, the Source, the Ground of all existence."[16] This is a popular starting point for discussions in eco-theology.

Sallie McFague is a theologian who has examined Christianity's traditional models of God and has proposed new ways of modeling our understanding of the Divine.[17] Her most recent model—the "universe as the body of God"—provides a metaphor that can be used to engage the ecological challenge. With the universe as the inspirited "body of God," God is recognized as the source, power, and goal of all that is, "the source, power, and goal of the fifteen-billion-year history of the universe." God is both the "creator and the continuing creator of this massive, breathtaking cosmic history" told as cosmogenesis.[18] God is the giver and renewer of the vast universe throughout the entire evolutionary process. Hence, all of creation depends utterly upon God.[19]

Thomas Berry connects this divine source, the Word, with the activity of the primordial fireball. Drawing upon Scripture, he reminds us that in John's Gospel we learn that the Word, through which all that is has been made, "by its own spontaneities brought forth the universe. . . . This spontaneity as the guiding force of the universe can be thought of as the mysterious impulse whereby the primordial fireball flared forth in its enormous energy, a fireball that contained in itself all that would ever emerge into being."[20] From the start, Berry identifies himself as a commentator on cosmogenesis who accepts that God brought the universe into being; other cosmologists might disclaim

15. Thomas Merton, *New Seeds of Contemplation* (New York: New Directions, 1961) 1, 26. See also Marilyn King, "'We Are Monks Also': Spirituality and Wholeness According to Thomas Merton," *Military Chaplain's Review* 16 (1987) 65.

16. Thomas Merton, "The Inner Experience," *Thomas Merton: Spiritual Master*, 326.

17. Sallie McFague is the Carpenter Professor of Theology and the former dean of Vanderbilt Divinity School. Her 1987 text, *Models of God*, was recognized with an Award for Excellence by the American Academy of Religion.

18. Sallie McFague, "An Earthly Theological Agenda," *Ecofeminism and the Sacred*, ed. Carol Adams (New York: Continuum, 1993) 94, 95.

19. Sallie McFague, *The Body of God: An Ecological Theology* (Minneapolis: Fortress Press, 1993) xi, 148, 151–2.

20. Thomas Berry, *The Dream of the Earth* (San Francisco: Sierra Club Books, 1988) 196–7.

this origin, but not Berry. He unequivocally attributes the single source of all being and life to the divine mystery.[21]

Merton, McFague, and Berry seem unanimous in recognizing God as the single source of creation.

The World Is "a transparent manifestation of the love of God, as a 'paradise' of His wisdom, manifested in all His creatures"

With God as the source of all of creation, it follows that creation would in some way reflect its creator. Consequently, Merton described the world in his letter to Carson as "a transparent manifestation of the love of God, as a 'paradise' of His wisdom, manifested in all His creatures." Merton is claiming that all of creation is a manifestation of the love of the divine mystery. As such, the mystery at the heart of all things participates in the gracious mystery of God. "The world is, as Merton writes in *Love and Living*, willed and held in being by God's love and is therefore infinitely precious in his sight. The cosmos is thus a revelation of the infinite love of the God who is 'Maker, Lover and Keeper.'"[22] If the cosmos is a revelation of God, then the experience of God is not restricted to extraordinary visions or experiences, but is to be found in the ordinary events of daily living.

This positive perspective on the revelation of creation and its manifestation of the divine represents an evolution in the understanding of Merton. In the 1953 volume *Bread in the Wilderness* Merton had posited that the fall of Adam had clouded the window of creation so that humanity could no longer see the natural world in the light of God.[23] By 1961, he had nuanced this outlook, noting that "in all created things we, who do not yet perfectly love God, can find something that reflects the fulfillment of heaven and something that reflects the anguish of hell."[24] In his letter to Carson in 1963, Merton had moved to an even more favorable position on creation, stating that "the whole

21. Thomas Berry, "The Dream of the Earth: Our Way into the Future," *Cross Currents* 37:2–3 (1987) 201, 210. See also Stephen Hawking, *A Brief History of Time: From the Big Bang to Black Holes* (New York: Bantam Books, 1988); Stephen Gould, *Wonderful Life: The Burgess Shale and the Nature of History* (New York: Norton and Co., 1989) 291.

22. Butigan, "Thomas Merton's Vision of the Natural World," 338. Butigan is quoting Thomas Merton, *Love and Living* (New York: Bantam Books, 1979) 159.

23. Kilcourse, *Ace of Freedoms*, 51.

24. Merton, *New Seeds of Contemplation*, 26.

world itself . . . has always appeared as a transparent manifestation of the love of God . . . manifested in all His creatures." The *theoria physica* of the Greek Fathers, who had significantly influenced Merton's more mature understanding of creation and the incarnation, had taught the monk that contemplation of God could be realized in created things through the ascetic gift of discernment.[25]

> Detachment from things does not mean setting up a contradiction between "things" and "God" as if God were another "thing" and as if His creatures were His rivals. . . . Rather we become detached *from ourselves* in order to see and use all things in and for God. . . . We love in all things His will rather than the things themselves, and that is the way we make creation a sacrifice in praise of God.[26]

If humanity failed to see and experience this divine Presence in creation, then perhaps it was because "man has lost his 'sight.'" The fault did not so much lie with the rest of creation, but with the human dimension. Indeed, humanity could confidently accept that the rest of creation was "doing the will of God, every single minute."[27] This creation, if untouched by human indiscretion, would not only nurture and sustain us; it would be a revelation of the divine. Creation, Merton observed, can inform our thoughts and prayers, acting as cables, medium, and message.[28]

Merton was echoing St. Teresa's observation that "all creation teaches us some way of prayer."[29] In one instance, he poetically reflected on the metamorphosis of six or seven black and russet caterpillars to their pupal state. Using such insect metamorphosis as a metaphor, he exhorts his reader to seek with similar "glad alacrity" transformation in Christ. He concludes that "we can learn such ways to God from creeping things and sanctity from a black and russet worm!"[30]

25. Kilcourse, *Ace of Freedoms*, 98.
26. Merton, *New Seeds of Contemplation*, 21, 25. (Merton's emphasis.)
27. Raymond Bailey, *Thomas Merton on Mysticism* (Garden City, N.Y.: Doubleday, 1974) 185. Bailey is quoting Merton's comments to novices while he was novice master.
28. Merton, *Cables to the Ace*, 7.
29. As quoted in Kilcourse, *Ace of Freedoms*, 27.
30. Thomas Merton, *The Collected Poems of Thomas Merton* (New York: New Directions, 1977) 184.

These themes—that creation is a manifestation of God's love, a revelation of the divine, and a way to approach our Maker—are also apparent in the thought of Thomas Berry, although Berry tends to push his conclusions further than Merton. Berry argues that if humanity is to value the planet and all of its inhabitants in any vital way, then a functional spirituality must emerge; that is, humanity must be inspired by a spirituality that is congruent with our understanding of cosmogenesis and simultaneously integrates us into the processes of cosmic evolution, emphasizing that we are formed and sustained within that dynamic emergence. Yet for such a functional cosmology to be successful, the "universe itself, but especially the planet Earth, needs to be experienced as the primary mode of divine presence."[31] That is, the living forms of this planet must be experienced as modes of divine presence, as voices of the divine. They are to be understood as our primary revelation of the divine, our primary scripture.

To reinforce this position, Berry appeals to Thomas Aquinas's *Summa Theologica,* (Prima Pars, q. 47, a. 1). Quoting Aquinas's reply, Berry notes that

> because the divine goodness "could not be adequately represented by one creature alone, [God] produced many diverse creatures, that what was wanting to one in the representation of the divine goodness might be supplied by another. For goodness, which in god [sic] is simple and uniform, in creatures is manifold and divided; and hence the whole universe together participates the divine goodness more perfectly, and represents it better than any single creature whatever." From this we could argue that the community of all the components of the planet Earth is primary in the divine intention.[32]

Berry is arguing from Aquinas that God not only desires and chooses to communicate with creation, but that this communication through the various forms of creation ultimately manifests as a participation of the divine. He concludes that the sum of the diversity of creation is the greatest measure of its perfection, since the greatest totality of the divine goodness, which is shared in part by each aspect of creation, most closely approximates divine perfection.

Because the natural world represents "modes of divine presence," notes Berry, we need to "perceive the natural world as the pri-

31. Berry, *The Dream of the Earth,* 120.
32. Ibid., 79.

mary revelation of the divine, as primary scripture, as the primary mode of numinous presence" and as the "primary subject of incarnation."[33] Merton has also emphasized the importance of experiencing the "numinous presence" of the divine, but he has limited this experience to humanity. Merton notes that the awakening of the inner or true self in each person will "not only enable us to discover our true identity 'in Christ' but [will] also make the living and Risen Savior present in us." We come to recognize "the sensation of a 'numinous' presence within us."[34] But Berry extends this encounter with numinous presence to the natural world, which he describes as the first revelation of God, the voice of the divine to creation. Consequently, for Berry, any obliteration of the planet by humanity is a destruction of the sacred presence within that reality; it is to "silence forever a divine voice."[35] Any wanton destruction of the natural world diminishes our experience and knowledge of God, since the way we come to know the world becomes the language by which we come to speak of God. Berry speculates that

> If we have powers of imagination, . . . if we have words with which to speak and think and commune, words for the inner experience of the divine, . . . it is again because of the impressions we have received from the variety of beings about us. If we lived on the moon, our mind and emotions, our speech, our imagination, our sense of the divine would all reflect the desolation of the lunar landscape.[36]

If the grandeur of the universe is diminished, then so too is our art, our dance, our language, our imagination; so too are our ways to express a sense of the divine who is grandeur beyond all other. As creation diminishes, Berry cautions, so too does our sense of the divine, to the extent that "if a beautiful earth gives us an exalted idea of the divine, an industrially despoiled planet will give us a corresponding idea of God."[37]

33. Ibid., 11, 37, 105.
34. Merton, "The Inner Experience," 328, 341.
35. Berry, *The Dream of the Earth*, 46.
36. Ibid., 11.
37. Berry, "Economics: Its Effects on the Life Systems of the World," *Thomas Berry and the New Cosmology*, ed. Caroline Richards (Mystic, Conn.: Twenty-Third Publications, 1987) 17. See also Thomas Berry and Thomas Clarke, *Befriending the Earth: A Theology of Reconciliation between Humans and the Earth*, ed. Stephen Dunn and Ann Lonergan (Mystic, Conn.: Twenty-Third Publications, 1991) 8–10.

This connection between our symbols—based upon our appreciation of nature—and the way we are able to speak of God was also apparent to Merton.[38] As we have already seen, Merton contends that nature informs our prayers, acting as cables, medium, and message. Creation has a sacramental quality, a quality also studied by Berry.[39]

Both Berry and Merton recognize that the created world can inform our prayer and language of God. Both consider creation to be a manifestation of the divine, and as such, a way of approaching the infinite mystery. Berry extrapolates these views to propose a functional spirituality for understanding our relationship with the rest of creation; i.e., he extends the implications of these views to engage the ecological crisis of today. To this point, the thought of Merton and Berry shows considerable convergence. However, Berry's notion that creation is our "primary scripture," our first revelation of the divine, was not a concept that Merton had entertained. Yet, one wonders if Merton would be less comfortable with Berry's language—i.e., primary *scripture*—than with the underlying concept that creation is a revelation of the divine mystery and a mode of that numinous presence. In any case, both Berry and Merton suggest that there is a sacred dimension to creation.

Creation Has a Sacred Dimension and Is Good

Merton notes that, with the exception of humanity, all of creation necessarily constitutes a holiness in the sight of God. Nonhuman creation exists exactly as intended by the love and art of God. Its unique identities and natures, completely fulfilling the will of God, become its sanctity. "Their inscape is their sanctity. It is the imprint of His wisdom and His reality in them."[40] This terminology and the theological reflection it articulates reveal the impressions that the thought of John Duns Scotus and the poetry of Gerard Manley Hopkins had upon Merton, influences that merit a brief pause for closer consideration.

Scotus wrote that God has given each being its own *"haecceitas,"* its own "thisness" or unique identity in the eyes of God, which accords each part of creation its special value and real worth. God's creative love has deemed that *this* particular person or creature should come

---

38. Kilcourse, *Ace of Freedoms*, 51, 74–75.

39. Merton, *Cables to the Ace*, 7. See also Thomas Berry, "The Passion of Mother Earth," *Passionists* 13:9–14.

40. Merton, *New Seeds of Contemplation*, 30.

into existence, and *this* singular identity would be reflected in its "haecceity."[41] It was Scotus's notion of haecceity which allowed Hopkins to develop his understanding of inscape. Writing in his journal in 1872 as he studied medieval philosophy in the Jesuit novitiate, Hopkins recalled his concept of inscape and remarked:

> At this time I had first begun to get hold of the copy of Scotus on the Sentences . . . and was flush with a new stroke of enthusiasm. It may come to nothing or it may be a mercy from God. But just then when I took in any inscape of the sky or sea I thought of Scotus.[42]

Hopkins' description of inscape as "the essential and only lasting thing . . . species or individuality-distinctive beauty of style" recalls Scotus's *haecceitas* and the subtle doctor's contention that each element in God's creative landscape is intrinsically valuable because its unique existence was willed into being by God. Consequently, the inscape of each part of creation, reflecting the creativity of God's intention, becomes its sanctity.

Because the various elements of nonhuman creation perfectly satisfy their identity, Merton remarks, they have no problem. It is humans, whom God has left "free to be whatever we like," who are challenged with finding salvation and sanctity through the discovery of each person's true self. But we are not alone in this task, for we remain sons and daughters of God who are "called to share with God the work of *creating* the truth of our identity."[43] Merton concluded that

> the world was made as a temple, a paradise, into which God Himself would descend to dwell familiarly with the spirits He had placed there to tend it for Him. . . . God made the world as a garden in which He himself took delight. . . . The love of God, looking upon things, brought them into being. . . . God creates things by seeing them in His own Logos.[44]

In view of God's continuous presence in creation, and since creation represents an outpouring of the Creator's love, creation is necessarily

41. Philibert Hoebing, "St. Francis and the Environment," (ms. from author) 14–15; later published in *Divine Representation, Postmodernism, and Spirituality,* ed. Ann W. Astelle (New York: Paulist Press, 1994).

42. Gerard Manley Hopkins, *Poems and Prose,* selected by W. H. Gardner (London: Penguin Books, 1988) 126. See also Hoebing, "St. Francis and the Environment," 6.

43. Merton, *New Seeds of Contemplation,* 31, 32.

44. Ibid., 290–1.

good. Merton recognizes this goodness of creation.[45] As early as 1948, in *The Seven Storey Mountain*, he vigorously rejected any claim that the created world was intrinsically evil, especially since such a notion cast a shadow of suspicion upon the fact and subsequent doctrine of the incarnation of Christ.[46] Echoing the opening chapters of Genesis, Merton heralds in *New Seeds of Contemplation*, "There is no evil in anything created by God. . . . The world and everything made by God is good."[47]

Thomas Berry shares this understanding of creation as sacred and good, and also comments on its continuing relationship with the divine. Berry reminds us that "the divine always appears in some embodiment; no one ever worshipped matter as matter. Whatever is worshipped is seen as a mode of divine presence."[48] Furthermore, with perhaps the exception of the modern era, humanity has generally tended to be aware of an all-pervading mysterious power present within the universe. We have tended to believe that there is an ineffable, pervasive presence of the divine in the world about us. And while every form of existence is subsequently considered to be a mode of divine presence, we recognize that each existence is not itself divine; there is a distinction and difference between the two. The planet itself and every other existence, while awesome, intrinsically valuable, and a sacred community in its own right, are not specifically divine; there is a difference between the sacred and the divine. Berry explains, however, that "if there were a difference in the sense of separation, the created world would not be. I could not exist except for a divine presence."[49] Without God, there simply is no world, no creation.

Sallie McFague arrives at the same conclusions as Berry and Merton, but travels that journey based upon her model of the universe as the body of God. If the universe is the body of God, then divine embodiment as the universe makes all embodiment in that universe sacred, because the universe is a place where God is present. The various bodies of creation, as the visible signs or sacraments of God's invisible grandeur, take on a sacred quality. They are a means through which God can become sacramentally present to us. Such bodies are therefore

45. Thomas Merton, "Poetry and Contemplation: A Reappraisal," *Commonweal* 59 (1958) 89.

46. Merton, *The Seven Storey Mountain*, 85.

47. Merton, *New Seeds of Contemplation*, 21, 24.

48. Berry and Clarke, *Befriending*, 19.

49. Berry and Clarke, *Befriending*, 19; cf. 10. See also Thomas Berry, "Creative Energy," *Cross Currents* 37:2–3 (1987) 179.

to be valued both as manifestations of the divine in an incarnated world and as a means through which we might seek an experience of union with God. The natural world is then understood to be "a concern of God and a way to God rather than limiting divine activity to human history."[50] The nonhuman dimension of the universe is subsequently too sacred and valuable to be desecrated; humans must live by an ecological ethic.

Once again our three interlocutors do not hold significantly different understandings of the sacredness of creation. The fundamentals are similar. Admittedly, both Berry and McFague employ a recognition of the sacredness of creation to address consciously the world's ecological status in a way that Merton has not. However, the reasons Berry and McFague believe that they can hold these positions mirror the fundamental concepts already found in Merton's works.

But before any further comparisons can be suggested, it is necessary to delve more deeply into Merton's christology. It is arguably impossible to comprehend this monk's life without discussing his understanding of our relationship with Christ. That relationship is central to Merton's identity and therefore to any appreciation of his thoughts. I will focus on the aspects of his christology that might suggest how he would speak to today's ecological issues.

Christology

Centrality of Christ

Merton asserted that "God's revelation of Himself to the world in His Incarnate Word forms the heart and substance of all Christian mystical contemplation."[51] "Faith in Christ, and in the mysteries of His life and death, is the foundation of the Christian life and the source of all contemplation."[52] It is through emptying ourselves in Christ, and in the discovery of who we are in Christ, that we arrive at our true self— the self that is one with God through Christ.[53] This understanding was

50. McFague, *The Body of God*, 54–55, 83–84, 128, 162, 184–5, 206. See also McFague, "An Earthly Theological Agenda," 95–96.

51. Thomas Merton, *The Ascent to Truth* (New York: Harcourt, Brace, 1951) 131.

52. Merton, *New Seeds of Contemplation*, 151–2.

53. Thomas Merton, *Zen and the Birds of Appetite* (New York: New Directions, 1968) 17–19.

central to Merton's writing and essential to the way he sought to engage life. He concluded that "whatever I have written . . . can be reduced in the end to this one root truth: that God calls human persons to union with Himself and with one another in Christ."[54]

Such a christocentric perspective can also be found in the earlier writings of Thomas Berry. In "Christian Humanism: Its New Universal Context" (1968), Berry states that

> The world of man is a Christian world. There is no non-Christian world. Christianity is an absolute inseparable from human existence itself. The People of God is mankind. It is not proper to define the People of God as the church in the narrow sense of the word. . . . There are . . . more or less developed Christians.[55]

As far as Berry is concerned, if Christ is the source of all that is in creation, and the numinous reality ever present in cosmogenesis, and additionally the goal of creation, then the world is a Christian world. On a universal, macrophase level, Christianity is identified with "that which bears an identity with man's total spiritual and human formation . . .; it infolds the entire world of man."[56] On a more microphase level, Christians are those who are baptized and institutionalized into the Christian churches, yet who bear within themselves this universal dimension, even if they are not aware of it.

Berry distinguishes between a universally Christian world within the context of Christ's presence in the world and a universally Christian world within the context of the Christian faith, particularly when this manifests within a specific individual. Berry states that "the Body of Christ is ultimately the entire universe. Otherwise neither the incarnation nor the redemption is complete."[57] Consequently, for Berry, there is no non-Christian world.

---

54. Thomas Merton, "Concerning the Collection in the Bellarmine College Library—A Statement, November 18, 1963," *Bulletin of the Merton Studies Center* (1971) 1:3. Quoted in George Kilcourse, "'Pieces of the Mosaic, Earth': Thomas Merton and the Christ," *The Message of Thomas Merton*, ed. Patrick Hart (Kalamazoo, Mich.: Cistercian Publications, 1981) 129.

55. Thomas Berry, "Christian Humanism: Its New Universal Context," *Riverdale Papers* (Riverdale, N.Y.: Riverdale Center for Religious Research, 1968) 2:2.

56. Ibid., 5.

57. Thomas Berry, "The Third Mediation: The Christian Task of Our Time," *Riverdale Papers* (Riverdale, N.Y.: Riverdale Center for Religious Research, 1979) 6:4.

Having recognized the centrality of Christ in the thought of both Merton and Berry, it is necessary to consider what role christology might play in the formulation of contemporary eco-theological thought. With this in mind, an overview of Merton's perspectives on the incarnation, the transformation of creation by Christ, and the cosmic Christ will be coupled with similar explorations of these same perspectives in eco-theological works.

The Incarnation

In *Ace of Freedoms: Thomas Merton's Christ*, George Kilcourse has observed that during the course of Merton's life, the monk's christology evolved through various stages—from a descending christology bordering on Docetism to a more integrated christology that included the fuller mystery of immanence-with-transcendence. He increasingly explored and experienced the kenotic dimensions of Christ's incarnation, discovering Christ in the "weakness and defencelessness" of both himself and the wider world.[58]

Gradually Merton's entire life felt the impact of his growing awareness of the humanity of Jesus, the mystery of the crucifixion, and the "groaning in travail" of all of creation (Rom 8:22). As a result, Merton's quandary was no longer to free his true self from his false self to be resolved within the comfortable confines of an abstract theory. Its resolution demanded that personal experience be contextualized and lived within the mystery of the incarnation. Because of that incarnation, Merton noted, humanity enjoyed an intimate and inseparable unity with Christ, despite its weakness and failings.

> [The] mystery of our vocation [is] . . . that the love of my man's heart can become God's love for God and men, and my human tears can fall from my eyes as the tears of God because they well up from the motion of His Holy Spirit in the heart of His incarnate Son.[59]

For this reason, humanity can accept its imperfections, seeking to be transformed through contemplation, so that the "ineffable and

---

58. Kilcourse, *Ace of Freedoms*, 4–9.
59. Thomas Merton, *Thoughts in Solitude* (New York: Farrar, Straus & Cudahy, 1958) 124, as quoted in Kilcourse, *Ace of Freedoms*, 103; cf. 27, 91–92, 102.

indefinable light of Christ" might penetrate its darkness.[60] Because of the dynamics of the incarnation, humanity can realize its divinization and overcome the failings of the modern world that challenge it.[61]

By virtue of Christ's entry into creation, Merton declared he was joyful to be a member of the same race in which God chose to become incarnate. Writing in *Conjectures of a Guilty Bystander*, a rather ecstatic Merton declares:

> It is a glorious destiny to be a member of the human race, though it is a race dedicated to many absurdities and one which makes many terrible mistakes: yet, with all that, God Himself glorified in becoming a member of the human race. . . . I have the immense joy of being *man*, a member of a race in which God Himself became incarnate.[62]

The contemplative monk was no longer turning his back on a despicable world. "The whole illusion of a separate holy existence [sealed within a monastic enclosure] is a dream."[63] In self-deprecating humor the reformed Merton notes in *Contemplation in a World of Action* that

> due to a book I wrote thirty years ago, I have myself become a sort of stereotype of the world-denying contemplative—the man who spurned New York, spat on Chicago, and tromped on Louisville. . . . This personal stereotype is probably my own fault, and it is something I have to try to demolish on occasion.[64]

Merton had come to believe that the good God had begun with creation was perfected through the incarnation. God's love, which had not only initiated creation and destined Christ's entry into historical time, was further expressed when that entry was realized in Jesus of Nazareth. Creation, coming forth from God, is transfigured in Christ, so that "all things manifest Christ and God's goal for creation."[65]

Berry shares Merton's appreciation of the magnitude of the incarnation. Berry describes the incarnation of Christ into cosmic history

60. Thomas Merton, *The Monastic Journey*, ed. Patrick Hart (Kansas City, Mo.: Sheed, Andrew & McMeel, 1977) 20–21.

61. Thomas Merton, *Seeds of Destruction* (New York: Farrar, Straus & Giroux, 1964) 176–83. See also Kilcourse, *Ace of Freedoms*, 98, 120.

62. Merton, *Conjectures of a Guilty Bystander*, 157. (Merton's emphasis.)

63. Ibid., 156; cf. 19, 51, 156–8.

64. Merton, "Contemplation in a World of Action," 376.

65. Kilcourse, *Ace of Freedoms*, 64; cf. 51.

as "the greatest revolution in the human order, the moment of the total recreation of man."[66] This is an event of such magnitude that Berry claims that Christianity itself has not grasped its full revolutionizing import. Had it done so, he insists, it would not have spent so much energy emphasizing the need for humanity to be redeemed from this world. It would have celebrated the entry of Christ into cosmic history and the immanence of the divine in the world, an immanence resident in a divine-human-nature communion. Indeed, Christianity would have espoused a more positive attitude toward the planet. For "if God has desired to become a member of the earth community, man himself should be willing to accept his status as a member of the same community."[67] If Christianity were to adopt such a positive perspective, and if it were to bring a fuller appreciation of the incarnation into its daily life, then, Berry concludes, the solutions to the planetary problems that beset humanity might be found in the context of a world pregnant with the presence of Christ. Humanity would come to realize that the incarnation brought divine presence to all aspects of creation.

McFague also extends the implications of the incarnation to this wider vision. She argues that "the primary belief of the Christian community, its doctrine of the incarnation [can] . . . be radicalized beyond Jesus of Nazareth to include all matter. God is incarnated in the world."[68] McFague reminds us that this is not a new understanding within the Christian tradition, since certain early Christian thinkers such as Origen held that the cosmos was "animated by the Word-Soul or the Logos of God," and that divine immanence pervaded all of the natural order, including nonhuman life forms.[69] Thus, God is present through the incarnation in every being of creation, and not only in those who hear the word. All of the cosmos subsequently becomes the dwelling place of God. Through this incarnation, McFague insists, "the entire universe is expressive of God's very being."[70] Matter is no longer inanimate substance, but throbs with the spirit of God.

66. Thomas Berry, "The Christian Process," *Riverdale Papers* (Riverdale, N.Y.: Riverdale Center for Religious Research, 1976) 4:8.

67. Berry, "The Third Mediation," 5.

68. McFague, *The Body of God*, xi.

69. Ibid., 35. See also Sallie McFague, "Imaging a Theology of Nature: The World as God's Body," *Liberating Life*, ed. Charles Birch and others (Maryknoll, N.Y.: Orbis Books, 1990) 211–2.

70. McFague, "Imaging a Theology of Nature," 211.

It is worth noting that McFague is not suggesting an animistic view of creation, because she is not claiming that each part of the universe is animated through its own means. Nor is she saying that each being is a god; rather, that each being can be considered to be a means by which God becomes present. She recognizes the power of God in each aspect of creation, not each being as independently powerful. God empowers or animates creation, but creation is not self-animated.

While Merton, Berry, and McFague agree on the fundamental importance and magnitude of the incarnation, the latter two push that doctrine into a less anthropocentric realm. While they expand our understanding of the incarnation in order to propose an ecological ethic, they do so by drawing upon the same convictions that Merton held. In fact, the wider vision of McFague's reflection on the incarnation is at least suggested in Merton's comments on the "transfiguration" of creation by the incarnation.

Creation Is Transformed Through the Incarnation of Christ

With a profound awareness of the impact of the incarnation upon all of creation, and a deep appreciation of the sacramentality of the cosmos, Merton relished the presence of the divine mystery pregnant in the paradisal world about him. For this contemplative monk, creation is transformed and reawakened by the presence of Christ. "The world *has* been transformed and illuminated" by and in the resurrection light, which is "in all things, in their ground, not by nature but by gift, grace, death and resurrection."[71] Once again readers of Merton encounter his affirmation of the goodness of creation. Just as he had affirmed creation's intrinsic goodness in *The Seven Storey Mountain*, Merton restates his case in 1959:

> In Christ the world and the whole cosmos has been created anew (which means to say restored to its original perfection and beyond that made divine, totally transfigured). . . . If God is "all in all," then everything is in fact paradise, because it is filled with the glory and presence of God, and nothing is any more separated from God.[72]

71. Thomas Merton, *The Hidden Ground of Love: The Letters of Thomas Merton on Religious Experience and Social Concerns*, selected and edited by William H. Shannon (New York: New Directions, 1985) 644.
72. Ibid., 566. Quoted in Kilcourse, *Ace of Freedoms*, 202.

While acknowledging the influence of Aquinas, Scotus, Bonaventure, and Dante, Merton restates this recurring theme in "Contemplation in a World of Action": in the work of these authors "we see a harmonious synthesis of nature and grace, in which the created world itself is an epiphany of divine wisdom and love, and redeemed in and by Christ, will return to God with all its beauty restored by the transforming power of grace."[73]

The fact that creation is transformed through the incarnation of Christ is clearly a consistent theme in Merton's work. But to speculate on how this transformation of the world might have eventually influenced Merton's apprehension of nature and the ecological challenges that presently beset us, I would argue that it is necessary to link his understanding of incarnation and this transformation with his thoughts on the cosmic Christ.

The Cosmic Christ

Two sources greatly influenced Merton's understanding of the cosmic Christ: the theology of Duns Scotus and the writings of the Greek Fathers.

Influenced by Scotus's notion that the incarnation was not primarily necessary because of sin, but was essentially inevitable because of God's love, Merton came to resonate with the subtle doctor's view that the cosmic Christ was not a postscript to the creative action proceeding forth from the mind of God. Instead, the cosmic Christ was God's first thought, forming the paradigm of creation. Creation, which was formed by the word and continues to manifest the word, is returned to full freedom through the additional epiphany of God's love in the incarnation of Jesus the Christ.[74] Philibert Hoebing, a Franciscan commentator on Scotus, recalls that the latter's belief in the absolute primacy of Christ meant that "every creature that comes from the creative act of God is marked by Christ and for Christ. Every individual is dignified by its relationship to Christ, who is the first of God's creations (cf. Colossians 1:15-20)."[75]

Drawing from the works of the Greek Fathers, Merton observed that from the beginning of time, God has permeated all of creation.

73. Merton, "Contemplation in a World of Action," 379.
74. Kilcourse, *Ace of Freedoms*, 31–32, 64, 110.
75. Hoebing, "St. Francis and the Environment," 17.

"God is everywhere. His truth and His love pervade all things."[76] He learned from these patristic theologians that even prior to the existence of humanity, Christ was the cosmic mediator who would additionally mediate the inclusion of all of humanity "in Himself in His Incarnation." Because humanity was intentionally created in the image of God, it was "already potentially united with the Word of God." Furthermore, God had "decided from all eternity to become man in Jesus Christ."[77] Biblical references such as Paul's depiction of Christ as the firstborn of all creation through whom all things in heaven and on earth were created also contributed cosmic elements to Merton's christology (see Col 1:15-17).

Similar "cosmic Christ" themes appear in the work of Berry. Berry argues that Christians need to "move from an excessive concern with the individual Jesus [of history] to the cosmic Christ in terms of St. Paul's Letter to the Colossians, [and] . . . the prologue of St. John's Gospel. This is the macrophase mode of the Christ reality."[78] That is, since the world originates in, through, and by Christ—the principle of intelligibility, the Word who is the creative context of all existence— there has been a Christ dimension to developmental time from time's very inception. The story of Christ is the story of the universe, not merely the story of a certain individual who lived at a particular historical period. Christ was not simply added to the cosmic history at some point fifteen billion years into its evolution. Christ has been part of the history of the universe prior to the emergence of humanity. According to Berry:

> The Christ reality as this numinous reality [guiding creation] is there from the beginning. In other words, all things emerge into being within this numinous context. . . . Only after the experience of the Incarnation and of the gospels could we have the name [of Christ] functioning in this way. It is our way of identifying something that has been there from the beginning. . . . Anything that was created was created in that context.[79]

Therefore, Christ is part of irreversible, cosmological, developmental time, not merely human, historical time. In Berry's eco-theological un-

---

76. Merton, *New Seeds of Contemplation*, 151.
77. Thomas Merton, *The New Man* (New York: Farrar, Straus & Cudahy, 1961) 134–6.
78. Berry and Clarke, *Befriending*, 77.
79. Ibid., 78.

derstanding, Christ is a continuous part of creation history, and Jesus the Christ is the microphase mode of the macrophase or cosmic Christ.

Therefore, the *redemptive* dimension of Christ, while not to be undervalued, is not the whole story; the *creative* dimension of Christ must also be considered. When we become more aware of this latter aspect, Berry notes, we recognize that "there is a Christ dimension integral to the numinous dimension of the universe" throughout the course of cosmic history. Christ is revealed to us in the universe; the natural world becomes our primary scripture, our first revelation of the divine, the context within which we can experience the divine manifestation.

In and through the earth, Berry claims, humanity is able to experience community with the entire cosmic process. If the universe were different in any way, then we would conceivably be different as well. The universal must be what it is for us to be individually what we are; change any part of cosmogenic history and we would be different today. Therefore, everything has its individual or microphase mode, as well as its cosmic or macrophase context. The cosmos is consequently represented in us just as we are a part of the cosmos; there is necessarily a cosmic, macrophase dimension to the human that reflects our participation within the order of the universe. The cosmic Christ, who acts as both the numinous source of creation and the mysterious guiding presence within cosmogenesis, is additionally the point of convergence toward which the earth process is striving. [80]

As a consequence of these features of the cosmic Christ and our growing awareness of community with the rest of the universe, Berry believes that humanity is moving toward cosmic consciousness and a closer unification with the divine. As humanity continues in cosmogenic evolution toward ever increasing complexification and unification, we move beyond individual self-reflective human consciousness toward cosmic consciousness. We are moving toward a fuller union with the cosmic Christ. Berry also asserts that this new collectivity is not limited to the human. Instead, the cosmic person will become "in a special way the realization of the fullness of the earth, the goal of

---

80. Ibid., 12, 73–76. When speaking, Berry sometimes refers to Carl Sagan's humorous yet insightful comment that it takes 15 billion years of cosmic history to make apple pie. Apple pies could not have existed prior to recent history. Their existence has required 15 billion years of cosmogenesis to unfold in just the way it has.

historical development" at the end of the cosmic process.[81] For most eco-theologians, this heroic journey toward this point of convergence in the cosmic person is not a spiritual journey of humanity alone, but the journey and story of the earth through its multiple transformations. The cosmic person of Christ has been present throughout the entire evolutionary emergence of the universe, present "in those elementary forms that are constantly striving toward their more complete fulfillment in the transforming experience toward which the cosmic process is moving."[82] It is this entire collective of cosmic evolution, not just humanity, that has been emerging and transforming toward an ultimate goal in Christ. Therefore, increasing unification with the cosmic Christ will involve all elements of the cosmos, not just the human dimension.

Merton also reflected upon increasing unification with Christ, but tended to limit his consideration to humanity alone. In "The Inner Experience," written in 1959 and revised intermittently but not published until after his death, Merton asserts that the resurrection and ascension of Christ permits the divinization of every person into the likeness of Christ through the action of the Holy Spirit. Revealing once again how the Greek Fathers influenced his work, Merton declares that through the mystery of the hypostatic union of Jesus Christ, the gap between God and humanity is bridged, allowing us to experience "our oneness with Christ" and to recognize "ourselves as other Christs." In fact, "God Himself must become Man, in order that in the Man-God, man might be able to lose himself as man and find himself as God."[83] Merton's bold statement admonishes each of his readers to seek his or her own "true inner face" or authentic self so that they might each discover their unique and true identity situated within the reality of God. For as humanity lost its sense of being one with the Creator and the rest of creation subsequent to the fall from paradise, humanity became an exile in the world. Its return to the true sense of being requires a return to its true identity in God.[84] And, Berry might add, humanity's return to its true sense of being also requires a reappreciation of our

81. Ibid., 17.

82. Ibid., 26.

83. Thomas Merton, "The Inner Experience," 327, 326. See also Merton, *New Seeds of Contemplation,* 157; cf. 150–51, 156.

84. Merton, "The Inner Experience," 325.

place within God's creation and a reengagement of the divine presence permeating all that is.[85]

During Merton's lifetime, the important consequences of viewing time as irreversible, evolutionary, and cosmological were not as developed as they would become in this last decade. Time was still primarily understood from within a human, historical perspective. The new understanding of time, emerging from astronomic sciences, was far from popular knowledge; few spoke of cosmic physics and the evolution of galaxies and planets. So it is not surprising that Merton did not engage Christ's cosmological dimension as much as he explored Christ's human incarnation. An understanding of irreversible, cosmological time is as necessary for grasping this fuller cognizance of the cosmic Christ as an understanding of the cosmic Christ is indispensable for probing the deeper meaning of irreversible, cosmological time. The two are interdependent.

But even if a new context has emerged for understanding the cosmic Christ, the foundational principles for our understanding of that dimension of christology are still to be found in Scripture and the works of Duns Scotus and the Greek Fathers, among others. Merton brought this foundational wisdom into dialogue with the context and issues of his day. Berry employs this same foundation within a contemporary, scientific understanding of the cosmos in order to address the present ecological crisis. Merton and Berry were writing for somewhat different eras, but each spoke to the important challenges of their time in order to reveal the deeper meaning of existence.

These dimensions of christology—the incarnation, the transfiguration of creation, and the cosmic Christ—have also influenced the formulation of eco-theological thought. Both Merton and contemporary theologians apply these perspectives to the issues before them. And in many respects they come to similar conclusions. However, the eco-theologians' reflections upon christology have caused them to push our understanding of the relationship among God, humanity, and the rest of the created world to new horizons; their reflections have drawn them to conclusions and consequences that Merton had not yet reached. Considering Merton's tendency to "push back the

85. Thomas Berry, "The Christian Process," *Riverdale Papers* (Riverdale, N.Y.: Riverdale Center for Religious Research, 1976) 4:19.

frontiers,"[86] one can only wonder how his evolving spirituality would have lead him to confront today's ecological issues.

Some Closing Thoughts

There are many more parallels between the thought of Thomas Merton and Thomas Berry, thoughts that Berry extends to a critique of our ecological crisis. Included among these are their shared discomfort with the technological, consumeristic focus of our society (what Berry labels as our technozoic era of Wasteworld), the primacy given to economics over social justice, the lack of mystical experience in the lives of people, our stubborn attachment to paradigms that have failed (Berry's "paradigm addiction"), and our autism to the rest of creation. Such parallels and their implications might be explored further. However, an additional common thread relates closely to our current discussion, although it is not stated within a specifically theological context.

In 1968, Merton's essay "The New Consciousness" was published in *Zen and the Birds of Appetite*. In that discussion, using categories Berry would also later adopt, Merton concludes that

> Christian consciousness today . . . will doubtless have to meet the following great needs of man: *First;* His need for community . . . with his fellow man. This will also imply a deep . . . seriousness in approaching those critical problems which threaten man's very survival as a species on earth. . . . *Second;* Man's need for an adequate understanding of his everyday self in his ordinary life. . . . Man needs to find ultimate sense here and now in the ordinary. . . . *Third;* Man's need for a whole and integral experience of his own self on all its levels, bodily as well as imaginative, emotional, intellectual, spiritual.[87]

These categories, although developed only for consideration of the human condition, reflect the three features of cosmic ordering that Berry has identified as a principle law of the universe, namely, community, subjectivity, and diversity. Berry argues that these three governing principles have directed the evolution of the universe from its

---

86. Jean Leclercq, "The Evolving Monk," *Thomas Merton, Monk*, ed. Patrick Hart (Garden City, N.Y.: Image Books, 1976) 102.

87. Thomas Merton, "The New Consciousness," *Zen and the Birds of Appetite* (New York: New Directions, 1968) 30.

explosive origin from the primal singularity fifteen billion years ago to the shaping of the earth and its present life forms. He notes that "every reality of the universe is intimately present to every other reality of the universe and finds its fulfillment in this mutual presence," although humanity has not adequately recognized its communion with the natural world. Second, each individual reality enjoys a mysterious interior depth that both determines its unique subjectivity or self and "enables each articulation of the real to resonate with that numinous mystery that pervades all the world." Finally, "reality is not some infinitely extended homogeneous smudge." Rather, reality is comprised of unrepeatable and irreplaceable unique articulations on a multitude of levels, which collectively comprise an integrated whole.[88]

While Merton is considering the elements that would constitute a Christian consciousness so that people might acquire a more mystical appreciation of creation and develop a more contemplative way of being, Berry is recognizing the principles that not only define the emergent properties of cosmogenesis, but also form the context for humanity to experience the mystique of the created world. If people were to experience such a mystique, Berry believes, humanity would be less inclined to partake in practices that devastate the planet and any of its inhabitants. While Merton's considerations are primarily focused on needs and mysticism for the human, Berry is providing a cosmological context and mystique of nature that integrates human action and reflection into a broader ecological perspective.

Rather than have his list appear to be too focused on the self, Merton pauses to suggest a fourth need for modern humanity. He contends that humanity must move beyond its "inordinate self-consciousness, [its] monumental self-awareness" in order that it might "enjoy the freedom from concern that goes with being simply what [it] is"—i.e., simply being, centered on God.[89]

Berry would undoubtedly welcome Merton's perspectives and recognize the common elements that they share. In fact, Berry has commented on one such mutual interest. In his *Riverdale Papers*, he wrote an essay entitled "Thomas Merton: His Interest in the Orient," in which Berry "pays tribute" to the way that Merton "mediated the difference between the Western prophetic and Eastern contemplative traditions, and thus enabled Christianity to emerge more completely

88. Berry, *The Dream of the Earth*, 44–46, 105–7.
89. Merton, "The New Consciousness," 31; cf. 24.

from its tribal context and enter more fully into the universal society of mankind."[90] As a recognized scholar on the Orient, having taught on these matters at Columbia, St. John's, and Fordham universities, Berry was well situated to review Merton's works on the spiritual traditions of the oriental world, namely: *Mystics and Zen Masters, Zen and the Birds of Appetite,* and *The Way of Chuang Tzu.* Berry applauds Merton's awakening to the spiritual traditions of the East in order to forge a more comprehensive spirituality that would facilitate humanity's attainment of fuller and truer being. He notes that Merton's reflections "assist in bringing about a sacralized universe, to enable the world to be in its full sense."[91] By entering into the mystique of the ordinary, Berry contends that Merton "sought an even deeper immersion in this realm of the sacred, in the silence beyond speech." As one who emphasizes the manifestation of the divine within the elements of the earth, Berry would tend to welcome Merton's appreciation of the sacredness and goodness of creation.

Were Merton alive today, it is plausible that his evolving spirituality would have brought him to many of the same conclusions as Berry. For example, Merton found certain aspects of Teilhard de Chardin's writings appealing, and Teilhard has strongly influenced Berry's cosmological constructions. Merton commended Teilhard's cosmic mystique and agreed with the Jesuit that "material things . . . are indispensable for our service and knowledge of Christ. The Lord not only manifests Himself to us in material Creation, He even gives Himself to us in matter sanctified and sacramentalized. . . . It is important to notice the sublimely eucharistic heart of the spirituality of Teilhard de Chardin."[92] Indeed, Merton echoes Teilhard's understanding of the evolution of matter when he asserts that "after a long precarious evolution matter has reached the point, in man, where it can become fully aware of itself, take itself in hand, control its own destiny."[93] This Teilhardian reference is also evident in Berry's claim that "the human is that being in whom the universe reflects on . . . itself . . . in its own unique mode of conscious self-awareness."[94] Further-

90. Thomas Berry, "Thomas Merton: His Interest in the Orient," *Riverdale Papers* (Riverdale, N.Y.: Riverdale Center for Religious Research, 1978) 5:17; cf. 3.

91. Ibid.

92. Thomas Merton, "The Universe as Epiphany," *Love and Living* (New York: Farrar, Straus & Giroux, 1979) 177.

93. Merton, "Contemplation in a World of Action," 382.

94. Berry and Clarke, *Befriending,* 21.

more, Berry claims that the Earth seems to have "given over to the mindsphere [noosphere] the major share of directing the course of earth development."[95] The parallels among Teilhard, Merton, and Berry seem quite clear on this matter.

These similarities notwithstanding, Merton was uncomfortable with Teilhard's optimistic appraisal of science and evolution; but in this concern he would again find a like-minded companion in Berry. Berry has also been critical of Teilhard's optimism, especially the latter's unconstrained confidence in scientific and technological progress.[96] And when Merton decried that the paleontologist's strong focus on evolution seemed to suggest that even God was becoming, or when Merton was critical of such notions in contemporary process theology, he would once again find a supporter in Berry.[97]

This camaraderie is not surprising. Merton and Berry have been fed by many of the same Christian authors; they both have had a fondness for Eastern literature and mysticism; they have employed similar writing styles and have been more practically and empirically orientated than theoretical. Both of their lives have been driven by meaningful reflection as they have sought to encounter their God in the midst of every moment. While formed by their respective Cistercian and Passionist traditions, they have nevertheless been compelled to engage the issues afflicting their times in order to offer the world a functional spirituality to deal with its malaise.

95. Berry, *The Dream of the Earth*, 19.
96. Berry and Clarke, *Befriending*, 25.
97. Ibid., 28.

Thomas Merton and Confucian Rites: "The Fig Leaf for the Paradise Condition"

John Wu, Jr.

Introduction: Seeking Personal Integrity

As it has been well-documented, in the last decade of his life Thomas Merton tirelessly pointed directly to the hidden potential of ancient Asian traditions. The Christian monk had an abiding love affair with Asia and saw in the Asian a repository of an older wisdom that he felt the West lacked. Yet, however optimistically he may have felt about Asia and her hallowed past, Merton was never blind to her contemporary problems. Although he was never a Christian of the triumphalist persuasion, Merton nonetheless saw clearly the role that a revitalized Christianity might play in future cultural and spiritual revivals in the East. His concerns are clearly indicated in the following excerpt from a letter to a Chinese priest in California:

> I fully realize the complexity of the problem today. The Asians have renounced Asia. They want to be western, sometimes they are frantic about being western. . . . They feel that there have been centuries of inertia and stagnation, and there is a reaction against the humiliations and misunderstandings of colonialism, calling for a defeat of the west at its own technological game. All this is dangerous but inevitable. Christianity of course has a crucial part to play in saving all that is valuable in the east as well as in the west.[1]

---

1. Thomas Merton, *The Road to Joy,* ed. Robert E. Daggy (New York: Farrar, Straus & Giroux, 1989) 323.

Elsewhere, Merton appears to be echoing Mahatma Gandhi when he writes that Western man "is communicating his spiritual and mental sickness to men of the East. Asia is greatly tempted by the violence and activism of the West and is gradually losing hold of its traditional respect for silent wisdom."[2]

Merton's writings on the East show a boundless concern for nearly anything Asian. Many of his later writings and talks to his novices centered around Zen Buddhism, philosophical Taoism, and Sufism. I will examine an interest of Merton's which up to now few Mertonian scholars have dealt with, notably, *Ju Chia,* or Confucianism. I will show that Merton was able to see in Confucianism a dimension much overlooked until very recent decades. His essay "Classic Chinese Humanism," in *Mystics and Zen Masters,* along with my father's work on Confucius and Mencius, initially opened my eyes to Confucianism as an exceptional philosophy of the person aimed at social and political harmony and anchored solidly on an idea of ritual whose function is to disclose the dimension of the sacred in human society. To Merton, the main thrust of the thought of Confucius and Mencius (the latter, the greatest Confucian after the Master himself) lay in recovering one's humanity and in restoring the order of things as they are; this, in fact, meant the recovery of what he called the "paradise condition," which I shall also examine.

In an enlightening tape appropriately entitled "The Search for Wholeness," Merton the novice master connects scriptural writings with the basic concerns of Confucius. The American monk enlists his

2. "Honorable Reader," preface to the Japanese edition of *Thoughts in Solitude* in Thomas Merton, *Honorable Reader: Reflections on My Work,* ed. Robert E. Daggy (New York: Crossroad, 1989) 115. See also *Beyond East and West* (New York: Sheed and Ward, 1951) in which my father, John C. H. Wu, writing of his beloved country two years after the Communist takeover, sings nostalgically of the old China and laments the new: "Now China has changed. She has been dragged into the swirl and whirl of the world. Like a leaf in the west wind, like a flower fallen upon the ever-flowing Yangtsze, she is no longer herself, but is being swept along against her will to an unknown destiny. I know she will survive all the storms and currents, and emerge victorious over all her trials and tribulations, but she will not recover the original tranquillity of her soul and sweetness of her temper. Her music will no longer be flute-like, reverberating with clear wind and running water: it will be turned into something metallic and coarse, like the Wagnerian masterpieces. To her son, she will no longer be the tender Mother that she was, but will be transformed into a stern Father, a Father who will be as severe as the summer sun. China my Motherland is dead, long live my Fatherland!" (16).

unique perspective by cutting through the hard-crusted, centuries-old paraphernalia surrounding the much-maligned old sage of China. He says:

> The philosophy of Confucius aims at developing the person in such a way that he is a superior person. But what do you mean "superior"? It's not that he is a superman or any of this kind of nonsense, and it is not at all that he stands out over other people by winning. . . . Confucius doesn't have a philosophy on how to be a winner. . . . In contrast, the superior man in Confucius is the self-sacrificing man, the man who is formed in such a way that he knows how to give himself . . ., that in giving himself, he realizes himself. This is what Confucius discovered, and this is a great discovery. . . . This is just as fundamental as anything can be.[3]

He goes on to say that Confucian love (*jen*), which we may also call humanheartedness or benevolence, implies full identification with and empathy for others. The proper carrying out of Confucian ritual or *li* (Merton, given his own experience as a monastic, understandably prefers the word liturgy) would in fact express the reality of humankind's relationship to the universe, in which we are given the insight into the way the universe is constructed; this is acted out in liturgy in both the sacred and secular realms, whose demarcation is, in fact, inseparable. Elsewhere in this same suggestive talk, Merton, compares (if not actually raises) Confucian *li* to Christian notions of sanctification and sacramentality.

Merton then suggests that the basic Confucian virtues (which include righteousness and wisdom) resemble what he colloquially calls the "Benedictine setup" traditionally based on an elaborate structure of formal relationships whose ultimate goal is the "fully-developed personality." In fact, he hints that if monks live according to these basic principles, they will become complete persons. He does not elaborate as to whether he means "complete person" in the Confucian or Christian sense, or even if such a distinction ought to be entertained. Merton says the importance of Confucian wisdom is that it makes everything interior so that when one loves it is because

> that is the way to be. . . . This is based on a vision of reality . . .
> and this means really a kind of contemplation of reality, a *contem-*

---

3. Thomas Merton, "The Search for Wholeness," Credence Cassette, Merton AA2370, Side 2.

plative awareness of the way things are. And this manifests itself in liturgy because a person knows how to express himself in liturgy (since it is something learned and/or handed down to him). *His liturgy is an expression of . . . love.*[4]

To the monk of Gethsemani, the Confucian vision of reality is "contemplative awareness" because he sees in it a preordained *wholeness* imprinted indelibly in the heart of the person at birth. Further, it is this deeply ingrained sense of wholeness, this sense of oneness of life, that informs the Confucian person's relationships with others and with heaven. The true Confucian never goes through ritualistic movements merely to fulfill personal and social duties: rather, personal fulfillment is the perfect exchange of love and compassion, of that deep commiserate feeling of identity with the other, to wit, an exchange of humanheartedness *(jen)* and good will at the sacred level of being.

Confucius shared with all dialogical thinkers the belief that though the seeds of wholeness or the paradisaic condition may indeed be part and parcel of man, we nonetheless depend *existentially* for our completion on others. There is, hence, the implicit belief in the perfectibility of the person, that through proper study and the learning and carrying out of rituals, the person may indeed come to fulfill that original state of being for which he or she was destined from the very beginning of his or her existence.[5]

To my mind, it is the spiritual and contemplative dimension and not its rather prosaic ethical and social dimensions that gives Confucianism its true value and appeal. Without its *given* and encompassing wholeness, *Ju* could easily degenerate—and as Chinese history so well attested to, has degenerated—into a rigid set of mechanized social rituals whose sole aim would be to preserve a dead social and political order or, at best, be a disconnected series of moral aphorisms, both of which have been its fate since nearly its inception.

A close reading of *The Four Books* would convince us that these early Chinese classics were initially conceived as an organic way of life

---

4. Ibid. Emphasis added.

5. A thorough investigation into this question can be found in Donald J. Munro, *The Concept of Man in Early China* (Stanford, Calif.: University of Stanford Press, 1969), in which the author's main thesis is that "men, lacking inner defects, are perfectible through education." And adds, "The educational environment determines whether or not men will be good or evil, and educational reform is a key to the solution of urgent social and political problems" (preface, vii–viii).

that long centuries of intensive systematization together with state-craft had emptied of their original energy and vision of wholeness. Merton's approach typifies his gifted ability to see through the deadly and choking provincialism of two millennia into what he felt was, at its core, perhaps, humanity's most universally-conceived *personalistic* philosophy.

When my wife, Terry, and I were at Merton's hermitage in June 1968, we noticed he had been reading Herbert Marcuse's *One-Dimensional Man*, which I too had just read for a college course. Nearly six months later, on the last day of his life on December 10, he was to make prominent mention of Marcuse in his last talk in Bangkok. At the time of our meeting, when I asked the monk why he was reading the neo-Marxist, instead of giving me the expected answer that Marcuse was "must reading" for his social and political thought—Marcuse then being the absolute darling on the more radical U.S. campuses—Merton confirmed for me what I, too, had hesitantly thought to be the real value of the book: Marcuse's fine critique regarding the utter usurpation and destruction of language by mass society, communistic *and* capitalistic. The socially prophetic Marcuse believed that society, with technology at its disposal, could order reality according to its own totalitarian or commercial ends, beginning with the control of the uses and abuses of language itself. The whole enterprise becomes ever more cynical when the services of psychology and other social sciences are enlisted to achieve their not-so-harmless aims. As the present world rides ever more enthusiastically on the shirttails of multinational enterprises that depend for their survival on the increasing utilization of language that is locked strictly into the language of the salesperson, we can see clearly the prophetic nature of Marcuse's warning of a coming world whose people have become immune to the inherent subtlety and beauty of words.

Beginning in the 1970s when I studied Confucianism in the Republic of China, I was reminded of Merton's interest in Marcuse and of his concern for the preservation of language, which, as I see it now, resembles the Confucian concern for *cheng ming* (正名) or what is conventionally accepted as *rectification of names*. This was the rather simple, common-sensical Confucian insight that the root of all social and political ills can largely be traced to the disharmony and personal and social alienation that ensue when we no longer give much thought to the importance of fitting names to realities. In a nutshell, we may say that disharmony and alienation occur when no one quite knows for certain who he or she is supposed to be; that is, when we have lost our identity or when, in the case of ideas, a concept such as love becomes for all practical purposes the dominant province of soap operas, ad agencies, and, most absurd and tragic of all, appropriated by totalitarian governments.

Both totalitarian regimes and capitalist societies (to which Merton fittingly gave the nicknames Gog and Magog, respectively)[6] abound with gross examples of such abuse. Societies as we know them could not flourish without conscious linguistic manipulations either by the state or Madison Avenue and Hollywood and, as I have suggested above, by worldwide multinationals in recent decades.

Confucius was able to see the root of both social and moral chaos in a person's inability to live according to who he or she is. The integral person—the famous Confucian gentleman, or what Merton calls the "superior man"—is the human being who has cultivated his or her ability to respond in a fully human way to each and every person and situation. This implies knowledge of one's identity and being free of all external coercion, political or commercial.

But cultivation also implies the understanding that there is in man and woman a constant growth in the realization of being, beginning with one's moral and aesthetic senses and finding its completion in spiritual fulfillment. The following well-known passage from *The Analects of Confucius* illustrates wonderfully the Confucian sense of moral and spiritual progress, perhaps the only progress that really matters and is intrinsic to persons. It indicates quite clearly the unlimited spiritual potential suggested throughout early Confucianism and

---

6. See Thomas Merton, *The Courage for Truth: Letters to Writers,* ed. Christine M. Bochen (New York: Farrar, Straus & Giroux, 1993) 179. Bochen writes the following introduction to Thomas Merton's letters to the Nicaraguan poet Pablo Cuadra:

"In 1961, Merton wrote an article in the form of a letter to Cuadra. The well-known 'Letter to Pablo Antonio Cuadra Concerning Giants' was published in Nicaragua, Argentina and El Salvador, as well as in Merton's *Emblems*. In it Merton denounced both the Soviet Union and the United States whom he labeled Gog and Magog. 'Gog is a lover of power, Magog is absorbed in the cult of money: their idols differ and indeed their faces seem to be dead set against one another, but their madness is the same. . . . Be unlike the giants, Gog and Magog. Mark what they do, and act differently. . . . Their societies are becoming anthills, without purpose, without meaning, without spirit and joy.' The letter was 'a statement of where I stand morally, as a Christian writer.' Merton wrote to Cuadra on September 18, 1961."

serves as a healthy counterbalance to notions of progress that govern our contemporary lives. To my mind, the progression the Chinese sage is pointing toward is a truer understanding of our being, for he is here resituating for us the entire notion of progress in the qualitative possibilities of life itself:

> The Master said, At fifteen I set my heart upon learning. At thirty, I had planted my feet firm upon the ground. At forty, I no longer suffered from perplexities. At fifty, I knew what were the biddings of Heaven. At sixty, I heard them with docile ear. At seventy, I could follow the dictates of my own heart, for what I desired no longer overstepped the boundaries of right.[7]

Rituals and the Wholeness of Life

Perhaps it is imprudent to lump together a monk/writer of the twentieth century with one of the paradigms of world history. Yet, one cannot help finding common ground in their thought. Like Confucius, Merton knew the importance of keeping the light of classical learning burning, which was, of course, an old monastic tradition. His talks and conferences to student novices and fellow monks are a testament of his respect for such studies. In fact, one of his main concerns with regard to his students was that, in entering monastic life, they had not sufficiently prepared themselves in either the basic classics or good literary works, past or present. To his credit, even though he was a religious, he did not find it necessary to make hard and fast distinctions between so-called sacred and secular literatures.

To Confucius, classical learning and all that it implies was the very lifeline of a race of people, the repository without which humans soon would degenerate into mere barbarians not only without social graces—which seems to have been the least of his concerns—but without any notion as to where he or she is rooted. In fact, one could conclude that his principal motivation was the very recovery of classical learning itself. For without classical learning—which Confucius considered the human person's essential didactic tool—one becomes morally and spiritually directionless. To Merton, too, an intimate knowledge and love of the classics was no less critical. Here is what he had to say regarding the relationship among classical learning,

7. Arthur Waley, trans., *The Analects of Confucius* (New York: Vintage, 1938) 88.

Confucian humanism, and the human personality, on the one hand, and his debunking of the shallow, modernist attempt to come to terms with the person, on the other hand:

> The foundation of [the] Confucian system is first of all the *human person* and then his relations with other persons in society. This of course sounds quite modern—because one of our illusions about ourselves is that we have finally discovered "personality" and "personalism" in the twentieth century. Such are the advantages of not having had a classical education, which would do us the disservice of reminding us that personalism was very much alive in the sixth century B.C., and that, in fact, it existed then in a much more authentic form than it does among us with our "personality tests" and "personality problems" [the ultimate carving of the Taoist uncarved block!].
>
> *Ju* (Confucianism) is therefore a humanist and personalistic doctrine and this humanism is religious and sacred.[8]

Then Merton seems to draw directly from his own experience as a member of a community of monks when he says:

> The society in which (men would once again be themselves, and would gradually recover the ability to act virtuously, kindly, and mercifully) must be very seriously and firmly held together by a social order that draws its strength not from the authority of law but from the deep and sacred significance of liturgical rites, *Li*.

And in the same vein, he adds almost rhapsodically: "These rites, which bring earth into harmony with heaven, are not merely the cult of heaven itself but also the expression of those affective relationships which, in their varying degrees, bind men to one another."[9] Finally, he reveals what to me is the quintessential humanistic Merton of the mid- and late-1960s, in which he speaks surely not only for Confucianism but for himself as well: "The Confucian system of rites was meant to give full expression to that natural and humane love which is the only genuine guarantee of peace and unity in society, and which produces that unity not by imposing it from without but by *bringing it out from within men themselves*."[10]

---

8. Thomas Merton, *Mystics and Zen Masters* (New York: Farrar, Straus & Giroux, 1967) 51.

9. Ibid., 52.

10. Ibid.

Confucianism in its purest form is a philosophy of the interior person and ought never to be associated with ideas that bespeak or are suggestive of determinism or social necessity. Merton's treatment of Confucian rituals may indeed be an idealization, but its great advantage is that it points out certain possibilities as to what rituals—particularly those that concern human relationships—may suggest when practiced to their fullest, that is, as vehicles revealing latent human tendencies that the Confucianists themselves may not have imagined existed. Merton points out the potentially rich *existential* content of what Confucius may have had only an inkling, but whose richly suggestive quality makes the idea worth exploring given the nature of its open-endedness.

Due to the sacredness with which Confucius regarded *any* ritual, religious or interpersonal, and the organic and holistic manner in which the early Confucianists naturally perceived the world—indeed, as *cosmos*, as had the Greeks—the potential for development of a truly flourishing and open-ended *personalist* philosophy of life would seem to be boundless. Merton helps us see the Chinese sage in an altogether new light.

The Confucian rectification of names and the notion of reciprocity[11] in human relations, rather than suggesting rigidification of the family and social strata, can be regarded as ideas that, when car-

---

11. As Confucius says in *The Analects*, trans. Arthur Waley (New York: Vintage, 1938): "The man of *jen* (仁) wishes to establish his own character, also helps others along the path" (VI, 28). For an explanation of the notion of reciprocity, see Y. P. Mei, "The Basis of Social, Ethical, and Spiritual Values in Chinese Philosophy," *The Chinese Mind*, ed. Charles A. Moore, 149–66 (Honolulu: University of Hawaii, 1967), in which the author writes:

"Confucius repeatedly spoke of his 'one unifying principle,' which is also rendered as 'an all-pervading unity.' This unifying principle is generally assumed to be *shu* (恕), reciprocity, which Confucius once said was the one word that might guide one's conduct throughout life. Reciprocity was stated to be 'what you would not have others do unto you, do not (do) unto others,' and this formula has usually been referred to as the Chinese Golden Rule. . . . *Jen* is . . . the cornerstone of Confucianism, and it may be assumed that reciprocity, . . . is an expression of *jen*, and that it is just as proper to regard *jen* as the one unifying principle of all of Confucius' teachings. Historically, *jen* is a distinct Confucian concept, a concept little used before his time" (152).

See also Wing-tsit Chan, "Chinese Theory and Practice," *The Chinese Mind*, trans. James Legge, 11–30 (Oxford: Oxford University Press, 1939). Chan writes the following regarding the Golden Mean, or what he calls "central harmony":

ried out with deference, benevolence, and deep charity, lend themselves to the gradual actualization of those hidden qualities in all of us. How? Through an unmasking process brought about by commonplace, everyday ritual practices. It is essentially related to the understanding of human personality, not exclusively in a psychological sense within which we modernists tend to confine the whole of it, that is, as largely behaviorist phenomena, but in deeply existential, moral, and spiritual terms that emphasize the process of self-effacement and self-emptying, which are basic concerns of both the Taoist and the Zen Buddhist and of nearly all mystical traditions in the West. Further, it is related less to the absorption by the other—which is suggestive of a psychologically coercive relationship—than identification with the other at the level of being. When performed with the proper attitude, the action would naturally disclose what is deepest and, in the process, transform the participants.

Hence, the key to the progressive unfolding of the true self lies in reciprocity, which we may broadly define as the willingness of a person to allow the deepest yet most natural, expansive, and magnanimous impulses to come into play in his or her life. It says plainly to the other, I want to give to you because in the giving is revealed my true self. Further, it lies in never permitting this sacred exchange between persons—an exchange, as I have suggested above, at the level of *being* rather than *having*—to degenerate into the endless giving and returning of external favors, a social cult quite unrelated to genuine filial or fraternal feelings born fully of the spirit of benevolence and love. Surely it is not rooted in familial, social, or political pressure or coercion, that is, in the conventionally tiresome and perfunctorily carrying out of duty for the sole purpose of fulfilling an obligation, and, at its crudest form, mere face-saving.[12]

"Confucius said that 'there is one thread that runs through my doctrines.' . . . The thread is . . . generally to be identical with the Confucian doctrine of central harmony (*chung yung*, Golden Mean). Indeed, the doctrine is of supreme importance in Chinese philosophy; it is not only the backbone of Confucianism, both ancient and modern, but also of Chinese philosophy as a whole. Confucius said that 'to be central (*chung*) in our being and to be harmonious (*yung*) with all' is the supreme attainment in our moral life" (35).

12. For a rather extensive but wholly interesting elaboration and documentation on the ubiquitous issue of face in Chinese society, see "Face Saving as a Way of Life" (305-376) in Richard W. Hartzell's book, *Harmony in Conflict* (Taipei, Taiwan, ROC: Caves Books Ltd., 1988).

To Thomas Merton, the person or human personality is a manifestation of human nature transformed and divinized and made hallowed by the inherent sacredness of life. But the sacred, as he learned in his monastic experience, can only be experienced through the concrete ritual act which, if performed with a sincere and humble heart and directed wholly toward the other, goes a very long way in humanizing those involved. Yet, ironically, the real boon of any ritual act that is part and parcel of this humanizing process is the natural coming together of the sacred and the secular, the experience of the wholeness of being in which we, in finding identity in the other, become one with the universe as well. This, I think, is Confucianism at its most profound and the reason Merton felt he could speak so affirmatively of classical Confucianism as having understood the meaning of true personality and universal harmony that mirror one another. Confucianists have never made any Procrustean distinctions about harmony found in people, society, and the universe.

In Merton's delightful essay "A Study of Chuang Tzu," preceding his "imitations" of the great Chinese Taoist sage, he says, "To give priority to the person means respecting the unique and inalienable value of the other person, as well as one's own" (17). No doubt "inalienable value" refers to that sacred element in the person without which rituals would be wholly empty, a mere going through the motion. In fact, the end of ritual is partial fulfillment of one's personality through a mutual exchange on a very deep level of the mystery of being informed by the guiding light of *Tien* (天) or heaven. The ritual act, while taking the two persons to an altogether different depth, makes the participants aware of the ground of being upon which their lives are anchored. The sacred is never "out there" as much as it is in us as a guiding principle of life; in fact, it is irrevocably there for all eternity, and the deference we show toward others in relationship is to predispose the ever-present sacred to show its face whenever it sees fit to do so. And if we understand Confucius correctly, we may infer that *Tien*—the sacred—when listened to "with docile ear," indeed can inform the heart in such a way that all words will find their rightful resting place in actions that will keep within "the boundaries of right," that is, within the measure and pivot of central harmony *(chung yung)*.

Perhaps for this reason the Sinologist Julia Ching has written so enthusiastically about the possible future revival of Confucianism, not as statecraft, but as perennial philosophy. As she puts it so aptly, "To survive and to be of use to modern man, Confucianism must become young again, as in the days of its first gestation."[13]

The material form of Confucian ritual may follow a certain well-defined pattern, but what is encountered in the ritual (for example, the lovely tea ceremony) is conditioned primarily by the right attitude of the heart the participants bring into the act. The spirit, in other words, is free and undetermined, and the degree to which this freedom roams depends very much on the freedom, maturity, and depth of the persons involved. And this is as it should be, for the ritual—seemingly stylized and rigid—is never mechanical and, if performed with correctness of attitude, is wholly personal. What is exchanged is *unspeakable* and beyond language; more significantly, it is never repeated. In fact, because in any true action language and the concrete act merge into one, the act is the language itself.[14]

Rituals, then, properly performed, can play the role of continuously helping to redefine the self in the most concrete and flesh-and-blood way, directing us to our proper place in the world and gradually

---

13. Julia Ching, *Confucianism and Christianity: A Comparative Study* (Tokyo/New York/San Francisco: Kodansha International/USA) 63.

14. Merton himself illustrates this point of *act as language*. In responding to my father's gift of Chinese calligraphy and the poem Mei Teng ("Silent Lamp"), a Chinese sobriquet that the older man gave the younger monk, Merton in a typically playful Zen mood replies:

"So it was moving to be 'baptized' in Chinese with a name I must live up to. After all, a name indicates a divine demand. Hence I must be *Mei Teng*, a silent lamp, not a sputtering one. . . . Your calligraphy fascinates me, and of course so does the poem. . . . I wish I could reply in kind, calligraphy and all. In desperation, or rather no, in considerable joy, I resort again to the green tea, and in fact the kettle is whistling by the fire right at my elbow, and the sun is rising over the completely silver landscape. *Instead of putting all this into a poem, I will let it be its own poem.* The silent steam will rise from the teacup and make an ideogram for you. Maybe sometime I will add a poem to it as an exclamation point of my own. But are such exclamation points needed?" (Thomas Merton, *The Hidden Ground of Love*, selected and ed. William H. Shannon [New York: Farrar, Straus & Giroux, 1985] 632; letter dated December 28, 1965.)

The above seems to be an extraordinary spiritual insight. Words can only serve as footnotes to what is. The action/act is always primary as long as it expresses the fullness of being. Hence the tree trees, the steam steams, man mans, brother brothers, etc. Anything less than "steam steams" is an alienation of/from being. In "man mans," man is both the substantive and the predicate, and, in the end, there is, in fact, only "man," a merging of the doer and the doing. And if we really took all this very seriously, the rest would be silence.

disclosing the latent potential that lies dormant in us, in others, and, in the process, in what is hidden in life itself. With rituals, life can assume a grace, dignity, and depth hitherto lost, even disposing us to true contemplation. For the final aim of ritual is not so much aesthetic or even moral, but realization of the deep mystery of being that unaccountably shapes each relationship.

Rituals, beginning with forgetfulness of self and informed by charity and deference toward others, remind us not to press forward aggressively with our plans and schemes, an attitude and behavior that would unwittingly shrink the possibilities of what lies before us and in us. On the contrary, in being deferential toward others, in learning to step back and refusing to impose our will—which is what interpersonal rituals encourage—we are able to see uncovering before us the full measure of dignity in each person so that in the process of discovering that dignity, we recover our own dignity as well. In that discovery lie the seeds for our transformation into our true selves, or, as it were, the Confucian gentleman, the *chun tzu.*

Confucianism and the Revival of Humanism

Confucius, at least for the more progressive Chinese today, has not and perhaps never will fully recover from the onslaught of the May Fourth Movement,[15] whose reverberations continue unmitigated to this day. In this century, no sage has been discredited and cast aside more often and indiscriminately than Confucius, first by the proponents of the May Fourth Movement, then by the Communists' ongoing polemic. How ironic it is, then, that it has taken Western thinkers such as Karl Jaspers, Donald Munro, Herbert Fingarette, Benjamin I. Schwartz, Merton, and others, or Asian thinkers trained in the West such as Wing-tsit Chan, my father, John C. H. Wu, Julia Ching, and Tu Wei-ming, to see in the Chinese sage the seeds of a future renaissance. Others, even scholars who perhaps should know better, seem to be caught in endless political squabbles over what ought to be done with

---

15. For a good historical discussion of this very important social and intellectual revolution in early twentieth-century Republican China, see Chow Tse-tsung, *The May Fourth Movement: Intellectual Revolution in Modern China* (Cambridge, Mass.: Harvard University Press, 1960) esp. 300–13, on the controversies surrounding the anti-Confucian movement, which seemed to have set the intellectual, social, and moral tone for the rest of the century in China.

Confucius. What we do know is that the old fellow refuses to go away.[16]

Toward the end of *Mystics and Zen Masters*, in the essay "The Other Side of Despair" Merton writes of the horrors of faceless or "mass man," a perfect contrast to what he felt was the essence of Confucian humanism and personalism:

> Mass society . . . isolates each individual subject from his imme-diate neighbor, reducing him to a state of impersonal, purely for-mal, and abstract relationship with other objectified individuals. In dissolving the more intimate and personal bonds of life in the family and of the small sub-group (the farm, the shop of the arti-san, the village, the town, the small business), mass society segre-gates the individual from the concrete and human "other" and leaves him alone and unaided in the presence of the Faceless, the

16. See Julia Ching, "Confucianism: A Critical Reassessment of the Herit-age," *Confucianism and Christianity: A Comparative Study* (Tokyo, New York and San Francisco: Kodansha International/USA) 34–67. Some choice excerpts will suffice:

"The critics today judge (Confucius) to have been 'irrelevant' to his own time, indeed, a reactionary and counter revolutionary who impeded the course of history. . . . His class-biased teachings can have no universal meaning, his thought was unoriginal, 'eclectic,' compromising, his scholarship was mediocre, and even his personal character is being assailed: he was no sage, but a hypocrite" (52).

"The fall of Confucianism as an ethical system is bringing about a total spir-itual vacuum. The alternative is to be the new, still evolving Maoist ethic, with its emphasis of serving the people. But the new ethic still lacks complete structuring and comes to the people, not from below, but from above. The message of Legalism is obvious. Faith in authority, that characteristic so much criticized in Confu-cianism, is not being assailed in itself. But the final arbiter of conscience has changed. It is now the state" (60).

Ching asks the question, "Is Confucianism relevant?", to which she gives the following rather upbeat comments:

"If we . . . mean by it a dynamic discovery of the worth of the human per-son, of his possibilities of moral greatness and even sagehood, of his fundamental relationship to others in a human society based on ethical values, of a metaphysics of the self open to the transcendent, then Confucianism is very relevant, and will always be relevant.

"And if, going further, we desire for Confucianism an openness to change and transformation, through confrontation with new values and ideas coming from other teachings—such as earlier from Buddhism—through a readiness to evaluate itself critically as well, then Confucianism is not only relevant but in possession of a future" (63–64).

collective void, the public. Thus . . . mass-man finds himself related not to flesh and blood human beings with the same freedom,
responsibility, and conflicts as himself, but with the idealized
typological images: the Führer, the president, the sports star, the
teen singer, the space man.[17]

One of Merton's chief concerns—and here I believe he was
prophetic as he was in so many other areas of concern—was his fear
that the milieu, "a certain cultural and spiritual atmosphere" that "favors the secret and spontaneous development of the inner self," has
disappeared. In contrast to ancient cultural traditions in both the East
and the West, which "favored the interior life and indeed transmitted
certain common materials in the form of archetypal symbols, liturgical
rites, art, poetry, philosophy, and myth which nourished the inner self
from childhood to maturity," Merton resigned himself into believing
that "such a cultural setting no longer exists in the West, and is no
longer common property."[18] And we might add with some trepidation
that with the dawning of modernization such a setting no longer exists
in the East either. In fact, what has happened in the East would have
confirmed his worst suspicions as to the direction the East has been
taking since his passing.

Merton, beginning with his own student novices, was very concerned with the rediscovery and the uncovering of common cultural
materials conducive to the recovery of the true self. He did not hesitate
to explore geographies of the mind and heart that appeared to be
esoteric and obscure to his readers. The monk was disturbed by the obsessive emphasis on discursive thought that he felt had disproportion-
ately contributed to the problems of the contemporary West. He
actively sought after more affective ways of thinking and living that
would help bring us directly back to both ourselves and God.

On the first leg of his journey to Asia, while speaking at the Center
for the Study of Democratic Institutions, a think tank in Santa Barbara,
California (October 3, 1968), Merton made his position rather clear with
regard to a society fostering a constant reductionism of the human person. Remaining in character, he made no effort to water down what he
had to say, even at the expense of touching a few raw nerves:

17. Thomas Merton, *Mystics and Zen Masters* (New York: Farrar, Straus &
Giroux) 274.
18. William H. Shannon, *Thomas Merton's Dark Path* (New York: Farrar, Straus
& Giroux, 1987) 117-8.

We are living in a society that is absolutely sick. And one of the reasons why it is sick is that it is completely from the top of the head. It's completely cerebral. It has utterly neglected everything to do with the rest of the human being: *the whole person is reduced to a very small part of who and what the person is.* . . . And Christianity has connived with this, you see. The official Christianity has simply gone along with this, that is, with this kind of repressive, partial, and fragmented view of the human person.[19]

I might add that in the West there is almost always the tendency toward one extreme orientation or another. One is either wholly mystical or intellectual or moral or practical and, as is so often the case today, even strictly psychological. By insisting on one extreme, we facilely and conveniently explain all the others away, as if it were really possible to live out of the tunnel of one of these extremes. And the East, of course, goes along with this aberration and creates its own caricatures of the fragmented self. Under such circumstances, there is rarely a healthy coming together of all the diverse elements and dimensions that naturally go into the making of the whole man and woman.

One has to wonder if there are indeed some built-in elements in contemporary life's milieu that would make wholeness impossible and fragmentation of the self inevitable. To Merton, steeped in the existential literature of the nineteenth and twentieth centuries, experiences of alienation and angst were commonplace, a given of contemporary life. Despite the wholeness and optimism of his own thought, he was never optimistic enough to believe that in his own lifetime such problems had bottomed out, or had even come close to it.

In the same session at the Society for Democratic Societies Center in which he spoke of monastic renewal, Merton made his ideas concerning the relationship between external restructuring of institutions and renewal of the inner self quite clear. He understood the shortcomings of trying to cure what is fundamentally interior by manipulating what is external:

You hear this talk everywhere, or you hear it in monasteries, about monastic renewal, and it is confusing because, too often, it is employed to talk about the renewal of an institution. But as soon as

19. Thomas Merton, *Preview of the Asian Journey*, ed. Walter Capps (New York: Crossroad, 1989) 48. Emphasis added.

people start talking in these terms, you can see that they are en-
veloped in what Sartre calls bad faith: if the life we are living is not
meaningful in itself, how are we going to make an institution
meaningful to other people?[20]

Rather than putting all its efforts into making its institutions
meaningful and relevant to the world, true monasticism, for Merton,
"is a question of *renewing an age-old experience,*" for the "real essence of
monasticism is the handing down from master to disciple of an *uncommunicable experience.*"[21] True education or learning in the classical
sense, East and West, is, indeed, this sacred handing down of a something that is uncommunicable. Though necessarily couched in words,
true words are always transparent words that point to that uncommunicable something that always is. What is authentic and vital can never
live fully in cold formulas alone.

Both Confucius and, later, Mencius regarded human relationships as the very cornerstone of society, the existential lifeline of an entire culture. In their writings, it astonishes readers that there are
essentially no obvious traces of either legalism or Machiavellianism
(which are both manipulative and concerned with control) in their
almost naive and pristine social and political schemes; we can only
attribute this to their remarkable faith not only in the human person,
but in that which both persons and nature are squarely rooted: upon
Tien itself. Confucius and Mencius were wise enough to leave *Tien* undefined and to accept it as either a universal metaphysical principle or
a personal or suprapersonal God, depending upon the context. More
concretely, they relied on what in the West we may call natural law that
emanated from an undefined and undifferentiated heaven.[22]

---

20. Ibid., 30–31.
21. Ibid., 34. Emphasis added.
22. The opening passage to The Golden Mean, or *Chung Yung,* one of *The
Four Books,* reads: "What is ordained by Heaven is called 'Nature.' Following out
this Nature is called the *Tao* (or the natural law). The refinement of the natural law
is called 'culture.'"

Mencius, as if giving a teleological form to this basic ontological insight,
says: "He who has exhaustively studied all his mental constitution knows his nature. Knowing his nature, he knows Heaven. To preserve one's mental constitution
and nourish one's nature is the way to serve Heaven." *The Four Books,* trans. James
Legge (Oxford University Press, 1939) 448–49. (Book 7, Part 1, ch. 1, art. 1).

My father comments: "Thus, the mandate of Heaven, human nature and culture form a continuous series. The natural law is to be found by the mind in human

Merton, writing of an institution of which he was an integral part for over half his life, lamented that "in the end monasticism (in the late Middle Ages) by a curious reversal that is so usual in the evolution of societies, identified the fig leaf with the Paradise condition" so that "freedom . . . consisted in renouncing nakedness in favor of elaborate and ritual vestments."[23] Here he could have very easily been speaking of Confucianism as well.

The Heart as the Basis for Social Reform

By way of parallel, when Confucianism was rationalized into a convenient vehicle and basis of statecraft in the Han Dynasty (202 B.C.E.–220 C.E.), it too could be likened to identifying "the fig leaf with the Paradise condition." If we examine the spirit of the *Analects* and the *Book of Mencius* carefully, especially in the light of what rituals and rites might have meant to ancient peoples in general and to the Chinese in particular, we can come to a better appreciation of these ancient books and what their authors and compilers might have had in mind even without their having spelled out in detail and depth the meaning of personal and social rites. My own conclusion is that the Chinese sages, seeing the chaos of the times throw the entire social fabric out of joint and into general confusion, thereby looked *inward* in an effort to find a solution to what nearly everyone else seemed to have felt were basically external political and military problems. Their true wisdom lay in their ability to view social and political chaos as mere symptoms of a deeper illness residing in humankind itself. This is doubtlessly what Merton meant when he spoke of Confucius's achievement: "This is a great discovery. . . . This is just as funda-mental as anything can be."[24]

---

nature itself, and to be further developed and applied by the mind to the ever-widening human relations under infinitely variable circumstances" (John C. H. Wu, "Mencius' Philosophy of Human Nature and Natural Law," *Christian Humanism and Christian Spirituality: Essays,* Asian Philosophical Studies 2, ed. Paul K. T. Sih [Jamaica, N.Y.: St. John's University Press, 1965] 17).

23. Thomas Merton, "Learning to Live," *Love and Learning,* ed. Naomi Burton Stone and Patrick Hart (New York: Farrar, Straus & Giroux, 1981) 8.

24. Julia Ching capsulizes the early fate of Confucianism in her *Confucianism and Christianity:*

"In 213 B.C. [the first emperor of the Ch'in dynasty, 221–206 B.C.] ordered the burning of all books except those which dealt with medicine, divination and

The writings of the sages make plain the demands they imposed on all of society, beginning particularly with the ruler down to the most humble. They called for nothing short of a total internal reconstruction, which, to Confucius and Mencius, was the only healthy and possible road toward the recovery of the lost and fragmented moral sense in the human person and of the spiritual and cultural milieu. Their sole aim was to save a society that they loved for the reason that their whole beings—the traditions and history that made them what they were and their love for the ruler down to the common folk—were inextricably bound up with the way they thought, felt, and lived. One cannot imagine their loving their people less than the way Socrates loved and wholly identified with his beloved Athenians even unto death.

---

agriculture. Allegedly, he also ordered the burying alive of 460 scholars, in order to put an end to criticisms of his rule. It is not known how many of these were Confucians.

"Confucianism remained underground, to be revived and dominant during the Han dynasty, where Emperor Wu (r. 140–87 B.C.) made it the state philosophy, supported by government patronage and an official educational system. But this could only happen at a certain cost to the teachings of Confucians themselves. The Confucianism that triumphed was no longer the philosophy of Confucius and Mencius. It had already absorbed many extraneous ideas . . . from Legalism and yin-yang cosmology and religious philosophy. It would emphasize—far more than Confucius and Mencius did—the vertical and authoritarian dimensions of the five moral relationships. . . . It was a triumph which has been described as a 'Pyrrhic victory'" (40).

Writing on the Legalists in his essay "The Individual in Political and Legal Traditions," in *The Chinese Mind*, my father says:

"By isolating the Rule of Law from the fundamental humanity of men [and women], [the Legalists] foredoomed it to a catastrophic collapse. Instead of securing the rights and freedom of the individual, as it normally should, it became actually a ruthless instrument for dehumanizing the people. . . . So far as China was concerned, this unhappy wedding spoiled the chance of a genuine balanced Rule of Law for over two millenniums.

"Of all these lines of thinking, the way of Confucius would seem to be the most balanced. It excels Mohism by its catholicity, and excels Buddhism by its sense of reality. It steers between the anarchistic tendencies of Taoism and the totalitarianism of the Legalists. It recognizes the need of unity, but at the same time it sees the desirability of diversity. As Confucius himself puts it, 'Men of superior quality aim at harmony not uniformity; while the small-minded aim at uniformity, not harmony.' This is in the best tradition of political wisdom, and is still a living ideal" (342–3).

Thomas Merton falls very much into this sapiential dimension so evident in the ancient sages, a wisdom centered on life as unity and harmony. In "Cold War Letter 25" to James Forest (dated January 29, 1962), a pacifist who continues to be politically active today, he talks of the necessity of "the complete change of Heart," of "inner change," of praying "for a total and profound change in the mentality of the whole world," of "application of spiritual force and not the use of merely political pressure," of "the deep need for purity of soul," finally concluding that "this [and all the above] takes precedence over everything else" when one is involved in a social and political movement.[25]

In a later letter to Forest in the same year, Merton speaks in a way that Confucius himself might have spoken on politics were the ancient sage living today:

> The basic problem is not political, it is apolitical and human. One of the most important things to do is to keep cutting deliberately through political lines and barriers and emphasize the fact that these are largely fabrications, and that *there is another dimension, a genuine reality, totally opposed to the fictions of politics.* The human dimension which politics pretends to arrogate entirely to themselves. This is the necessary first step along the long way towards the perhaps impossible task of purifying, humanizing and somehow illuminating politics themselves.[26]

The thought of the early Confucians reflects an abiding faith in the "interiority of man" that is based first on the more fundamental and implicit faith in the basic goodness of humans and, second, in the intimately personal relationship between human persons and heaven, which they regarded as a given, that is, as both preordained and inherent in the very structure of life itself.

The fact that such a vision never got off the ground and failed to materialize in Chinese society is surely less the fault of the sages than that of later Confucianists who shifted the emphasis from a remarkably balanced philosophy of life and society where rituals are constantly informed by the spirit of love and benevolence, to a one-sided emphasis upon the mere carrying out of rituals as a means of securing social and political order. Chinese humanism seemed to have quickly degenerated into a system and thought devoid of that all-important

---

25. Merton, *The Hidden Ground of Love,* 262.
26. Ibid., 272. Emphasis added.

organic feel for the wholeness of life. It substituted for this original wholeness a rather lame notion of an impersonal cosmos without a warm, throbbing heart at the center of the universe. Moreover, it was marked principally by an overwrought and obsessive emphasis on filial piety and ancestor worship that favored looking backward rather than emphasizing a dynamic present and future.

This nearly deterministic opting for a narrower notion of social order over and against what initially held great promises of developing into a potentially powerful personal, social, and even spiritual philosophy was indeed an identifying of "the fig leaf with the Paradise condition." The cult of the family, great and important as it has been in China, alas, never seemed to have overcome the blight of the tribal and the provincial; in the end, the cult sapped whatever natural energy and inclinations the Chinese might have had for true brotherhood, which, I am convinced, was the original vision of the early sages. The Chinese Communists have tried to bring about "universal brotherhood," but have, in its agonizing train, summarily torn the heart out of the human person. Indeed, one wonders exactly how long the new fatherland can last.

The quiet and subtle Confucian vision of true brotherhood based on a healthy sense of personalism draws each generation to reappraise Confucianism not as a system conceived for statecraft and its preservation, but as an indispensable way of life with sacred and universal principles at its very core. Without such abiding principles that these sages fathomed at the heart of nature and heaven, Confucianism would be no more than a quaint cultural remnant from the dead past; as, indeed, Christianity would be if we were to identify its merely external structures, hierarchy, Canon Law, or moral theology as the whole of it.

In this generation, the East owes a great debt to Thomas Merton for reminding Easterners of a priceless treasure that a good number of us, anxious not to be left off the irrepressible express freight of modernization, have already abandoned. He saw in classical Confucianism part and parcel a paradise condition, the very roots of which lie dormant, yet, in fact, are very much alive in every man and woman. It remains vigorous because Confucius hit upon a principle of love that is rooted not in society, but squarely in nature, by way of *Tien* itself. Therefore, it is not a positivistic principle whose reality and validity are strictly dependent on social environment and reforms.

Both Confucius and Mencius were able to speak very confidently of the basic goodness of humanity only because they saw the unmistakable signature of heaven in the center of humankind's being. Any fruitful exchanges between Confucianism and Christianity would center on an investigation between the Confucian *Tien* and the living God of Christianity.[27]

In August 1967, Pope Paul VI requested that Merton write a "message of contemplatives to the world." What resulted was a wonderfully rich outpouring of humanistic sentiments supported by love and compassion. Like Confucius' faith in heaven, Merton's faith in the living God by the late sixties was so profound that he was able to see God's epiphany everywhere. The following may indeed be seen as a beautiful flowering of Confucian humanism couched in the language of a twentieth-century monk whose sentiments would have done even Confucius proud:

> If we once began to recognize . . . the true value of our own self, we would see that this value was the sign of God in our being. . . . Fortunately, the love of our fellow man is given to us as the way of realizing this. For the love of our brother, our sister, our beloved, our wife, our child, is there to see with the clarity of God Himself that we are good. It is the love of my lover, my brothers or my child that sees God in me, makes God credible to myself in me. And it is my love for my lover, my child, my brother, that enables me to show God to him or her in himself or herself. Love is the epiphany of God in my poverty.[28]

The basic message of Thomas Merton is that we are not alone and that both social and political harmony and moral and spiritual salvation demand the constant help of everyone we know.

---

27. For an excellent discussion on the affinities and disparities in the Confucian and Christian notions of God, respectively, see chapter four, "The Problem of God" (112–50) in Ching's *Confucianism and Christianity*. Ching notes, for example, "the Confucian Classics clearly enunciate a belief in God as the source and principle of all things, the giver of life and the protector of the human race" (118).

28. *The Hidden Ground of Love,* 157 (letter to Dom Francis Decroix).

WORKS CITED

The Analects of Confucius. Trans. Arthur Waley. New York: Vintage Books, 1938.

Arendt, Hannah. *Men in Dark Times.* Orlando, Fl.: Harcourt Brace Jovanovich, 1968.

The Chinese Classics. Trans. James Legge. Oxford: Oxford University Press, 1939.

The Chinese Mind. Ed. Charles A. Moore. Honolulu: University of Hawaii Press, 1967.

Ching, Julia. *Confucianism and Christianity: A Comparative Study.* Tokyo, New York, and San Francisco: Kodansha International/USA, 1978.

Chow Tse-tsung. *The May Fourth Movement: Intellectual Revolution in Modern China.* Cambridge, Mass.: Harvard University Press, 1960.

Fingarette, Herbert. *Confucius: The Secular as Sacred.* New York: Harper and Row, Harper Torchbooks, 1972.

The Merton Annual. Vol. 1. Eds. Robert E. Daggy et al. New York: AMS Press, Inc., 1988.

Merton, Thomas. *Conjectures of a Guilty Bystander.* Garden City, N.Y.: Image Books, 1968.

_____. *The Courage for Truth: Letters to Writers.* Sel. and ed. Christine M. Bochen. New York: Farrar, Straus & Giroux, 1993.

_____. *The Hidden Ground of Love.* Letters sel. and ed. William H. Shannon. New York: Farrar, Straus & Giroux, 1985.

_____. *"Honorable Reader": Reflections on My Work.* Ed. Robert E. Daggy. Foreword by Harry James Cargas. New York: Crossroad Publishing Company, 1989.

_____. *Love and Learning.* Ed. Naomi Burton Stone and Patrick Hart. New York: Bantam Book published by arrangement with Farrar, Straus & Giroux, 1981.

_____. *Mystics and Zen Masters.* New York: Farrar, Straus & Giroux, 1967.

_____. *Preview of the Asian Journey.* Ed. Walter Capps. New York: Crossroad Publishing Company, 1989.

_____. *The Road to Joy.* Letters sel. and ed. Robert E. Daggy. New York: Farrar, Straus & Giroux, 1989.

_____. "The Search for Wholeness," Credence Cassette (Merton AA2370).

_____. *The Way of Chuang Tzu.* New York: New Directions, 1965.

_____. *Zen and the Birds of Appetite.* New York: New Directions, 1968.

Munro, Donald J. *The Concept of Man in Early China.* Stanford, Calif.: Stanford University Press, 1969.

Shannon, William H. *Thomas Merton's Dark Path.* New York: Farrar, Straus & Giroux, 1987.

The Wisdom of the Desert Fathers. Trans. Thomas Merton. New York: New Directions, 1960.

Wu, John C. H. *Chinese Humanism and Christian Spirituality: Essays.* Asian
    Philosophical Studies, no. 2. Ed. Paul K. T. Sih. Jamaica, N.Y.: St. John's
    University Press, 1965.

Thomas Merton and Zen

Robert Faricy

In the book *Contemplative Prayer*[1] Thomas Merton presents his mature thought on Christian contemplation. The problem is this: Merton's last and most important writing on contemplation can be, and often is, misunderstood. Contemplative prayer, as described by Merton in the book, can appear solipsistic, self-centered, taking the center of oneself as the object of contemplation, taking the same person contemplating as the subject to be contemplated. This, of course, has little or nothing to do with Christian contemplation, and would fall into a category sometimes denominated "natural mysticism." But, on the contrary, Merton has no intention of proposing a kind of natural mysticism. Nor does he propose some sort of solipsistic meditation, nor a contemplation that takes the form of just simple or heightened consciousness. *Contemplative Prayer* is about Christian contemplation, about real prayer in the Christian tradition and framework.

Unfortunately, even a close reading of the book can and sometimes does give a wrong impression. Personally, until 1992, I had trouble with *Contemplative Prayer*. I misinterpreted Merton's final theology of contemplative prayer, concluding that it had been badly influenced by his interest in, and perhaps practice of, Zen. I dropped my interest in Merton after a last rereading of *Contemplative Prayer.*

I came back to Merton, and particularly to *Contemplative Prayer*, after I examined, studied, and—most importantly—experienced Zen myself. I began to have an interest in Buddhist meditation, and particularly in Zen, in the late 1980s. I read everything I could. Over a

1. New York: Doubleday Image, 1971. Further page references will be to this American edition of the book.

period of years I talked with Buddhists, with and without interpreters, as well as with Christian experts in Buddhist meditation, in Rome, Tokyo, Kyoto, Bangkok, and Seoul. Then, in 1992, I came across a book on Korean Zen. I do not have the patience for soto Zen. And I had dabbled in rinzai Zen, with the generous and kind help of K. T. Kadawoki at Sophia University in Tokyo; but I was a poor pupil, got nowhere, and gave up quickly.

I found Korean Zen, a form of rinzai, more aggressive; it insists on questioning. Sitting in the Loyola Marymount University library in Los Angeles, reading a book on Korean Zen, I experienced enlightenment. And it lasted. Later, my library experience was verified independently by two Korean Zen masters as an authentic Zen enlightenment experience.

In the spring of 1993, after several months of teaching as a visiting professor at Sogang University in Seoul, I went into the mountains not far inland from Korea's southern coast to a hermitage of the main monastery of the Chogye order, Songwang-sa, for three weeks of Zen meditation. It was an intensive and profound experience. Among other things, it brought me back to another reading of *Contemplative Prayer*. This time, I think I understood it.

What went wrong in the writing of the book? Why are not the ideas sufficiently clear? How can one read Merton's most important book on prayer with understanding? In this study, I would like to briefly answer those questions. We know that in the years when Merton was putting *Contemplative Prayer* together, he suffered from poor health (chronic dysentery, severe dermatitis—especially of the hands—bursitis, and a bad back), and he went through considerable turmoil concerning monastic obedience, his vocation, and his personal relationships. As if all this were not enough, a further problem comes from Merton's methodology in *Contemplative Prayer*. He describes contemplative prayer not in abstract categories, but according to the *experience* of contemplation.

I suggest that the book is confusing because of how Thomas Merton put it together and because of its unfinished nature,[2] and that the book must be read with the knowledge that Merton wrote it strongly influenced by how he understood Zen meditation. In conclusion, this paper sketches the main outlines of Merton's final theology of prayer.

---

2. Basil Pennington gave me this information in June 1995.

The Lack of Clarity of the Book

Contemplative Prayer has nineteen chapters; it is really two books.[3] Chapters one through five, eleven, fourteen, and sixteen through eighteen originally comprised a booklet called *The Climate of Monastic Prayer*, fifty-eight pages long, circulated privately, and then published in 1969 by Cistercian Publications. The booklet aimed at a monastic audience, professional monks. The other chapters—six through ten, twelve, thirteen, fifteen, and nineteen—come from a 1959 manuscript, never published as such, entitled *Prayer as Worship and Experience*. This second book or manuscript aims apparently at a broader audience than does the booklet *The Climate of Monastic Prayer*. Sometime after 1965, Merton broke up the manuscript *Prayer as Worship and Experience* and inserted the various parts of it into *The Climate of Monastic Prayer*. The resulting book was published in 1969 by Cistercian Publications as *The Climate of Monastic Prayer*, and by Herder and Herder as *Contemplative Prayer*.

Merton thought considerable revision necessary on the part of the publishing house editors at Herder and Herder to make the book accessible to the nonmonastic reader.[4] *Contemplative Prayer*'s principal editor agreed, but in fact almost no revising took place. Basil Pennington and Merton had the firm and planned intention to work together on *Contemplative Prayer* after Merton's Asian trip, to get the book in order and to clear up ambiguities. Merton died in Asia before he could really finish the book. The fact stands that Merton's theology of contemplative prayer, especially as presented in *Contemplative Prayer*, remains open to misinterpretation.[5]

Merton's Understanding of Zen

There are, of course, varieties of Zen Buddhism, and every kind of Zen opens itself to various ways of understanding it. Merton

3. This information comes from William Shannon, *Thomas Merton's Dark Path* (New York: Penguin Books, 1981); see especially ch. 7, "The Climate of Monastic Prayer (Contemplative Prayer)," 164–88.
4. Basil Pennington in June 1995 personally gave me the information in this paragraph.
5. Good examples of a theologian's complete misreading of Merton's theology of contemplative prayer are two articles by Catharina Stenqvist: "Thomas Merton and His View on Contemplation," *Studies in Spirituality* 2 (1993), and "Merton, Zen, and Phenomenology," *Studies in Spirituality* 4 (1994). Stenqvist finds

learned about Zen mainly through the writings of D. T. Suzuki.[6] Not a Christian himself, Suzuki interprets Christianity in his own way, sees it from a thoroughly Zen perspective. He shows great appreciation for Meister Eckhart who, like Zen and therefore like Suzuki himself—and like Merton—has a principally noetic theology of contemplation.

Suzuki identifies the God of Christians with "the Absolute Present itself."[7] Does Suzuki, from a Christian point of view, have an adequate idea of God? He naturally has no place for the incarnation and the cross and resurrection. But, as Suzuki himself realizes, his idea of God is close to, consonant with, the strongly noetic current in the Christian mystical tradition represented by Meister Eckhart.[8]

For Suzuki, *satori* means "seeing into one's own nature." And that means "seeing into the Buddha-Nature, or the Absolute." Merton will use the term "the true self" in a similar and quite parallel way to mean "the self as in Christ."[9] When Suzuki writes about *satori*, does he

---

that Merton has a nonintentional idea of contemplation, that contemplation for him is simply a state of just being conscious. This shows how badly Merton can be misunderstood.

6. Some important titles by D. T. Suzuki that especially influenced Merton are: *Mysticism: Christian and Buddhist* (New York: Macmillan, 1957); *Zen Buddhism: Selected Writings of D. T. Suzuki,* ed. W. Barrett (New York: Doubleday Anchor, 1956); *Manual of Zen Buddhism* (London: Rider, 1950). For Suzuki's notion of Christianity, see Roger Corless, "In Search of a Context for the Merton-Suzuki Dialogue," *The Merton Annual,* vol. 6 (Collegeville: The Liturgical Press, 1993) 76–91. For another view of Suzuki on Zen, one that compares him with different members of the Kyoto school, see Fritz Buri, "The True Self in the Buddhist Philosophy of the Kyoto School," *Buddhist-Christian Studies* 12 (1992) 83–102, esp. 88–90.

7. *Living by Zen,* ed. Christian Humphreys (New York: Samuel Weiser, 1972) 12.

8. See Suzuki, "Meister Eckhart and Buddhism," *Mysticism: Christian and Buddhist,* 11–32. But is not Zen Buddhism atheistic? I suppose it can be. Suzuki's Zen is not. I have found Chinul, the founder of Korean Zen (numerically at least the most important current of Zen practice today), to have an idea of God (although Korean Zen refers not to "God" but to "True Mind" and "the Buddha Nature") not completely incompatible with and, although the metaphysical framework is entirely different, in some ways even similar to Thomas Aquinas' idea of God in *Summa Theologiae.* See Hee-Sung Keel, *Chinul: The Founder of the Korean Son Tradition,* Berkeley Buddhist Studies Series (Seoul: Po Chin Chai, 1984).

9. See Gal 2:20: "I live, not I, but Christ lives in me." See also Christopher Nugent, "Satori in St. John of the Cross," *Bulletin of Monastic Interreligious Dialogue,* n. 14, May 1993, 13–18.

think he is talking about what Christians talk about when they say infused contemplation? He seems to.[10] One could think that Zen contemplation, when it occurs, necessarily falls into the category of
natural mysticism or takes the shape of only a metaphysical intuition
of being. Suzuki does not seem to think so.[11] Merton does not criticize
Suzuki on these points. He seems to accept them; they concur with
Merton's own views:

> There is a natural metaphysical intuition of being, even of
> Absolute Being, or of the metaphysical ground of being. . . .
> There is no difficulty in relating this metaphysical intuition to the
> *satori* of Zen.

10. See Suzuki, *Mysticism: Christian and Buddhist*, 63–72, on Eckhart's "divine
spark" or "little point of light" in the soul. Suzuki compares hitting this "little point
of light" to *satori*.
    11. The point seems impossible to prove one way or the other. For different
opinions, and for opinions other than mine of what Merton thought about this, see:
Thomas King, *Merton: Mystic at the Center of America* (Collegeville: The Liturgical
Press, 1994); and Annice Callahan's review of the same book in *The Merton Annual*,
vol. 6, 205–8. See in particular William F. Healy, "Thomas Merton's Evaluation of
Zen," *Angelicum* 52 (1975) 385–409. This article has as its basis the author's doctoral
dissertation at the Collegium Pontificium Angelicum, defended in 1974. Healy
writes in his dissertation that, for Merton, Zen cannot be contemplation in the normal Catholic sense, not even acquired contemplation, because "it is not supernatural contemplation" (400) and "it is not a matter of grace" (89).
    As to the question of the difference between Christian contemplation and
Zen meditation see: Heinrich Dumoulin, *Zen Buddhism in the Twentieth Century*,
trans. J. O'Leary (New York and Tokyo: Weatherhill, 1992); H. M. Enomiya Lasalle,
Zen Meditation for Christians, trans. C. Maraldo (Lasalle, Ill.: Open Court, 1974), especially ch. 6 on Zen and Christian meditation. Dumoulin and Lasalle have the
opinion that the main difference between Zen and Christian contemplation lies in
the fact that Zen is impersonal—rather, apersonal—and Christian contemplation is
personal, to a personal God; and, further, that Zen contemplation is a natural mysticism (Dumoulin) or acquired contemplation (Lasalle). See also J. K. Kadowaki,
Zen and the Bible, trans. J. Rieck (London: Routledge and Kegan Paul, 1980), although Kadowaki does not so much compare Zen and Christian contemplation as
write about his own experience with both.
    See William Johnston, *Christian Zen* (New York: Harper, 1971), where
Johnston tries to show what Christians can learn from Zen. Also by Johnston, *The
Mysticism of the Cloud of Unknowing* (New York: Desclee, 1967), where he shows
how Christian contemplation and Zen differ. In *The Still Point* (New York: Fordham
University, 1970) Johnston brilliantly compares Christian contemplation and Zen,
and finds that the difference does not lie where so many (e.g., David Loy, "Comparing Zen *Koan* Practice with *The Cloud of Unknowing*," *Buddhist-Christian Studies*

Whether there is in non-Christian religions a truly mystical or supernatural vision of God may still be debated, but the best theologians have admitted its possibility. Nor is there any real difficulty about this, in theory, since we know that men of good will in all religions, who follow the dictates of an upright conscience, can certainly attain to holiness and union with God because they receive grace from Him to do so.[12]

Merton does not say that Zen's *satori* remains only a metaphysical intuition; he states that it is possible that Zen contemplation be truly supernatural contemplation, and that there is no real problem with this. Nor does Merton ever claim that Christian contemplation and Zen contemplation are the same. The Zen that influenced Merton was mainly the Japanese rinzai Zen of D. T. Suzuki. His belief that Zen and Christian contemplation are alike in an important way, that they both are or can be supernatural contemplative union with God, gives him a basis for working out a theology or theory of Christian contemplation that incorporates Zen insights.

Zen is not Kerygma but realization, not revelation but consciousness, not news from the Father who sends His Son into this world, but awareness of the ontological ground of our own being here and now. . . . The supernatural Kerygma and the intuition of the ground of being are far from being incompatible. . . . Zen is perfectly compatible with Christian belief and indeed with Christian mysticism (if we understand Zen in its pure state, as metaphysical intuition).[13]

Earlier, Merton had written about the question of Zen and supernaturality: "In Christian terms, one can hardly help feeling that the illumination of the genuine Zen experience seems to open out into an unconscious demand for grace—a demand that is perhaps answered without being understood. Is it perhaps already grace?"[14]

---

9 [1989] 43–60, esp. 58) think it does: between the Zen void and the Christian necessity of clinging to a concept of God. On the contrary, the Christian mystic positively ought not to cling to any image or concept, especially of God.

12. Merton in the introduction to Johnston, *The Mysticism of the Cloud of Unknowing*, x.

13. Thomas Merton, *Zen and the Birds of Appetite* (New York: New Directions, 1968) 47.

14. Thomas Merton, *Mystics and Zen Masters* (New York: Dell, 1961) 228.

John Francis Teahan, in his doctoral dissertation "The Mysticism of Thomas Merton: Contemplation as a Way of Life," finds that Merton in his later years increasingly believed in the possible supernatural character of Eastern mysticism in general and of Zen in particular.[15] Here is how Merton compares the experiences of Christian contemplation and of Zen:

> In the Christian tradition, the focus of this "experience" is found not in the individual self as a separate, temporal, and limited ego, but in Christ . . . "within" this self. In Zen, it is Self with a capital S, that is to say precisely *not* the ego-self. This Self is the Void.[16]

And that Void is the ground of being, absolute being, what Christians call God. Since Jesus' act of existence is one, only, and divine, his human nature inheres in that one divine act of existence. In Zen terms, Christ is the Buddha-nature, he is the ground of being. Merton understood this.[17]

In 1993, while in Korea and Japan for several months, I asked the same question of four Catholic experts on Zen: "What do Zen adepts attain when they meditate? God, or themselves, or nothing, or what?" I asked Sister Kim, a Korean Sister of Charity who has a Harvard doctorate and who teaches comparative mysticism at Sogang University in Seoul; Heinrich Dumoulin, S.J., the foremost historian of Zen; William Johnston, S.J., author of books on Zen and on Christian mysticism; and K. T. Kadowaki, S.J., Zen master. These last three were all members of the Sophia University Jesuit community. The four experts all gave me the same answer: Those adept at Zen do attain, in some way, transcendent Truth. This, from a Christian point of view, we

15. Princeton University, 1976, 46. The whole section on Eastern religions (39–52) is good. To the best of my knowledge, this truly outstanding manuscript has never been published.

16. Ibid., 74.

17. In one of his last conferences before his death in 1968, Merton said, "Even before the Lord dwells in us by his Spirit there is a deeper presence which comes in a certain sense from the fact that we are created in him, and, as we read in Colossians, live in him—our being is in Christ even ontologically. . . . Our true sense of who we are consists entirely in this response to Christ, but the most important thing is that this response is to someone we really do not know. We know him; yes, we know him and we don't know him. . . . We respond to someone unknown" ("Conference on Prayer," on the Feast of Christ the King [Conference of Religious of India, 1968] 2).

can identify with God. Do they pray when they meditate? Zen monks would say no. The four people I consulted with would say, from our Catholic point of view, yes. I agree with them.

Merton, however, never did really work out conceptually his later theology of contemplation, at least not fully. He recognized Zen as an authentic way of contemplative prayer. He tried to express what he understood about Zen in *Contemplative Prayer* in a Christian framework and as part of a Christian understanding of contemplative prayer.[18]

Merton's Theology of Contemplative Prayer in *Contemplative Prayer*

Parker Palmer, writing in the *Dictionary of Christian Spirituality*,[19] sums up Merton's theology of contemplation: "No matter how widely Merton reached in his spiritual search, he remained grounded in the personal experience of God in Christ. For Merton, the spiritual search is deeply inwards, towards the Christ in each of us who is also our True Self." This experience of God in Christ becomes, in contemplation, subjective. I am one with him. He is my most profound "I." "I-Thou" no longer has a place in the contemplative experience. Merton on contemplation evokes T. S. Eliot, who believes that contemplation is like "music heard so deeply / That it is not heard at all, but you are the music / While the music lasts."[20]

Merton understands contemplative prayer as prayer of the heart. He understands the heart as "the deepest psychological ground of one's personality, the inner sanctuary where self-awareness goes beyond

18. Can Christian theology be separated out from the Greek metaphysics which it has, however imperfectly, assimilated? Can the egg be unscrambled? See J. Fredericks, "The Kyoto School: Modern Buddhist Philosophy and the Search for a Transcultural Theology," *Horizons* 15 (1988) 299–315, esp. 314. Merton, like others including Bede Griffiths and Henri Le Saux (Swami Abhishiktananda) in India, have tried to do just that for Christian mysticism, for the Christian theology of contemplation. Our positive appreciation should be that they have thus contributed to the true "catholicity" of Christian teaching on contemplation.

19. London: SCM Press, 1983, 265.

20. "The Dry Salvages," ll. 211–3, *Four Quartets* (New York: Harcourt Brace Jovanovich, 1971) 44. Eliot refers to the point of intersection of the timeless with time, to incarnation, and the analogy with music can as well be applied to contemplative union with Christ.

analytical reflection and opens out into metaphysical and theological confrontation with the Abyss of the unknown yet present—the one who is more intimate to us than we are to ourselves."[21]

The heart, for Merton, is not so much the seat of the affections; contemplation is not essentially a matter of felt love given and received. Like Meister Eckhart, like Suso and Tauler, the followers of Eckhart, like the author of *The Cloud of Unknowing*, and like John of the Cross, Merton is firmly in the apophatic tradition of Christian contemplation.[22] Apophatic mysticism is the way of negation, of the denial that anything we know on earth can be God; God is "not that." The opposite of apophatic mysticism is cataphatic mysticism, the way of affirmation by analogy that the good, true, unified, beautiful that we know on earth can be affirmed in a purified and analogous way of God. Apophatic and cataphatic describe different kinds or qualities of experience, as well as different modes of talking about mystical experience. Famous examples of the apophatic and the cataphatic are, respectively, John of the Cross and Teresa of Avila. For Merton, contemplation is a mainly intellectual activity, a primarily noetic state, an emptiness, a mental vacuity.[23]

Contemplation takes place in an obscurity where knowing is not knowing, in a darkness, and not essentially nor at all necessarily in the light of love.[24] The way to union with God, for Merton, is the way of darkness, night, emptiness. It stands in the void; real contemplation is mute in the empty silence of the void. The lights are out. Merton in his apophaticism is closest to Eckhart, and to Zen. "On the psychological level," Merton writes, "there is an exact correspondence" between the Zen void and the dark night of John of the Cross.[25] And, for Merton, the normal contemplative state is the dark night.

21. Merton, *Contemplative Prayer*, 33.

22. From the Greek *apophasis*, "negation" or "denial." On the apophatic in Merton, Teahan is excellent ("The Mysticism of Thomas Merton," 158–91).

23. See Robert E. Doud, "Emptiness as Transparency in the Late Poetry of Thomas Merton," *Horizons* 21 (1994) 269.

24. Love itself acts in emptiness, is a kind of emptiness. "The man who has truly found his spiritual nakedness, who has realized he is empty, is not a self that has *acquired* emptiness or *become* empty. He just 'is empty from the beginning,' as Dr. Suzuki has observed. . . . He is one with God, and identified with God, and hence knows nothing of any ego in himself. All he knows is love." *Zen and the Birds of Appetite*, 71.

25. Merton, *Mystics and Zen Masters*, 242.

Merton's personal contemplative experience was clearly dark, empty, a desert experience.[26] His material in *Contemplative Prayer* on emptiness in general and on "dread" in particular surely comes out of his own experience of not just emptiness and darkness but of real desolation in the face of limits and finitude.[27]

Through and in darkness and emptiness, passing through dread, one arrives at that darkness in which one no longer knows oneself apart from God, one finds one's true self.[28] The true self, then, is not self only; it is the self in Christ, the self in union with Christ in God in the self. The parallel concept in Zen would seem to be the self as nothing, but in—part of—the Buddha Nature, the True Mind, universally transcendent in its immanence, standing in and above all being and all nothingness.

What then is the purpose of Christian contemplation? This:

> To come to know God through the realization that our very being is penetrated with his knowledge and love for us. Our knowledge of God is paradoxically not a knowledge of him as the object of our scrutiny, but of ourselves as utterly dependent on his saving and merciful knowledge of us. It is in proportion as we are known to him that we find our real being and identity in Christ. We know him in and through ourselves in so far as his truth is the source of our being and his merciful love is the very heart of our life and existence. . . . There is no true knowledge that does not imply a profound grasp and an intimate personal acceptance of this profound relationship.[29]

The whole purpose of Christian contemplation "is to deepen the consciousness of this basic relationship of the creature to the Creator, and of the sinner to his Redeemer."[30]

---

26. See, for example, *The Sign of Jonas* (New York: Harcourt Brace, 1953). There is ample documentation of Merton's interior darkness in prayer.

27. See especially *Contemplative Prayer*, ch. 16, 120–8.

28. Ibid., 104.

29. Ibid., 83. "Christ is King, but he controls by love. This love is the very root of our own being. . . . Our true sense of who we are consists entirely in this response to Christ, but the most important thing is that this response is to someone we really do not know. We know him; yes, we know him and we don't know him. . . . We respond to someone unknown" ("Conference on Prayer," 2, 4).

30. Merton, "Conference on Prayer," 2, 4.

"Teaching Is Candy":
Merton as Teacher at
Columbia and Bonaventure

Thomas Del Prete

In one of his inimitable letters to literary soulmate Bob Lax, Merton, referring to his experience as an instructor in English composition in the extension program at Columbia in the fall of 1939, playfully exclaims, "Teaching is candy. Wotta happy clars!"[1] Precisely one year later, having spent several months teaching three sections of English literature to ninety sophomores at St. Bonaventure's College, he reflects in his journal, "Literature is hard to teach. You cannot explain what is good easily, any more than you can explain Faith easily, or Love easily."[2] This contrast in perspective suggests that Merton, though preoccupied in his search for spiritual and vocational direction during this time, was both engaged and challenged as a young teacher. It helps frame the effort to understand what being a teacher meant to him prior to entering Gethsemani, what he understood his work as a teacher to be, how he approached it, and what impact it had on him and his students.

In what sense might teaching have been "candy" for Merton? How did his experience teaching literature at Bonaventure differ from his experience teaching writing in the extension program at Columbia? What part, if any, did teaching play in his intellectual and spiritual de-

---

1. Thomas Merton to Robert Lax, December 3, 1939, Friedsam Memorial Library, St. Bonaventure University, Olean, New York.
2. Thomas Merton, *Run to the Mountain: The Story of a Vocation,* ed. Patrick Hart, (New York: HarperCollins Publishers, 1995) 274.

velopment at the time? How, conversely, did his prevailing intellectual and spiritual concerns, not to mention his intense search for vocational direction and identity in the religious life and as a writer, affect him as a teacher? What kind of a teacher was Merton? Does the young beginning teacher of 1939, '40, and '41 project any of the concerns or characteristics of the monastic mentor of the sixties?

By drawing on his reflections in his correspondence, journals, and *The Seven Storey Mountain,* and on the recollections of former students and colleagues, we may sketch Merton's first teaching experiences and begin to answer some of these questions. What emerges as an overarching theme is his concern for linking learning in an academic sense to more existential matters. For Merton formal learning appears more often than not to provide a context for addressing fundamental life questions; it becomes an integral part of the process of discerning what is real or what matters in life, and something of one's personal identity and purpose. If this is Merton's overriding interest, even at this initial stage of his journey as a teacher, there are other matters of import as well: how to help others learn to read and write, to think clearly and form solid ideas, to understand, appreciate, and learn from art and literature. These concerns combine with the larger one to shape his pedagogy and his students' experience.

Columbia

Apart from work as a Latin tutor during the previous year, Merton had no formal teaching experience prior to serving as an instructor in English composition for three nights a week in the Columbia extension program during the fall of 1939. Teaching seemed a logical enough pursuit for someone who had recently earned his masters degree in English literature, who had begun study toward his doctorate in the same field, and who had spent the summer feverishly turning out pages of a projected novel. Merton tells us in his autobiography that he "liked teaching very much. . . ."[3] Yet it did not necessarily hold the most prominent place in the hierarchy of his vocational interests. Even as he declared to Lax that teaching was "candy," he makes clear that he was interested in continuing in it only as a secondary option. As he explains it in Merton/Lax-talk:

---

3. Thomas Merton, *The Seven Storey Mountain* (New York: Harcourt Brace Jovanovich, Inc., 1948) 274.

I got a chance to work full time as an instructor to Barnard College for girls only I don't think that will make me quit the [Franciscan] monastery because there is right now only violence or some sudden adverse judgement on the part of the monks could keep me out, and I guess if I wasn't to get into the monastery I would not be a cheerful fellow at all. Also I wish I knew when it was going to begin, because I am sick of novels, and although I am not sick of teaching, but like it better every time. Only I want to be a monk first and then teach and write next.

But still I am going to see the english dept guy about it . . . and I will make no attempt not to be hired, just in case there are delays about the monastery or trouble. And if I wasn't going into the monastery I would certainly like very much to teach in Barnard because I think it would be mild and suave and pleasant to instruct maybe one fine dame like Burton or Reilley or Eaton in a whole class of Camilles, even.[4]

If becoming a Franciscan was Merton's chief interest at this time, the prospect of teaching was by no means distasteful. Teaching engrossed him more deeply in subject matter he loved, invariably drew him into the experience of others, and confronted him with challenging intellectual and pedagogical issues. Midway through the teaching term at Columbia, the twenty-four-year-old instructor relates to friend Lax what he was discovering:

It is interesting and instructive to teach a class: it is not true that any of them are crazy at all, but nor is it true that many of them can write English. Also it is true that they are beginning to write better than before once they can write about their families and their summer vacations, which is nevertheless what they started out with. It is much easier to get them to write saying they really want to be blessed than saying they want to be smart, which as a matter of fact they do not so much care about, but were only told to care about in High School. Thus I love my class very much, individually more than in a lump and will in the future make a ges-

4. Merton to Robert Lax, December 3, 1939, Friedsam Memorial Library, St. Bonaventure University. It took a good while for Merton to recognize teaching as an integral part of his life. After many years of teaching as both the master of scholastics and master of novices at Gethsemani, he reflected in his journal in 1962, "I usually ignore this element in my own vocation, but obviously I am a writer, a student and a teacher as well as a contemplative of sorts, and my solitude etc., is that of a writer and teacher, not of a pure hermit."

ture of biting off my tongue before I talk about crazies or stoopies for one minute.[5]

Merton seems to have been genuinely affected by his students' earnestness, by the need for identity and meaning that emerged in their struggle to write. That he tapped their desire to be "blessed" rather than "smart" is not surprising; it is telling, however, insofar as it points to Merton's role in fostering the openness necessary for nourishing this kind of self-disclosure and self-searching. To the extent that this is true, we can say that a person-centered philosophy drove Merton's teaching, what he might describe much later and with much greater understanding as a philosophy oriented to self-discovery; Merton, in other words, was concerned with linking learning how to write to the process of developing one's own ideas, and learning who one was and what matters in life.

As an instructor of English composition, Merton saw as his specific tasks teaching "students how to get up enough interest in things to write about them," and also teaching them how to read.[6] He encouraged students to trust and tap their own personal experience as a motivational source for writing. He records in his journal the advice he gave them, advice he would follow faithfully himself: "I have spent weeks telling my class to write out of their own experience: and they write best when they do, too. They write almost good autobiographical short stories sometimes."[7] To help them along, he provides them with examples of published autobiographical material, such as James Thurber's *My Life and Hard Times*.[8]

Merton established a clear pedagogy in grounding the process of learning to write in his students' personal experience. But his understanding of writing and language at this stage required something more besides, even for students at a beginning level of confidence and artistry. The act of writing implied a conscious and reflective stance on life. Merton reminds himself in his journal to tell the class how important a "writer's attitude towards life is," how much this attitude affects the way someone writes.[9] Merton challenges his students to consider

---

5. Thomas Merton to Robert Lax, *The Road to Joy: Letters to New and Old Friends*, ed. Robert Daggy (New York: Farrar, Straus & Giroux, 1989) 151.
6. Merton, *The Seven Storey Mountain*, 274.
7. Merton, *Run to the Mountain*, 92.
8. Ibid.
9. Ibid., 108.

writing not as an abstract or formulaic exercise, and not simply as a way to represent personal experience, but also as an expression of something fundamental about themselves.

While Merton's own experience as a writer was no doubt relevant, his reading and his reflection on teaching clearly interact in the formulation of his view of writing, and consequently in the development of his pedagogy as a writing teacher. He paraphrases William Saroyan's preface to *The Daring Young Man on the Flying Trapeze* in his journal when he observes, "if [someone] writes remembering we must all, at some time or other, die, it is very important."[10] He says he will probably read the Saroyan preface to the class; if he in fact did, then his students would have heard that Saroyan's "number one" rule was not to follow the rules laid down by others, and then the following:

> A writer can have, ultimately, one of two styles: he can write in a manner that implies that death is inevitable, or he can write in a manner that implies that death is *not* inevitable. . . . If you write as if you believe that ultimately you and everyone else alive will be dead, there is a chance that you will write in a pretty earnest style. . . .
>
> The most solid advice, though, for a writer is this, I think: Try to learn to breathe deeply, really to taste food when you eat, and when you sleep, really to sleep. Try as much as possible to be wholly alive, with all your might, and when you laugh, laugh like hell, and when you get angry, get good and angry. Try to be alive. You will be dead soon enough.[11]

Merton adds that, beyond attitude, belief is important, noting specifically that whether a writer believes in God and in the redemption of the world by Christ would certainly be important. He then discusses his effort to get his students to understand the attitude toward life reflected in a particular piece (Thomas Stanley's *Exequies*), noting the lightheartedness in it, presumably in the deference paid to the "kinder flowers" that "can take no birth or growth" from the "unhappy earthe" of the speaker's grave.[12] Here is a concrete example of how Merton links learning to read with learning to write, and sets both against the background of a basic existential consideration of life.

10. Ibid.

11. William Saroyan, *The Daring Young Man on the Flying Trapeze and Other Stories* (New York: Random House, 1934) 12–13.

12. Merton, *Run to the Mountain*, 108–9.

It is unclear, beyond this example of how they interrelated, how else Merton acted on his belief in the importance of learning how to read in relation to learning how to write in the Columbia class. We can be reasonably sure that he was referring to learning about what is meaningful and substantive in good writing, and how that is communicated, more than learning about style per se, and definitely more than learning about the rules of grammar. At one point in his journal he writes, "Everybody has been educated to read and write, but nobody has been educated in the things a man reads and writes *about.*"[13] In a letter written in 1963, he states that "the real joy of reading is not in the reading itself but in the thinking which it stimulates and which may go beyond what is said in the book."[14] Teaching may very well have helped to nurture these insights.

As a teacher, not surprisingly, Merton was challenged as a learner, and particularly as a reader. During his first semester at Bonaventure he mused, "I often wonder if teaching literature hasn't been the first thing to make me really read the stuff. I feel as if I never had read any literature before!"[15] To ensure that he was reading well, Merton took extensive notes, working through the thoughts his reading had stimulated. In a later journal entry he reveals: "I have been learning how to read. . . . Learned how to read Blake's 'To the Muses.' I read it to my sympathetic evening class. They shook their heads. I explained 'the green courners of the earth.' They fainted."[16] It was one thing to learn yourself, quite another, particularly in the realm of literature, to enable others to do the same; as Merton said, "Literature is hard to teach."

In his first teaching experience Merton seems to have quickly reached the conviction that one learned to write not in the abstract according to prescribed rules, but first of all by deciding on something important to write about, in connection with personal experience and some of the big questions of life. This premise put at serious risk the primacy of grammar in the writing curriculum. Merton writes in his journal, "Filled with ideas to talk to the class about—grammar and usage. That grammar is not the art of speaking *correctly* but of speak-

---

13. Ibid., 144.

14. Thomas Merton to M. R. Chandler, *Witness to Freedom: Letters in Times of Crisis,* ed. William Shannon (New York: Farrar, Straus & Giroux, 1994) 165.

15. Merton, *Run to the Mountain,* 258.

16. Ibid., 271.

ing *logically.*"[17] Merton developed a strong belief in the importance of the "innate logic of language" over and against the mere correct and standardized usage typically implied by grammar. Indeed, language for Merton, as he works it out in response to the challenge to develop a working philosophy for the teaching of writing, had an organic quality; it was "a living, growing thing" with its own life. The "logic of language . . . is something like experience: it follows it closely, is not rigid but supple, imitates life."[18] To constrain it too tightly by the imposition of rules and arbitrary structure was akin to subverting the natural order, and represented the kind of external control over mind, conscience, freedom, and spirit to which Merton then and later so strongly objected. Merton was concerned more for helping his students learn to write according to what was "logical and in good taste," in keeping with the particular context of the writing. Correct writing "is simply proper to its surroundings—its context," he wrote.[19]

By emphasizing grammar as the art of saying things rationally, Merton challenged students to consider the relationship of language to meaning, idea and their personal experience, and thus to relinquish any dependence on external formulas, thus in some sense to learn while exercising responsibly their independent judgment and freedom. He concludes his discourse on grammar on an anti-modernist note, "The modern incomprehension of the *kind* of thing grammar really is reflects the modern incomprehension of *respect for liberty and life.*"[20] This would not be the first time that Merton would work through intellectual issues in his journals to help orient his teaching. In this instance, there was a very practical result. Merton declined an opportunity to teach grammar in the spring semester, asserting that "grammar was something I knew absolutely nothing about, and only the most constant vigilance had kept it out of sight in the composition class."[21] He puts it differently to Lax, "I lost my section of English composition, and they were going to give me a class teaching spelling to old ladies instead, and I declined, saying no thanks for the offer of that stupid spelling class."[22]

17. Ibid., 41.
18. Ibid., 83.
19. Ibid., 41.
20. Ibid., 42.
21. Merton, *The Seven Storey Mountain*, 274.
22. Merton, *The Road to Joy*, 152.

Based on his own description, Merton seems to have taught with a bit of serendipitous flair at Columbia, in his words, spending

> most of the time throwing out ideas about what might or might not be important in life and in literature, and letting them argue about it. The arguments got better when they also included discussion of the students' favorite ideas, as expressed on paper. It soon turned out that although they did not all have ideas, they all had a definite hunger for ideas and for convictions.[23]

Here Merton confronts in his own teaching the challenge of helping others produce their own explicit ideas and to establish their own inner certitude, a challenge he felt his mentor Mark Van Doren met so adroitly.[24] In striving to meet this challenge himself, he learned with some surprise the extent to which a teacher can influence students, in particular the ease with which a teacher can preempt a student's own thinking. As a case in point, we can take Merton's example of how a student responded to his insistence on "concrete and tangible evidence, in describing places and things" by blossoming out from a state of bewilderment

> with a fecundity in minute and irrelevant material detail that it was impossible to check. He began handing in descriptions of shoe factories that made you feel as if you were being buried under fifty tons of machinery. And I learned, with wonder and fear, that teachers have a mysterious and deadly power of letting loose psychological forces in the minds of the young. The rapidity, the happy enthusiasm with which they responded to hints and suggestions—but with the wrong response—was enough to make a man run away and live in the woods [a statement that grew in irony over time!].[25]

If Merton discovered something of the power of the teacher, he discovered it in relation to his students' "hunger for ideas and convictions." Merton fed this hunger by assigning writing topics such as "My Favorite Movie Star" and "Is It Possible To Be Happy Without Money?"[26] It was his students' ready response to topics such as these

23. Merton, *The Seven Storey Mountain*, 274.
24. Ibid., 139.
25. Ibid., 273–4.
26. Thomas Merton, *The Secular Journal* (New York: Farrar, Straus & Giroux, 1959) 98.

that prompted his remark to Lax that "Teaching is candy. Wotta happy clars! They write essays about the funny sheet and the movies and now precisely I got them writing a big dirty argument whether money stinks and defiles the hands like pitch or not, and whether everybody ought to love everybody."[27]

In Merton's teaching at Columbia we see at work in rough and embryonic form what might be described as his modus operandi as a teacher, and what is perhaps at the heart of all great teaching: his gift at framing learning not only as a process of attaining intellectual understanding and clarity and appreciation, but as a way to discover what is meaningful, real, and true in oneself and in life. By linking grammar, construed as the art of saying things rationally, and the question of one's basic "attitude towards life," to experience, he provided students with a path to learn that was in some sense respectful of life—and of their own particular lives—and subject to care and discipline. The personal and universal seem to have had a significant interplay in Merton's approach to teaching, even as they did in his writing, and even as they would so compellingly when he was master of scholastics and novice master.

As a student, Merton had noted with admiration Mark Van Doren's capability in helping others discriminate what was genuine in thinking and writing.[28] In later years he is explicit about cultivating this capacity as a teaching priority, and more explicit, in his few reflections on the subject, in placing the whole person at the center of education. To a bookstore manager in 1965 he writes that "a man or a woman goes to college not just to get a degree and a good job, but first of all to find himself and establish his true identity"; he says that this implies a capacity and freedom to choose from real possibilities, in turn implying a capacity to judge and to think. He goes on to say that "truth is important and the whole purpose of thinking is to be able to tell the difference between what is true and what only looks good."[29] These themes are amplified in his essay "Learning to Live," written in 1967 and published posthumously in 1969.[30] If we were to trace Merton's teaching through the monastic years we would see his gift at

27. Merton to Robert Lax, December 3, 1939.
28. Merton, *The Seven Storey Mountain,* 139.
29. Merton to Mr. L. Dickson, *Witness to Freedom,* 169.
30. Thomas Merton, "Learning to Live," *Love and Living,* ed. Patrick Hart and Naomi Burton Stone (New York: Farrar, Straus & Giroux, 1979).

connecting learning and life at work over and over again, whether it be in asking novices in his written introduction to a course on the monastic vows in 1955, "How does one judge the value of [a person]?" or in introducing a talk on St. Bernard in the 1960s by saying, "What I really intend to do is not to talk about St. Bernard exclusively but to talk about *us*."[31]

Bonaventure

At St. Bonaventure it was not unusual for Merton or students to hitchhike to the center of town. One of his former students remembers somewhat abashedly going to town with friends and on the way picking up Merton, in his saddleback shoes, on the Saturday before the beginning of the fall term. The group good-naturedly "gave [Merton] a hard time," not realizing until the following Monday that the twenty-five-year-old newly appointed assistant professor, sitting cross-legged on his desk, clad in a corduroy sports jacket (Merton typically wore a tweed coat, according to another former student) with patches in the arms, tan pants, and the same saddleback shoes, would be their instructor in English literature.[32] In another instance, Merton hitchhiked to town with a group, there joining them for conversation, he drinking a coke, they beers. (Merton did make Bonaventure the place for purging himself of what he then considered bad habits, a view, at least as it pertained to beer, he later, under monastic influence, revised!) According to a student in the group, Merton was always saying, "What do you want to do with your life?" Reflecting the times, this former student adds, "We never gave very good answers because we all knew if we got through college, then we'd go to the war."[33]

This story seems more emblematic than apocryphal, both because the question pressed dramatically on Merton himself during this time, and because it exemplifies in some sense his belief that college ought to help students in realizing their true identity. It also strikes a neat parallel with Merton's accounts of the importance of his own personal encounters with teachers such as Dan Walsh and Mark Van

---

31. Thomas Merton, "An Introduction to the Vows," *The Collected Essays of Thomas Merton* (Thomas Merton Studies Center, Bellarmine College, Louisville, Kentucky); Thomas Merton, "Love Casts Out Fear," Conference Tape (Kansas City, Mo.: Credence Cassettes, 1988).

32. Interview with Robert Fenzl, May 18, 1995.

33. Interview with Cornelius Donovan, May 9, 1995.

Doren. This is not to say that the formation of students' identities was Merton's chief concern while at Bonaventure. He was intent on his own interior journey even while he was in the role of teacher, "very pensive," "kind of a loner," and "a little introverted," in the words of one former student;[34] "shy, bashful-acting," and "a quiet man," in the words of another.[35] Others retain this same image: "After class he seemed to be a loner. . . . He walked alone on campus;"[36] he was "other worldly, walked by as though in a trance."[37] A colleague remembers, "He never said too much. . . . He wasn't a recluse or anything like that; he just kept quiet for the most part."[38]

If Merton seemed meditative and removed when alone, pondering life and his vocation, and, as he puts it, getting his soul "in harmony with itself and with God," his quietness when in a group was not necessarily detachment.[39] "He always listened very carefully," noted a colleague.[40] Nor was he shy about making noise on occasion. Both former colleagues and students remember his periodic playing of bongo drums at night in Devereux Hall, where lay faculty who needed housing and virtually all of the students lived. Recalls one, "He turned out not to be the best neighbor. . . . He played bongo drums. Bill Glynn [would yell], 'Cut out the bongo drums, Professor Merton, cut it out!'"[41] Jim Hayes, a fellow lay faculty member, confirms that "he would go on sometimes for fifteen minutes, one-half hour. . . . He would lock the door—he was very good at it."[42] His playing "used to annoy those of us who were studying. . . . [The sound] would reverberate throughout the corridor," declares a hallmate who lived three rooms down from Merton.[43] Perhaps Merton felt that his drumming would not grate any more than the yelling for "Cassidy," which he tol-

34. Interview with Edward M. Horey, January 5, 1994.

35. Interview with James F. Magill, May 15, 1995.

36. Interview with James Battaglia, May 9, 1995.

37. Interview with Leo Keenan, January 5, 1994.

38. John Gussom, videotaped remarks (St. Bonaventure Conference on Thomas Merton, 1988), Friedsam Memorial Library, St. Bonaventure University, Olean, New York.

39. Merton, *The Seven Storey Mountain*, 305.

40. John Gussom, videotaped remarks (St. Bonaventure Conference on Thomas Merton, 1988).

41. Interview with James Barnhurst, May 15, 1995.

42. Jim Hayes, videotaped remarks (St. Bonaventure Conference on Thomas Merton, 1988).

43. Interview with Fr. Joseph A. Ciaiola, May 9, 1995.

erated as part of the telephone communication system in the dorm.[44] James Peters remembers that Merton loved jazz, which he played on the same portable phonograph he had used as a student at Oakham, recalling specifically his fondness for "Big Noise from Winetka," a "Bob Crosby and the Bobcats" album.[45]

Taken collectively, the impressions of former students (formed, it should be remembered, at the age of about nineteen, and offered fifty-four or more years later) portray Merton's classroom demeanor as a mixture in some proportion of distance and approachability, informality and seriousness, patience and animation. Marion Weis Horey, one of the few women who had Merton as a teacher (there were little more than a handful of full-time female students at Bonaventure at the time, and they were assigned to the night classes), recalls him as "a man apart, a very gentle, pleasant person, [but] in class kind of remote, almost in a world by himself, [though] very friendly."[46] Robert Fenzl puts it somewhat differently, describing Merton as "a nice man, very quiet, very knowledgeable; he wasn't an outspoken man, not an aloof man at all, but kept to himself."[47] Horey felt that Merton really did not know much about her, something, it is apparent, she wished could have been different. Her perception of the difference between Merton's understanding of literature and her own may also account for her sense of remoteness. As she explains it:

> We'd read something, and he would see so much more in it than I saw. I realized from his class that I had a lot to learn. . . . He just did operate on another plane. I never felt that I could read poetry and get from it the thousand levels of meaning that he got.[48]

Fenzl, for his part, remembers some of Merton's liveliness. "Oh, God, he was great," he enthusiastically comments. "He read *The Canterbury Tales* like they should have been read. . . . I didn't always understand all of them. . . . He explained it so thoroughly. . . . [He] made it seem easy. . . . [It was] not so hard as I thought."[49] Merton tried to help students in their effort at reading and understanding Chaucer by having

44. Merton, *The Seven Storey Mountain*, 304.
45. Interview with James Peters, May 18, 1995.
46. Interview with Marion Weis Horey, January 5, 1994.
47. Interview with Robert Fenzl, May 18, 1995.
48. Interview with Marion Weis Horey.
49. Interview with Robert Fenzl.

them put some of the tales into modern English, noting that "this will probably severely tax their brains, and do violence to their tempers."[50]

There can be little doubt that Merton was enamored with his subject. He tells us that the task of preparing his classes gave him significant "health and satisfaction and reward."[51] His extensive class notes, kept in a neat notebook, attest to his diligence in preparation and to his thorough background in the classics of English literature. He begins the course with a discussion of language, focusing in particular on the origin and development of English as an Indo-European language, as a prelude to work on Anglo Saxon poetry, *Beowulf,* and *Sir Gawain and the Green Knight.* Chaucer and Milton receive considerable attention. Historical and literary timelines periodically appear in his notes; at one point, there is an elaborate page "PLAN for Treatment of Elizabethan Drama," which includes lists of relevant works under headings such as "Romantic Drama," "Tragic Tendency," and "Domestic Drama."[52] Merton's class notebook reveals a careful and traditional treatment of his subject. In this respect he seems to have remained quite true to the description of the course provided in "The St. Bonaventure College Bulletin" for the 1940–41 sessions. English 201–202 was "a survey course of the chief periods of English Literature to define the more important forms. Aims to give the student an intelligent appreciation of the best literature and at the same time to provide him with the general literary background pre-requisite to the special courses in literature."[53] In commenting on his teaching responsibility, Merton mentions his "happiness" to be steeped again in the literature that had enthralled him as a child. He felt that he communicated something of this world to his students, concluding that "because they saw that I myself liked my own subject matter, they tolerated it, and even did a certain amount of work for me without too much complaint."[54]

James Barnhurst corroborates Merton's view, declaring him "an inspired teacher. He really knew English literature and could get it

50. Merton, *Run to the Mountain,* 255.

51. Merton, *The Seven Storey Mountain,* 305.

52. Thomas J. Merton, "English Lit. Class" (notebook), Friedsam Memorial Library, St. Bonaventure University, Olean, New York.

53. "The St. Bonaventure College Bulletin," vol. XIV, January 1941, no. 1, Friedsam Memorial Library, St. Bonaventure University, Olean, New York.

54. *The Seven Storey Mountain,* 306.

across to us. . . . Some of the big husky football players of the Pennsylvania coal country were equally smitten; he got them interested in English literature . . . a tribute to his ability as a professor."[55] Rita Ballard, herself for several years an English teacher, remembers Merton as "casual, laid back" and his class as "very interesting, lively, not very formal. . . . He always . . . made you want to do [the reading] without being very demanding. . . . [He had] an easygoing way, but did expect you to do it . . . [and] never embarrassed you if you didn't understand what he was trying to get to."[56]

If he was motivating without being demanding, he seems also to have had a strong sense of deserving quality. Merton told Catherine de Hueck Doherty of a nun in his class who wrote an essay about what impressed her about St. Bonaventure, not least of all the visit of Baroness de Hueck herself, with whose views she evidently agreed. Merton goes on to say, "Well, I nearly gave her an A on the strength of this, but I didn't. Charity is one thing, art another." Any doubts he might have had about this assessment were erased when he discovered this student's too ardent affection for the understanding of grammar, which Merton mistrusted. "A for charity, B-plus for technique was what I gave the sister, only the first grade remained unspoken, and that was just as well too, because today she gave me a big argument about some obscure point of grammar."[57]

In her recollections, Rita Ballard also notes with a trace of lingering indignation that "some of the profs [were] not too happy about having women in the classes . . . [but Merton] accepted us as part of the class."[58] Maurice Crisman describes Merton as "very patient" and "well-respected by all of his students."[59] He remembers as a sign of his thoughtfulness a compliment Merton gave him on an essay on the word "light," which he wrote in response to an assignment to write on one word.

Though quite at home with English literature, Merton was challenged as a teacher to read ever more carefully and to consider more closely the meaning and significance of what he read and what he had

55. Interview with James Barnhurst.

56. Interview with Rita Ballard, May 9, 1995.

57. Merton to Catherine de Hueck Doherty, October 6, 1941, *The Hidden Ground of Love: The Letters of Thomas Merton on Religious Experience and Social Concerns,* ed. William H. Shannon (New York: Farrar, Straus & Giroux, 1985) 4.

58. Interview with Rita Ballard.

59. Interview with Maurice Crisman, May 9, 1995.

his students read. He wondered, as I have noted, whether "teaching literature [was] the first thing to make [him] really read the stuff." Issues arose in his classes that demanded careful reading and clarification. To cite an example, he wrote in his journal:

> I have been very exercised about "literary truth" and "belief" since my classes thought that because Sir Gawain and the Green Knight was *truer* than Beowulf, it was because it was "more realistic." But a man riding around with his head cut off, holding it by the hair, and talking to people, is not realism.[60]

Many years later, in the monastery, Merton would introduce novices to art and poetry, and to the truth illuminated about human experience to be found in literature.

Teaching at Bonaventure was not quite "candy" for Merton. Literature proved "hard to teach." It was hard to explain what was good and to avoid cliches in teaching an appreciation of literature. This difficulty was a sign of Merton's own respect for literature, of his determination not to reduce it to something less than what it was, but to let it speak somehow for itself. It was also perhaps Merton remembering the standard of teaching set by his mentor Mark Van Doren, who, he wrote, "being employed to teach literature, teaches just that: talks about writing and about books and poems and plays . . . [and teaches students] how to read a book and how to tell a good book from a bad."[61] Marion Weis Horey provides a clue regarding how Merton managed in his effort to represent literature well in his teaching: "My impression [was that he] went out of himself in these writings. [You were] watching a man take a piece of literature and eat it up [and] let you enjoy the work with him. If you were up to it, good . . . he didn't show you how to do it."[62]

Like Van Doren, Merton did not want to preempt students' thinking about and direct appreciation for literature, but instead foster it. Indeed, Merton's own artistic sensibilities in some sense demanded this educational stance. Toward the end of his first semester at Bonaventure, on a short visit to the Boston Museum of Fine Arts, he noted with indignation "a class of high school girls, sitting on all the benches and even on the floor while their teacher dictated information,

---

60. Merton, *Run to the Mountain*, 256.
61. Merton, *The Seven Storey Mountain*, 139.
62. Interview with Marion Weis Horey.

all of which they busily and humbly took down in their notebooks."[63] The students never actually looked at the pictures in the museum. Art was a matter of seeing and responding, of learning about how to see and what to see and responding to it. A year before, after a visit to the art exhibit at the World's Fair, Merton had lamented in his journal those who read the names of painters off the frames and neglect to look at the pictures themselves. He faults a course in aesthetics at Columbia and the "new darling" in "Humanities" for promoting the same kind of art noneducation: "Columbia succeeds in remembering a list of names: that is all."

His tone in the passage about paintings shifts from sarcastic to admiring as he describes Breughel's *Wedding Dance*, retracing vividly the path of his own eye through the formal arrangement of the picture: "You start by seeing the dancers in a round in the foreground, their whole group is like a living organism: in a pyramidal arrangement." It is the form of the picture—the gaiety and life it conveys—that captivates him. He concludes that this is what attracted others to the work as well, "no matter what they said."[64] In discussing the Fra Angelica *Temptation of Saint Anthony*, he writes, "Looking at the picture is exactly the same thing as praying." Again it is the form of the picture that communicates and which he sees; the point at which the Saint's movement is captured is "still," evoking a sense of the eternal and of a kind of ineffable prayer.[65] Many years later, as he introduced the subject of art to them for the first time, Merton would emphasize to novices at Gethsemani that it was not as important "to have some kind of self-conscious knowledge of what art is about" as it was "to be able to respond to beauty in life." Reminiscent of his response to *Wedding Dance* and *Temptation of Saint Anthony* twenty-five years earlier, he opens the monks to considering art as an aspect of a broad orientation to life, rather than solely in terms of who or what.[66] He thus fortifies rather than simply embellishes the monastic curriculum; learning to see the beauty of life through art and understanding beauty as a matter ultimately of being, as he tells the novices, supports the development of a Christian if not contemplative view of the world.

63. Thomas Merton, "Brown Journal," November 26, 1940, Friedsam Memorial Library, St. Bonaventure University, Olean, New York.

64. Merton, *Run to the Mountain*, 51–55.

65. Ibid.

66. Thomas Merton, "Beauty and Art," 8-12-64, Tape #175 Side B, Thomas Merton Studies Center, Bellarmine College, Louisville, Kentucky.

Merton's account of his visit to the art exhibit includes not only his own detailed observations of different paintings, but also his commentary on the observations of others he overheard; he was concerned with how people were looking at and interpreting the art. He could not understand, nor could he condone, the empty exercise of looking for the painters' names, anymore than he could simply talk about literature. If Marion Weis Horey's description is indicative, then he chose to teach literature in part by entering into it and in this way, like Van Doren, to communicate it as it was meant to be, inviting his students to understand it and engage it likewise. For students like Robert Fenzl this approach worked.

Horey, Fenzl, Barnhurst, Ballard, and Crisman represent the students about whom Merton says little in *The Seven Storey Mountain*, those he does not rank with either the football players or the seminarians as among the "best elements" in his classes. If he has overlooked them in his account, then he has overlooked students who respected his knowledge, appreciated his European background, and who were attentive to, and grateful for, his teaching. They understood the challenge Merton had in teaching literature to a mixture of students, many of whom were not there by choice, and appreciated his patience in doing so. As James Magill puts it, "[He] handled us all quite well, both the football players and the scholars, and all thought him an OK guy."[67]

Merton's teaching responsibility combined with his daily prayer, writing, and study to establish a discipline, order, and satisfaction in his daily life lacking before. But, as we know, he was stirred by a deeper spiritual longing. After a little more than a year at Bonaventure he agonizes that

> teaching English is not enough—nor is writing novels in double-talk. Both of these are sidetracks, and this place is too remote from the places where people suffer most, and cry out in agony for some kind of help. Besides that, I imagine I can teach people here something that will turn them towards helping those others. But how can I? How do I know what I am talking about?[68]

Here he is in the throes of deciding whether to go to Friendship House in Harlem to serve the poor. A month later he writes to Lax, "Harlem

---

67. James Magill to author, May 16, 1995.
68. Merton, *Run to the Mountain*, 450.

isn't it, for me. Nor is any college. Nor is New York."[69] Within days, desiring to "belong entirely to God," he would leave his teaching notebooks behind—but not, as it turns out, his teaching career—as he made his way to Gethsemani.

69. Merton to Robert Lax, *The Road to Joy*, 163.

The Abbey Center for the Study of Ethics and Culture Conference: To Develop a Just Peacemaking Theory

Edward LeRoy Long, Jr., Glen Stassen, and Ronald Stone

For sixteen centuries we have debated about restraining or limiting war, using two paradigms: pacifism and just war theory. Many thoughtful persons say it is now past time to develop a third paradigm—a just peacemaking theory—that focuses not only on restraining war, but on creating peace. We have needed it before, but we need it especially now, to guide us in our newly hopeful and newly dangerous world context.

In their pastoral letter *The Challenge of Peace,* the U.S. Catholic Bishops say:

> Recognition of the Church's responsibility to join with others in the work of peace is a major force behind the call today to develop a theology of peace. Much of the history of Catholic theology on war and peace has focused on limiting the resort to force in human affairs; this task is still necessary, . . . but it is not a sufficient response.[1]

Official statements of the United Church of Christ, the United Methodist Church, and the Presbyterian Church (U.S.A.) have also called explicitly for a just peacemaking theory.[2] So have books by

---

1. U.S. National Conference of Catholic Bishops, *The Challenge of Peace* (Washington, D.C.: United States Catholic Conference, 1983) paragraph 23.
2. Susan Thistlethwaite, ed., *A Just Peace Church* (New York: United Church Press, 1986) v, 134; United Methodist Council of Bishops, *In Defense of Creation* (Nashville: Graded Press, 1986) 13, 24; General Assembly, *Peacemaking: The Believers' Calling* (New York: The General Assembly of the United Presbyterian Church in the United States of America, 1980) 20.

many of the panelists who participated in the Abbey Center for the Study of Ethics and Culture Conference at the Abbey of Gethsemani October 28–30, 1994.

The conference included eighteen scholars who had drafted the major Church statements on peacemaking during the past decade, written books arguing the need for a just peacemaking theory, or offered special expertise: Steven Brion-Meisels, John Cartwright, Michael Dyson, Duane Friesen, Alan Geyer, Gary Gunderson, John Langan, S.J., Edward LeRoy Long Jr., Patricia McCullough, Peter Paris, Rodger Payne, Bruce Russett, Paul Schroeder, Michael Smith, Glen Stassen, David Steele, Ronald Stone, and Susan Thistlethwaite. In addition, Bryan Hehir, David Hollenbach, and Barbara Green are participants in the project who were unable to attend the Abbey Center Conference. Abbot Timothy Kelly served as host. Peter Paris served as moderator.

In addition there were twenty invited distinguished guests, mostly from the Louisville and Lexington area, who provided community feedback, stimulation, and reality-testing on the practicality of the proposals that emerged.

It was a working conference, not merely an exchange of ideas. The purpose was to probe whether we might be able to work toward consensus on the ingredients of a just peacemaking theory.

At Vigils at 3:15 a.m., the monks and those conference participants who were awake prayed these words: "O God, give justice to thy kingdom; Let the mountains show forth peace. . . . Give pity to the meek, and justice to the poor." This prayer dedicated our conference.

What Is Just Peacemaking Theory?
How Does It Relate to Pacifism and Just War Theory?

Like just war theory, just peacemaking theory is a set of principles for evaluating policy.[3] Just war theory evaluates the rightness—or wrongness—of a policy to make war. Just peacemaking theory evaluates the adequacy of a government's initiatives—or its lack of initiatives—to make peace. We believe it is inadequate to limit debate to whether it is right to make a particular war; we want to focus debate on initiatives to make peace so war will not be the only resort. So just

---

3. Dana W. Wilbanks and Ronald H. Stone, *Presbyterians and Peacemaking: Are We Now Called to Resistance* (New York: Advisory Council on Church and Society, 1985) 44.

peacemaking theory is an expression of ethical principles affirmed by a church for evaluating governmental policies that promote or hinder international peace and justice. Some Christians recognize the source of just peacemaking principles to be revelation in Scripture, others regard them as a discernment of the moral law of the universe or the logic of moral discourse, others take them as grounded in study of the historical processes that lead to peace, and most base their just peacemaking theory in some combination of these scriptural, philosophical, and historical/empirical sources.

A just peacemaking theory should supplement, not replace, pacifism and just war theory. The relationship will be dialectical and neither simplistically symbiotic nor merely polarizing. The imperative of taking initiatives to make peace is implied in both pacifism and just war theory. But when pacifism and just war theory debate, the debate naturally focuses on their point of disagreement: Is it permissible to make war? They lose focus on the initiatives to make peace. Just peacemaking restores that focus. It highlights and magnifies the concern for peacemaking initiatives that is implied by pacifism and just war theory, and that most pacifists have emphasized. Just peacemaking will not always succeed, however, and we will still need pacifism and just war theory to guide the debate if just peacemaking fails.

Just-peace thinking must be a new creation that respects the concerns of pacifists and just war theorists for the restraint of particular evils, yet seeks to prevent the development of the very crises to which they offer criteria for a moral response. Focusing early and determinedly on steps of just peacemaking may provide the space for pacifism and just war theory to do their work before the momentum of war gathers such strength that their debate is too late.

Just-peace theory can be embraced with equal integrity by pacifists and nonpacifists. Under just-peace thinking the burden of proof shifts from those who would resort to violent conflict as an extraordinary means to those who do nothing to seek justice and peace in the daily course of events—or those who claim to be seeking peace but are not taking the essential steps for peace.

Just peacemaking has a place in the formation of public policy at every time and place and not merely at times of tension. Just peacemaking not only responds to crisis situations, but also creates an ongoing agenda for normal times as well as crises. Governments and citizens—and churches and people of faith—have an obligation to support these peacemaking practices both in long-term work to build conditions that make peace more likely, and in crisis situations where peacemaking initiatives can make war less likely. In crisis situations they specify initiatives that should be tried before governments resort to war. We believe they are a test of the sincerity of governments' claims that they are trying to make peace. They can guide people in prodding governments to take peacemaking initiatives. We sense that our world is at once more dangerous, more in need of peacemaking initiatives, and also more open to initiatives to make peace. At the same time, we must say realistically that our world has forces that resist peacemaking initiatives. Therefore people need to encourage and prod their churches and their governments to push for peacemaking initiatives where there are opportunities.

The idea of justice governing just peacemaking is not primarily the forceful restraint of those who have violated some standard of civil decency, but creative, engendering, and liberating—focusing attention on achieving fair, open, trusting relationships between groups and freeing us from vicious cycles that drive us toward war. The mode of reasoning in just peacemaking is not primarily the means-and-ends reasoning of just war theory, but diagnosis of causes of unpeace and prescription of essential steps for *shalom*.

Just peacemaking seeks the reconciling path of cooperation with others in a blending of wills, rather than forcing others; but it, too, must wrestle with the need to grow an international network that resists tyrants and aggressors. It seeks to maximize cooperation rather than submission; "power with" rather than "power over." It engenders initiatives at every stage, attempts reconciliation in every situation, and seeks joint achievements of righteousness rather than a coerced blocking of malfeasance.

In sum, there will be many similarities and also some significant differences between just war theory as it has developed across the years and a theory of just peacemaking as we envision it:

- Both are concerned with the advancement of human well-being through political processes.

- Both are premised on a belief that political affairs are subject to moral guidance and constraints.

- Both are situation-pertinent, but not situation-specific; that is, while they enunciate general principles that can be applied to concrete decisions, they do not set forth an analysis or set of mandates for one particular historical situation.

- Both are systems of ethical reflection that employ general wisdom and ordinary experience to the problem they address rather than an exegetical use of biblical modes of thinking.

- Just-peace theory will likely be proactive rather than reactive. It will attempt to furnish guidance for taking hopeful initiatives rather than to provide restraints and strictures over problematic impulses and vitalities. While just war thinking employs the concept of "last resort" to signify the conditions that warrant the use of force, just peace thinking will concentrate on the steps that ought to be taken to alleviate conditions that lead to hostilities.

- Just-peace theory will foster and cultivate activities that are fruitful and creative (even remedial) in purpose and quality rather than concern itself with limiting or proscribing activities that are punitive and/or potentially destructive.

- Just-peace theory is primarily concerned with what can be accomplished by persuasion, whereas just war theory has been mainly concerned with what conditions require coercion or threat of coercion. This distinction cannot be complete and total, since forms of peacekeeping are developing that depend upon the employment of military force to maintain agreed-upon commitments. But peacekeeping activities are low-level uses of military presence, far different from overt war between nations.

- Just peacemaking provides criteria not only for heads of state, but for the callings, involvements, and activities of all persons, voluntary associations, congregations, church or faith groups, and nongovernmental organizations. These all need criteria for guiding their own peacemaking, for prodding governments to take steps for peace, and for seeing through governments' claims to be seeking peace when they are insincere or ineffective. The essay by Duane Friesen that follows this essay explains the importance of organized faith-groups working for peacemaking. Just peacemaking is directed to communities of faith and people's advocacy groups, as well as to decision-making processes within the international community (including officials of bodies like the United Nations and the World Court or World Bank) and not only to the leaders of nation-states.

- Just-peace thinking relates to other spheres of moral concern (particularly to concerns for liberation, for political freedom, for social justice, and for ecological responsibility) and cannot deal with conflict as an isolated moral problem.

Why Is Just Peacemaking Theory Emerging Now?

Over fifty years ago the world was stunned by the horror and devastation of World War II and the threat of atomic and nuclear weapons. The reality of that universally perceived threat persuaded people and institutions to develop new networks and practices to try to prevent another world war and the use of nuclear weapons. Many of these new networks and new practices have not been widely noticed, or have been seen as small and imperfect contributions in the face of such a large threat. Now fifty years have passed and we have avoided those two specters—world war and the use of nuclear weapons. New practices, such as the spread of democracy and human rights; conflict resolution methods; sustainable economic development; arms control and reduction; the step-by-step building of international networks politically, economically, and culturally; the nonviolent direct action that has brought the remarkable changes in the Philippines, Eastern Europe, and South Africa; and the independent initiatives strategy that has brought a rapid reduction of nuclear weapons, are actually getting results in ways many have not noticed. These are not disembodied ideals disconnected from power considerations, but historically situated processes or practices that actually function, though imperfectly, to discipline power—a bit here and a bit there—and they add up. Working together, they are in fact pushing back the frontiers of war. France, Germany, England, and Western European nations—once the igniters of world wars—have now moved well beyond making war against each other. No democracy has fought another democracy in this century, and democracy is spreading. We believe we are now at a moment of *kairos* when it can serve useful purposes to name these actual processes, to call attention to them, to support them ethically. This is the contribution we hope to make.

At the same time, the threat and the reality of war are still enormous. The destructive power of weapons still continues to grow. Civil wars are rife, and can be unimaginably genocidal. Our generation is using up essential, nonrenewable resources as if there were no future to be concerned about, and the resulting scarcity can be a major cause of war. War by other means—especially economic—causes millions to die and millions more to live in misery. The enormity of the threat spurs us on to strengthen the steps of just peacemaking because they are so badly needed.

At the abbey conference, Tom Mullaney, chair of the board of the Abbey Center, offered a moving meditation in the words of Thomas Merton. At one point he read these words:

> Finally, we must be reminded of the way we ourselves tend to operate, the significance of the secret forces that rise up within us and dictate fatal decisions. We must learn to distinguish the free voice of conscience from the irrational compulsions of prejudice and hate. We must be reminded of objective moral standards, and of the wisdom which goes into every judgment, every choice, every political act that deserves to be called civilized. We cannot think this way unless we shake off our passive irresponsibility, renounce our fatalistic submission to economic and social forces, and give up the unquestioning belief in machines and processes which characterizes the mass mind. History is ours to make. Now above all we must try to recover our freedom, our moral autonomy, our capacity to control the forces that make for life and death in our society.[4]

We want to avoid either fatalism or ahistorical idealism. When we speak of the practices of just peacemaking, we are speaking not merely of what *ought* to happen ideally, but what is actually in process of happening in our time of historical change because it serves functional needs in the midst of the power realities of our time. We name and encourage these practices because they do demonstrably function to reduce causes of war and to grow peacemaking processes. We hope to make a contribution by naming their moral importance. We hope to say something that is not merely a wish, but an encouragement of redemptive processes that are emerging in our time and a choice to participate in them, to add our energy to them.

Just peacemaking is emerging now in Church statements from different traditions, calling for a positive theology of peace and not only a negative restraint on war. These statements are being written because of the influence of prophets like Thomas Merton and Pope John XXIII, because of discernment of the signs of the times, and we believe because of the work of the Holy Spirit among us.

Just peacemaking theory is evolving through ecclesiastical processes and moving toward consensus.[5] The ethicists who came to

4. Thomas Merton, *The Nonviolent Alternative* (New York: Farrar, Straus & Giroux, 1980) 78–79.

5. Glen Stassen, *Just Peacemaking: Transforming Initiatives for Justice and Peace* (Louisville: Westminster/John Knox Press, 1992) 209–30. Ronald Stone, a Presbyterian, wrote the following paragraphs, but here cites Stassen.

the abbey conference are participants in these ongoing discussions; they are part of a developing expression of church thought and practice. The recent Presbyterian Church (U.S.A.) statement is evidence of the ecclesiastical movement toward consensus:

> The church in the nuclear age must shift its energies from considerations of just war to the urgent and primary task of defining and serving a just peace. A nuclear stalemate, or even the elimination of all nuclear arms, is still far from God's shalom. Shalom is the intended state of the entire human race. It involves the well-being of the whole person in all relationships, personal, social, and cosmic. Shalom means life in a community of compassionate order marked by social and economic justice. Peace without justice is no peace; that is why the Bible so often reflects God's special concern for the poor and powerless.
>
> The great biblical visions of global peace—swords into plowshares, every family under its own vine and fig tree—are fundamental to thinking about just peace. Such a peace is ultimately God's gift; we need to avoid the proud illusion that we can create it by human effort alone. But Christian obedience demands that we move toward that peace in all possible ways: by extending the rule of law, advocating universal human rights, strengthening the organs of international order, working for common security and economic justice, converting industry to peaceful production, increasing understanding of and reconciliation with those we identify as enemies, developing peacemaking skills, constructing concrete manifestations of just peace across barriers of conflict and injustice, and other means.[6]

Understanding our work from a Presbyterian and Niebuhrian tradition,[7] one can see continuity between our work now and the work of the Federal Council of Churches fifty years ago, in 1940–1947, on a just and durable peace: *The Statement of Guiding Principles*, with thirteen principles of peacemaking, and the more politically oriented *Six Pillars of Peace*.[8] That period of the Federal Council of Churches' work

---

6. *Christian Obedience in a Nuclear Age* (Louisville: The Office of the General Assembly, The Presbyterian Church U.S.A., 1988) 8.

7. As Ronald Stone, who wrote these words, does.

8. See: *A Righteous Faith for a Just and Durable Peace* (New York: Commission to Study the Bases of a Just and Durable Peace, 1941); Jessie J. Burroway, "Christian Witness Concerning World Order, 1941–1947" (Ph.D. dissertation, University of Wisconsin, 1953) 14–17.

on international relations was probably the high point of public policy influence in international relations of Protestant churches in this country. The principles developed then provided a strong basis for churches' work to prepare U. S. public opinion to support the United Nations and to lobby the Senate to vote for the United Nations. Recent Church statements and our work on a just peacemaking theory carry on a strong Church tradition, both Protestant and Catholic, since the beginning of World War II.

What Practices Are Emerging as Essential Steps of Just Peacemaking?

The process of developing a consensus just peacemaking theory is not yet finished, and the practices of just peacemaking are not yet finally decided. But we have continued our work since the abbey conference. We are working toward another conference in which we hope to agree on a consensus just peacemaking theory. Papers are being written on ten essential practices of peacemaking, a sort of peacemaking Ten Commandments:

1. Talk with the adversary, respect their valid interests, and use methods of conflict resolution.

2. Respect and support nonviolent direct action for justice.

3. Take independent initiatives to reduce threat and distrust.

4. Respect and support international peacekeeping, peace enforcement, peacebuilding, international law, and perhaps humanitarian intervention.

5. Act so as to strengthen the growing international linkages that weave nations together and reduce international anarchy.

6. Reduce offensive weapons and weapons trafficking.

7. Acknowledge wrong and practice forgiveness.

8. Spread human rights, religious liberty, and democracy.

9. Foster sustainable economic development that meets basic human needs.

10. Respect and support people's movements—organizations of citizens independent of governments.

Can You Explain a Few of These Practices, if Only Briefly?

The commitment to international law and international organization, expressed in Church statements of fifty years ago, is also a present commitment of recent Church statements on peace and war. Similar commitments to strengthening the United Nations are found in all of our traditions. Basic themes of covenantal government, covenantal responsibilities, universal will of God, and law from a central source are all imperfectly represented in the existing machinery of international relations, in international law, and the United Nations. This principle of just peacemaking theory may be stated: "To be regarded as fulfilling the principles of just peacemaking, a governmental policy must not contravene international law or the will of the universal community of nations as expressed by the United Nations."

Many policies of the United States clearly fall within normal expressions of such a principle. The principle would provide a clear norm for opposing U.S. war actions in Nicaragua and Panama, and the nonpayment of United Nations assessments by recent U.S. administrations. It is a principled way of recognizing the representative of the voices of most peoples and of limiting sovereignty. It is of course arguable that the principle should be put positively rather than negatively: Just peacemaking requires compliance with international law and the will of the universal community of nations as expressed by the United Nations.

We can also learn from the historical clash between Paul Tillich and John Foster Dulles. Tillich criticized the work of the Federal Council of Churches Commission on a Just and Durable Peace and clashed with its lawyer, chairman John Foster Dulles.[9] Dulles was right in emphasizing law, international organization, and in moving the churches and indirectly the government to develop the United Nations. Tillich, however, was right in emphasizing the dynamic nature of life; he contended that no status quo could be made durable. Tillich did not oppose order, but he was more concerned that in a world in revolution the imperative of social-economic security be achieved. Today we recognize it even in our cities. If hope for socioeconomic security or justice is lost, peace is lost. A divided world of affluence and malnutrition is neither stable nor peaceful. The principle

---

9. Paul Tillich, *A Theology of Peace* (Louisville: Westminster/John Knox Press, 1990) 73–87.

could be expressed: "To be regarded as fulfilling the principles of just peacemaking, a government policy must not, in its expression in treaties, international monetary policies, and international economic strategies, reduce the social-economic welfare of the suffering."

This principle, like the previous one, allows for humanitarian policies, rational economic planning, and international agencies, but it denies them the freedom to inflict more suffering through imposition of unemployment or anti-welfare or encouraging long-term dependency roles. It is congruent with work in the churches going forward under norms of sustainable economic development that meets basic economic needs justly. It does not negate privatization of inefficient state corporations, but it prohibits policies that can be shown to reduce health, food, housing, and transportation for the poor.

A third peacemaking practice we focused on is the new strategy of independent initiatives devised by the social psychologist Charles Osgood to reduce threat and distrust. The strategy of independent initiatives is a partial response to the opening words of Thomas Mullaney's reading from Thomas Merton: "At the root of all war is *fear.*"

The practice of independent initiatives is designed to de-escalate hostility when the sense of distrust and threat are major causes of that hostility. One side takes a series of initiatives—visible actions, not mere words—independent of the slow process of negotiation—to decrease the other side's distrust or perception of threat. It may pull back some troops or weapons or open up some trade or halt nuclear testing. Although independent initiatives should decrease the threat to the other side, they should not leave the initiator weak, because the initiating side would then become driven by fear. The timing for each initiative should be announced in advance and carried out regardless of the other side's bluster: to postpone confirms distrust. There should be clear explanation of the purpose: to shift the context toward de-escalation and to invite reciprocation. There should be a series of initiatives inviting reciprocation and increasing if the adversary does reciprocate significantly.

The method of independent initiatives is successfully being used by governments to resolve antagonisms and produce mutual disarmament. It is spreading. It is a feedback loop with positive feedback because it works; it resolves conflict.

It was used by the United States and the Soviet Union to achieve freedom and neutrality for Austria in spite of the Cold War, rather than leaving it divided between East and West as Germany was. It was advocated by peace movements, eventually persuading the U.S. Congress, President Gorbachev, and President Bush to take independent initiatives to rid the world of medium-range and shorter range nuclear weapons, and reduce long-range nuclear weapons from 35,000 to 6,500. It was used to create the atmosphere for beginning talks between Israel and the P.L.O.

The problem is that it is not widely understood, so when it succeeds, often we do not see what is occurring, and those opposed to reducing tensions characterize it as giving away everything to an enemy. We need to spread the knowledge of it not only so we can encourage antagonists internationally and interpersonally to take independent initiatives, but so we recognize it when it occurs and can give thanks and tell our neighbors.

God's grace is about as independent an initiative as there is. At vespers, the monks at the abbey read from 1 John 3:

> This is the proof of love,
> that he laid down his life for us,
> and we too ought to lay down our lives for our brothers.
> If anyone is well off in worldly possessions
> and sees his brother in need,
> but closes his heart to him,
> how can the love of God be in him?
> Children, our love must be not just words or mere talk,
> but something active and genuine.

Independent initiatives cannot be mere words; there is too much distrust and fear for mere words to heal. They are actions, visible actions to distrust and fear.

If we see our sister/brother adversary in need of being freed from distrust and fear, and we are well off in the capacity to take an initiative to decrease that need, and instead we close our hearts to our adversary, how can the love of God be in us?

In the following essay, Duane Friesen develops another dimension of just peacemaking more fully: Respect and support people's movements—organizations of citizens independent of governments—with particular attention to groups grounded in religious faith.

A People's Movement as a Condition for the Development of a Just Peacemaking Theory[1]

Duane K. Friesen

As the United Church of Christ document *A Just Peace Church* states: "Just peace requires peacemakers."[2] I believe that a just peacemaking theory presupposes not only individual peacemakers, but a community of peacemakers.

The norms of a just peacemaking theory should not assume that the only or primary agents of action are heads of state or the leaders of revolutionary groups vying for power. Making peace is increasingly a function of a combination of many actors within the international system: people's movements, nongovernmental organizations, leaders of nation states, and international organizations. Later in this article I will focus upon how the world's religions, in particular, have contributed and can contribute to a people's movement of peacemakers. The development of a just peacemaking theory, in fact, is largely possible because there exists on an increasingly growing worldwide scale a people's movement that shares an implicit set of norms. The goal of just peacemaking theory is to make explicit the norms that are already shared by a network of interlocking groups of people at a more grass-

1. Portions of this essay have been published as "Religion and Nonviolent Action" in *Protest, Power, and Change: An Encyclopedia of Nonviolent Action from ACT-UP to Women's Suffrage*, ed. Robert S. Powers and William B. Vogele (New York: Garland Publishing, 1997), a project of the Albert Einstein Institution, Cambridge, Massachusetts.

2. Susan Thistlethwaite, ed. *A Just Peace Church* (New York: United Church Press, 1986) 60.

roots level. I cannot here describe this relatively new phenomenon in history, but the following developments (among others) can be cited:

1) a growing knowledge, awareness, and experience (recently evident in the collapse of the Soviet Empire) of nonviolent movements for social change in the traditions of Gandhi and King;

2) an interlocking network of NGO's and INGO's that bring pressure to bear on governments all over the globe on everything from human rights to arms control and reduction;

3) an increasing networking and cooperation worldwide of people across confessional and religious boundaries and barriers;

4) the coming together of these people into clusters of local organizations, peace and justice groups in churches, and interfaith committees—not just isolated individuals;

5) a strengthening of international governmental organizations that may be able to work more effectively on common human problems (perhaps we may be seeing the emergence of a United Nations World Disaster Relief Force [UNWDRF]);

6) increasing awareness and study of the vast repertoire of processes and skills by which most people make peace most of the time, and with that knowledge the possibility of extending those processes to an ever wider sphere of human interaction.

Having said this, however, I must acknowledge that the worldwide network represents a small minority (especially those who work at the peacemaking vocation intentionally) in a world that is in a rather desperate situation. The world is threatened by a number of major unresolved armed conflicts, people living in desperate situations of poverty and hunger, serious abuses of human rights, as well as major environmental problems. These desperate world-needs require that we extend and expand the global peacemaking network. One way that network can be expanded is for ethicists to seek to identify those norms that can provide a framework for increased cooperation and mission in the world by people of diverse cultural, national, and religious orientations. I come to this worldwide network of persons as a Christian pacifist. That vision continues to shape my orientation and my sensitivities, but I am less and less interested in defining the pacifist position over against other positions. I seek for more of what I have already experienced, increasing convergence among points of view. There is also a fundamental pragmatic (and ethical) reason for seeking to identify those norms that can be a basis for convergence among positions. We must find a way to develop a "global civic culture," to use Elise Boulding's phrase, if we are to have any chance of meeting the serious challenges of our globe.[3]

Why is a citizens' movement of peacemakers and peacemaking groups so important? What do they do?

1) A transnational network of people who are organized to learn from each other and act in concert can partially transcend the narrow self-interest and myopia that often characterize groups in conflict.

2) A citizens' movement, committed more to peacemaking processes than to defense of governmental or bureaucratic interest or to quick fixes (often with armed force) in a single conflict, can help keep before people the long view, the kind of perseverance that is needed so that a just peace can emerge over generations.

3) Citizens' groups can be advocates for the voiceless, especially those who are poor and powerless.

4) A transnational people's network has less investment in defending what has been. Persons in the movement can free our imaginations to think of alternatives to established patterns of behavior and the narrow range of options we often consider in resolving conflict.

5) People within a citizens' movement can play a servant role, working behind the scene in mediating conflict without needing to be in the limelight or take credit. People without strong attachment to governments or people who do not bring to a conflict a strong self-interest can gain the trust of parties and serve in a mediating role.

6) Citizens' movements can help to initiate, foster, or support transforming initiatives, an idea developed especially well by Glen Stassen,[4] where existing parties need support and courage to take risks to break out of the cycles that perpetuate violence and injustice. Stassen tells the fascinating story of the role of citizens groups in encouraging the adoption of the zero solution in the late 1980s on intermediate-range missiles in Europe.

7) A citizens' network (particularly as that is institutionalized in voluntary associations) can sustain concern and interest when the media and world opinion are unaware, forget, or flit about from one thing to the next. One year it is Somalia. Earlier it was Iraq. Where will our attention be next year?

3. Elise Boulding, *Building a Global Civic Culture: Education for an Interdependent World* (New York: Teachers College, Columbia University, 1988).

4. Glen Stassen, *Just Peacemaking: Transforming Initiatives for Justice and Peace* (Louisville, Ky.: Westminster/John Knox Press, 1992).

8) A citizens' network of NGO's and INGO's can often be a source of information and knowledge that persons in positions of governmental authority lack. I am convinced that perhaps the primary service performed by the Washington D.C. Office of the Mennonite Central Committee is to circulate returned workers from around the globe to the U.S. Congress. I have seen the power and significance of such testimony on a number of issues, as well as their impact in informing their home communities.[5]

9) Citizens' groups can also resist governments when they behave unjustly, or are short-sighted or arrogant, thinking they know more than they do, or thinking they can control futures that are in fact not under their control.

10) Churches and other religious groups can serve a special role in nurturing through worship a spirituality that sustains courage when just peacemaking is unpopular, hope when despair or cynicism is tempting, and a sense of grace and the possibility of forgiveness when just peacemaking fails.

Religion, while often contributing to violence in our world, can also be a source for building a network of peacemakers. To build a global civic culture of peacemakers, we must find ways to transcend religious differences in order to find common themes among the plurality of religions that can nurture a peacemaking culture.

Religion nurtures, supports, and contributes to nonviolent action in four fundamental ways. First, religion can legitimate strategies of peacemaking and nonviolent action (and delegitimate violence) through its symbols, myths, belief systems, and ethical norms. Second, religious institutions (the small cell, congregation, ashram, base community, interfaith organization, mosque) can give leadership or provide "space" in a society for the development and practice of nonviolence. Third, religion can foster a spirituality of truthfulness, hope, courage, patience, and willingness to suffer to sustain a movement of nonviolence under difficult conditions of struggle for change. And finally, religion contributes to the repertoire of methods of nonviolent action (prayer, fasts, vigils, love, talking with the enemy).

One of the major ways religion supports nonviolent action is to legitimate nonviolence and delegitimate violence. The legitimation of

5. See the documentation of this impact in the research of Keith Graber Miller, *American Mennonites Engage Washington: Wise as Serpents, Innocent as Doves?* (Washington, D.C.: University Press, 1996).

violence is deep and pervasive in all the major world religions. The ancient mythologies of Babylonia and Greece honored tribal war gods. Both the Hebrew Bible and the Qur'an have holy war traditions. After Constantine, the Christian Church aligned itself with empires and kings and supported the crusades, inquisitions, and religious persecution. The virtues of the warrior are glorified in the Zen Buddhist traditions of Japan or the Bhagavad Gita of India. The dominating paradigm of most religious traditions is the "myth of redemptive violence," that peace and justice are best won or maintained through the use of violent means. Religious traditions also have a strong interest in legitimating the prevailing political authority. This happens in the Christian tradition in many interpretations of texts such as Rom 13:1-7 (submit to the authorities) or in the concept of the Divine Right of Kings. In Hinduism the Laws of Manu legitimate the existing caste system.

The religions also contain stories and teachings that support peacemaking and nonviolent action and challenge the myth of necessary violence to preserve the existing order. During the last several decades especially, many religious traditions have experienced a conflict over interpretation, as groups claim religious traditions for support of nonviolent struggles for justice while others deny them that claim. Since the myths, symbols, and belief systems of religions are ways of interpreting the world, nonviolent struggles are often battles with opposing views to define the world in ways that are consonant with peacemaking and justice.

Religions can legitimate nonviolent action several important ways. Religious belief systems provide a transcendent frame of reference that empowers people to challenge the conventional view that violence is necessary for maintaining or transforming the existing social order. They also provide alternative visions of a peaceful order, an alternative dream or vision of how the world can be constructed. Religions develop universal conceptions of the human race that undermine conventional divisions between insider and outsider, friend and foe. And they enliven the human imagination and open the human spirit to consider ways to risk conflict by nonviolent means. They give hope for achieving justice and reconciliation nonviolently.

The Eastern religious traditions tend to search for an alternative to violence through a personal inward quest. Gandhi reinterpreted violent warfare in the Bhagavad Gita symbolically, as an inward spiritual struggle of the soul between light and darkness. The contemporary Vietnamese monk Thich Nhat Hanh drew from the resources of the Buddhist tradition of right mindfulness and meditation to resist the Vietnam War with the spirit and practice of nonviolence. Buddha's teachings reflected in the Dhammapada are profoundly nonviolent. The Buddha views the root of violence as ego-centeredness. Through detachment from self-centeredness by means of the eightfold path, human beings can achieve "right mindfulness," a state of calm that brings humans into peaceful relations not only with fellow humans, but with the whole universe. The *Tao te Ching*, a classic Chinese text, became popular during the 1960s in the youth counterculture of the West because of the way it turns a central value of Western culture on its head: it advocates peace through humility and meekness rather than through striving and the quest for power.

The monotheistic traditions search for the answer to violence by seeking a right relationship with God. Though the Hebrew Bible seems to legitimate violence by God's chosen people against God's enemies, it also contains stories of "outsiders" like Hagar and Ishmael who are objects of God's compassion and who also receive God's promises. Many interpretations, especially theologies of liberation, claim that the Hebrew Bible primarily takes the side of the poor and oppressed. Such a view can undermine existing unjust social systems, though liberation theologians differ as to whether violence or nonviolence is the appropriate means to pursue justice. The Hebrew prophets challenged nationalism and war as well as the power of elites who acted unjustly. The universalism of the Hebrew Bible is reflected in the prophet Jeremiah, who calls on Jews carried into exile to Babylon to seek the *shalom* (well-being) of their enemy, Babylon. Jewish rabbis of the Diaspora interpreted faithfulness to the Torah to be the practice of deeds of loving kindness. This view became the fundamental foundation for Jewish ethics as the Jewish community lived for centuries as a nonviolent minority in the context of repression and persecution.

Christians are reappropriating the early church before Constantine and the life and teachings of Jesus as a model of peacemaking and nonviolence. Scholars such as Walter Wink are challenging the view that Jesus advocated nonresistance or passivity before enemies in the face of injustice. Instead they see in Jesus' Sermon on the Mount as a model of nonviolent confrontation, a third way between violent revolution and passivity.[6]

6. Walter Wink, *Engaging the Powers: Discernment and Resistance in a World of Domination* (Minneapolis: Fortress Press, 1992).

After St. Augustine the just war theory served to legitimate the use of violent force to preserve some semblance of order and justice in a world of sin. This view seems to be in tension with the example and teaching of Jesus, though not all scholars agree that Jesus taught and practiced absolute nonviolence. The horrors of modern warfare and the skepticism about the efficacy of revolutionary violence have caused many in the twentieth century to reassess the "just war" tradition. This tradition has become more a moral framework to foster just peacemaking and practical nonviolence and increasingly less an instrument for the justification of war. This peacemaking theme is central in Pope John XXIII's encyclical *Pacem in Terris* and in the 1983 pastoral letter of the U.S. Catholic bishops, *The Challenge of Peace*. Within the World Council of Churches the reassessment of nonviolence is reflected in the 1973 study document *Violence, Nonviolence and the Struggle for Social Justice*.

A new challenge to the legitimation of violence has been advanced by many feminist theologians who believe that violence is rooted in patriarchy and the mythology of a patriarchal God. They reinterpret Christianity and other religious traditions by the development of alternative symbols and stories that emphasize equality and mutuality rather than dominance and submission. A practical example is Rigoberta Menchu's nonviolence, which is nurtured both by her own indigenous culture of Guatemala as well as by stories from the Bible.

The common perception, especially in the West, is that Islam is a religion of violence. But this interpretation has been challenged by many Muslims. Muslims can cite the example of the prophet Muhammad during the Meccan period, before his flight (Hegira) from Mecca to Medina, when he struggled nonviolently against those who wanted to suppress the faith. The Sufis and contemporary peace-minded Muslims have also emphasized that for the Qur'an the greater jihad (holy war) is the inner struggle of a person to be in submission to God, much more central than the lesser jihad of external war. The Indian Muslim Ghaffar Khan, a contemporary of Gandhi, developed a principled nonviolence.

Though religious symbols, myths, and belief systems play a critical role in shaping human behavior, these ideas are often powerless if they are not institutionalized. The ashram was central to the success of Gandhi's nonviolent struggle in India. Bishop Desmond Tutu and the South African Council of Churches have been in the forefront in advocating nonviolence in the struggle in South Africa. Religious institutions, the leaders of religious organizations, and ordinary people who practice religion daily play a very important role in nurturing and sustaining nonviolent action. As movements come and go, and the popularity of a cause begins to wane, religious organizations and leaders often provide key support and staying power. Religious institutions represent a "space," even in the most repressive societies, that is not easily controlled by the dominating political system. They can thus become a center for teaching and organizing. Religious institutions can also model alternative ways of living that put the lie to so-called inevitable hatreds by bringing together persons of diverse religious, national, racial, ethnic, ideological and economic background. Out of intense loyalty grounded in the authority of religious tradition, ordinary people act and shape social reality regardless of whether they are always conscious of how they impact the world.

In the Philippine struggle against Marcos and the numerous nonviolent struggles in Latin America, archbishops, bishops, priests, nuns, and Christian base communities have played key roles. In the Philippines, for example, Sister Milar Rocco was teaching her students about active nonviolence when she learned that defense minister Enrile and General Ramos had defected and were expecting to be bombed. Together with her students they encountered the soldiers still loyal to Marcos by offering them food and talking to them. Fifty of the soldiers said they wanted to surrender, so the nuns formed a chain around them to "protect" them and led them to join Enrile and Ramos. In the Philippines the International Fellowship of Reconciliation provided leadership and training in nonviolent action. Daniel Buttry's recent book, *Christian Peacemaking: From Heritage to Hope* (Judson Press, 1994), is especially helpful in documenting the widespread employment of nonviolent direct action and conflict resolution, often based in religious groups, to resolve conflict nonviolently.

In Vietnam, Thailand, and Burma, Buddhist monks have given leadership in protest of human rights violations and movements for nonviolent social change. Aung San Suu Kyi, daughter of Burma's national hero, winner of the Nobel Peace Prize, and advocate of nonviolence and democracy, connects her struggle explicitly to the teachings and institutions of Buddhism. The Tibetan nonviolent struggle for human rights is inspired by the exiled Dalai Lama.

The revival of Islam nurtured in the mosques throughout Iran was critical in the overthrow of the Shah in 1978–79 by nonviolent direct action. Islamic women played a vital role in the mass protests. In the Palestinian Intifada, mosques became organizing and teaching centers. Frequently marches and demonstrations began at mosques, or were linked to key religious rituals.

The civil rights struggle in the U.S. in the 1950s and 1960s was centrally linked to the African American church and the African American preacher, who was the most important leader in the community. Rosa Parks and other African American Christians did not just learn nonviolence in 1954. They had been nurtured in nonviolence through the singing of spirituals and through biblical preaching.

In 1981 a youth pastor and some young people started weekly Monday prayer services for peace at the St. Nicholai Church in Leipzig, East Germany, one of the small seeds planted early that contributed to the crumbling of the Berlin Wall. In 1988 these prayer services became the locus of increasingly larger groups of East German citizens who gathered to discuss social issues and organize marches. By October 1989, 300,000 persons gathered in Leipzig to demonstrate despite police harassment and arrests.

Religion also nurtures a spirituality that is essential to nonviolence. Critical to nonviolent action is the willingness of persons to cross the barrier of fear, to be able to say "no" to illegitimate authority without fear of sanctions and death. Vaclav Havel's courageous action in communist Czechoslovakia is a profound demonstration of what it means "to live within the truth" rather than "living a lie."

The motto of Quaker nonviolent action has been "speak truth to power." Religion nurtures virtues that are central to nonviolent movements such as courage and the willingness to suffer, overcoming hatred of the enemy and enduring abuse without retaliation, hope and patience during a long period of struggle, trust in the possibility of the miracle of transformation when the evidence for change appears bleak, joy even in the midst of suffering and pain, realism that guards people from disillusionment by making them aware of the depth of human evil and the persistence of systems of domination and injustice, and humility about their own lack of knowledge and need for wisdom.

Gandhi's nonviolence was integrally tied to his awareness that each position he took was an "experiment with truth." He prepared himself for action by fasting, meditation, and prayer. Dorothy Day was able to practice "the harsh and dreadful love" (one of the mottos of the Catholic Worker Movement) of Father Zosima in Dostoyevsky's

Brothers Karamazov by drawing sustenance from daily participation in the Mass. The icon of the Russian Orthodox Church kept alive the spirituality of the Russian people during the dark days of communism. Thich Nhat Hanh practices disciplines of meditation and breathing exercises in order to maintain internal control and calm in the midst of hatred.

Numerous nonviolent movements draw inspiration and courage from the examples of martyrs who have died for the cause. The music of the black spiritual was central in both the joy and endurance of people in the civil rights struggle. One could name a host of religious thinkers, saints, and also artists and creators and makers of music, who nurture the spirituality of movements of nonviolence such as Martin Buber, Abraham Heschel, Simone Weil, Julian of Norwich, St. Francis, Thomas Merton, Kathe Kollwitz, hymn writers from many traditions, and many others.

Religion also provides nonviolent movements with a repertoire of actions. Simple deeds of kindness and charity in the context of hatred and violence can disarm an opponent or undermine his morale. A symbol (a cross, salt, the spinning wheel) can become a powerful unifying force in a movement. Nonviolent movements frequently utilize the power of prayer, fasting, meditation, silence, sanctuary, religious processions, key festivals or religious rituals, remembrance of martyrs or saints, funerals, songs and chants, gatherings at churches, mosques, temples, or other sacred sites. Any genuine religious act is potentially an act of nonviolent protest because it brings people into relationship with a transcendent reality and power that challenges systems of injustice and violence.

One of the challenges for the world's religions is to overcome their violence toward each other. The "commitment to a culture of nonviolence," signed by around 150 religious leaders at the 1993 Parliament of the World's Religions in Chicago, may signal an era of more peaceful relationships among religious traditions. Though religious traditions have contributed and continue to contribute to warfare and violence, the world's religions have a marvelous history with common themes of nonviolence and peacemaking that can contribute to development of a people's movement to nurture and sustain a global culture of peace. A just peacemaking theory will be powerful and impact the world only if it is supported and sustained by a worldwide network of actors ready to put into practice the processes of just peacemaking.

The Dalai Lama and Abbot Timothy Kelly visit the grave of Thomas Merton at the Abbey of Gethsemani, April 25, 1994. (Photo by Amy Taylor, The Kentucky Standard. Used with permission.)

"The Great Honesty":
Remembering Thomas Merton
An Interview with
Abbot Timothy Kelly, O.C.S.O.

Conducted by George A. Kilcourse, Jr.
Edited by Kimberly F. Baker

*T*he following interview was conducted on January 25, 1996, at the Abbey of Gethsemani. Abbot Timothy Kelly entered the Cistercian life in 1958, and Thomas Merton was his novice master during the years 1958–60. From 1965 until the summer of 1968, he studied canon law in Rome, where he received his J.C.L. degree. His responsibilities include being master of novices at Gethsemani from 1969–73. Timothy Kelly was elected abbot in 1973 and continues to serve the community in this office.

Kilcourse: Could we begin with questions about your own entry into the abbey in 1958? Can you tell us something about your decision to leave Canada and become a Cistercian monk in Kentucky?

Kelly: I originally thought of being a monk when I was in high school, but my family was very opposed to it. They thought it was a waste of a life, so instead I did a year of college at what was then Assumption University of Windsor. Then I went to the Basilian novitiate [in Toronto], which was the initial study to be a priest in the Congregation of St. Basil which operated Assumption University. I did novitiate, and then I did three more years with them and, in fact, came back to Assumption and the University of Windsor and finished a degree in philosophy and history. I taught a bit in a high school and became convinced that I was not a teacher. I wanted to do something

193

other than be an administrator, so I decided that I should try being a monk at Gethsemani since the Canadian monasteries are all French-speaking and my French is a bit awkward. So, on the strength of that, I applied to Gethsemani after college graduation in June of 1958.

In fact, the French element enters into my life when I was much younger. I used to go around with a French-speaking girl in the Windsor area, which was all right as long as I had my French-speaking friend go in and pick her up. One night her father caught me bringing her home and so my career, my love life, was brought to an end! What else could I do but come to a monastery?!

Kilcourse: Sounds like a familiar monastic biography! From something that I recently read, your family did have some mixed reactions.

Kelly: They were very opposed to my coming to a monastery. They thought it was a waste of a life and were just very opposed to it, but I persevered.

Kilcourse: Didn't your father do something dramatic?

Kelly: My father worked for the Canadian lighthouse service and also for a company that supplied lake freighters, and so they flew a flag at his lighthouse. When I went to the monastery, he flew it at half-mast. One of the ship captains asked who was dead, and he said, "My son."

Kilcourse: He's become a Trappist monk! Could you tell us something about what Gethsemani was like in those days when you arrived here.

Kelly: I suppose that my first impression was that it was a very crowded place. There were over 200—210 or so—in the community when I came. It was summer; it was late August and very hot. That was when the church was crowded with monks, and at the end of a hot day in Kentucky (we worked in the fields and so on), you were aware of a lot of bodies present in the church. So my first impression was crowdedness. Not so much noise, but just an awful lot of people and certainly activity. When you're the introvert that I am, you're inclined to want your corner and hold on to it for survival.

The refectory was crowded and busy and the food was more or less our own produce from the garden. It was nourishing but not that appetizing. One of the great observations of my mother was how could I ever live there since I was so finicky about food. The first day I arrived, my plate was served. There was the plate before me with mashed potatoes and watery spinach, just this great big goop in the middle, and I thought, "Well, either I'm going to have to say my mother's right or do this."

Kilcourse: It's an act of liberation, is that it?

Kelly: Yes!

Kilcourse: How many would have been in the novitiate in those days?

Kelly: There was a lot more movement in and out, candidates coming in, candidates leaving. Probably we had a central core of fifteen who were more or less stable. There were fifteen or twenty and then back down to fifteen or so. This was the end to the big influx of vocations.

Kilcourse: In the hey-day, how many would have been there?

Kelly: At 10:00 some morning in July, I think in 1954 or something, there were approximately 275 people! The number fluctuates, but that's about correct.

Kilcourse: Do you remember your first contact with Thomas Merton?

Kelly: I do. I was in the guest house for a week or so, which was normal when new people arrived for entry, and just washing dishes and living there. One evening the guest master said, "The novice master will come to see you." I didn't know Thomas Merton was novice master. And so, this one evening the guest master said, "Be in your room at 6:30, the novice master will come and see you."

And so I was up there, and the novice master came and knocked on the door and introduced himself as the novice master and asked the usual questions a novice master would ask. Since I'd been involved a little bit at the University of Toronto, he was interested in the Medieval Institute and the people there like Etienne Gilson. He was asking me about that, and then he said, "Well, what do you know about the life?" And I said, "I've read all of Merton's published works and all of Fr. Raymond's published works and have a certain amount of historical awareness and so forth." And he said, "What do you think of the books?" And I said, "They're both rather romantic, although they have different perspectives." I said, "Certainly, Merton's style is much easier to handle than Raymond's." And he said, "Yeah, you really have to be careful what you read." With that the interview ended.

Kilcourse: That was the novice master!

Kelly: Yes, and the next morning the guest master said, "Oh, did you see Thomas Merton, did you see Thomas Merton?" I said, "I saw the novice master." And he said, "Well, that's Thomas Merton." "Oh-h-h."

Kilcourse: That's an interesting first step.

Kelly: A few hours later, I was brought to the novitiate, and I was a bit embarrassed when I met him and he said, "Ah, good to see you," or something like that. That's life!

Kilcourse: Merton was also the master of scholastics as well as master of novices.

Kelly: He had been master of scholastics before master of novices. I came in 1958. I think he had only been novice master then for about a year. He'd just finished his time as scholastic master.

Kilcourse: What kind of a teacher was Merton?

Kelly: He was a very enthusiastic teacher, a very excellent teacher. His conferences were always very well-prepared, and often they were parts of some article he was writing. He called forth a lot of enthusiasm from his students. He would wax eloquently on some Latin father, and when you went to read it on your own, it just didn't quite have the same gripping interest. Of course, it was a time of silence in the community, and he didn't evoke much interchange with the students and didn't seem, in one sense, to appreciate questions.

He was well-prepared and had a certain amount of material he wanted to present. He wasn't that desirous of student commentary. That was an impression, but again the community had a very strict regime of silence in those days, and that would also be a part of his teaching method to avoid conflict.

Kilcourse: Less controversy on his part. Part of his persona?

Kelly: Yes, he also didn't want to gather disciples around him. He was always very objective in his teaching and if someone showed a bit of interest in his own person, who he was and so on, it was generally a sign that the person wasn't going to be around that much longer. It was just a part of his desire that *he*, Merton, not be attracting them to the monastic life but rather that the novices find their own basic monastic identity.

Kilcourse: You were away for a good while in Rome. Those would have been what years?

Kelly: 1965 to 1968, just when Fr. Louis completed his last year as novice master. I had been his assistant during that last year. They, or rather the abbot, was willing to let Merton move to the hermitage full-time. And so it was time for the assistant to go also. I went to Rome to study. I'd just been ordained that summer.

Kilcourse: And you came back as novice master?

Kelly: I came back in the late summer of 1968, and then in April 1969 I was made novice master. I was novice master until 1973.

Kilcourse: So you saw him only briefly when you came back before he left for Asia?

Kelly: Very briefly. At the time I was teaching moral theology having just returned from Rome. We were doing studies on justice and peace. Completely unwittingly, the night before he left for Asia (I knew nothing about his trip), I met him going in the library, and I asked him, "Hey, we're just dealing with peace issues in class and you're one of the most vociferous of the peace people around, why don't you come to class tomorrow?"

Now, in retrospect at least, I can see this anxious look on his face, but I didn't really read it at all. He just said, "Oh, there's not much you couldn't say about peace that I could say," and gave a rundown of the basic principles of the peace and justice questions. And he said, "I'm sure you can do a more than adequate job and it'd be kind of hard for me to fit it into my schedule at this point," or something, and he went off. The next morning he left for Asia.

Kilcourse: So you didn't really have a chance to say good-bye?

Kelly: No, I didn't.

Kilcourse: You wrote an essay about Merton in the *Canadian Catholic Review.*[1] As I recall, there was a wonderful story about

1. Timothy Kelly, "My Brother Thomas: Merton at Gethsemani," *Canadian Catholic Review* 3 (Sept. 1985) 290–5.

Merton's humility in the wake of a visit by a Scripture scholar. Is that the story that you tell?

Kelly: Yes. Barnabas Ahern used to come to the community—oh, once a month or whenever he could come—and give these wonderful scriptural conferences which were introducing us to modern scriptural exegesis. For Barnabas Ahern to stand up in the midst of this community and talk about whether the magi were historical figures or not was quite admirable in 1963–64. But with his own giftedness as a teacher and truly holy man that he was, he was quite able to pull it off.

In those conferences, at one time or another, he talked about Jonah as midrash. I'm quite sure most of us didn't understand what the term really meant. The next Sunday, Merton was giving the novices and juniors a conference based on the Scripture reading for the night office; we were reading the book of Jonah at the time. He waxed very eloquently in a poetic way about Jonah, who was a very special person in his own life. It is in *The Sign of Jonas* (1953) in "The Firewatch" he talks about Jonah and the mercy upon mercy that is our gift.

One novice kept raising his hand, and finally, he acknowledged him. He said, "Fr. Barnabas said Jonah's nothing but midrash." And with that, Merton closed his books, and he walked out and for a year or so never gave another Scripture conference. He said something to the effect that modern biblical scholars are ruining the culture of Christianity. I wouldn't say that's an exact quote, but it is something along that line.

Kilcourse: He took umbrage.

Kelly: He took a very grave umbrage.

Kilcourse: That's a wonderful story, though.

Kelly: Never made anything out of it, never condemned Barnabas Ahern or anything, but just was upset.

Kilcourse: Barnabas Ahern and he had corresponded, hadn't they?

Kelly: Oh, yes, in fact, when Barnabas came for conferences, he would also spend some time with Fr. Louis. I think Ahern helped Dom James understand Merton. Certainly Merton would be the last person who would negate scholarship.

Kilcourse: Barnabas did help him, I recall, in his own struggles about his monastic identity.

Kelly: He did.

Kilcourse: It's an interesting twist, though. . . . One of Merton's responsibilities was assigning work for the novices. He also combined that with his responsibilities as chief forester here. He did a lot of work in the woods?

Kelly: Yes, he used to go out and plant trees and thin trees, and it was always an enjoyable time just being out of the tight enclosure and seeing the big, wide world. A lot of the trees out around what we call Dom Frederic's lake, one of our reservoirs, would be trees planted by Thomas Merton.

Kilcourse: I've heard that he nearly decapitated one of the novices once when he was driving the Jeep.

Kelly: That was before my time. He was not a very mechanical person, not at all. That's why none of us who knew him had any trouble believing the story that he was electrocuted by a fan. We wouldn't expect anything else to happen. He just wasn't mechanical, and so the stories are innumerable about his close misses, by himself or with novices.

Kilcourse: And machinery?

Kelly: And machinery! There are various myths about brothers having tried to teach him how to drive.

Kilcourse: We talked a little bit earlier about Merton being impatient with people who were preoccupied with his notoriety or celebrity in the monastery. He didn't have much patience for that. But he did have prominent visitors and friends. Did they interact with the community?

Kelly: If they could fit in with what we were about, he was always very generous with getting them to give conferences to the novices or to the wider community, if it seemed proper. Also, I can remember when I was undermaster, being aware of these very famous guests here to see him, and he'd be visiting with them. But when time came for him to see a brother for spiritual direction, he would leave and go to see him. He was always very conscious of his service to the community. He didn't use his notoriety as an escape from the day-to-day life of the monastery.

Kilcourse: He combined the temperament of an artist with an enormous capacity for self-discipline. I always think of the hermitage years as being the culmination of that.

Kelly: He was even more disciplined in the community. In those days the schedule was cut up into little sections, and he always was very disciplined and used every moment. He tried to inculcate this discipline into the life of novices. He encouraged us to know what we were going to do, what we were reading, what we were working with when the schedule gave us time; not to waste time, but to start immediately.

He was an excellent example of this. When it was time for reading, he would begin reading and read very assiduously, and when it was time to do something else, he did that very assiduously, too. He would even say that in the old schedule, in the very truncated, cut-up schedule, he actually thought he got more work done than he did in the great empty periods in the hermitage, which I don't think is quite accurate. Even at the hermitage he was always a very disciplined worker.

Kilcourse: How would you characterize Merton's personality, his approach to life as you experienced him?

Kelly: Always really alive! I wouldn't want to say exuberant, that would be too strong, but always "up." You really never experienced him as being down about something or negative. Always very positive, always very present to life, very present to the moment. Always seeing the humor of the present moment and also the pathos of it, and always very, very conscious and very alive to the place, to what he's doing and so on.

He was a scholar and a poet by temperament, yet one never really ran into him when he was preoccupied by other things. He was always really present. If you were speaking with him, he was very present to you. If he was doing something else, that's what he did. For example, because we eat in silence at some meals, brothers would bring a book to read at the meal. Fr. Louis would say, "Don't do that. When you eat, eat, and be present to what you're eating. Enjoy it, be aware of what you are eating. When finished eating, go do the reading."

Kilcourse: That is really a great contemplative streak.

Kelly: Yes, very Zen.

Kilcourse: John Eudes Bamberger commented once in publication about Merton's rare, but poignant references to his own woundedness as a young person,[2] which in many ways was a catalyst for his experience of God's mercy and his own vocation flourishing.

---

2. John Eudes Bamberger, "Wrestling With God," *Commonweal* 111 (Oct. 19, 1984) 555–7.

Kelly: Yes. I don't recall his speaking that much about his own life. Fr. Eudes was a little before my time. One thing you'd say, Merton was always growing. That would be one of his weaknesses, even as a novice master. He didn't repeat himself. He was always having new visions or new ways of seeing things.

The only incident that comes to mind is one Christmas time, on the feast of Thomas à Becket, when he read us great pieces of Eliot's drama *Murder in the Cathedral*. I can remember him getting very choked up with emotion and in fact, ending the conference at that point where Becket speaks about the greatest treason is to do the right thing for the wrong reason. He did a little speech on that, and he basically broke down, saying that this is one of the great dangers in life, one of the great trials in life.

That would be about the only time I really recall much personal show of emotion. He would often refer in a very general way to the fact that we all have things to do penance for, reasons why we struggle with life now because we made such a mess of it earlier or something like that. It wasn't a recurring theme, or at least I didn't pick it up as a recurring theme.

Kilcourse: I've heard divergent opinions from monks here in the monastery about their assessments of the hermitage years, 1965–1968. Some emulate him for his eremetical life. Others describe the experience as a failure. What do you say?

Kelly: Well, having been absent during those years, I guess I'm free!

Kilcourse: You've been exonerated?

Kelly: I've been exonerated from commenting on it! I think he himself would be slow to describe his own life as "hermit life" and would see it more as a life apart and a life used more for intellectual pursuit or scholarly pursuit. I would say I had heard him say that, but I realize there are a number of his fans who would not agree with my comment at that point. I would say again his great honesty would make him say something like that because he certainly did use the time to do a lot of very good work in his own pursuits but at the same time, for the most part, lived a very rigorous life or a very disciplined life. So it was an interesting mixture of a life that had both a very real spiritual quest as part of it, and also this very intellectual interest. It was a great time of transition in his own life, a great time of transition in the Church, so he couldn't help but be aware of a lot of the questions that were coming.

I remember I was in Rome at the time, and in many ways I would say we were friendly, but I had never really written to him or sought his direction. I was somewhat under a cloud in Rome, and Abbot James and I had had some disagreements, so I wrote to Merton about my concerns. A lot of my concern was that they were doing a lot of renovating at the monastery and I felt they weren't asking the community enough. They weren't being aware enough of some of the traditions of simplicity in the order and so on. And so, I presented him my concerns wondering if I had a place at Gethsemani. He responded that he hadn't entered into the real questions involved at the monastery because he felt like his own life was then beside the community, so he wasn't really aware of the dynamics or whatever that were involved.

But then he brought me to task and said, "But, you know, you're doing the same thing as these people you are accusing. You are saying they don't have the answers and you do, and they are saying you don't have the answers and they do." He said, "The one thing I've learned in my twenty-five years of monastic life is that one has to compromise." He continued, "I realize it is a very bad word for some in a spiritual discipline, but it is a reality that is also gospel." And with that, I felt chastened.

Kilcourse: He was still being novice master.

Kelly: He was still being very much novice master.

Kilcourse: If you were to pick out a single memorable experience of Merton in the community that epitomizes his life as a monk of Gethsemani, what would it be?

Kelly: Well, the story that comes to my mind that epitomizes Merton as I would have known him isn't about a "living Merton" but is a story of a small incident at the time of his death. The day his death was announced to our community, it was announced in the refectory at the main meal. In those days, we used to get our mail put at our place in the refectory. There was an old monk; Fr. Alphonse was his name at that time. He had changed his name; it used to be Idesbald. He was Belgian by birth and had come to this country in 1917 or so, right after the First World War, and never really learned English. He was only in the country for about a year when he joined the community here. So as an old man, he really didn't have a language. He'd forgotten his Flemish, if anyone could speak Flemish here, and he never really did learn English, and he didn't know that much French. He was a person who had certainly a lot of frustration in his life. I guess nowadays you'd put it in terms of anger. But a real character in the community. Always a bit marginal, but just a "character." It is the only word I can use, a good person but someone to whom you didn't pay that much attention.

So the day Merton died, it was announced in the refectory. Fr. Alphonse comes up to me with a postcard in his hand trying to understand it. He said, "You know, they said he died, but I just got this postcard from Fr. Louis." And I thought, "Wow!" It was true. He had a postcard sent from Thailand just saying, "Hi, how are you? I hope it was not too much work with cheese and fruitcake this year, and I'm going to be with the monks in Hong Kong for Christmas," and ended up by saying, "Behave yourself now," or something like that. Here is Merton over meeting the Dalai Lama and doing all these things he wanted to do, and he sent this postcard to this old man. I was in Rome for three years and I never sent Alphonse a postcard. And so I always think that was the true Merton. Very much aware of people in the community and especially the marginal people, and very willing to acknowledge their presence in just a simple show of friendship.

Kilcourse: That's really stunning, that on the day of his death that would be made manifest.

Kelly: Yes, and to this particular person.

Kilcourse: Beautiful.

Kelly: And I would say a lot of the brothers would say that. They all had a type of personal relation with him. When he had the occasion, he would be present to them as he was, as they were. He would always meet them where they were, he wasn't a person of any pretense.

Kilcourse: Let's talk a little bit about Cistercian life, contemporary Cistercian life and Merton's impact on that. John Griffin once said that Merton restored intellect to the Cistercians.

Kelly: In a sense, he certainly advocated a more serious reading, a serious study. There always was a lot of fatigue in the life. Part of it, I think, because of the way the schedule was broken up into just pieces, and part of it, too, the diet was not all that good. So there was a lot of fatigue.

There was an inclination to read pious literature that wouldn't be all that demanding. But he advocated very much reading of the Fathers and going to the sources of the Cistercian spirituality and spirituality in general. He didn't really fly a banner or something like that, but just by persistence and urging, encouraged us to do more serious work.

I would say yes, he did change a perspective or point of view in the ways of Gethsemani's life. Serious study of our tradition wasn't that common in this country; it was being done in Europe at the time. So, yes. I would say he had an influence on it.

Kilcourse: He also challenged the monastery to help monks cultivate their contemplative lives.

Kelly: He did, he was always a vociferous critic of the industrialization of Gethsemani and always opposed machines and becoming more and more industrialized. He thought we were losing our connection to the earth. And this was typical of the contradictions in Merton. I remember when he had to go to the doctor or something in the days when I was his assistant, he'd say, "Now, I gotta go to the doctor today. You get the Caterpillar up to the hermitage and clean up around there." And I'd say, "Yeah, but that's a machine." "Well, I'm not going to be there. It's okay." And so, we always teased him about this contradiction.

Kilcourse: We never forget that Merton's own teacher Dan Walsh was an important source for teachings and insights here, too.

Kelly: Yes, in the early 1960s he came and lived here in the monastery for the most part. He and Merton got together on a regular basis and discussed philosophy. I think he, Dan, was a good catalyst who pushed Merton on or helped him become aware or showed him paths of awareness that were going on in the larger intellectual world at the time. At the same time, Dan taught some of us philosophy and generally was available to the other brothers. He taught some philosophical courses to the community, not making great demands on them, but just introducing them to the ways of philosophy and Dan's own particular brand of philosophy and Duns Scotus.

Kilcourse: Merton never really traveled a great deal. I know he went to Collegeville back in 1956, but he never really traveled to the other monasteries. Yet is it fair to say that his influence would be felt in formation programs, certainly in Cistercian circles as well as others?

Kelly: I would say yes, but that's not something I've studied. I think there was an influence just because he wrote so much. On a couple of occasions, they had meetings here of novice masters and abbots, and he was always a part of those meetings in some sense or other and was always very generous whenever people would write him from one of the other communities to respond very fully. Certainly, I would say he did influence them to some extent. There was a great admiration of him.

Kilcourse: The abbey here at Gethsemani has exercised a considerable impact on Cistercian life when monks from this house have been selected as abbots at the other monasteries. Merton taught and helped in the formation of many of these who are now abbots, yourself included. How would you assess his influence in this regard?

Kelly: I'd say it's obvious in some sense that the people whom he trained would have a respect for the intellectual side of the spiritual journey, would have a respect for persons. That would be what in many ways I think epitomizes Merton's formation: that he always respected the person and wanted the person to find the roots of his monastic vocation within his spiritual life and not be just modeling principles from other people.

I suppose also his willingness to look at the whole breadth of other spiritual disciplines, the whole culture, the traditional culture. These would be elements that were always part of his teaching. So those of us who were trained by him would not feel these were alien or would not feel these other influences as detrimental to the spiritual development. I think there's been a positive influence. I would say that when I first came to Gethsemani, what we picked up as a spirituality would have had a very strong emphasis on doing a lot of *things,* pious acts, extra penance, obviously fulfilling the obligations. It was just *doing* a lot. He would not encourage this, although he was always very disciplined and always very respectful of the structures. Rather, he would speak of it in other terms. He would remind us that we weren't just doing such things because they were penitential or doing these things because they curbed our self-will or something. He would speak of it more in terms of freedom. You did these things in order to become free from those other elements in your life that held you back or that confused you, or whatever it is. He subtly put a different emphasis on a lot of monastic practices, which made them much more realizable, or much more positive than just something done as an exercise. They were really for growth and for knowing yourself.

Kilcourse: And so now we have new abbots who are spiritual masters in this tradition.

Kelly: Well, I don't think we've reflected on it that way, but I guess you can claim that.

Kilcourse: One of Merton's more effective reforms was, at least I've heard, the arrangement of the monastic schedule here.

Kelly: He certainly advocated it, but really it was Fr. Flavian [Burns] who changed it. Fr. Flavian was very much a student of Fr. Louis and was trying to create these blocks of open time for us to spend some serious efforts in study and prayer. So yes, that would be something that Fr. Louis would have advocated and something that did come about.

Kilcourse: Just to broaden our horizon for a moment to the International Cistercians, is there any way to gauge the influence of Merton beyond these shores?

Kelly: Not really, except that you do find that at General Chapters Meetings of abbots in the order there are always people who ask you about him, always people who are aware of him and know something about some of his works. So obviously he has been read or has influence in some way.

Kilcourse: Did Merton ever evidence what you would think in retrospect to be some blind spots about some of the directions of monastic renewal that he was talking about?

Kelly: I would say that he and Jean LeClercq (the Benedictine from Luxembourg) both would be very enthusiastic about a lot of experiments, and especially if they had an eremitical bent; but such experiments proved in the long run not to work. I would say that perhaps I could understand their enthusiasm in the sense of trying to create, trying to find those new ways to give expression of the monastic life. Perhaps a bit more discretion might have been helpful. I say this obviously influenced by my present service as an administrator.

Kilcourse: I was going to ask you: I've heard that discretion is supposed to be the great virtue of abbots.

Kelly: Obviously we think it is!

Kilcourse: We'll read between the lines on that! Let's move on to the community at Gethsemani. Now in two years it will be forty years since you entered the monastery. You belong in some ways to that bridge generation. As you say, you were there in the last wave of the big days. What would be the three most significant changes since the time you entered?

Kelly: Liturgically, the language of the liturgy. We entered in an all-Latin liturgy, and the discipline of prayer in that context is much different from the vernacular. I suppose also just the ethos of the community, we always talked about monasticism as enclosure and separation, which has an unconscious tendency to create a sort of dualistic world, a "we" against "they," and I don't want to say the "saved" against the "unsaved," but there's that underlying little temptation there. I think that is altered considerably, and I think Fr. Louis' influence helped alter it. And to be really mundane, the diet. While still vegetarian more or less, it's a bit more free, a bit more ample. They are not weighing your two ounces of bread for breakfast anymore.

Kilcourse: Like our old Lent.

Kelly: Oh, yes, we were just old Lent 365 days of the year!

Kilcourse: I remember Dan Walsh once talking about him and Merton disagreeing about the house and the gift shop here. Merton said people should only come out to pray, and Dan said, "Well what if they buy cheese and fruitcake and books and pray too?"

Kelly: That is still a cause of controversy in the monastery. There's always the group who feel a store would be an added attraction to the monastery. Again, we could make available the products we produce and also decent religious literature.

Some of the brothers who work at the "gate" say that a store is a constant request. People do come to places like this and want to buy something. So the brothers do get tired about hearing the same recurring question about why we do not sell our goods here. Obviously, we haven't a store yet, so you know which side I'm on.

Kilcourse: Another dimension of the abbey's life is the change about the guest house. There are no longer structured retreats at the guest house, and I think of the decision to allow women.

Kelly: Part of the change really came in the immediate post-Vatican II regime. Retreats did change a lot and moved to more family-oriented or husband-and-wife-oriented, and our facility just wasn't available to do it. At the same time, Fr. Flavian became abbot and was very strong on the contemplative dimension of the life and said that a monastic guest house should really just *be* and not be a retreat center, but rather offer the possibility for people to share in some sense the contemplative dimension of the life. So I think those two things working together somewhat changed, you might say, the approach.

Guests at the monastery have always been a reality. Our retreat house, in particular, goes back to the early part of the century. Abbot [Edmund] Obrecht [(+1935) who preceded Dom Frederic Dunne] really got involved with the local Knights of Columbus and organized it by parish-by-parish retreats. It was a real help for the monastery. In its most simple way, it helped just becoming somewhat known and also being a part of the local church. I think it was a very good thing that it did happen. Vatican II changes altered that somewhat, and our retreat movement did take more of the form of just being available for a more quiet type of retreat. With the renovation of the facility, since we did ask for contributions from benefactors to help us and since the question was often asked if women would be able to use the facilities, it seemed that justice demanded it. So we did it.

Our experience alternating men and women on an every other week basis has been very positive. The persons who come on retreat are here very seriously and do spend their time well sharing in the liturgy as far as they are able using the time and facility. It's booked up far in advance, and again we're grateful. It's a good example for us; to see people take time from very busy lives to come apart to a monastery is an encouragement to the monks. It helps us realize the gift we have. It helps us to enter into it more seriously.

Kilcourse: Let's talk about your two predecessors—Dom Flavian and Dom James. Two very different persons. In one of the earlier interviews that was done for *The Merton Annual*,[3] one monk described Dom James as "authoritarian, holy, and shrewd." You can recognize who probably said that. Dom James' relationship with Merton was complex to be sure. Could you comment first about your experience of

---

3. Matthew Kelty, "Looking Back to Merton: Memories and Impressions: An Interview," *The Merton Annual* 1 (1988) 55–76.

Dom James and the role that he played here—Harvard Business School, former Passionist?

Kelly: I think the three words sum up Dom James very well. He was complex, yet he had a very, seemingly simple, spiritual life. The passion was very much essential to his own understanding of life. And so, he understood monastic life very much as a way of sharing in the burdens that Jesus carried and sharing in his redemptive act. So the more burdens the monks carried, the more they would share in this redemptive reality for the sake of the world and the more they would be transfigured into the image of Jesus. And he preached that in season and out of season, with a little statement which added a balance, you might say. He used to always talk about doing things, "All for Jesus through Mary with a smile," which was a bit much! But the smile part of it, as corny as it sounds, was important because life here was pretty harsh. Adding that element of brightness to it, I think, and making it part of the on-going spiritual asceticism was a value or had a place. Some of his natural wisdom.

He took over the community, I think, historically at a time when they really didn't have any money. Not that Dom Frederic [Dunne] had been a bad administrator, but they'd done a couple foundations and the community really was just a subsistence farming community until the late 1940s or early 1950s. The influx of all these vocations demanded that they had to change their ways, and so the Harvard Business School man was probably very much the proper person for the time. He organized the work, which became more productive, and he was a good investor and that certainly helped the community in many ways.

In relation to Merton, I don't know. He just didn't have his perception of life, his education. He had an entirely different vision than Merton, yet he had a respect for him. I think Dom James was always torn between some sense of the ideals of a monastic life as he knew it, and some of the things where Merton was always pushing the edges. So, I think in that way it was often difficult for him to discern what to do with Merton.

He took a very hard line relative to his going out or his being available. At the time, I would certainly say he took a hard line. Looking back, he may have had an insight that was helpful because he certainly did keep Merton productive. One could imagine Merton dissipating his energy and just doing lots of things not too well, whereas keeping him in somewhat of a direction and working in areas of spiritual formation I think, was helpful.

For years, Merton went to see him regularly. Merton was James' confessor. Merton himself had an ambivalence; certainly he had a certain respect for James. He would never allow novices to criticize the abbot. I was corrected on that on various occasions, but not in a blind way or anything, but just demanding a true respect. It was good. It was an interesting relationship. I would say that in all my time with Merton as novice master, I was never really aware of his struggles as we read of them in his books. He never really left James' office and came over and gave vent to his anger to me or any of the other novices. He certainly didn't do any of that, and I was surprised to recognize that here I was dealing with him at the same time that he was really having some traumatic experiences. But again, that was Merton. He was a very private person. I think there was a mutual respect between Dom James and Merton, also a mutual suspicion. But I think it produced a life for both of them. I think Merton really influenced James in a very real sense, too.

Kilcourse: So the symbolism isn't lost that they are buried next to one another in the cemetery?

Kelly: No, it's a study!

Kilcourse: Dom Flavian?

Kelly: He obviously was much more in Fr. Merton's intellectual understanding of things and was a real "disciple." Certainly he admired everything that Merton did and wrote, always the earlier material. Flavian has trouble with the later Merton, I think.

Kilcourse: Did you want to say something about that?

Kelly: His social materials—he said Merton just did that for friends' sake. I would disagree with him completely. I think Merton was always evolving, always moving and coming to his perceptions of social issues. I believe this was a very deep part of his own monastic vocation as I understand his vocation. I would suspect that Merton's death rites, within the first year of Fr. Flavian's time as abbot, was a real difficulty for Fr. Flavian. He did see Merton as someone who would help him to perceive how monastic life can develop at this time.

Kilcourse: Well, in a matter of weeks, you're going to have the twenty-third anniversary of your election as abbot.

Kelly: I was at a conference the other day at St. Meinrad, and this young monk got up who mentioned that he was twenty-five years old, and a monk sitting beside me said, "Just think, he was two years old when you became abbot!"

Kilcourse: A senior statesman!

Kelly: That sounds terrible!

Kilcourse: Peaks, valleys? Anything that you're particularly grateful for in those twenty-three years, or anything that still troubles you as a challenge?

Kelly: I'm grateful to have gotten through them. I can't say that I started out with some great project that I wanted to do. I'm grateful for the brethren and how much they always actually do want to live a very serious monastic life, so that in many ways it makes it simple enough to be abbot. There's always a concern of how do you continue to call people and more, yourself, to a more profound spiritual journey. And what are the images one uses, what are the ways to evoke that depth of living, a depth of reality where one does share in the passion of the Lord Jesus. I suppose that's probably one of the on-going burdens, how to find the vocabulary, how to have the vision to continue and to be called and to call others to live that life.

Kilcourse: I pulled a couple of things here. I wanted to read at least this one passage to you. Merton refers to you and your ordination in *A Vow of Conversation.*

Kelly: I don't remember it very well.

Kilcourse: There are two related references just to jog your memory a little bit. The first is a letter written in August 1967 to you and Brother Patrick Hart in Rome. You never got the letter because he writes back a couple weeks later to Patrick, "I forgot Fr. Timothy wasn't there." He ends the letter by talking about the church and the renovations here, and then he says, "I'm not crazy about the altar which is either Aztec or juridical. I'm not sure which but anyway, it's designed for bloody and possibly human sacrifice. All joking aside, I think there's absolutely only one hope for Gethsemani, for those of us who have some brains to hang together (hang is a badly chosen word, it might be all too true) and trying to salvage what we all came here for by hook or by crook and to keep things going. The most Dom James can and ever will do will be to hold things together as they are and implicitly prevent any real change."[4]

But then he talks about the election at the end of 1967 and here's where he mentions you. "Flavian is the only candidate likely to get it." He's writing to Fr. Felix in Rome. "Flavian's the only candidate likely to get it who has a mind of his own and won't be dominated by someone else, certainly not by Dom James. Flavian's year as hermit has done him a great deal of good. He's intent on the right things." And he goes on, "And I still think Tim has no chance, but none, this round. His turn comes next."[5] I must find this next passage. He says wonderful things about you. Do you remember that?

Kelly: No, I don't. Find it, please!

Kilcourse: "Tomorrow Frs. Timothy and Barnabas are to be ordained priests." (This is June 11, 1965.) "I shall concelebrate with Fr. Timothy on Trinity Sunday. He has been the most competent and reliable of all my undermasters in the novitiate. Already Fr. Abbot is speaking of sending him to Rome this year and getting him ready quickly for the Norway Foundation."[6] I wanted you to at least hear those good words again.

Anything in particular that Merton taught you that proved especially valuable to you as abbot later?

Kelly: I would say the respect for persons, to encourage others— I always use the "true self" and that type of vocabulary which was an underlying theme in all his teachings—to help a person come to know really what it is that he wants to do with his life, how it is that he best can live the gospel. Merton was always encouraging novices to come really to that understanding rather than accepting a form of life because it supposedly is perfect and supposedly is very good. No, no! Finding what it is, where you can use your talents or you can be yourself most honestly is the essential. To some degree, I've endeavored to do that or hoped to do that as abbot. I've tried to have the monks and

4. August 23, 1967, to Father Timothy Kelly and Brother Patrick Hart, *The School of Charity* (New York: Farrar, Straus & Giroux, 1990) 343–4.

5. December 28, 1967, to Father Felix Donahue, *The School of Charity*, 359.

6. June 11, 1965, *A Vow of Conversation: Journals, 1964–65* (New York: Farrar, Straus & Giroux, 1988) 189.

those who come to join us to come to see whether this is really the best way they can serve the Lord and helping them to discover how they can do that in this context.

That that would be something I would attribute to his influence because I think as a younger person I was rigid and much more rigorous in my ideas of what should be and shouldn't be. I would have been more inclined to support a narrow, institutional response to most questions. I would say Merton added an element of breadth, the seeds of trying to broaden my scope of perception.

Kilcourse: Having listened to many of his tapes, I recall Merton occasionally mentioned a particular person who decided to leave the community. His attitude was reflected in what he would say to the novices: "Well, so-and-so's left, but, you know, we hope things go well. Let's just be really grateful for the time that they were here."

Kelly: Yes, he was always very supportive and encouraged people to find their way. We were talking about the spirituality earlier, and I'm reminded that there was here, very much, the axiom that you were saved while you were here, but if you got off Noah's Ark, the devil's right at the front door there waiting to attack you as soon as you walk out the door. Merton did not agree with that at all.

Kilcourse: Let's turn to the future of monasticism. I'm curious about your sense of experiments of monastic life in the twenty-first century. You've got Dom Bernardo as the Abbot General, that's significant, isn't it?

Kelly: Certainly. He's from Argentina, which creates a whole new perception of the order and its roots in the whole culture of North Europe. To have someone from Argentina, very much Argentinean, as Abbot General should alter the perception.

I would suspect that our relation to the Church, to the wider Church, is something that will possibly be more visible. We've always claimed our exemption from the bishop, which I hope we keep, but our awareness of the oneness of the Christian community will be greater. And all of us, each of us lives the vocation in a little different perspective.

I think I would say the present use of our guest house is a good example of the inner penetration and the seriousness of living a Christian life. We find support from that community, and the community hopefully gives the retreatants some sense of support. I suspect that monastic life will be made more conscious, or our type of monastic life will be more conscious of awareness.

Kilcourse: Two years from now will mark the one hundred fiftieth anniversary of the Gethsemani community. What are the community's plans for that?

Kelly: We're not able to create much excitement quite yet.

Kilcourse: None of the originals are still around?

Kelly: None of the originals are around! We are doing a book, a history of the one hundred fifty years. We discussed in the community whether to do a video or a book. I had contacted a very fine crew from Canada which I thought could do a very good historical video. What the abbot really wants, if he really directly pushes for it, he very rarely gets. I don't know if it was because they were Canadian or whether the community really just didn't feel video would be the best presentation. We are having this book researched and written as a tribute to the one hundred fifty years.

Kilcourse: I understand the author is a person who has a great feel for the monastic life, Dianne Aprile.

Kelly: Yes, Dianne Aprile.

Kilcourse: She's already done some wonderful writing about the monastery.

Kelly: She has. She's been working in our archives now and interviewed some of the monks and will visit the foundations and Melleray, our founding house. I think Fr. Clyde Crews is going to help her with the history, to flesh out or respond to some of her concerns.

It's something for the sake of the whole U.S. Church because, as you mentioned, we're the oldest abbey. By some strange quirk we became an abbey rather quickly, although some of the Benedictine foundations are older than we are. All those foundations began in the 1840s or thereabouts. We were founded in 1848. Some of the others are a bit older than we are, but they didn't become an abbey right away, so that's one of these little . . .

Kilcourse: That's your claim.

Kelly: Yes. We're also a minor basilica, you know. Fr. Matthew pushes for acknowledging that a bit more. I'm not one for pushing for the "great cope."

Kilcourse: Two or three years ago, we had a group of Bellarmine students here. You received them and spoke briefly with them and gave a very good orientation. One of the things I remember you saying, and I hope I'm quoting you right here, you commented that monks were "weaker" than people in the world and needed the structure and support of the monastery. Can you elaborate on that?

Kelly: I would repeat the statement again. I think we choose or we find this the way that is most congenial to who we are or how we can live the gospel. And often it is precisely because we're too dispersed in our intellectual abilities or just not disciplined enough maybe to live in a social milieu that gives constant choices to make. So we choose to take a life that has a structure in it, that gives us a direction, that frees us from a lot of other type of decisions. I think it's also maybe part of our weakness which we bear in recognizing that the monastery is the way for us. And in saying that, I'm trying to demythologize a bit; monks aren't better people or extraordinary or anything like this. We really are people who need more structure than a lot of other Christians to be faithful.

Kilcourse: Eugene Laverdiere, the biblical scholar, when I met him here five years ago, was telling me that his perception was that monks have two senses of time. They think on one hand in terms of centuries, and then they think of today's schedule. Next week doesn't mean anything to a monk.

Kelly: That's very true. Time's a funny thing around here.

Kilcourse: That's why the bells ring and you know you have to be in choir.

Kelly: The days go rapidly but the years . . .

Kilcourse: What about the future of Merton's legacy? Maybe one place to start would be 1963 with the beginning of the archives, the Thomas Merton collection at Bellarmine. I was always amused by the story they tell about Dom James that he was persuaded that that was a good decision in part because the monks wouldn't have to fool with these scholars but especially because women would be coming. Is there any truth to that?

Kelly: That's probably a quote, a real quote, and I think it was a wise decision on James' part and on Merton's part because it freed us, and rightly so, of a lot of the decisions relative to publishing and making his works available. Because he is our brother and you're not always inclined to take your brother's things that seriously, we probably wouldn't have been the best judges on how to respect his legacy. Not only is it freeing us from a burden in that sense, but I think it also is giving the Thomas Merton Legacy Trust a better opportunity to have its effect in the wider society. So, a prudent decision. Pragmatically, a good decision, too.

Kilcourse: Would you like to say anything about the publication of Merton's journals?

Kelly: Yes, that's going to be certainly, as I understand it, the publication of everything. Every jot and tittle of his works should be finished with the publication of these journals and then the notebooks. Of course, someone may uncover a waste basket somewhere that hasn't been emptied or rifled! I think, too, that the new generation of Merton Legacy Trustees will have to work in some different direction. It won't just be getting everything in print, but it will be . . . I don't know quite what . . .

Kilcourse: They'll have to make decisions about, "Do we put it on CD-ROM?"

Kelly: That's true.

Kilcourse: Merton on the Internet! There's a new thought. . . .

Kelly: Surely, if he has any influence, he'll put static on it!

Kilcourse: Some people have the impression that the royalties from Merton's publications and paraphernalia support the monastery with an influx of dollars.

Kelly: I would say, not really. There is a steady flow. It has been constant over the last several years. For the most part, we use that type of income for charitable work. We aren't really dependent on the Merton legacy or the Merton Trust to finance the monastery in any way. I would suspect that it did help in the very early days when *The Seven Storey Mountain* came out. It was also a time of great influx into the community. There was a certain cash flow problem, and I think the royalties probably did help a lot. At this point in our history, we're grateful for it, and we try to administer it with a proper Christian perspective, but it's not essential to our survival.

Kilcourse: One of the more recent initiatives you've taken here was the Abbey Center for the Study of Ethics and Culture meetings in 1992, 1993, and another coming in the fall of 1996.

Kelly: That certainly was, I suppose, inspired in some ways from Merton, but really Fr. Francis [Kline], who is now abbot at Mepkin, is probably more the visionary in that particular perspective. It was trying to follow through Merton's thought, to find the place where monastic communities can be influenced by the serious thinking that's going on in the wider society. At the same time, those persons can become more aware of monastic life and monasticism as a place of finding wisdom. I think, due to the fact that Fr. Francis went to be abbot at Mepkin, the Center really hasn't progressed with any strong impetus. It continued to be in its original vision, but I think there is space for it someday to develop into a more living type of relationship with the community and the wider world of persons with a contemplative instinct.

Kilcourse: Two years ago the Dalai Lama visited. I think in many ways that this event illustrates Merton's influence because of his own profound engagement with interfaith issues. Would you describe your impressions or memory of that day the Dalai Lama visited?

Kelly: He was a very easy person to be with. Actually, we had met the day before. We'd had a luncheon at Berea College with their president and trustees. At that luncheon, they seated me beside the Dalai Lama, I guess so we could talk monastic stuff. It was interesting. Also interesting, I wore my habit, just to be noticed. And he right away picked it up and recognized me as being from Merton's monastery. He mentioned this recurring thing he says about Merton—that Thomas Merton taught him most about what Christianity was—which is an admirable statement from such a person.

He asked me structure-type questions about our monastic communities and compared them to his own experience of monastic life. He asked me, surprisingly, "Are your monks celibate?" I said, "Well, it's not really something I ask them each day!" But his real interest was the whole difficulty of young boys who may join a monastery as young boys and then discover that it isn't really their way of life. How we dispense them from vows was what the question really concerned. And so we talked about that, and he talked about how, yes, that they often had to let the young men go out and become fathers, with the understanding that they would come back and take up their life again as old men. So it was an interesting interchange. And we talked about the Trinity (and I'm sure I fell into some heresy). What else did we talk about? Yes, and we talked about politics and his own situation in Tibet.

When he came here the next day, we had a simple ceremony, and he was very responsive to us. He asked that we pray at Merton's grave. After he got up from the grave, I don't remember the term he used, but he said, "I have now prayed [I guess it would be the prayers of the dead that they say in their own tradition] for Merton, and our spirits are one again!"

Kilcourse: We've had decades of trying to coordinate Merton activities, publications, and conferences. Now with the birth of the Thomas Merton Center Foundation, it seems to offer a lot of possibilities. Would you tell us more about that?

Kelly: Like yourself, I hope it will pull together a lot of divergent activities and perspectives and just sort of "unify," in the best sense of the word, our efforts.

Kilcourse: You've invested a lot of your own energy and influence in this.

Kelly: Yes, I've always wished I'd been more disciplined or more regular in my pushing in that area.

Kilcourse: In 1967 Merton did something very unusual. He granted an interview for *Motive* magazine.[7] It was very rare that he'd do that sort of thing, but he included the pungent reminder that he reserved the right to resist being turned into a myth for parochial school children. How do we keep from mythologizing Merton that way?

Kelly: That's the real danger; everybody's always trying to make him into some type of a myth. I wonder if his voluminous writing isn't part of his own effort to keep from becoming a myth, so that the Legacy Trust's willingness to publish everything is a good way to follow up Merton's own desire. Because, if you read it all, there's a lot for edification, but there's also a way that one recognizes a very human, in the best sense of the word, person. Perhaps that's the best service we could do for him, that his whole work be known.

7. Thomas P. McDonnell, "An Interview with Thomas Merton," *Motive* 27 (Oct. 1967) 32–41.

It's interesting how brutally honest he is in writing about his own life. I think in some sense it makes him a much more acceptable person or model because one can find in him a lot of one's own reality—I wouldn't say struggles, but his own difficulties, something to relate to and something to find hope for. If this man could hold together such divergent and disparate views and bring them together, bring them to some type of resolution, then we too are hopeful for spiritual integration.

Kilcourse: You get a wide array of visitors and Merton visitors here at the guest house. You get the kind of spiritually-wounded people who are searching and who come to pilgrimages to his grave. How does the community here deal with this phenomenon?

Kelly: I think, for the most part, unless you're involved in the guest retreat house, you really don't encounter them. So the community isn't that aware of how many people are coming and going who are interested in Merton. So it really hasn't infringed in that way on us.

Kilcourse: Some of us have written that the essence of Merton the monk still eludes the biographers and commentators. How do you see that dimension in Merton studies?

Kelly: It would take someone with a lot of ability and a lot of patience to go through many of the works he read as an early monk. Someone would need to find those passages that he indicated in some way and so do a lot of work within the sources that influenced his own thinking. I think that though he wrote so much, he himself was still a very private person. No one really knew him. That may be a bit too dramatic, but he was a very, very private person. The depth of his own spiritual journey or what really were the workings there, I don't think were ever explicated totally.

I think he was and we see him as a very modern person, but yet at the same time, he was very steeped in the classical culture. The classical Latin church culture was something he always held very dear. A lot of Vatican II's changes were difficult for him, or he made light of them. So, I think there was in him this very profoundly classical Christian who held dearly to very traditional values in Church life, in Church expression. He saw them as life-giving. Certainly, he was always trying to find new ways, too. And I think that's what we're very much aware of, his pushing the boundaries all the time, but we don't know where the anchor was. How to find that would be interesting. Who could?

Kilcourse: Well put, well put. I like that. What's the most important thing to remember about the Thomas Merton you knew?

Kelly: I suppose the great honesty always with himself and with others. Not honesty in the sense of being arrogant about it, or being demanding of the truth, or that he had the truth. But very honest about where he was or what he understood, what he believed. Yes, an honesty and directness. That would be what came to mind.

Editing the Journals of Thomas Merton

Patrick Hart, O.C.S.O.

When I was asked to write an article for *The Merton Annual* on editing the original Thomas Merton journals, I thought it would afford an opportunity to reflect on our approach to this long-range project. Thus far the first volume, *Run to the Mountain*, which I edited, was published in June 1995; in January 1996 the second volume, *Entering the Silence*, edited by Jonathan Montaldo, was published, and in June 1996 the third volume, *A Search for Solitude*, edited by Lawrence S. Cunningham, appeared. The fourth volume, *Turning Toward the World*, planned for January 1997, is being edited by Victor A. Kramer. HarperSanFrancisco has scheduled the seven volumes to appear at six-month intervals. So by the new millennium all seven volumes will be available.

Until a publisher was chosen by the Merton Trust, it was not possible to decide definitely on the editorial policy for the entire project. If a university press were chosen, there was a possibility of doing something closer to a facsimile edition of the journals. But with HarperSanFrancisco as the publisher, it became clear that a very readable series of Merton journals was wanted, much like Merton himself might have published, but without inclusion of deletions and additions and/or rewritings, often done by Merton to satisfy censors of the order. Our thought was to publish the journals just as Merton wrote them with minimal editing. Footnotes would be allowed only for essential explanations of persons or events not comprehensible to the reader. Foreign language phrases were translated and placed in brackets immediately following the text. As John Loudon at Harper explained at the outset, he did not want something resembling a German doctoral dissertation on the Scriptures, with more footnotes than text.

After my appointment as general editor in the spring of 1990 I began a search for all the extant Merton journals housed in the various archives around the country. The majority of these were located at the Thomas Merton Center of Bellarmine College in Louisville, Kentucky. I had become aware of a number of journals located at St. Bonaventure University Library, especially the pre-monastic journals Merton had given to his friend Mark Van Doren and some transcripts of journals he had given to another friend, Richard Fitzgerald. Columbia University in New York inherited the Sister Thérèse Lentfoehr's Merton collection, which is quite extensive.

The Merton Legacy Trust agreement, drawn up in 1967, the year before Merton's death, includes the indenture that the journals may be published "in whole or in part" at the discretion of the Trust, but not until after the official biography had been published and twenty-five years had elapsed since his death. The biography, *The Seven Mountains of Thomas Merton* by Michael Mott, was published in 1985, and December 10, 1993, marked the twenty-fifth anniversary of his death, so the journals could begin to appear anytime after that date.

During his lifetime Merton drew upon these journals, choosing excerpts for a number of his books, including *The Secular Journal, The Sign of Jonas,* and *Conjectures of a Guilty Bystander.* He edited heavily, omitted a great deal of material, and substituted fictitious names in the monastic journals to preserve the anonymity of monks in particular. After his death several books based on his journals appeared: *A Vow of Conversation, Woods, Shore and Desert, The Alaskan Journal,* and, finally, *The Asian Journal.*

As I explained in the introduction to *Run to the Mountain,* "There is no denying that Thomas Merton was an inveterate diarist. He clarified his ideas in writing especially by keeping a journal. Perhaps his best writing can be found in the journals, where he was expressing what was deepest in his heart with no thought of censorship."

Run to the Mountain

The first volume of the Merton journals covers the years from May 1939 through December 1941, the earliest journals discovered from his pre-monastic years. The first part, which has been called "The Perry Street Journal," begins with an entry dated May 2, 1939: "This is May. Who seen any birds?" I find it amusing that he should begin with an ungrammatical question, followed by reflections on Cicero and Augustine.

This early journal reflects the life of a young intellectual living at 35 Perry Street in the Village and teaching at Columbia University Extension. He had received his master's degree from Columbia in 1938 writing on "Nature and Art in William Blake"[1] and was contemplating a doctoral dissertation on the poetry of Gerard Manley Hopkins, but the latter never became a reality. We see here a twenty-four-year-old writer, clearly ambitious and eager to be published, offering his first novels to any number of publishing houses, only to be greeted with rejection slips. Some of the more compassionate publishers actually read the manuscripts and commented on them, encouraging Merton to continue writing.

As far as we know, after his reception into the Catholic Church in 1938, he must have destroyed his previous journals, as he mentions in the introduction to *The Secular Journal:*

> These are a few selections taken from a diary that I kept when I was a layman, a graduate student at Columbia, teaching in University Extension there, and later when I was an Instructor at St. Bonaventure University. This was written, like most diaries, informally, colloquially, and in haste. The whole diary filled two or three large manuscript volumes. Only one of these still exists, the others were thrown away or destroyed after I had typed out a few excerpts which are given here, along with parts of the surviving volume[s].[2]

Merton was mistaken in the above statement, since there were two holographic journals given to St. Bonaventure's University archives by Mark Van Doren to add to their collection of Thomas Merton's notebooks and art work. These two journals appear to be the first and third of what must have been three pre-monastic journals. The first begins on May 2, 1939, and ends February 13, 1940. The third journal, which has come to be known as the St. Bonaventure Journal, begins on October 19, 1940, and ends with an entry for December 5, 1941.

But what about the missing journal, from February 13, 1940, to October 10, 1940? When packing his bags at St. Bonaventure's in early

---

1. See Appendix I in *The Literary Essays of Thomas Merton,* ed. Patrick Hart (New York: New Directions, 1981) 385–453.
2. *The Secular Journal of Thomas Merton* (New York: Farrar, Straus & Cudahy, 1959) vi.

December 1941, preparing to enter Gethsemani, Merton was passing out manuscripts, poems, and drawings to friends; one of these, Richard Fitzgerald, a seminarian who had been on friendly terms with Merton, was given a treasure trove. Many years later Fitzgerald, having retired from the ministry, was living in Florida. He wrote to St. Bonaventure's asking if they might be interested in these unpublished Merton materials. Fr. Irenaeus Herscher, a Franciscan friar and librarian at St. Bonaventure's University, was delighted to receive the gift. And so are countless Merton scholars today.

Among the contents of the so-called "Fitzgerald File" at St. Bonaventure's was a transcription of parts of the missing journal. It included Merton's month in Cuba, which, together with the manuscript Merton had sent Catherine Doherty when he was about to enter Gethsemani, came to be known as "The Cuban Journal." There were other articles, for example, one on the lay apostolate recently published in *The Merton Annual 7*.[3] In this same file were discovered fragments of unpublished novels, such as *The Labyrinth* and the opening part of *The Man in the Sycamore Tree*. We can only conjecture here that Merton himself made the transcription of a part of, or the whole of, the missing holographic journal that was then apparently discarded.

One question still remained: Were these actually transcriptions of the missing journal, or did Merton work them over as he typed them up, hoping that at some future time he might incorporate them or transform them into a novel? Or were they fragments of one of his autobiographic novels on which he was working at the same time at the cottage? This was to be a pattern in his later writings, for the most part to please the censors of the order. This dilemma was finally solved with the assistance of Robert Lax. This journal was written at a time when Lax and Merton were very close friends, and during several summers when the friends had stayed at the cottage near Olean, New York, which belonged to Gladys and Benjamin Marcus, Bob Lax's sister and brother-in-law. I felt strongly that if anyone would be able to help discern the authenticity of these journals and their chronological sequence, it would be Lax.

For nearly twenty years, Lax had been living in self-imposed exile on the Greek island of Patmos. I wrote him asking if I might visit him in an effort to establish some order in these transcriptions of journals found at St. Bonaventure's, and he readily agreed. In the spring of

---

3. See *The Merton Annual 7* (Collegeville: The Liturgical Press, 1994) 1–13.

1992 I set off for Athens, and then embarked on the ten-hour-long ferry ride out to Patmos in the Aegean Sea.

After going through these transcriptions page by page, Lax and I agreed on the transcriptions that were made directly from the "raw" holographic journals and not reworked at a later date. The immediacy of the writing convinced us that the transcriptions were authentic and could be included in this pre-monastic journal. Several transcriptions were not included because they were obviously reworkings of already existing entries that we considered "raw" journal.

The third part, known as the "St. Bonaventure Journal," was written for the most part at St. Bonaventure's while Merton was teaching English and creative writing. Before leaving St. Bonaventure's for Gethsemani, Merton had given Mark Van Doren two bound volumes of journals, along with other materials for an anthology of poetry, and a few typewritten pages from a journal. In January 1944, Van Doren wrote to St. Bonaventure's asking if these journals might find a home there. They were indeed welcomed, and on January 15, 1944, the two journals that comprise this volume were transferred to St. Bonaventure's for safekeeping. It was only years later, when Michael Mott, the official Merton biographer, wrote of having discovered these journals and other Merton manuscripts in the library at Olean, New York, that I realized what a gold mine was to be found at St. Bonaventure's Library archive.

Toward the end of the journal there are references to the Baroness, who had given a talk to the friars and students at St. Bonaventure's on her lay apostolate with the poor at Friendship House in Harlem. As the journal brings out very well, Merton was torn between a possible vocation as a volunteer staff worker at Friendship House and a vocation to become a friar or monk. The matter was finally resolved as the journal closes and he departs from St. Bonaventure's for the Abbey of Gethsemani in the knob country of Kentucky, where he would spend the last twenty-seven years of his life.

A Postscript:
Four Merton Journal Transcriptions

During the International Thomas Merton Society meeting held at St. Bonaventure's University in June 1995, Dr. Paul Spaeth, the director of the library, discovered some transcriptions of Merton journals that were filed in a folder called "The Brown Journal." While doing my research at St. Bonaventure's in 1990 I was not aware that such transcriptions existed, apart from what was unearthed in "The Fitzgerald File." Four of these dated entries coincided with pages Merton had torn out of the journal he was keeping and presumably discarded. We are grateful to Dr. Spaeth for calling these omissions to our attention. After studying them carefully, it was decided to make these available to Merton readers as soon as possible. What follows are the four transcriptions, which we considered authentic "raw" journal entries. Fortunately, they have been included as an Appendix in the forthcoming paperback edition of *Run to the Mountain*.

(1) July 13, 1940; Olean

[1941 is the year given by Merton, but the text of the letter leads one to believe it was actually 1940, when he was spending the summer at the cottage that belonged to Bob Lax's sister and brother-in-law, Gladys and Benjamin Marcus.]

At noon I went out to sit in the bright sun and write, but the sun was too bright to sit and write in.

The paper says we will all be in the army by October 1st. Nobody has beaten any drums, and probably nobody would believe them if they did.

All I know is that the weather today was bright like the fall of the year: bright and cool. Last night, the night was cold, and a lot like a night in fall, with the sky very full of bright stars. You could have been led to imagine that the cars climbing the hill were on their way back from football games.

Now, very clear, from down in the valley, comes the sound of barking dogs.

I haven't read any of the books I brought up this hill a month and a half ago.

(2) July 23, 1941; St. Bonaventure

"Son, believe not thine own affection that now is, for it soon shall be changed into another. . . . But above all these things standeth the wise man and well taught in spirit, taking no heed what he feels in himself, nor on which side the wind of unstableness bloweth, but that all the intention of his mind may profit to the due and best end. For so he may abide, one and the same, unshaken, with the simple eye of intention directed to Me without ceasing, among so many diverse chances."

Imitation of Christ 3:38

This is the whole of ethics, from a psychological standpoint. It is the only thing anybody needs to surely know how to do, in order to be happy, and holy, which are exactly the same thing. It is saying in psychological terms, "Forsake everything, take up thy cross, and follow Me!" It is saying what the following of Christ means, in anybody's experience, and what forsake everything means: and it gives the reason why we have to forsake everything, psychologically.

No matter how we feel, subjectively, happy or sad, devout or not, healthy or sick, our feelings are unimportant, but our intentions are all that matter, if they are still directed only to God. And they are directed to Him when they drive us always to do good actions, to think good things, according to God's commandments and counsels.

This also is the basis of the *credo ut intelligam* [I believe so that I can understand] in philosophy. If philosophy is to be the search for truth, instead of mere curiosity, it must go out with this humility and this obedience to God: ignoring everything that merely pleases or flatters or amuses us, or merely defeats somebody we dislike. Unless we possess this humility and intense singleness of vision, we go to find truth somewhat like those Jews who "sometimes came into Bethany to Martha and Mary not for Jesus alone, but for they would see Lazarus."

(3) November 9, 1941

Baudelaire was never really comprehensible to me until I became a Catholic. He is not intelligible unless you are aware of what it is to love God, and what it is to consciously rebel against God, believing Him to exist to be rebelled against. When I lived in my mild, anarchic, Epicurean universe at the age of sixteen I could hardly see what Baudelaire was talking about. I thought I knew what he meant by *ennui*. If I had for one moment felt at that age the *ennui* of Baudelaire instead of the *ennui* of anybody who was ever sixteen, I would have died on the spot and crumbled into ashes.

I had the pleasure of finding out later something of what he was talking about, however: but I didn't understand what it was either until more recently still.

To understand the degradation he describes, you have to know at the same time the infinitesimally short distance between grace and sin, life and death, which is, at the same time, the immensely large, the infinite distance between heaven and hell.

There is a certain terrific incorruptibility about Baudelaire's writing and his clarity in hell that makes his writing about damnation almost holy in its honesty. He has a poem on the denial of St. Peter that kills me with sorrow and anguish and I can hardly read it, it is so terrible: and its terror is that it is the denial of St. Peter seen from the point of view of Judas, and *praised.*

—Ah Jésus, souviens toi du Jardin des Olives!
Dans ta simplicité tu priais à genoux
Celui qui dans son ciel riait au bruit des clous
Que d'ignobles bourreaux plantaient dans tes chairs vives.

[Ah Jesus, is that memory still fresh—
How in the Garden of Olives guilelessly you prayed
To Him who in his heaven, undismayed,
laughed at the sound of nails that pierced your flesh?]

It combines all the desolation of the "My God, My God, why hast thou forsaken Me!" with the terrible twist of meaning that this is how the cry sounded in hell: hell, which did not understand, believed that Christ's cry was hell's victory, and began to sympathize with Him triumphantly as if he actually were no more than a man, and a failure.

But it is that actual cry: the cry that shook heaven and earth and hell, and Baudelaire, in hell, heard it: which many of us, in grace, never bother to listen to!

Putting down Baudelaire I realized that the whole of Dante's *Inferno* is nothing but a schoolboy's fancy compared to what is described in the *Fleurs du Mal.* Dante fancies himself in a kind of hell, and described it according to the textbooks. And all the other writers who described the howling of the damned and their terrible torments have been silly compared to Baudelaire who saw that the most terrible thing about hell was the attractiveness of what is horrible, and not its unattractiveness!

In all evil, there is something holy perverted. The dialectic between the good that underlies evil and the evil into which this good is perverted is frightful. In every evil act of Baudelaire's life, God was present to remind him of exactly what he was doing, who he was crucifying. That is the greatness and the terror of the *Fleurs du Mal*, and it is proved by the fact that Baudelaire finally admitted it, and gave in to God [whom] he had killed all his life.

And anybody who can't see the intimate connection between Baudelaire's love of evil and his return to the love of God, had best leave him strictly alone. What terror is in that book! God, save me!

To fear to lose God is the worst of all fears—it is [at] the same time the most salutary and the silliest. We can only lose Him by our own stupidity and ill will. To know how great is our own stupidity and weakness is to have everything in the world to fear, but to know the strength of God's grace is to have nothing in the world to fear. As long as we live, we remain balanced between fearlessness and terror.

(4) November 17, 1941

It was a nice sunny day, to be a pilgrim and an exile. I went into town and deposited my monthly paycheck in the bank: which did nothing whatever to make me happy. For, in spite of the sun, there is no real peace in this place, only inertia, and inertia is never the same as peace: peace is a kind of active order and harmony. It is vital, and not inert.

Everything here seems totally neutral. Not unhappy people, who are not happy either, stand in the sun and talk about absolutely nothing; and time passes. Sun shines in the windows of the stores, upon the big gaudy showcards, upon the grins of the hefty, moronic blonde queens (always the same empty grins, everywhere, as if it were a blasphemy not to be grinning all the time) as they point their cardboard hands at the refrigerators and the electric ranges, or salute (and grin falsely, still) as if to say: "We are ready, Uncle Sammy, with our bottles of ketchup, our cheap toothbrushes, our ersatz good humor and cheap products, to support anything so long as we only have to make faces and never have to think, as long as we live."

It flashed into my mind a comparison between the inertia here, which is spiritual, and the inertia of any small town in Europe, which might be economic. But economic inertia is no inertia at all compared to this, which is really deadly. And even though there is no end of spiritual inertia in Europe (especially in England), that stagnation doesn't seem so bad in places where there are some signs that there was some life in the past, once. On the other hand, when the spiritual decay of something that was once very vital sets in, it is more terrible than the inertia of something that was never really lived at all. (I just remembered Oxford and Cambridge.)

There is often no real reason for preferring one place to another: metaphysically, it doesn't matter what town you happen to be in; you can work out your salvation in it, and find peace there if you want to, because the peace we need we have to look for in ourselves.

Psychologically, there are great differences between places, though, and the limits they put upon your own spirituality are often very significant. I am beginning to think it was good, being quiet here for a year, but now, perhaps, I have used up the resources for recollection that the mere inertia of the place gave me. Maybe if I stayed here, what I now seem to possess as peace would cease to deepen itself, and turn into inertia (if such a thing is possible).

Perhaps there is in place a certain value: they make it possible for you to seek and find certain things in your own soul. When you have found them, you begin to know the place has served you: and if the place is pleasant and pretty doesn't mean much anymore: it has only one further value: the value of a sacrifice. The only good thing that can be done with the place, the type of life, is to give it up. Renounce the temptation to keep what you have got as if it were now a possession, and hold on to it in inertia.

There was a rich young man in the Bible who had learned to keep all the commandments. Being rich, he had nevertheless used his riches wisely and justly. But they had done him all the service they could: they had only one further service, the value they would have if he freely renounced them, and gave everything to the poor. Unless he did this, from this point on, all his justice would be mere inertia, and to a Christian, inertia must be intolerable—it is hiding the talent that will become useless as soon as it is idle!

Christ told the young man what he should do. But he loved his security, and loved the peace that had already ceased to be peace (since he was restless enough to ask what to do) and become inertia. He turned away in sorrow, says the Gospel, for he had great possessions. And yet most Catholics who frequent the sacraments are "good people." Some are pharisees, no doubt, because there are pharisees everywhere where pride is possible, and that is everywhere on earth. But most practicing Catholics are good, worthy men and women, not willfully unkind, not more nervous and short tempered than anybody else, often much less so—but what is all this? These things are insults: to say Christians are *no less* uncharitable than everybody else. If they are not men who are consumed with the intense desire to love God and their neighbor, they are salt without savor. If they merely are in a sort of negative state of grace, not doing any wrong but not doing any good either, are they actually in grace at all? What about the man who took the talent and buried it? What will happen to him when the Lord comes and asks what we have done with our talents that he left with us? What will happen to us if the grace in us doesn't bring forth any fruit and is allowed to remain idle from our own lack of work and of charity?

When the aim we know is our highest aim in life, the salvation of our souls by means of loving God and our neighbor, is followed after with so much indifference by us (at best we merely keep out of a state of sin), how will the writing of poetry ever command any intense devotion from us?

No doubt we mean furiously to be good poets, and rage about our literary opinions, just the way we fume over our religious and political arguments too: we have enough energy to argue, but not enough to act. We can roar and rave against communists, but we have not the strength to go out and be charitable to the poor. We can rage against atheists, but we do not try to become saints ourselves, and we rage against the writers who are said to be technically good but write about things that really hurt us and offend us (like Joyce), but we do not devote ourselves to learning how to write, or even to read like Joyce did, and great writers must. We want it to be easy. We want to learn to be saints without giving up our whole lives to the Love of God.

In the same way, we think we can learn to be writers without loving the best and deepest and greatest poetry as a total and intense experience of the whole intellect and imagination, united in an act of contemplation, for contemplation means nothing to us any more, either spiritually or intellectually!

The one Catholic writer in this century who knew that being a writer meant following a vocation through tribulation and poverty and persecution was Leon Bloy. And Eric Gill went about being an artist with the same kind of attitude, too, prepared to suffer anything for what he knew was true and good and holy.

Two Missing Sheets of Merton Journal Discovered

In his research while reviewing *Run to the Mountain*, Dr. Patrick O'Connell, president of the International Thomas Merton Society, was able to compare the published text with the manuscripts and transcriptions at St. Bonaventure University Library. In addition to the typographical errors he noted, and for which we are most grateful since they have been incorporated into the new paperback edition, he unearthed two sheets that were previously torn out of the holographic notebooks.

When I did my research there in 1990, these pages were not available. Through some mystery of "providence" the pages were returned to St. Bonaventure's and were made available to Dr. O'Connell. Whether Merton himself or someone else removed the pages, we will never know for certain, but we must be grateful that they have been retrieved. They make more comprehensible this particular part of the journal.

The first of these sheets (69–70) of the "St. Bonaventure Journal" manuscript would fit into *Run to the Mountain* on page 300 as a continuation of the preceding dialogue:

besides the plot?

A: Alas, no. Even in one story the plot was nothing, either.

Q: What about characters?

A: Ninnies, the whole crazy pack of them. Stoopids. Clods. Blocks. Logs. Stones. Earth.

Q: Come, come. That's bad.

A: You said it. That's what comes of cheating.

Q: What are you going to do with the stories?

A: First send them to Westbrook's Business College to be typed out neat and tidy. Then mail them to Naomi Burton, England's jewel, down at Curtis-Brown Lit. Agency, 347 Madison Ave, New York City.

Q: And supposing they sell like hot cakes?

A: I'll cry like a boy with a mouthful of mustard.

Q: And why?

A: Love of poverty.

Q: Couldn't you take the dough and give it to the poor?

A: That would be cheating. Aint I poor too? Robbing Peter to pay Paul. Who am I to give money to the poor? Leave it alone in the first place.

Q: Aw, you're crazy.

A: You said it. But I don't feel clean, writing a story with a plot, and selling it. Especially when it isn't even autobiographical.

Q: Lousy Platonist.

A: I hate the word: admit the fact. I fear stories that are all technique and lies. Better truth and no technique, eh?

Q: Ha ha! You'd look silly saying that in public.

A: Anyway, I wasted time. I could have been doing something profitable, like reading Euphues.

Q: Yes, or T. S. Eliot's essays on The Elizabethans!

A: Sneering dog!

Q: Well, come on, you farcical writer: what do you like writing?

A: Joyce language; that's what I like writing. I'd like to write that all the time.

Q: Why don't you? Because you think you'd make money the other way?

A: No. But I can't. I can't write Joyce talk all the time. And my style is changing. It is getting clear, even stupid. Too terse, too. Too sharp. Too darn precious.

Q: When did you ever write Joyce talk since the spring and summer of 1939?

A: I wrote three pages of it in a letter to Lax. And I liked writing it, too. That's the way I want to write. And it can't be sold. Just because it can't be sold doesn't mean it can't be read. I could mimeograph it and send it around. I have a clean stencil, right here in my room. And I don't mean send it around to just anybody: only to people I know. Jinny, Lilly, Lax, Gibney, Rice, Knight, Van Doren, Dan Walsh, even (those mad) professors in the Graduate School of English at Columbia. That's what I want to do. Write like poor Joyce. I pray he comes to heaven. I was sorry to read he went so long without marrying his wife. He just did that to be funny!

As to Lax: Lax's father came up to me in the lobby of the New Old Lompoc house, beaming like a golden statue, and told me of Lax's new job on [the] *New Yorker.* That is a sweet new job. Ten minutes a day, ten cents: but I guess what he wants to do. I don't think he'd even want to be editor, but it would be a good thing if in the future all the editors were to listen to him, and maybe the *New Yorker* would get good again. And what I think is, maybe they will.

Macaronic Lyric

Mens sana (nerfs de café)
Corpore sano (défense de fumer!)
"What are ces mots of advice you have sung us!
Mens feeble in corpore fungus?"

Mens grandma in corpore grandpa
Comes never to lovers of rhumba and samba:
La vie carries on plus heureuse, also longer
With mens sana in corpore conga!

There are palabras far besser to teach:
"Mens happy in corpo felice!"

No! Joys of the sense
Ruin corpus and mens!
Your corpus is drunk and reason is dense!
So please to pensare some thoughts of demain:
Mente di coucou in corpo migraine!

Feb. 2, 1941

"In numerous minds is to be found the coexistence of faith and
atheism, of anarchy in the sentiments and of some doctrine of order in
the opinions. On the same subject, the majority of us will have several
theses, which, at the same moment, are without difficulty mutually in-
terchangeable in our judgements according to the passing mood."
—Paul Valery, *Variety.* p. 188.

"A modern man—and it is in this that he is modern—lives on
familiar terms with a quantity of contraries lingering in his mental
penumbra and taking their turn on the stage."

The second missing sheet from the journal is pp. 75–76, which
fits into *Run to the Mountain* in the middle of page 304:

condescension, and in him there is no condescension, but perfect
friendliness, which is perfect because you have absolutely no feeling of
being, yourself, singled out by it, but that it is for everybody, and the
same—and in some way you know here is a man that loves all men as
himself, because his friendliness is not friendliness, it doesn't step out,

and show itself, it is part of a simple unity, part of calmness, part of immense patient curiosity about meanings of words and symbols, of liturgy, of everything, part of a no doubt immense knowledge of language, and an immense memory, I don't know.

He was disturbed because they had changed, in the Easter Morning Epistle, "leaven" to "yeast," and had all sorts of different reasons, linguistic as well as reasons of delicacy. I hope he gets the change annulled.

As for Mgr Reugel— he is a very reverend person. I think it was just his saying "Good day, son" that put into my mind, from somewhere, the movement that ended in the poem I wrote down about the Passion of the Lord.

If I were not so mad with my own vanity and selfishness and petty cares for the ease of my flesh and my pride, I would see clearly how perhaps nothing I have ever done, of any good, was mine, or through me, but given by God through the love and gifts and prayers of people who have given their whole life in fruit for me to pick and take or spoil according to my indifferent and cursed selfishness. And that fruit has only nourished me in grace in spite of myself, so to speak, and accidentally given me a little health.

Look how the whole life of my grandfather, all his work of years was poured out for my brother and myself, buying me what hundreds of things, Italy, France, England, Cuba, Bermuda, food and clothing and care and hundreds of curious books and besides that all the things I hate to think of. But Pop worked from a boy in an Ohio town, for sixty years, in order that I should run down Bridge Street, Cambridge, in the middle of the night, terrified because I had just thrown something, a bottle, a shoe, a brick, I don't know, through a shop window. And he worked his whole life so Bill Finneran and I should lean on some poisonous little bar on 52nd St. in a half empty place picking a fight with some (long,) callow, drunken kid whom some swept up lousy old dames in the place seemed to prefer to us.

And look how he spent his whole life in working so that I could sit at the foot of the flag pole outside Columbia, in 1935, with a great (pleasure and surprise in me) about a girl I thought I was in love with. [cancellation of one and one-half lines] That's nobody's affair.

What else did he buy for me with his blood, for not only Christ gave his life for me, but all who ever loved me have sacrificed some of their life's blood for me. How easily I take that gift, as if I were a god, to be sacrificed to—as if the sacrifice really could be mine, and not God's.

My grandfather bought me the day I came into the bar of the American Merchant, going up the channel, around 3:30 in the morning, after I had fallen [on] my [berth] with all my clothes on around ten, and passed out. So I find this dame talking with the Ship's doctor. That was a fine humiliation, me with vomit on my black pants. That was what I gave him back for loving me even with his life, and my grandmother too.

If father had not died ten years ago, how much would I have hurt him in that time? How could I spoil and waste so much love and so much care and so many gifts?

At Aunt Maud's funeral: I realized it was dramatic and was only secretly vain of it, and congratulated myself that here I was down from Cambridge and nobody knew the secret of where I had been the night before, not that it was anything terrible, but I made it so in my imagination, that I should come among the sober relatives, at a funeral, and could still taste this dame's perfumed mouth in my own mouth. So when good Aunt Maud, a saint, was buried, I had, I supposed, some decent regret she was dead, because I did love her, but was just as full of my own private seventeen year old drama that I applauded for a magnificent adventure, I am sure! That was what her love for me brought her at her funeral! For she had made it possible by her patient care, for me to get to Oakham, and then to Cambridge.

All these things are easy to say: and the Lord suffered in everyone who ever loved me for Love's sake and was turned upon by my vicious ingratitude and pride, for I hated even to be loved in any such way.

Posthumous Prolificacy:
A Bibliographic Review Essay

Michael Downey

If it is true that Merton has always been difficult to pigeonhole, the same can be said about Merton publication and scholarship. The range of material by or about him released during 1995 defies easy categorization.

For many readers of *The Merton Annual*, 1995 will be remembered as the year of the journals—or at least the first of the "complete" Merton journals. But there is much more. There are translations of Merton's works (or portions of his works) into Spanish, Polish, Dutch, Hungarian, Chinese, Japanese, and Czech. For benefit of the visually impaired and others, *Bread in the Wilderness, Contemplative Prayer,* and *The Way of Chuang Tzu* are now available on cassette.[1] Credence Cassettes (Kansas City, Mo.) released twenty Merton tapes in 1995, covering topics from patience to poetry to T. S. Eliot to prayer. Two recently published titles were released in paperback editions: Merton's *Witness to Freedom: Letters in Times of Crisis*[2] and Ron Seitz's *Song for Nobody: A Memory Vision of Thomas Merton.*[3] Merton may indeed be the most prolific posthumous author in our day. Writings by him and about him keep on coming.

The task at hand calls for arranging the 1995 works by and about Merton in some orderly fashion. Without forcing the range of material into predetermined categories, noteworthy Merton scholarship and publication for 1995 is here arranged in light of six guiding

1. London: Saint Cecilia's Guild for the Blind, 1995.
2. New York: Harcourt Brace and Co. (A Harvest Book), 1995.
3. Liguori, Mo.: Triumph Books, 1995.

images evoked by some common features that emerge from the writings: (1) Merton as Kindred Spirit, (2) Merton as Model, (3) Merton à la Mode, (4) Merton in the Margins, (5) Merton as Guide: At Home and Abroad, (6) The Original (?) Merton.

Merton as Kindred Spirit

Three selections from 1995 suggest a strong kinship between Merton and other spiritual figures. In "To Merton Through Augustine: Images, Themes, and Analogies of Kinship,"[4] John Albert, O.C.S.O., compares Merton and St. Augustine. The first part focuses on images and themes in the life and thought of Augustine. Then the article investigates Merton's thought on Augustine during the period of his conversion and early years at Gethsemani. In the third part, Albert presents a selection of writings that illustrate Merton's growing awareness of himself as an acknowledged representative of the Catholic Church, with particular attention to the introduction he wrote for St. Augustine's *The City of God* in 1950.

Albert's analysis is limited to Augustine's two most celebrated works: *Confessions* and *The City of God*. In the first of these, Albert sees a threefold pattern: (1) personal narrative, (2) articulation of Augustine's struggle as the struggle of humankind, (3) the critical engagement with the major systems of thought of his day. He discerns a shift during Merton's early years in the monastery, a movement from identification with the Augustine of *Confessions* to the Augustine of *The City of God*. If in *Confessions* Augustine addresses the ramifications of a commitment to God for his personal life, in *The City of God* he provides an eschatological theology of the whole Church. Like Augustine, Merton made a choice for the Catholic Church in a process of conversion that was all encompassing—cultural, moral, intellectual, and religious. In other words, Albert suggests that *Confessions* illustrates the dynamics of an interior, more personal conversion; *The City of God* illustrates the ramification of such conversion for the external, that is, the social, ecclesiological, and political realms.

In "Born 'On the Borders of Spain': Thomas Merton and John of the Cross,"[5] Christopher Nugent examines the deep resonance between Merton and St. John of the Cross. He sees in these "two great

4. Conyers, Ga.: Holy Spirit Abbey, 1995.
5. *Mystics Quarterly* 21:3 (Sept. 1995) 91–100.

contemplative theologians" an abiding commitment to the "apophatic" way, a type of knowledge of God by way of negation. Nugent suggests that even though Merton's writings give evidence of a sporadic yet certain attraction to the kataphatic or affirmative way, especially as he found it in the writings of Julian of Norwich and others of the English school of mysticism, the way of darkness and unknowing holds a place more central in Merton's thought and writing. Nugent suggests that Merton was, from early on, profoundly influenced by the life and legacy of the Spanish mystic. Merton's own writings, especially *The Ascent to Truth*, wherein he attempted to correlate the insights of the scholastic theology of Thomas Aquinas with the mystical theology of John of the Cross, give evidence of the importance of the Mystical Doctor in Merton's early work. But Nugent sees the influence as more enduring and all-pervasive. For Nugent it was the influence of John of the Cross that shaped Merton's understanding of the way of contemplation as a dark path. And it was John who laid the foundation by which Merton was able to make the seemingly natural and predictable transition from the apophatic, dark way of Christian spirituality to the wisdom of the East. D. T. Suzuki's "zero equals infinity" is affirmed by the mature Merton because of his early recognition of the truth in John's insight, gained in the dark path of unknowing, that God is at once *todo y nada*, all and nothing.

The theme of the dark path of contemplation is taken up by Peter King in *Dark Night Spirituality*.[6] The author treats the lives and writings of Thomas Merton, Dietrich Bonhoeffer, and Etty Hillesum in view of what he judges to be their common approach to contemplation. Thomas Merton's view of contemplation is well known. And many will be familiar with the Lutheran pastor and theologian Bonhoeffer, whose writings from a prison cell during World War II provide a testament of endurance and hope in the face of his profound experience of desolation and the absence of God.

Although Etty Hillesum has gained a wide readership in recent years, she is not nearly as well known. Born on January 15, 1914, Esther Hillesum was a Dutch Jew with little formal religious training. Our knowledge of her is based primarily on eight notebooks in which she penned her diaries between March 9, 1941, and October 13, 1942. In addition, her letters from Westerbork describe daily life in a transit camp that was the last stop for Dutch Jews en route to Auschwitz and

6. London: SPCK, 1995.

other Nazi death camps. On November 30, 1943, the Red Cross reported the death of Etty Hillesum at Auschwitz. The Hillesum diaries and letters give evidence of the transformation of a soul through the dawning realization of the reality of God's presence and activity, even and especially amidst the horrors of World War II and the evil of the Nazi's Final Solution. The luminosity of Hillesum's soul only intensifies as the darkness of the age engulfs her neighbors, friends, and family.

King's thesis is that each one—Merton, Bonhoeffer, and Hillesum—has something to offer by way of insight into the nature of contemplation. He maintains their understanding of contemplation is rooted in an experiential knowledge of some "dark night." However, there are real differences in the experience of these three representatives of dark night spirituality, differences that deserve fuller attention than King manages to give in this slim volume. That Merton came to some knowledge or understanding of God by way of unknowing is not at issue here. And that he discerned God's nearness in a dazzling darkness certainly makes him a fitting representative of dark night spirituality. But can he or should he be yoked together with two figures whose lives were threatened minute by minute by forces of evil that would eventually prevail and result in their extermination? Their luminosity and hope in God in the face of their impending destruction makes of Bonhoeffer and Hillesum representatives of a dark night spirituality substantially different from Merton's, whatever similarities there may be in their approaches to contemplation.

Merton as Model

Four authors look to Thomas Merton's life specifically as worthy of emulation. Fred Herron is a high school religion teacher. In "Meeting the Rhinoceros: Thomas Merton Makes a Valuable Role Model for the Spiritual Journey of the Adolescent Rhinoceros,"[7] Herron takes his cue from both Merton and long-time high school educator William O'Malley, S.J. In an effort to pierce the tough hide of the rhino, that is, the indifferent adolescent in the high school religion class, with some sort of religious insight, O'Malley suggests that the religious educator (1) rely on stories, (2) honestly grapple with experiential questions rather than pass on dry-as-dust theories, (3) attend to the dynamics of personal conversion, and (4) share deeply held con-

7. *Momentum* (Feb.–Mar. 1995) 60–62.

victions. Because Merton personified these characteristics in his life and writings, he is, for Herron, a model for both educator and adolescent in the religion class.

The appearance of the relatively new *The Merton Journal,* published by the Thomas Merton Society of Great Britain and Ireland, is a clear indication of growing interest in Merton "across the pond." Several pieces in the journal deserve attention. But of particular interest is "Fr. Louis' Mertonoia"[8] by Hilary Costello, O.C.S.O. Costello's essay looks to Merton in view of his quest for holiness. But Costello's Merton is not immune from critique. Recognizing that Merton's life was unsettled and in many ways highly conflicted, he is quick to point out some of the conflicts. For example, Costello judges Merton's longstanding desire to live as a hermit to be at odds with his deep need to be in steady communication with others. And he speaks rather directly of Merton's affection for the nurse Margie Smith as being at odds with the monastic vocation. But in a note of candor Costello admits that he too has fallen in love in the course of his monastic life, a compelling reason for Costello to be drawn to Merton as exemplar. The deeper reason for Merton's appeal to him is that, in the midst of all the conflicts that riddled his life, three values and interests remained stable: (1) mysticism as the ideal of Christian life, (2) a longing for solitude, and (3) a fierce attachment to freedom.

Portraying Merton as exemplar, warts and all, is also one of the aims of Monica Furlong's *Merton: A Biography.* Now available in a new edition,[9] there is in fact very little new here save the introduction to this edition. But her second thoughts about Merton are quite valuable. First, Furlong laments that she may have been too sympathetic to her subject and overly critical of his abbot in her portrayal of the relationship between Merton and James Fox. She now claims that Merton may have been very difficult to live with, indeed something of a prima donna, which she maintains is true of many of the clergy she has come to know. Second, she writes that Merton's view of the hermit life was shot through with romanticization and idealization. She compares his dreamy ruminations about the solitary life with the daily struggle of millions of elderly and otherwise socially marginalized people who are trying to come to terms with the pain of solitude and darkness day in and day out. For Furlong, revisiting her subject years after the original writing, the solitary

8. *The Merton Journal* 2:1 (Easter 1995) 11–20.
9. Liguori, Mo.: Liguori Publications, 1995.

life is a mystery about which Merton theorized but did not, in fact, actually live. Third, because of the information that has been brought to light about Merton's real struggle with his affection for Margie Smith, Furlong's respect and admiration for him has increased rather than diminished. Finally, she suggests that Merton's "subversion" needs more attention than it has hitherto been given. In her telling, toward the end of his life at Gethsemani, many saw virtually everything Merton did as subversive. For Furlong, this may have been caused by his reluctance to notice the root cause of his ongoing distress, namely, "that he was in many ways a square peg in a round hole"[10] at Gethsemani.

Tim Dutcher-Walls draws upon the work of Ernst Troeltsch in "Thomas Merton: Model of Integration."[11] For Dutcher-Walls, what makes Merton a model of integration is that in him the "church," "sect," and "mystic" ideal types described by Troeltsch in his celebrated *The Social Teaching of the Christian Churches*[12] were held in creative tension. Merton was and remained a Roman Catholic (the church type), a Cistercian monk, (the sect type), and a religious individualist (the mystic type). Though assigning a certain superiority to the mystic religious type, Troeltsch maintains that all three need to be held together in a noble tension. This is no small task since the three ideal types tend to be at odds with one another. The religious individualist (mystic) resists both the restrictions of the sect and the compromise of the church with the world. The sect demands a surrender of individuality, and rejects the compromise of church. The church, with its universal appeal, tends to mitigate against the individual integrity of the mystic and the communal witness of the sect. In Dutcher-Walls' presentation, Merton is preeminently the mystic type, but this is significantly modulated by his contact with and appreciation for the other two. In this age of individualism, religious and otherwise, Merton is for Dutcher-Walls a model of the integration Troeltsch was pointing toward.

In "Contemplation: A Universal Call: Merton's Notion of Contemplation for People in the World,"[13] James Conner suggests that Merton is a model for contemplatives "in the cloister" and "in the world." Here Conner is particularly concerned with the contemplative

10. Ibid., xxiv.
11. *Spiritual Life* 41:4 (Winter 1995) 207–13.
12. Louisville, Ky.: Westminster/John Knox Press, 1992.
13. *Monos* 7:3 (May–June 1995) 1–4, 9.

call of those in the world "forced to live that [contemplative] life in greater poverty and spirit"[14] because of the lack of communal or institutional support. These "masked contemplatives" living in the world will find a model in the person of Merton who, Conner claims, was himself something of a masked contemplative even though he was explicitly committed by public profession to the contemplative life in a monastic context. Indeed, Merton's masked contemplatives need models. Further, there is a need for a clear articulation of the nature and demands of their contemplative call. But what Conner does in this short essay is simply assert rather than offer an analysis of the notion of contemplation for people in the world. His definition of contemplation is hazy: "For God is always with us in every circumstance of life and where God is, there is love. And where love is, there is contemplation."[15]

Merton à la Mode

In 1995 authors continued to bring Merton's legacy to bear on specific contemporary problems. In James Conner's presidential address at the meeting of the International Thomas Merton Society at St. Bonaventure's University in June 1995,[16] he hails Merton as a prophet for the next century while lamenting the political climate of our day. Politicians are false prophets and those who buy into their agendas are fools. Merton is a surer bet. His insights about the problems of the 1950s and 1960s are "just as applicable today as before." Why? In Conner's view, "the circumstances of our world of today have basically not changed that much since the time when Merton was writing."[17] This is an arguable claim, at the very least. Granted that there are certain constants that human beings have had to face throughout the ages, but are we not, in fact, living in a very different world from that of Thomas Merton?

Our deepening awareness of cultural diversity is but one of the factors that poses unique challenges at this point in history. Patrick O'Connell engages this issue in "Thomas Merton and the Multiculturalism Debate: Cultural Diversity or Transcultural Consciousness?"[18] He argues that Merton maintained strong roots in his own

14. Ibid., 9.
15. Ibid.
16. "Thomas Merton: A Prophet for the Twenty-first Century," *The Merton Seasonal* 20:3 (summer 1995) 4–8.
17. Ibid., 5.
18. *Cithara* 34:2 (May 1995) 27–360.

Christian and European tradition and at the same time was open to and respectful of other cultures. The author is persuaded that Merton holds a key to overcoming the tendency toward cultural imperialism and dominance, on the one hand, and cultural relativity and fragmentation, on the other. For O'Connell, Merton speaks to this dilemma because he recognized both the limitations and the contributions of diverse cultures, his own as well as others, in his attempt to give shape to a more just social order, as well as in his effort to articulate a common understanding of shared human existence.

If there are two poles in the multiculturalism debate, O'Connell sees Merton on the side with those striving to reach common ground between and among diverse cultures. He emphasized what different cultures have in common rather than what makes them unique and particular. This is evidenced in Merton's selection of the term "transcultural consciousness" as a more accurate way of describing his concern in this regard. O'Connell treats six interrelated aspects of this "transcultural consciousness." But in the end, even though O'Connell aims to bring about greater clarity to the current debate on multiculturalism and tries to move toward mutual understanding and convergence of insight, his proposed synthesis does not do justice to the complexity of issues raised by the proponents of cultural pluralism.

Perhaps it is the same concern for unity and coherence that underpins the fascinating study of Waclaw Grzybowski, "Epistemology, Poetics and Mysticism in Thomas Merton's Theory of Poetry."[19] The author conducts his investigation in view of the polemics of phenomenological, structuralist, and deconstructivist poetics. He maintains that Merton understood poetry as a way of recording his spiritual, existential, and cognitive experience. For Grzybowski, Merton's poetry reestablishes the metaphysical and theological character of poetry. In the author's understanding, poetry expresses, according to Merton, a unique metaphysics. That is to say that poetry discloses an ontic mystery. And though the metaphysical truth in poetry does not yield to rationalization, it nonetheless is given in the poem. Thus metaphysics finds confirmation and expression in poetry.

Grzybowski extrapolates Merton's theory of poetry from a reading of what he judges to be Merton's most important works. But the latest of Merton's works investigated is *The New Man* (1961). In an effort to demonstrate that Merton's poetics expresses a unified world-

19. *Filologia Angielska* 8 (1995) 105–27.

view in which everything hangs together and makes sense in view of a larger whole, Grzybowski overlooks Merton's later poetry, the "anti-poetry." Scholars are still debating the evidence of any "givenness" or ontic structure in the anti-poetry. To what extent do Merton's later words crack rather than disclose, interrupt instead of confirm the ontic mystery?

Merton in the Margins

In two noteworthy essays Merton has a significant albeit marginal place. In "The Lure of Catholicism,"[20] Avery Dulles, S.J., addresses the issue of "conversion" to the Roman Catholic Church today. Originally given as the Thomas Merton Lecture at Columbia University on November 16, 1994 (the fifty-sixth anniversary of Merton's reception into the Catholic Church), Dulles offers a profile of the pre-World War II "convert" in contrast to the post-World War II convert. With respect for the real differences between them, Dulles likens his own conversion to Catholicism to that of Thomas Merton, one of dozens of young intellectual converts of the late 1930s.

The pattern of converts in Merton's generation, Dulles suggests, was relatively constant. Most were attracted to the work of living Catholic philosophers like Gilson and Maritain, who were striving to recover the principles of Christian philosophy represented by such thinkers as Thomas Aquinas. And all were enamored of the high Middle Ages. Now how do the motives of converts today differ from those of Merton and his contemporaries? Dulles suggests that, instead of seeing their conversion to Catholicism as a rejection of previously held beliefs, today's converts more often see it as a completion or fulfillment of their previous commitment. According to Dulles, the deep attraction to Catholicism for most converts resides in its ability to integrate three dimensions: the intellectual, the liturgical, and the social. If the draw of Catholicism for Merton's generation was the golden era of the high Middle Ages, the draw today is Catholicism's living legacy of wisdom, worship, and community.

Donald R. Canton's "The Quality of Mercy"[21] is a brief personal narrative in which the author seeks to uncover the authentic meaning of mercy with an eye to embodying the mandate to be merciful in his

20. *New Oxford Review* 62:2 (Mar. 1995) 6–14.
21. *Living Prayer* 28:4 (July–Aug. 1995) 9–13.

own life. After exploring the various common sense meanings of the term, Canton looks to the writings of Thomas Merton, especially *No Man Is an Island,* for a fuller and deeper explanation. He maintains that "the Christian concept of mercy is, therefore, the key to the transformation of the whole universe." Canton concludes on the basis of his reading of Merton: "Mercy is an act that travels both ways, from heaven to earth, an act that, through faith and prayer, inspires courage, even when our hearts seem to fail us."[22]

Merton as Guide: At Home and Abroad

Several publications in 1995 focus on Merton as spiritual guide. Two of these portray Merton as offering a guided retreat. Basil Pennington's *On Retreat with Thomas Merton*[23] is a reprint of his earlier *Retreat with Thomas Merton* (1988). Anthony Padovano's *A Retreat with Thomas Merton: Becoming Who We Are*[24] is part of the new "A Retreat With" series featuring Jessica Powers, Job and Julian of Norwich, Gerard Manley Hopkins and Hildegard of Bingen, and others, as spiritual guides for retreats at home. Designed for those who cannot afford the time or expense of a more formal retreat away from home, this volume is constructed in such a way that Merton, whose life and legacy are here arranged in light of seven crucial movements, may "speak" to the retreatant over the course of seven days. Acting as an unseen narrator and codirector, Anthony Padovano selects facets of Merton's story, inviting retreatants to get in touch with their own life story and spiritual journey. An opening prayer begins each session. Questions for reflection and a closing prayer conclude each chapter, or day of retreat.

For three writers, Merton serves as an able guide to the thought and practice of peoples of distant lands. Cyrus Lee's *Thomas Merton and Chinese Wisdom*[25] is more about Lee than about Thomas Merton. This collection of ten essays written in freestyle celebrates the delight that Merton took in harmonizing different sources of Chinese wisdom. The author speaks of Merton's understanding of Confucianism, Taoism, Zen Buddhism, Chuang Tzu, Hanshan Tzu. There is a meditation on life, death, and reincarnation. Even though Lee never met

22. Ibid., 12.
23. New York: Continuum, 1995.
24. Cincinnati: Saint Anthony Messenger Press, 1995.
25. Erie, Pa.: Sino-Chinese Institute, 1995.

Merton, what we have in these pages is a personal sharing of dreams, conversations, intuitions, and insights about Merton, as well as a sustained expression of the joy that the author takes in introducing others to Thomas Merton. In brief, this is a "veritable stir-fry of Chinese delights."[26]

John Wu, Jr., in "Thomas Merton as Teacher and Guru: 'In Praise of Divine Folly,'"[27] presents Merton as a thinker who instinctively understood the limits of both the intellect and discursive reasoning. Because of this recognition, he was able to allow God free reign in communicating the truth in others and in other traditions. It was this openness that made Merton a writer who enriched his own tradition and, in the process, both stimulated and revitalized other traditions. For Wu, Merton was able to be "spiritually venturesome" only because he was wholly wedded to a living orthodoxy and tradition. Standing within his own religious tradition, Merton took a spiritual posture "of forcing nothing on reality and allowing God to play in *his* field and by *his* rules so that the unexpected, the mysterious and the unanticipated what, how, and why are understood to be all beyond one's reckoning."[28]

Merton's turn to the East is the subject of ongoing discussion, research, and publication. But Paul Ruttle, C.P., reminds us that Merton had an interest in other traditions and cultures as well. Ruttle's "Voice of the Stranger: Merton's Penetration of the Mystery of the Maya"[29] charts Merton's thought regarding this extant people with roots in pre-Columbian Mesoamerica. Suggesting that Merton's early naive and somewhat disparaging remarks about this people were based upon partial and inaccurate information, Ruttle argues that Merton's interest in the Maya was enduring and his appreciation of their culture and spirituality considerable. In an effort to deepen the reader's appreciation of the Maya, Ruttle provides a synopsis of the story of this people from the pre-Columbian era, through the Conquest, to the modern period. This forgotten and marginalized people still numbers five million throughout Central America. But Ruttle's main objective is to show that, despite his misconceptions about them, Merton was able to grasp intuitively the vitality of the art and spirituality of this people. Even though he knew of their art and

---

26. Ibid., v.
27. *Cistercian Studies Quarterly* 30:2 (1995) 114–40.
28. Ibid., 127.
29. South River, N.J.: Privately Printed, 1995.

spirituality mostly through books and pictures, Merton was able to penetrate the secret of "the children of the sun" because he himself was an artist and a contemplative.

The Original (?) Merton

Some of the "original" Merton that appeared in 1995 has already been available in earlier editions and collections. The new edition of Ernesto Cardenal's *Abide in Love*[30] contains a foreword written by Merton for the original Cardenal volume *Vida en el Amor.*[31]

Similarly, *Passion for Peace: The Social Essays of Thomas Merton*[32] contains a good measure of what is already available in other forms, but is either out of print or not readily accessible. What makes this new volume noteworthy is the arrangement of the essays in chronological order with editorial remarks (though uneven in length and quality) introducing each essay. The volume illustrates that Merton was passionately concerned about the whole gamut of social concerns that shaped the political climate of the 1960s. In addition to guidelines for establishing peace, he addressed the issues of war, social justice, civil rights, racism, and nonviolence. Because many of the essays were developed in view of particular historical manifestations of social evil and sin, for example, those of the 1960s in the United States, some might be inclined to judge Merton's message as irrelevant to the pressing exigencies at the dawn of the new millennium. But there is enduring value in Merton's central intuitions regarding the social problems about which he was so passionately concerned. If the benefits of his legacy are to be reaped to advantage, however, what is required is not a fundamentalist appeal to his message and its meaning as applicable to all problems in all places at all times. What is needed is a critical recovery of some of Merton's guiding insights with an eye to addressing very different social circumstances and problems that often call for different and more refined solutions than the ones he himself proposed.

The five volumes of Merton's selected letters under the general editorship of William H. Shannon have been a welcome addition to the Merton corpus. But since the volumes have made available only Merton's letters and not those of his correspondents, reading through

30. Maryknoll, N.Y.: Orbis Books, 1995.
31. Buenos Aires: Ediciones Carlos Lohlé, 1970.
32. Edited with an introduction by William H. Shannon (New York: Crossroad, 1995).

the letters is a bit like listening in on one side of a telephone conversation. With the publication of *At Home in the World: The Letters of Thomas Merton and Rosemary Radford Ruether*,[33] we are privy to both sides of the conversation. We also now have available correspondence between Merton and Ernesto Cardenal,[34] which adds to the growing body of "both sides" of correspondence. Hopefully, there will be more "two way" correspondence published in new editions in the near future. There is a world of difference between reading someone's personal mail, even a whole ton of it, and reading an exchange of letters.

The editor of this collection has gathered the letters exchanged during 1966–1968 between Merton and Ruether. At the time of this correspondence Merton was a well-known writer and celebrated monk. Ruether was a young, progressive theologian just beginning her work, but her influence was already being recognized. Their letters occasion a volley of new ideas. At the beginning Ruether seems drawn to Merton's spiritual maturity and his commitment to live out his monastic life with integrity. For his part, Merton appears fascinated with the intellectual acumen of this young theologian-in-the-world. It is precisely this difference between Merton the monk and Ruether the woman theologian-in-the-world that underpins the correspondence, making it very engaging. Their real differences provide the opportunity for each to invite the other to relinquish tightly held preconceptions. Merton is bent on demonstrating to Ruether that monasticism is indeed still a meaningful Christian vocation even in the face of the pressing demands of the contemporary world and the gospel mandate to transform the world in accord with God's purposes. Ruether, on the other hand, keeps challenging and criticizing what she judges to be Merton's preconceptions about women, materiality, and the nature of contemplation. But what is most inviting about the correspondence is Ruether's unrelenting pursuit of the truth. She speaks forthrightly and directly, calling forth the same from her correspondent. Ruether continually sets the terms of their conversation by telling Merton time and again to clarify his theological positions and to speak candidly of his trials and tribulations as a monk in a rapidly changing world. This did not come through when we only had access to Merton's letters to Ruether.

33. Ed. Mary Tardiff, intro. by Rosemary Radford Ruether, afterword by Christine M. Bochen (Maryknoll, N.Y.: Orbis Books, 1995).
34. *The Merton Annual* 8, ed. Christine M. Bochen, trans. Roberto S. Goizueta (Collegeville, Minn.: The Liturgical Press, 1996) 162–200.

Undoubtedly the most significant original Merton material to be published in 1995 is *Run to the Mountain: The Story of a Vocation.*[35] It is worth noting that portions of these journals had already appeared. Shortly before his unexpected death in 1968, Merton gave instructions that his journals could be published, in whole or in part, twenty-five years after his death.

This is the first of seven volumes of Merton's complete journals, and it reflects the decisions to make available all of the extant journals with minimal editing. The first volume contains most of the earliest surviving journals, beginning in May 1939 and concluding in December 1941, when Merton entered the Abbey of Gethsemani. There are, in fact, three quite distinct sections in the volume: the first covers the period while Merton lived on Perry Street in Greenwich Village; the second was kept during his brief visit to Cuba; the third and perhaps most important journal was written while living a sort of quasi-monastic existence and teaching English at St. Bonaventure's University in Olean, New York. It is in the St. Bonaventure journal that we watch Merton agonizing over the question of his vocation. The issue is finally resolved as the journal is brought to a close on December 5, 1941, and he departs for Gethsemani.

The value of this volume, for general readers and for scholars alike, lies in the insight it offers about Merton's vocation both as a man of God and as a writer. In these pages he writes freely, without restraint, sometimes hastily. He gives evidence of powers of sharp observation, clear expression, and deep commitment to the craft of writing. He is often preoccupied with the task of establishing himself as a serious writer. Rejection slips from publishers hurt him. But he continues to hone his skills in these journals by means of jotting down enticing questions, reflections, soliloquies, quotations from various writers, his flights of fancy. In some of the most delightful sections of the journals he scribbles lists of all sorts: book titles, names of political figures, wishes, deep desires, artists, works of art, titles of songs, lines from songs, "out of the way and uninteresting things," "things I never really could believe existed," places "I am glad I am not in," and so on. This sort of "stream-of-consciousness" rambling is not something Merton set aside as he grew as a writer. His playful correspondence

---

35. *The Journals of Thomas Merton, Vol. I, 1939–1941,* ed. Patrick Hart (San Francisco: HarperSanFrancisco, 1995). See the review symposium in this volume of *The Merton Annual.*

with Lax and his anti-poetry strike a similar chord as these lists of everything under the sun.

Merton comes across as an earnest, vigorous, and intellectually gifted young convert and college teacher. But the real story line in these pages is his dissatisfaction with life on Perry Street and at St. Bonaventure's, and his growing attraction to and readiness for something much more than the life he was leading. In the crux of this desire is formed a writer of enduring appeal through the cultivation of a singleness of purpose in pursuit of God. At the same time we glimpse, in bud, much of what continued to concern him throughout his life: the need to publish, the desire for God, prayer, social responsibility, war and peace, race relations, the poor, the draw of satire, a feel for the poetic.

With the endorsements from such spiritual luminaries as Thomas Moore, HarperSanFrancisco announced the publication of *Run to the Mountain* with the bold claim: "After twenty-five years, the final literary legacy of the most important spiritual writer of the twentieth century." This gives rise to an observation and a question that may serve to wrap up this roundup of Merton publication and scholarship in 1995. First, Thomas Merton may indeed be the most important spiritual writer of our century. But the claim is arguable. The claim would have been less subject to dispute had the publisher made a more modest claim in terms of Merton's significance as a *Western* and *Christian* spiritual writer. Second, is this really the first of the last? In what sense are the journals Merton's final literary legacy? There is more—much more—to come. Even after the publication of *Run to the Mountain*, editor Patrick Hart was informed of further journal entries from Merton's pre-monastic years that properly belong in this first volume of journals, and which are scheduled to be included in the paperback edition.[36] Twelve volumes of Thomas Merton's "Monastic Orientation Notes" await publication, though there is some indication that the project is about to get underway. It is not likely to stop there, however. There is a myriad of letters, tapes, various manuscripts, and the voluminous working notebooks. The journals have been hailed as the last and best of the Merton legacy. But there is more to come, even of the original Merton.

---

36. See Patrick Hart, "*Run to the Mountain:* Four More Journal Entries by Thomas Merton," *The Merton Seasonal* 20:4 (Fall 1995) 4–8. See also his response to the review symposium in this volume of *The Merton Annual*.

Reviews

Thomas Merton and Rosemary Radford Ruether. *At Home in the World: The Letters of Thomas Merton and Rosemary Radford Ruether.* Edited by Mary Tardiff with an introduction by Rosemary Radford Ruether. Maryknoll, N.Y.: Orbis Books, 1995. xix + 108 pages. Paper. $12.95.

Reviewed by Clare Ronzani

This engaging correspondence between Thomas Merton and Rosemary Radford Ruether unveils a lively exchange between Ruether, a theologian at the outset of her career, and Merton, a seasoned monk of twenty-five years. Contained in this slim volume is dialogue on a wide range of topics, including monasticism, authority, the situation of the Church in the late 1960s, and the value and meaning of the contemplative life. Merton readers will be aware that he addresses various aspects of these issues in such works as *Contemplation in a World of Action,* published a few years prior to the writing of these letters, and the perhaps lesser-known *Springs of Contemplation,* which records a retreat with a group of contemplative prioresses in 1967–68. Readers of Ruether will recognize that the questions she continues to raise regarding authority and infallibility have been with her since her earliest days as a theologian.

The correspondence covers approximately a year and a half, extending from August 1966 to February 1968. What is new in this book is Ruether's side of the correspondence; Merton's letters to her were previously published in *The Hidden Ground of Love* (William Shannon, ed., 1985). To have a record of the exchange that went on between the two provides some marvelous insights into each of them at a time when both were dealing with significant questions and were seeking one another's perspective.

Ruether, for her part, looks to Merton as one

> with whom I could be ruthlessly honest about my own questions
> of intellectual and existential integrity. I was trying to test in this
> correspondence what was the crucial issue, for me, at that time:
> whether it was, in fact, actually possible to be a Roman Catholic
> and to be a person of integrity (xvi).

Merton, too, deals with questions of integrity, particularly in relation to his life as a contemplative and hermit. (The reader may recall that he had recently been involved in a relationship with a young nurse, which had no doubt deepened these questions in himself.) It is perhaps the mutual quest of each of these correspondents for a depth of integrity in their lives that makes their letters so challenging to each other and to the reader.

If, in the correspondence, Ruether is seeking to explore with Merton the crucial question of integrity within Catholicism, Merton, for his part, reveals quite directly at one point what *he* is looking for in corresponding with Ruether. He states:

> It happens that you, a woman, are for some reason a theologian I
> trust. . . . And I do think I need the help of a theologian. Do you
> think you could help me once in a while? . . . I have no great pro-
> ject in mind. I just need help in two areas where I have serious
> trouble and where I have simply been avoiding a confrontation:
> the Bible and the Church.

The personal and interactive way in which both correspondents deal with these and other issues comprises one of the most engaging aspects of this volume. The quality of interchange between Merton and Ruether goes beyond intellectual discussion and reveals exploration on their parts, in the late 1960s, of issues that have grown in significance in subsequent decades. For readers, who, now as much as then, are struggling to live with integrity in the midst of the changing Church and world, the correspondence offers an implicit invitation to explore such questions fully and deeply, with perhaps some measure of comfort gleaned from the exchange between these two searchers.

The content and style of the letters varies. Ruether, especially, explores issues more from the point of view of the theologian. It is clear that Merton is interested in her writing and welcomes the exchange of ideas it offers. Readers may agree with Merton when he finds some of her letters "very dense and tight and solid." Yet there are splendidly candid exchanges on both their parts, and the letters lack neither wit nor wisdom.

Given the genre, and the personalities of the two correspondents, as much is communicated through the *tone* of these letters as through the content. Some readers will enjoy this book because of the insights it gives into Ruether at the beginning of her career and/or Merton toward the end of his. But more perhaps, will appreciate the lively debates and the places where they run into each other's edges as two human beings struggling for authenticity.

For Merton, the locus of the dilemma is with the role of the monk in the world. Ruether consistently challenges him to look at the question personally. What ultimately comes through is her intuition that Merton faces a significant point of change in his life. The young theologian puts it squarely to the monk:

> I . . . get the strong impression . . . that you are in some period of crisis whose implications you are fighting off with long arguments. . . . The crisis I sense is not primarily to do with monasticism as an answer in general, but with *you*, with the rhythm of your personal development. You seem to me to have reached a crisis point in that development where you need a new point of view. This is a crisis, because if it is not met adequately, it will surely mean a regression to a less full existence for you, while if its meaning is properly discerned, it will be a new *kairos* leading to a new level of perception.

Ruether's sometimes relentless questioning of Merton, which she acknowledges (in the introduction) might reflect "a certain shocking style of frankness," sparks further reflection on Merton's part. Neither lets the other "off the hook," and their tone is often one of lively sparring. An example of this is their difference of opinion regarding the value of monastic life in the contemporary era. Ruether makes it clear that "I am radically out of sympathy with the monastic project." She confronts Merton: "You say that you have no trouble with your vocation, but, if that is really true, maybe you should be having some trouble with your vocation." Merton, in his turn, accuses Ruether of being "a very academic, cerebral, abstract type," to which she replies, "If I weren't a woman would it have occurred to you to accuse me of being cerebral? Interesting resentment there."

As critical as Ruether becomes, Merton takes her critiques seriously and responds by letting her know that he has given her ideas further thought. Ruether: "Do you realize how defensive you are, forever proving, proving, how good your life is, etc. . . . you seem too threatened at the moment to discuss . . . objectively." Merton: "I am really very grateful for your last letter . . . and I am sorry for being such a creep, but it is true that you did make me feel very defensive. . . . So don't give up on me, I will be objective."

Despite their sometimes turbulent character, these letters ultimately reveal an attitude of equality on the part of both Merton and Ruether. In her introduction, Ruether states:

> Merton from the beginning addressed me as an equal. (This did not surprise me at the time, since I saw myself as an equal, but it is more impressive in retrospect.) . . . Never did he take the paternalistic stance as the father addressing the child, which is more typical of the cleric, especially in relation to women.

This attitude of respect for those with whom he corresponds is wonderfully evident in other letters as well, as those who have delved into other volumes of Merton's correspondence will recognize.

One final note: the actual correspondence between Ruether and Merton is enhanced by the introductory and concluding sections of the book. Mary Tardiff's preface provides valuable background information, especially in regard to Ruether, as does Christine Bochen's afterword in regard to Merton. And Ruether's introduction adds very helpful contextual information. One image she offers is especially revealing as she states candidly:

> I see Thomas Merton and myself somewhat like two ships that happened to pass each other on our respective journeys. For a brief moment we turned our search lights on each other with blazing intensity. Then, when we sensed that we were indeed going in different directions, we began to pass each other by.

Readers will be grateful for the passing of these two ships.

Thomas Merton. *Passion for Peace: The Social Essays.* Edited and with an introduction by William H. Shannon. New York: Crossroads, 1995. 338 pages with index. $29.95.

Reviewed by Richard D. Parry

This book is a collection of essays written by Thomas Merton between 1961 and 1968. They cover the major social issues of the day—

the threat of nuclear war, the war in Vietnam, the civil rights movement, and nonviolence. Here we see Merton articulate positions that
now have lost their revolutionary edge; at the time they were innovative enough to evoke some misgivings by his Cistercian censors,
among others. Indeed, as William Shannon points out in his introduction, in 1961 no well-known priest or bishop in the United States had
spoken out against war. So the reader must be careful in reading these
essays to put them into their proper historical context. In them Merton
appears as a prophet, both in the sense of someone who stands against
the corrupt moral assumptions of his time and in the sense of someone
who looked into the future to the consequences of not correcting these
assumptions.

It is reflection on the former role—the prophet who stands
against moral corruption—that is an undercurrent of these essays.
Clearly Merton sees himself in this role. It is how he saw the role that
will help us to frame an appreciation of this collection. The monk of
Gethsemani had retired from the world at the beginning of the cata-
clysmic Second World War to become a contemplative. In his studies
of monasticism and essays about contemplation, he fostered a generation of Catholics who idealized "the hidden life." His occasional attempts to defend the contemplative life from unfavorable comparison
to the active seemed to many of his readers beside the point; he had
already convinced them of the value of the contemplative life by the
beauty of his own eloquence. However, the title of his 1966 book
Conjectures of a Guilty Bystander tipped his hand. In the twentieth century, at least, a contemplative is a bystander to the appalling events of
the most violent century yet—but a guilty bystander. How can the contemplative life—the hidden life, the nonactive life—be justified in the
face of two world wars, the Nazi holocaust of fourteen million humans, a Soviet sacrifice, of similar proportions, to their own version of
social planning, and a threatening nuclear war that would put even
these preceding events in its shadow for sheer murderous brutality?

Merton's answer is that a contemplative can be a prophet because, in part, of his or her unique perspective, outside the world (148).
Detachment from the world, then, is not a way of ignoring it but a way
of seeing its problems by offering a distance that allows proper assessment. One might add that being detached is not just a question of geography; renunciation of power and wealth is the heart of detachment.
And it is the embrace of these that most corrupts the perspective of
those in the world. Finally, detachment implies a radical reliance on

the will of God; the one who renounces power and wealth becomes most like the lilies of the field and the birds of the air, whose welfare is completely dependent on a benevolent God. If it is this perspective that allows one to be a prophet in the first sense, it too frequently undermines one's claim to be a prophet in the second sense—one's claim to foretell the consequences of not following God's will. It does credit to Merton to see how well he has endured under both senses of prophet. It even does him credit to note that his ability to expose moral corruption is greater than his ability to foresee consequences.

The first section of essays is devoted to the morality of nuclear war. Here especially one needs to remember the context because so much of what Merton urges and argues for has now become Church teaching. However, at the time, before the forthright condemnation of nuclear war by the Vatican Council II, it was still possible for Catholic theologians to argue for the morality of nuclear war. In fact, James Douglass in *Commonweal* (Oct. 11, 1991) relates a fascinating story about moral theologian Austin Fagothey, S.J. In the years before the council, Fagothey was writing a dissertation at the Gregorian University in Rome defending the position that nuclear war is morally acceptable under the just war doctrine. In these days before the council, then, Merton is trying to put together papal pronouncements, and draw out their conclusions, in order to show that authentic Catholic teaching could not countenance such a war. One can feel the urgency —almost desperation—in his writing. The Church simply could not be indifferent or ambivalent about the prospective destruction of civilization, perhaps of humanity itself. Indeed, it is worth noting in this new era of ecclesiastical attempts to stop debate on other issues that the abbot general of the Cistercian Order eventually forbade Merton to write on this topic.

What was Merton urging about nuclear war? First of all, that an aggressive nuclear war is immoral on the face of it (59); that a defensive nuclear war is immoral because it cannot discriminate between combatant and noncombatant (60); that a limited nuclear war of defense is immoral because it cannot be limited (88–89). The first two of these positions were vindicated by the forthright condemnation of the council: "Any act of war aimed indiscriminately at the destruction of entire cities or of extensive areas along with their population is a crime against God and man itself. It merits unequivocal and unhesitating condemnation" (*Gaudium et spes*, no. 80). Not only the council but, more particularly, American Catholicism reflected Merton's thinking on this topic. In 1983, the U.S. Bishops' Pastoral *The Challenge of Peace* elaborated on this condemnation to say that it ruled out both offensive and defensive nuclear war, since both are aimed at civilian populations (nos. 147 and 148). The bishops expressed grave doubt about limited nuclear war because it seems unlikely that any nuclear exchange could be limited (nos. 158 and 159).

One is, nevertheless, struck with how cautious in one way Merton's thinking was on the issue of nuclear war. He did not advance beyond the topics mentioned above to the more radical one of calling for immediate nuclear disarmament (89). He did say that we must pursue disarmament, but he did not condemn the possession of a nuclear deterrent force as in itself immoral. Yet, if offensive and defensive nuclear war is morally wrong, the very notion of a policy of nuclear deterrence comes into question. Such a policy is simply the intention to wage a defensive nuclear war under certain conditions. But if it is morally wrong to wage a nuclear war, then it is wrong to intend to wage a nuclear war—provided that it is wrong to intend to do what is morally wrong. Of course, it is a staple of Catholic moral thought that the intention to do an immoral action is also morally wrong. For instance, since murder is morally wrong, it is morally wrong to intend to commit murder. It is, of course, notorious that the bishops did not draw this obvious conclusion about our own policy of nuclear deterrence; in their peace pastoral they did not condemn nuclear deterrence but rather they gave it "a strictly conditioned moral acceptance"— conditioned on the assumption that it is part of a process that leads to real disarmament.

The bishops aside, one can see how radical would be the condemnation of nuclear deterrence. For the United States to renounce nuclear deterrence would be for it to become vulnerable to nuclear aggression and nuclear blackmail. From the theological perspective it would call for a radical declaration of dependence on the will of God. As a nation we would renounce what is contrary to God's will, casting ourselves on divine protection. It is the step that the bishops were not willing to take, although Merton might well have been more favorably inclined because of his perspective as a prophet. His analysis of war and the conditions that justify war required a more radical adjustment of attitude in order to become a peace maker. It required a renunciation of power and wealth. To someone deeply enmeshed in the world and its values, such a renunciation seems impossible; to a contemplative, detached from the world, the renunciation might well seem possible.

This more radical analysis of war begins with Merton's review of the prison meditations of Father Delp, a priest imprisoned and executed by the Nazis. Father Delp, from his prison cell—a place both detached and fraught with the meanings of contemporary social and political life—saw the problem as humanity's refusal to recognize its spiritual crisis, its alienation from God. Modern humans are alienated from God because they believe in their own power and in their material means to exercise that power. Merton quotes with approval:

> Either he (man) still hopes in matters (sic) and in the power he acquires by its manipulation, and then his heart is one to which "God himself cannot find access, it is so hedged around with insurance." Or else, in abject self-contempt, alienated man "believes more in his own unworthiness than in the creative power of God" (139).

We must then return to the spiritual springs of faith to overcome the illusions of self-sufficiency and to discover the creative sufficiency of God. However, Merton emphasizes Father Delp's insight that returning to the well springs of faith must not be confused with a "negative, lachrymose, and 'resigned' Christianity" (139). One thinks immediately of the seductive appeal of the contemplative life, uninvolved in the turmoil of the active. Rather, Father Delp says that what is needed "is not simply good will and piety, but *truly religious men ready to cooperate in all efforts for the betterment of mankind and human order*'" (141). Such cooperation is not, however, just enlisting in the cause of human progress, espoused by any self-respecting secular humanist; rather it is "the decision to become *totally engaged in the historical task of the Mystical Body of Christ* for the redemption of man and his world" (146).

It would be hard to imagine a more bold call to the active life. It is also one that is quite familiar to anyone who lived through the heady days of the Vatican Council II, with its stirring calls for activism on behalf of the poor and the oppressed. Merton, however, goes somewhat beyond these moral exhortations. The historical task of the mystical body of Christ is not just a neat way of summing up the liberal Democratic agenda—at least that of the pre-abortion era. There is a good deal more mystery to the mystical body of Christ, and it is war, once again, that uncovers the mystery. In his review of Jacques Cabaud's biography of Simone Weil, Merton meditates on nonviolence. Again he is troubled by the notion that Christianity encourages passivity. Simone Weil has been associated with nonviolent resistance, yet she decided to join the French Resistance after the invasion of her homeland. The problem is how to resolve this contradiction. Merton notes a distinction between ineffective and effective nonviolence. The former is simply passivity in the face of evil; the latter is a creative attempt to overcome evil without engaging in violence. Gandhi's successful fight for the independence of India is, of course, the outstanding example of the latter. On the other hand, everyone who takes seriously nonviolence as a means for overcoming evil must face the possibility that the most determined nonviolent campaign can fail to overcome the evil at which it was aimed. In Merton's understanding, Weil faced this very situation in her own country and decided "that if this nonviolence had no hope of success, then evil could be resisted by force" (233). Somewhat confusingly, Merton then ends the review by saying that Weil "did not change her principles. She did not commit herself to violent action, but she did seek to expose herself to the greatest danger and sacrifice, nonviolently" (234). Yet surely, she came to approve of the work of an organization that did use violent means to overcome the evil of Nazism. In this passage we can see enshrined the temptation to believe that such undertakings as eradicating Nazism is part of the historical task of the mystical body of Christ and that if violent means are the only way to achieve this goal, perhaps they can be countenanced in some provisional way.

In the essay "Blessed Are the Meek," Merton faces this problem squarely. Nonviolence may mean failure in the face of overwhelming evil. Nevertheless, recourse to violence is not possible for the Christian; the proper response is to trust in the working of God in history:

> The Christian can renounce the protection of violence and risk being humble, therefore vulnerable, not because he trusts in the supposed efficacy of a gentle and persuasive tactic that will disarm hatred and tame cruelty, but because he believes that the hidden power of the Gospel is demanding to be manifested in and through his own poor person (251–2).

Merton here approaches the fundamental principle of nonviolence. It seeks not efficiency but truth (325). Even in its failure, Christian nonviolence shows what the truth of the gospel looks like. In his tribute to Gandhi, Merton puts the point this way: "Political action therefore was not a means to acquire security and strength for one's self and one's party, but a means of witnessing to the truth and the reality of the cosmic structure by making one's own proper contribution to the order willed by God" (205). If witness to the truth is more important than efficacy, then one does not have to value success over nonviolence. What must be meant, then, is that suffering defeat in a nonviolent campaign to end injustice still has value because suffering defeat in a nonviolent way incarnates the vision of the gospel. If truth is more important, then resorting to violence obscures the truth—the truth that God's will is a human order based on love, not on hatred and its manifestations, war and violence.

Here we have an attitude to the world and its values that only a prophet could love. Only someone for whom power and possessions were no longer important could see clearly enough to appreciate that the essential task is witness to the truth of the gospel, not efficiency in carrying it out. It must go hand in hand with another attitude—that no matter what one's own efforts might produce, it is ultimately up to God to fulfill the promises of the kingdom. Finally, one must believe that failure as the world understands it will be overcome by the resurrection. In order to follow this way of living, one must see the things of this world in an entirely different way. Not only must we not be seduced by the power and possessions of the mighty of this world we must also divorce ourselves from those conceptions of success and failure that are integral to the vision of this world. We must give up the very notion of success even for the gospel's vision of peace if that success must be bought at the price of violence. One must believe that there is a reality behind the obvious one of success and failure and that this reality means that the gospel will triumph, but in its own way. To acquire and nourish this view of reality it would be necessary to look at our world from a place different from the place most occupy. This view of reality is God's view, doubtless; but it is one whose acquisition requires humans to be detached from the world and its concerns. Only from the perspective of a Dorothy Day, a Thomas Merton, or a Mother Theresa could this view of reality be strong and clear.

Nevertheless, to many, the difficulty of acquiring and maintaining this perspective is not a sign of its uselessness or of its deficiency. To many, reliance on that perspective is the essence of the gospel. It is hard to grasp and it is harder to live; but that fact does not lessen its hold on one's allegiance. Still, it is a hard truth. It seemed most appealing at the height of the Vietnam war. Here was a war that had all the signs of an excess of fascination with power and wealth.

The gospel vision of nonviolence seemed an appealing alternative to whatever the vision which informed that adventure. Again, the gospel vision of nonviolence seemed more appealing than the vision that saw nuclear holocaust as an acceptable means of defense. In a way it was a more demanding vision because it required some dangerous concessions to the moral claims of disarmament; but we might be able to square these claims with national survival by canny reasoning not unlike that of the bishops. It was altogether then an ennobling vision, and Thomas Merton was certainly one of its proponents in this country.

This position on war and the causes of war is one that goes beyond the just war theory, of course. The just war theory allows violence under certain, supposedly strictly limited, conditions. But the kind of nonviolence Merton was talking about was pacifism; it was the refusal to countenance the use of violence to achieve even—or especially—the kingdom of God. It seemed to be the notion that nothing could be used to establish the kingdom of God which would not be compatible with what that kingdom would look like once it was established. Here is a radical thought. Christianity has never wanted for those who admire and even love the kingdom of God as something to be established in the millennium; then we can live as brothers and sisters, when the lion lies down with the lamb. In the mean time, according to these Christians, it is necessary to live and survive in the world as it is, where the lion eats the lamb. It may even be necessary to kill in order to preserve the Church to whom the promises of the kingdom were given. However, those Christians who have said that the means must be consistent with the end have not been as numerous, especially in the days of violent persecution. Perhaps in our century, then—perhaps the bloodiest in the history of humankind—it was at last time to recapture the nonviolent tradition of Christianity. Perhaps Thomas Merton could be enshrined as one of those who worked to restore this tradition. Indeed, after his death, there was a spring time of nonviolence, from Manila to Eastern Europe. The corrupt Marcos regime was ousted by a massive turnout of street demonstrators who did not carry guns. The crowds in Czechoslovakia held their hands in the air to show that they were not armed. The tired regimes, so long reliant on repression and violence, gave way before such superior moral force.

As always, events have conspired to undermine this view—however inspirational and appealing. As long as we were talking about Vietnam and nuclear war, the issues were clearer. However, the tribal warfare of Rwanda and the ethnic warfare of Bosnia make the option of nonviolence less certain. It is one thing for those of us living in the United States to attempt to renounce violence, to put power and wealth in its proper perspective. It is another thing to counsel the people of Bosnia to renounce violence and reliance on power and wealth—and another thing still to urge our government to pursue a Bosnian policy not dependent on violence. Even if we try to filter out what the media has added to the reporting about that civil war, there seems to be enough left to outrage any moral person. If we assume that the refugees of Bosnia do not have the superior moral strength required to stop by nonviolent means the murders and rapes, for us to renounce violence as a means to contain those to whom ethnic cleansing seems like a good idea seems only to cooperate in this ethnic cleansing. Nor can we take refuge in the thought that the refugees' suffering is of the sort that reveals the truth of the gospel vision; it simply looks like another chapter in the dreary history of the bloodiest century. The trouble is that the Christian may take nonviolence to be a way to lead his or her own life; we may even urge it on our own country when it seeks to defend itself. We may also counsel nonviolence on our own country when it seeks, for its own goals, to interfere in another country—for instance, in the case of our intervention in Vietnam or in Kuwait. To others who say that our involvement was not entirely self-regarding and that we had an obligation to help the oppressed in these two countries, it might even be possible to say that the oppression suffered by the Vietnamese or by the Kuwaitis was not severe enough to require violence. As morally chancy as such a judgment might be, it seems impossible to make a similar judgment about murders numbering in the hundreds of thousands in Rwanda and in Bosnia. If a U.S. led bombing campaign will stop armed thugs from murdering and raping unarmed civilians, if the unarmed civilians are not engaged in nonviolent resistance—if they are simply pathetic victims—then to oppose the bombing campaign because it is violent seems wrong. If we oppose the bombing, we seem to have lost something in the translation of nonviolence from the gospel to the complexities of the modern age. One feels once again the pull of the just war theory—not the theory that has been used to justify every frightful war ever fought, but the theory that justifies war as the only alternative, in certain highly restricted conditions, to keep from being complicit in the most appalling savagery.

Here the prophetic role has broken down. We are no longer so confident that we know the way to go in these new times. We seem to be closer to the situation faced by Simone Weil as Germany—with its earlier version of ethnic cleansing—invaded France. In an apparent attempt to excuse her siding with the Resistance, Merton says that "her notion of nonviolent resistance was never fully developed. If she had survived . . . she might possibly have written some exciting things on the subject" (233). It is a measure of Merton's stature as a prophet that we feel the same about what he might have written about post-Cold War violence and the possibility of nonviolent resistance to it.

Thomas Merton. *The Merton Tapes: Sixth Release of Lectures.* Kansas City: Credence Cassettes, 1995. 8 cassettes (60 minutes each). $8.95 per cassette.

Reviewed by Thomas Collins.

---

1) "Belonging to God" AA 2805

2) "The Straight Way" AA 2801

3) "T. S. Eliot and Prayer" AA 2808

4) "Poetry and Religious Experience" AA 2804

5) "The Spirit of Poverty" AA 2807

6) "Poverty: The Vocation of Work" AA 2806

7) "The Thirst for God" AA 2799

8) "True Freedom" AA 2803

These tapes are recordings of Merton's talks to novices at the Abbey of Our Lady of Gethsemani during the early 1960s. Recorded at the suggestion of the abbot so that the talks would be available to other monks, the tapes constitute a remarkable set of cultural artifacts that document Merton as teacher. Through these talks, insight can be gained into the monastic subculture of the time and into the mind of one of the central figures in American Catholic religious thought.

The format of the recordings presents some problems. Sessions often start with topics important for the good of the novitiate, but unrelated to the title or the subject of the tape. A good deal of the time is "off topic." Sessions often come to an abrupt close, ending with prayer when time is up. References to topics already discussed or to be discussed in the future are frustrating to the present listener. One hopes, when all the tapes are published, that there will be some collation by topic, so that one could choose all tapes on religious vows or on prayer and the interior life or on poetry and the religious experience, for example.

"Belonging to God": This tape records an interesting discussion about prayer for the dead, especially for those mentioned in monastic chapter. The heart of the tape is Merton's explanation of how God's people come together in biblical times to praise Yahweh Lord, and how they belong to him in a covenant relationship. Side two of the tape is a related lecture discussing St. Thomas' reflections on imitating God.

"The Straight Way": Here Merton discusses the need to find a center, to keep focused, and to try to be as independent as possible of external circumstances. Sufism is presented as similar to monastic life in that in both cases individuals are seeking a certain detachment. If one is focused enough, one is better prepared to cope with change. Side two presents similar insights from Islam, using texts from the Koran.

"T. S. Eliot and Prayer": Merton stresses that modern poetry can give us insight into the meaning of life. Although some might link poetry with the emotional and romantic, the better modern poets offer new perspectives and challenge the reader to adopt a new angle of vision. Merton explicates this point with careful readings of several of Eliot's poems. Both sides of the tape are on this topic.

"Poetry and the Religious Experience": Merton begins this tape with a comment about the need for a more humanistic education for the clergy, then he demonstrates how this might be done by insightful readings of Rilke. Merton argues that the poetic experience is analogous to the religious experience. The poetic experience is an imaginative function of the intellect, creating and re-creating. The viewer or listener must contact the work of art. The religious experience is similar, but deeper. Being alive to the beauty in works of art heightens one's sensibility and awareness. Rilke, a poet of great sensibility, re-created perceptions of reality and challenges the reader to do so. The cultivated interior life should be a real response to real life, not just in the imaginative realm. Side two of this tape is a lecture on sanctity.

"The Spirit of Poverty": The tapes on poverty are especially interesting. While much that is discussed is from a monastic perspective, Merton puts it all in a much broader perspective. He reminds us that faith is fundamental. We need to constantly remind ourselves that without faith life is meaningless. Monastic poverty also helps keep the focus on essentials. Merton discusses things given to all monks and things for which a monk has special permission. He reminds the novices that the spirit of poverty would lead one to accept refectory food with gratitude, especially since really poor people in the world would be glad to get it. Novices who do not like their work assignment are reminded that poor people often have work that is messy and unpleasant, dull and tedious, if they have work at all. The admonition in the epistle of James that those who have an abundance in this world ought not harden their hearts against their brothers, Merton notes, applies to groups as well as to individuals.

"Poverty: The Vocation of Work": Much on this tape is unrelated to the title. There is some fascinating information about monastic bloodletting in the Middle Ages. The novices are given an admonition to avoid a worldly attitude toward culture and not to worry about keeping up with the latest novels. They should focus on more spiritual books. Experiences should be shared with the directors, not because they can offer the novice a formula to be adopted, but because the directors can be a guide as novices find their own ways. Side two begins with a discussion of the Trinity and the Incarnation. With regard to poverty, is it important to let superiors decide what is necessary, then accept their judgment. The spirit of poverty, therefore, renounces proprietorship. There should be no independent acts of ownership.

"Thirst for God": This is an elaboration on the theme that the central reason for existence is to develop a deep union of love with God. Side two, surprisingly, deals with a letter about civil rights and the death of Martin Luther King, Jr.

"True Freedom": In this talk Merton stresses that true freedom lies in asceticism. One must deepen consciousness and focus on what life is really all about. In that context asceticism is liberating, since it frees one from much that is peripheral and can lead to real purity of heart.

Michael Toms, producer. *Thomas Merton Remembered: Dialogues with Various People Who Knew Him.* Radio Program no. 2476 of *New Dimensions: The Sound of a New World Emerging.* San Francisco: New Dimensions Foundation, 1994. 1 Cassette (2 sides) 60 min. (P. O. Box 410510, San Francisco, CA 94141-0510)

Reviewed by Dewey Weiss Kramer

The *New Dimensions* radio series, of which this tape is program no. 2476, aims to transform the world by transforming human consciousness. As "one of the few genuine spiritual masters that America has produced," Thomas Merton clearly belongs in the series.

Producer and host of this program Michael Toms hopes to uncover the reason for Merton's increasing popularity decades after his death. Accordingly, he asks each of the six friends of Merton whom he interviews to consider this question among other matters, and concludes each interview with an invitation to express the overriding impression Merton left with each of them. This probing sheds new light on the nature of Merton's influence on latter day readers. Thus, while the tape is intended as introduction to the man and his work, it goes far beyond that modest intent.

As Introduction

It *is*, however, a fine introduction to the man and his work for several reasons. First, the connecting apparatus by Michael Toms offers basic orientation, facts on life and works, even a minimal bibliography. Second, it does a good job of placing him in his context. The connecting interludes of Gethsemani prayer give a better-than-usual sense of the monastic climate, with its liturgy, concern for the world, humor, and art. Third, since Toms is interested in Merton's status as potential *guide* for seekers, his questions draw out information that informs on an existential level. Finally, the balanced and representative choice of interviewees informs listeners of Merton's diverse roles and interests: the monk and his community (Abbot Timothy Kelly, Br. Paul Quenon, Fr. Matthew Kelty, Br. Patrick Hart, three of whom were novices under Merton); the monk-poet (poet Ron Seitz, Quenon); the metier of writing (Patrick Hart); and the tie to the extra-monastic world of families and children as well as the Merton "literary business" (Tommy O'Callahan, Hart, Seitz). These persons played key roles in his life, and capturing them on tape provides a valuable archival service.

New Insights

Each interview is interesting. But those with Quenon and Kelty are especially important. For in the course of their presentations, both men talk their way toward a dimension of Merton as he exists today, a dimension that has not previously been articulated so well.

Paul Quenon's interview begins with reference to the typical monastic day, and his reflections on Merton continue within the monastic framework—Merton present within the Gethsemani community, working for it, furthering it, forming it into a "communion of charity." Merton brought to this community "a confidence you live with the rest of your life, that there *is* a loving God. He convinces you. That is what he said, and what remains." Quenon's conviction of this on-going presence is supported, "proven," as it were, by his concluding story. On the evening that the community learned of Merton's death, Quenon returned to the chapter room and found a holy card lying there. And on the reverse side, in Merton's handwriting, was written: "Charity does not fall away." Producer Toms, recognizing the singular significance of that event, prefaces the entire program with this portion of Quenon's interview.

Matthew Kelty's reminiscence starts out somewhat disappointingly for someone acquainted with his own work. The recounting of humorous anecdotes illustrative of Merton's ineptitude in practical matters seems to belie the profound author of *Flute Solo* and *My Song Is of Mercy*. Similarly, his initial answer to host Tom's *leit-motific* question is also rather predictable—Merton is a modern man.

But then the gifted speaker breaks through. Musing on what "modern" means here, Kelty throws out phrase after fragmentary phrase of loss and alienation and suffering, the very fragmentary nature of the musing imaging forth the broken reality of the world from which Merton came and to which he turned his compassionate concern. It is a moving evocation of Merton as "the man for others."

In his final comments, Kelty articulates even more clearly the *representative* nature of this man Merton, drawing on T. S. Eliot's

powerful image of Christ present in the world. Merton was "wounded
. . ., the wounded healer . . .; who is, of course, . . . the perfect man
of compassion." Quenon and Kelty both develop, therefore, as source
of the continuing and increasing popularity of the *writings*, the ongoing presence of the *man* as real presence, a presence not restricted to
the memories of those who knew him but actual to those whom he
continues to enfold in his charity.

Skillful Editing

The placement of Quenon's "Charity does not fall away" as
motto to the whole program is an instance of the careful editing at
work here. The interludes between speakers are both graceful and substantial—Ron Seitz reading his poem on Merton, Gethsemani Vespers
or Compline, etc. Perhaps the most striking, though subtle, instance of
how the interludes further the content is provided by the one following the Kelty interview. Kelty ends with reference to absence of a
mother's love suffered by Merton. The interlude then leads directly
into Vespers, recording the Gethsemani community as it chants, "For
the mothers of all monks of this community, let us pray to the Lord,"
and continues with petitions for those various groups of persons who
are (still) suffering from and in the world. It is precisely that suffering
which Kelty cites as crucial to Merton's make-up. And it is the presence of that suffering, experienced and articulated for others, that lets
Merton lead others beyond it to the awareness, cited by Quenon, of a
loving God.

M. Basil Pennington. *Thomas Merton, My Brother: His
Journey to Freedom, Compassion, and Final Integration.* Hyde
Park, N.Y.: New City Press, 1996. 208 pages. Paper.
Approximately $15.

Reviewed by Raymond Wilkie

Fr. Basil Pennington is well-known to Merton scholars and
International Thomas Merton Society members, as well as to many (including the reviewer) who have attended his popular lectures and

read his books on spirituality and centering prayer. For more than two decades Father Basil has written prolifically on prayer and spirituality and, as founder and one-time editor of *Cistercian Publications*, he has edited the works of other writers, including Thomas Merton. His own writings about Merton (most of which emphasize Merton's conception and practice of prayer) include twenty-four essays, six book reviews, and four books. The most recent of these is *Thomas Merton, My Brother*, a collection of reprinted essays (Father Basil calls them "vignettes") that supplement his 1987 biographical volume *Thomas Merton, Brother Monk: His Quest for Freedom.*

The first two essays in *Thomas Merton, My Brother* are a summary of the 1987 companion volume and a bridge to the rest of the essays. The next two essays briefly describe Merton's journals and his circular letters. Three essays deal with Merton's intellectual relationship to the Cistercian tradition and, especially, to Bernard of Clairvaux. Two are concerned with spirituality and centering prayer and two are on Merton as educator and spiritual director. One essay is about Merton's trip to India and the last two essays trace the evolution of his spirituality and worldview.

Although these collected essays and the 1987 biographical essay differ in style and purpose, they have nearly identical titles and cover designs. They are also alike in that each includes a chronology of Merton's life and a selected bibliography of his major publications. The 1987 volume includes a bibliographic essay (as an appendix) that another reviewer considers the book's most valuable contribution. The essays have an appended bibliography of Father Basil's writings on Merton telling the interested reader when and where each essay was originally published. Both books emphasize Merton's conception and practice of contemplative prayer and its grounding in the writings of the Greek, Desert, and Cistercian Fathers. Also discussed in the essays, but not equally, are Merton's compassion for all humankind, his openness to increased monastic freedom, and his opposition to closed-minded authoritarianism in the Church. Little is said about Merton's prophetic critique of modern society, his poetry, or his literary essays.

Three of the reprinted essays (unlike the 1987 biographical essay) are descriptive summaries of Merton's journals, of his "Circular Letters," and of *The Spirit of Simplicity*, his translation and commentary on the 1925 Cistercian General Chapter. Most of the essays include extensive Merton quotations. Merton enthusiasts (such as this reviewer) will appreciate such quotations, but in some of the essays they are excessive. For example, the essay entitled "Thomas Merton and Centering Prayer" contains more quotations than commentary. The purpose of such extensive quoting in this essay is to show the essential identity of Merton's conception and practice of contemplative prayer with Father Basil's conception and method/technique of centering prayer, an effort that is not convincing.

The introduction points out that Pennington's essays were written for widely differing purposes and occasions, but does not give any specifics. It would have been helpful if each essay's context —its publication history, original purpose, and intended audience— had been included on its title page. With such background information the reader would understand why each chapter/essay does not follow (logically, rhetorically, or aesthetically) from the preceding one.

Father Basil's writing on Merton is based on a thorough knowledge of his work, a deep respect and admiration for Merton's thought, and the shared experience of being (like Merton) a post-Vatican II, American, Cistercian monk. Making these essays accessible in paperback is a valuable service. But the title, *Thomas Merton: My Brother,* is somewhat misleading and the subtitle, *His Journey to Freedom, Compassion, and Final Integration,* compounds the problem. These essays constitute neither a biography (as the primary title implies) nor a narrative account of Merton's spiritual journey (as the subtitle implies).

An additional problem with the title is that the phrase "my brother" implies that Father Basil had a particularly close personal relationship with Merton—that might have yielded unique insights into his thought or character. This impression is reinforced by the book's excessively frequent references to Merton as "Tom." To the contrary, however, no encounters or other events described in the essays (nor in Merton's published letters to Father Basil) evidence such a close personal relationship.

Father Basil exudes enthusiasm for Merton and his interpretations are in the mainstream of Merton scholarship. But Father Basil's viewpoint, and these essays, are better appreciated if accompanied (or preceded) by the reading of his 1987 biographical essay *Thomas Merton: Brother Monk* and by his 1980 *Centering Prayer.*

Richard B. Patterson. *Becoming a Modern Contemplative: A Psychospiritual Model for Personal Growth.* Chicago: Loyola University Press, 1995. 120 pages. Paper. $9.95.

Frank X. Tuoti. *Why Not Be a Mystic.* New York: Crossroad, 1995. 192 pages. Paper. $10.95.

Reviewed by Paul Wise

For Richard B. Patterson, contemplation necessitates a "movement *into* life and not *away* from it" (xii). Living a contemplative life involves moving back and forth from the inner to the outer, a withdrawal and return (69). Patterson applies the term "contemplative psychology" to the study of contemplation, meditation, and its effects, methods, and results, its "spontaneous experiences of wonder" (xii).

In chapter one, Patterson states that to become a modern contemplative (as opposed to an ancient one, perhaps), one must adopt certain stances in preparation for the journey. These stances include: (1) simplicity, not asceticism but a substitution in one's life of quality for quantity, substance for appearance, a reassessment of our attitudes about acquiring things and about the poor, and a willingness to become inwardly poor; (2) self discipline or the performance of "certain actions that may ultimately benefit us but which we are disinclined to perform"; (3) sensuality, an awakening and appreciation of the senses, including sexuality; (4) detachment, ceasing to try to control others or to desire riches, prestige, or the need to be unique (14); and (5) gratitude.

Patterson believes the means to achieve the contemplative state are "grounded in experiences that are available to us all" (61) such as journaling (in a helpful chapter that suggests writing down dreams and which explains the symbology of dreaming), recovering solitude, finding sacred places of retreat and reverence (which can include a church or an herb garden), and discovering a companion with whom to share our journey. Such companions can include spouses or lovers, friends, mentors, and therapists or spiritual directors. One of the greatest dangers to avoid on the mystical path is arrogance, thinking that one has "discovered all the outer and inner territory there is to chart" (49).

Chapter six of Patterson's book deals with five phases the contemplative movement has assumed, those of the meditator, the contemplative, the mystic, the prophet, and the clown. These phases are manifested constantly by contemplatives in everyday life. Being the meditator involves quieting the mind in order to achieve relaxation, not only of the physical body, but, more importantly, the letting go, at least temporarily, of the ego, the need to be in control, which is based upon fear. This relaxation response can be very healing and ultimately deepens self awareness and creates humility.

Becoming the contemplative involves reflecting upon the existence of others, of "beholding," suggesting the existence of an emotional response to what one sees or thinks about constituting a state of wonder. The mystic involves himself or herself with discerning the existence of God in all creation, of seeing the potential in situations, of viewing life simultaneously as it is and as it should be. The mystic also experiences the dark night of the soul, mainly loneliness and a feeling of the absence of God. Through love, however, the mystic can feel connected to all creation. The prophet is the hero returning from the quest. Often one has to deal with one or more temptations, which include burn-out, fame, rigidity and self-righteousness, persecution, and the use and/or abuse of anger and power. The clown is the aspect of contemplative movement that provides comic relief and can include any or all aspects of that individual or movement. The clown is able to integrate all aspects of the individual or movement.

Chapter seven suggests places to start and ways to begin the pilgrimage of the modern contemplative. Patterson suggests making an inventory of what has motivated and inspired one so far, such as works of literature, music, or art. He includes his own list of such works as an example. He suggests several "trail heads" or starting points for the inward journey, designed for each of the four spiritual "types."

Patterson, a clinical psychologist, clearly sees the modern contemplative as a figure who must maintain involvement with the outer world. He rejects the image of the lone, solitary ascetic who cuts off all ties to the world as a means to fasten all attention upon the ultimate or nonmaterial. Instead, Patterson suggests seeing the ultimate in all things. The "narrow way that leads into life" might include any of life's innumerable manifestations.

Patterson views mysticism and contemplation through the eyes of a psychologist. His discussion of the dark night of the soul, as well as the qualities of inner experience in general, sounds like an array of clinical symptoms to be minimized and brought under control by a positive attitude, instead of as profound disruptions that such experiences can actually be. One wonders how Patterson, as a clinical psychologist, might interpret an out-of-the-body experience or a case of "divine" illumination where the participant in religious ecstasy thought the room was aglow with a ruddy light. Patterson's book, however, is inspiring, especially to those who are more extroverted and can feel the presence God just as readily at the helm of a sailboat, for instance, as with their eyes shut in meditation while viewing the interior depths.

* * *

Frank X. Tuoti's book *Why Not Be a Mystic* emphasizes a more inward, traditional approach and methodology than Patterson's book, as well as quotations, restatements, and synopses of classical works of mysticism applied to the modern would-be mystic. He quotes extensively from Thomas Merton's essay "The Inner Experience" and other writings by Merton. Tuoti frankly acknowledges his dependence upon other sources, wishing only to "recast in existential and contemporary language what has been handed down, lived, and treasured since the earliest Christian centuries" (24). Tuoti's purpose and method makes his book seem a bit like a *Reader's Digest* of mysticism, and that is not meant as a disparaging term. He states that the book is intended for "those who are already 'pray-ers' but who have an unexplainable hunger for something deeper and more experiential" (20). Tuoti states the purpose of commitment to the mystical life is not the same as taking up a hobby such as basketball or studying astronomy, science, philosophy, or the arts, but it is to "'see' God in an obscure yet most real experiential interior vision" (23). The viewing of this "luminous obscurity" is what Tuoti terms contemplation.

The book is divided into four parts and includes thirty-four chapters. In part one, "A Treasure Lost: Recovering the Pearl of Great Price," Tuoti takes up the definition of mysticism and contemplation, two "bloodied words" (25), according to Tuoti, who wonders why we are not instructed in the "art of meditation" by the Church. He believes that without this lost art the "'inner eye' of the soul cannot be open to the Reality within it" (36). Stressing the importance of the inner journey, Tuoti believes we have lost the true discipline of the "imageless wordless prayer" (36). Tuoti believes that since the middle ages the Western Church has lost the "living waters" of contemplation (35).

Part two, "Contemplative Prayer, Beyond Words and Images," deals briefly with the nature, techniques, and discipline of contemplative prayer. Two basic approaches to contemplative prayer are discussed: discursive and nondiscursive prayer. Which method one uses depends upon one's personality and what works. Nondiscursive prayer can be achieved by the use of a mantra. Both methods aim to quiet the mind and achieve inner silence, the language, according to Meister Eckhart, that God speaks.

The ultimate form of prayer, says Tuoti, is when the Holy Spirit prays to God through the individual. This state is achieved by first quieting the "monkey mind" (ch. 12). In chapter seventeen, "Prometheus Chained," Tuoti says the cages we build for God with our own limited concepts become our own prison. We can escape this prison through "silent, wordless, formless prayer" (96).

Part three, "Night Birth: The Awakening Heart," concerns an aspect of apophatic mysticism, the dark night of the soul. Tuoti recounts the mystical truism, paraphrasing Gregory of Nyssa, that the spiritual journey is "a passage from light to darkness into light" (102). Quoting extensively from St. John of the Cross, Tuoti manages to make the same point as St. John of the Cross that the dark night really is not darkness at all but, paradoxically, greater illumination. Tuoti's description of the soul caught in such a state is quite graphic and useful to the contemplative who finds himself or herself in actual metaphysical darkness.

Part four, "Sentinel at the Gate: Guarding the Heart," outlines some of the spiritual diseases that can inhibit spiritual growth, such as attachment to the mundane and petty, needless activities, idle curiosity about everyday events and affairs. Concern for the superficial, the ordinary, and the transient is part of the illusion of this world brought about through the false self. The true self is the soul in union with God. However, one must have a balance between the "Mary" and the "Martha" forces in one's life.

In chapter five Tuoti quotes Carl Jung: "'It is high time' Jung wrote, 'that we realize *it is pointless to praise the light if nobody can see it*'" (Tuoti's emphasis, 42). If so, instead of referring to the light recounted and expounded upon in so many mystical writings as "luminous obscurity" (a descriptive term taken from *The Cloud of Unknowing*), one wonders why Tuoti, writing in the post-inquisition era of the twentieth century, does not refer to it as actual, tangible light, instead of covering it up with some kind of metaphorical significance. The light of God, if it exists, is not simply a metaphor for the knowledge or understanding it conveys. It exists apart from the understanding, according to St. John of the Cross. If it is actual light we are supposed to witness, Tuoti might be more specific about where and how we as aspiring mystics are to see it, or else state that the light is indeed metaphorical. The Bible does not say that St. Paul was blinded for three days on the road to Damascus only by great understanding or knowledge, though overwhelming knowledge and understanding certainly did accompany the light and the voice from heaven. St. Paul actually *saw* and *heard* something. The light of God is not merely a figure of speech but is beyond words, a point Tuoti would like to make against "deconstructive postmodernism" (21). However, the situation does improve, and Tuoti makes his case for an actual light more strongly in chapter sixteen, "The Garden of Night."

Another inconsistency in Tuoti's book resides in his dual condemnation of, and yet his dependence upon, symbol as a signpost to spiritual consciousness. His constant use of Christian symbology to deal with a subject (mysticism) that incorporates experience that is in no way confined to the Christian or to any other religious tradition limits the concept of universality he says mysticism achieves. Tuoti claims that mystics will eventually form a "Church of the little flock." The truth is that mysticism has always been the interest of the few, not the many, of every religion, and the Church of the little flock that Tuoti envisions where a "large number of perfunctory Catholics will defect" has already formed, only it is the mystics who have defected. The rest have simply stayed where they are, taking the symbol for the reality instead of what the symbol supposedly symbolizes.

Tuoti's chapter entitled "The Woman Who Weeps" paraphrases Carl Jung, a Protestant, who "sees the rejection of devotion to Mary by his fellow Protestants as an opportunity lost." Supposedly, worship of Mary as feminine principle, Jung's *anima*, would be good for mystics, at least male ones. But, again, Tuoti is in danger of confusing the symbol with what it is meant to symbolize, referring to Mary as "Our Lady" and "Holy Virgin," lending a powerful symbol a quality of mystery, while at the same time debunking Marian groups for excessive sentimentality. One wonders why other female symbols could not do just as good a job of playing the role of *anima* as well.

The positive side to Tuoti's use of so much orthodox rhetoric to make his point is that already mystically-inclined church members may be given insight into the mystical origin of the Scriptures. It was spirit that created symbols, not the other way around. Tuoti's book may help some Church members see through the rhetoric and the symbolism of religion to discover the living truth the symbols attempt to embody. Tuoti sometimes makes deliberate use of Christian rhetoric to illustrate his (mostly) more universal points. But mysticism is the essence of all religions, not just Christianity. One could wish that not only Frank Tuoti, but other writers on the subject of mysticism could be more explicit about what these symbols mean.

Cyrus Lee. *Thomas Merton and Chinese Wisdom*. Erie, Pa.: Sino-American Institute, n.d. vi + 138 pages. Paper. $14.95.

Beatrice Bruteau. *What We Can Learn from the East*. New York: Crossroad, 1995. 126 pages. Paper. $11.95.

Reviewed by Roger Corless

These are two very personal books. The reader who wishes to meet the authors, empathize with their points of view, and then think for him- or herself will find much nourishment here. One who comes looking for new scholarly insights will be disappointed.

Cyrus Lee is a philosopher and psychologist who was born in "China" (the biographical information is no more specific than that, but it appears to mean the Republic of China, or Taiwan), has lived and taught in the West for many years, and is currently active in inter-cultural and transpersonal research.

Thomas Merton and Chinese Wisdom at first appears to be a collection of papers read at academic meetings, but soon reveals itself as actually a series of Ignatian style contemplations—exercises of the imaginative will in which one places oneself in the context of a past event or puts oneself in the presence of a dead personality and acts and converses (performs a colloquy) as if the person were alive or the event contemporary. Those with whom colloquies are performed include, first and foremost of course, Merton himself, and, almost as prominently, John C. H. Wu (who taught Chinese Philosophy at St. John's

University, Long Island, New York, and was Lee's teacher), then the standard list of Chinese worthies—Lao Tzu, Chuang Tzu, Confucius, and, last but not least, Mo Tzu, whom most Chinese have forgotten because he taught (unrealistically, as it seemed to them) that one should love everyone as oneself, but whose work is, just because of this teaching, routinely praised by Christian missionaries as *praeparatio evangelica*.

Lee is quite open about never having met Merton, but he is unapologetic about recording colloquies with him because, he says, "I did meet him quite a few times after his death [although] only in my dreams." Lee claims that "Tom and I . . . have a lot of common interests and dreams" (2). In accord with this approach, the cover features a drawing by Lee of a very Sinitic Merton in a Confucian scholar's coat entitled, in Chinese, "A picture of the Honorable Teacher Merton," and the book closes with the exclamation, "Rapoche [sic: Rinpoche, perhaps?] Merton, Pray for us!" (135).

The question that most urgently presented itself to this reviewer was, "Why?" and the answer seemed to come in terms of Chinese Euhemerism. Many Chinese deities began their careers as humans, living lives that were sometimes humdrum but always focused and dedicated to an overall *Lebenswerk*. Their deaths were sometimes violent or occurred under mysterious circumstances. After death their presence was felt, like that of incipient Catholic *beati*, to continue in the human realm, and their forms were seen in visions and dreams. Then, it was often maintained, not only should such a spirit, whose power had shown itself, be worshiped, but (and here Chinese Euhemerism differs from Roman Catholic *processum*) the more the spirit was worshiped the more worshipful would the spirit become—because of, as it were, *liturgia deificia*, the spirit would mature into a deity, gaining, in the most famous cases, imperial recognition. Merton then, whose life and death accord with the accepted Chinese pattern, is becoming, in the mind of Cyrus Lee, a Chinese *shen*. This is a way of bringing Merton's insights into a fully Chinese cultural context, since a *shen* is more like a Catholic saint than a rival to the Christian God.

If Lee's book is the writing of a disciple, Beatrice Bruteau's book is the teaching of a *magistra* (we cannot say "master," since she is a woman, and the title "mistress" gives altogether the wrong impression). Bruteau put us all in her debt by her careful and illuminating study of the extraordinary comparisons between Pierre Teilhard de Chardin and Sri Aurobindo Ghose (*Evolution toward Divinity* [Wheaton, Ill.: The

Theosophical Publishing House, 1974]). She is the founder and resident teacher of Schola Contemplationis (formerly Philosophers' Exchange), an unofficial secular institute, we might say, centered in the wooded subdivision near her home near Winston-Salem, North Carolina, and reaching out to others via its spirituality newsletter. Based in the Roman Catholic tradition but not limited to it she is developing, in dialogue with other religious traditions, her own powerful insights into a rejuvenated, lay-centered, mystical Christianity. Not all will agree with her teachings, but no one can be unaffected by them.

What We Can Learn from the East contains transcripts of five addresses to retreatants and reprints of two journal articles. The collection is best characterized by Bruteau's remarks that "our planetary world has become so accessible" (1) that interreligious dialogue is no longer like the meeting of strangers who are exotic to each other, but is more like neighbors "entering one another's kitchens, swapping recipes, and sharing confidences over a cup of coffee" (very much what was happening when this reviewer visited Schola Contemplationis some years ago). Bruteau's great strength is that she revives the medieval approach to the Bible, honoring the *sensus litteralis* but seeing through it to the *sensus plenior,* and makes the exegesis credible to a twentieth-century, post-critical audience. She appeals straightforwardly to her audience's mythological sense, confident, as was Joseph Campbell, that they will intuitively recognize the truth both in her words and in their own deepest selves. But more subtly than Campbell, she regards myth as multi-layered, so that "as one progresses in understanding, the mythical events (including basically historical happenings that carry the meanings of the mysteries) show themselves as more and more universal and therefore paradigms of the essential experience of everyone" (111). She laments that "the modern one-dimensional mind, weaned on scientific fact and newspaper reporting . . . cares only for the putative historical happening, and either neglects or rejects the universal application of the mystery so presented" (111). *Ecce! Bernardus redevivus!*

Using this hermeneutics, Bruteau re-presents, for example, the Johannine pericope of Jesus and the Samaritan Woman (John 4:1-30) as Christian yoga (the seven husbands are the seven chakras), two synoptic logia about prayer (Mark 6:31 and Matt 6:6) as enstatic meditation (the closet is the self), and the doctrine of the Immaculate Conception of the Blessed Virgin Mary as the teaching not simply that Mary was miraculously preserved from original sin ("the limited and particular sense taught by its official custodians," 112), but "that there is . . . the unimpaired unity, still present and available" (110) to all humans.

Bruteau's weakness seems to be her tendency, despite her clear recognition of planetary neighborliness, to use "the West" to mean "us," meaning Western Christians (Catholics and Protestants, but not Orthodox, and certainly not Jews, Muslims, or atheistic philosophers), and "the East" to mean "them," or Vedanta Hinduism. (There are some references to Zen Buddhism, largely in its sanitized Western-import form, but they are interpreted, as is routine in Vedanta exegesis, as a variant of Vedanta, and there are no references to any other eastern hemisphere systems.) The book should more accurately be titled *What Western Christians Can Learn from Vedanta*—although that might not be as catchy.

More seriously, what we end up with is a kind of Vedanticized Christianity, or perhaps a Christianized Vedanta. Whether this is a Christian heresy or an exciting new development in re-presenting the Gospel in non-Semitic and non-Hellenistic terms, only time will tell. In any case, Bruteau's voice is worth hearing.

Bernard McGinn. *The Foundations of Mysticism: Origins to the Fifth Century* and *The Growth of Mysticism: Gregory the Great through the Twelfth Century*, vols. 1 and 2 of *The Presence of God: A History of Western Christian Mysticism*. New York: Crossroad, 1991–94. xxii + 494 pages. $39. 50. xv + 630 pages. $49.50.

Reviewed by Paul Lachance, O.F.M.

One of the striking and unexpected phenomena of our age is a mushrooming interest in mysticism. Initially, to be sure, the impetus came from the attraction exercised by Eastern religions, but more recently it emerges from the reappropriation of the Christian mystical tradition. This interest is all the more amazing since the religious strand of our culture generally takes mysticism only half-seriously (e.g., Catholics have been told to shun mystics and Protestants to consider them aberrant) and the scientific strand tends to repress it as irrational. Furthermore, our entire society is increasingly and alarmingly caught in a vortex of mimetic desires manipulated to seek satisfaction at their most immediate and trivial level. It is a wonder that space and time can be found for receptivity to the presence of the one love that can provide the complete and true joy that the human heart longs for.

Evidence of the lure to connect with the great tradition of those who have testified about having "heard, seen, looked upon and touched the word of life" (1 John 1:1-2) is nowhere more apparent than in the abundance of current publications, both scholarly and popular, which present either individual mystics or facets of the mystical tradition and process. One also gets the impression, while perusing libraries and book lists, that geographic location has a role to play in deciding which mystics are to be favored. In France, for instance, Elizabeth of the Trinity and Thérèse of Lisieux are at the forefront; in England and English-speaking North America, Julian of Norwich and Hildegard of Bingen; in Quebec, Mary of the Incarnation; in Italy, Catherine of Siena and Francis of Assisi; in Sweden, Brigit; and in Germany, Eckhart and the Rhineland mystics.

Among English publications, certainly one of the most significant ventures is the publication of the Classics of Western Spirituality Series (Paulist Press) initially foreseen as ending with the sixtieth volume, but now about to publish its eighty-fifth with a sizable backlog ready for the press. Two important anthologies are also available, *Light from Light: An Anthology of Christian Mysticism,* ed. Louis Dupré and James A. Wiseman, O.S.B. (New York: Paulist Press, 1988) and a more complete one (includes Merton!), *An Anthology of Christian Mysticism,* ed. Harvey Egan, S.J. (Collegeville: The Liturgical Press, 1991). On the international level, for the first time efforts are being made to provide histories of mysticism. In Germany, the eminent scholar Kurt Ruh has published the first of a projected three-volume study of the history of the Christian mystical tradition (with a bias toward the German mystics and their antecedents): *Geschichte der abendlandische Mystic,* vol. 1. *Die Grundlegung durch die Kirchenvater und die Monchstheologie des 12. Jahrhunderts* (Munich: C. H. Beck, 1990). In Italy, two likewise highly respected scholars, Giovanni Pozzi and Claudio Leonardi, have provided introductions for and edited an anthology of Italian women mystics: *Scrittrici mistiche italiane* (Turin: Casa Editrici Marietti, 1988). A team of Franciscans from Bologna has just edited and published the first of a projected ten-volume history and anthology of Franciscan mystics: *I Mistici: Scritti dei mistici Francescani: secolo XIII* (Bologna: Editrici Francescane, 1995). In France, the articles on mystical authors and themes in the multivolume and multiauthor *Dictionnaire de Spiritualité*, even if some are now dated, remain an indispensable reference. Impressive as all these contributions are for the renewed interest in mysticism none can match the depth, breadth, and boldness of enterprise (single-handedly foraging the entire range of twenty centuries of sources) of Bernard McGinn's *The Presence of God: A History of the Western Christian Tradition*, whose first two volumes (initially projected as four but now foreseen as at least five), *The Foundations of Mysticism* and *The Growth of Mysticism* have just been published.

Critical acclaim for McGinn's monumental study has been universal: "A summa of mystical thought of unsurpassed value" (Jean Leclerq, O.S.B.). Among the many other accolades, at the time of this writing, three major reviews have appeared by leading scholars in the field of mysticism: Michael Sells in a feature article, "From a History of Mysticism to a Theology of Mysticism" for the *Journal of Religion* (73:3 1993); Louis Dupré in *The Thomist* (59:1 1995); and Barbara Newman, the most rhapsodic, "The Mozartian Moment: Reflections on Medieval Mysticism" in the *Christian Spirituality Bulletin* (3:1 1995).

The task of writing a history of mysticism is a daunting one. The term "mysticism" itself is fraught with ambiguities and has been subjected to myriad definitions, none conclusive. In order to trace a furrow in this extensive and complex field McGinn, in his general introduction to *Foundations*, provides a heuristic definition: "The mystical element in Christianity is that part of its belief and practices that concerns the preparation for, the consciousness of, and the reaction to what can be described as the immediate or direct presence of God" (xvii). This definition has the merit of demarking the mystical as one element of the Christian personality or community and not necessarily its essence as so often claimed. It allows for the presence of theoretical interpretations of mysticism (e.g., Origen, Eckhart, Bonaventure) without an explicit experiential component. It departs from a too exclusive emphasis (the contemporary bias) on altered states of consciousness and paranormal phenomena, which in the popular mind are often associated with mysticism but which great mystics down through the ages have asserted represent accompanying phenomena but do not constitute the core of the mystical encounter with God. Finally, and this is McGinn's great strength, it enables focus on the mystical text itself—and its ecclesial and social context—rather than the fluid and not easily validated category of experience. McGinn's approach, fidelity to the text, has the added advantage of steering clear from preconceived theological, philosophical, and psychological categories that mar so much of contemporary mystical studies.

Foundations begins with three chapters demonstrating mysticism's roots in its Jewish matrix (the Judaism of the second Temple period), in the early Greek contemplative ideal (Platonism down through the time of Proclus), and in the New Testament and other texts of early Christianity. Even if it is beyond the purview of his purpose, namely the development of the *Western* Christian mystical tradition, two long chapters are dedicated to the early Greek and Eastern Fathers because of their decisive influence on the West. One chapter treats the complex and controverted contribution of Gnosticism and then presents some of the major orthodox spokesmen—Justin, Irenaeus, Clement of Alexandria, and the great master of early Christian thought, Origen, whose achievement is brilliantly synthesized. The other chapter of this section treats the "monastic turn" Greek mysticism took, highlighted by appraisals of Anthony, the hagiographical literature (the "Sayings,") of the desert tradition, Gregory of Nyssa, Macarius the Great, Evagrius Ponticus, and the intricate dialectics and apophaticism of Dionysius, whose theology has had an inestimable impact on the entire Christian mystical tradition. The two following chapters provide entry points into the main avenue of McGinn's history: the Western Christian tradition and how three major movements—monasticism, virginity, and Neoplatonism—affected the shape of early mystical thinking and experience. Ambrose of Milan, Jerome, and Cassian appear in one chapter, and another chapter, "Augustine: The Founding Father," is arguably the best one in this volume.

What especially marks the consciousness of divine presence in this first and foundational period, as McGinn repeatedly observes, is its close ties with exegesis, a consciousness then "cultivated within the exercise of reading, meditating, preaching and teaching the biblical text, often within a liturgical or quasi-liturgical context" (64). It is fascinating and informative to detect the initial soundings of mystical themes and formulations that the later tradition will adopt and adapt ("the layering effect") in an almost infinite variety of ways. Among the many such themes: flight of the alone to the alone; becoming one spirit with the Lord (1 Cor 6:16-17); the goal of life as vision of God or deification; the relation between action and contemplation (roles of Martha and Mary); the erotic and mystical symbolism of the Song of Songs; the soul as virgin and mother; the interlocking of love and knowledge in the ascent toward God; the role of the spiritual senses; the apophatic and kataphatic tendencies; the dialectics of presence and absence in the mystical journey.

The final section of *Foundations,* as well as so many of the presentations of various authors and spiritual systems, could easily be read as a separate monograph. In the form of three appendices (nearly a hundred pages), McGinn demonstrates his mastery of current scholarship in mysticism by surveying the literature concerning the theological, philosophical, comparatist, and psychological approaches to mysticism. These appendices provide a veritable guide and detailed map to the terrain. The thought of each contributor to this vast field is synthetically presented with an appraisal that is consistently fair and balanced along with an abundance of footnotes (close to five hundred) for easy referral. Interestingly, Evelyn Underhill is the only woman mentioned in these appendices as having contributed to contemporary understanding of mysticism. Though it certainly can be argued that women have not yet made a substantial contribution to mystical theory within the parameters set here by McGinn, their contribution, which will likely be increasingly noted in subsequent volumes, is undeniable in shifting the current agenda of mystical studies to gender related issues, as well as playing an incalculable role in the divulgation of mystical texts, in particular medieval ones. For instance, it is noteworthy that the founders of three recently issued periodicals publishing mystical studies are all women: Ritamary Bradley and Valerie M. Lagorio for *Mystics Quarterly;* Margot King for *Vox Benedictina,* and Mary Giles for *Studia Mystica.* Of further significance is the fact that the vast majority of scholars presenting quality papers on the mystics at the annual International Congress of Medieval Studies held at Kalamazoo, Michigan, are women.

In the final section, devotees of Thomas Merton will be pleased to notice a brief appraisal of his contribution, "one more difficult to evaluate in any simple fashion" (283), with promise of more elaborate treatment in the final volume. It is very unlikely, given his methodology, that McGinn will try to resolve whether Merton was a mystic or simply a mystical author, albeit a highly influential one.

The Growth of Mysticism, the second volume of McGinn's historical study, covers the period from Gregory the Great to one of the high moments of its evolution, the twelfth-century Cistercians, especially Bernard of Clairvaux and William of St. Thierry, and two

Victorines, Richard and Hugh. The hallmark of what McGinn continues to consider the "first layer" of the history of mysticism (both the
first volume and this one were initially conceived as one) is the ongoing nexus between reading and meditating the Scriptures with the
mystical encounter with God and its monastic character, that is, its setting and embodiment in mainly monastic institutions and authors.
Chapter one in the first part of this volume, "Early Medieval
Mysticism," treats the cultural context usually described as the era of
Christendom. The next chapter provides a presentation of Gregory the
Great, bishop and later Pope, who was to provide a major resource for
medieval contemplation (the term most often used then for the practice of the presence of God and the attainment of the higher stages of
the Christian life). Chapter three is devoted to a lesser known but important bridge figure between Eastern and Western mystical theory,
John Scotus Eriugena. As a sort of prelude for the flourish and volup-
tuosity of the twelfth century, chapter four mentions the contribution
of some of the minor monastic writers, in addition to developing some
of the spiritual themes that were predominant between 800 and 1100:
Solitudo/ Silentium; Lectio/Meditatio; Oratio/Contemplatio.

The Cistercians have been McGinn's area of specialization and
one can almost sense a certain palpitation, a quickening of the heart
rhythm that lies behind the exposition of twelfth-century mysticism,
which Barbara Newman has felicitously referred to as the "Mozartian
moment." *Ordinavit in me caritatem* (Song of Songs 2:4). McGinn suggests that "He has ordered charity in me" is the leitmotif overarching
this rich innovative moment of the mystical heritage. The litmus test,
he further suggests, for whether this ordering by the beloved has indeed taken place will be the *"liber experientia,* the book of experience."

In the first chapter of part two of this volume, likely the most
successful chapter so far, McGinn sets forth Bernard of Clairvaux's
doctrine of the love of God, the sublimation of eros in theory and in
practice, as it appears not only in his masterpiece, *Sermons on the Song
of Songs,* but throughout the entire gamut of the Bernardine corpus. A
subsequent chapter treats Bernard's friend and biographer, William of
St. Thierry, followed by a chapter on some of the other Cistercian masters: Guerric of Igny, Isaac of Stella (the subject of McGinn's doctoral
thesis), Gilbert of Hoyland, Baldwin and John of Ford, and, finally,
Aelred of Rievaulx, whose development of spiritual friendship *(amici-
tia spiritualis)* adds a significant new note to the monastic "ordering of
love." Even if these latter voices do not match those of Bernard and

William, their commonality, nonetheless (and here McGinn quotes Merton), "can be summed up in one great theme: the union of the soul with God" (274).

The twelfth century, however, was not the monopoly of the Cistercians as demonstrated by the authors in chapters eight and nine. The Benedictines and the Carthusians produced a host of witnesses who not only continued the great monastic contemplative tradition, but who brought new elements to bear upon it. One of these innovations has to do with an important and controversial issue in the history of mysticism: the role of visions. The question is, as McGinn puts it: "Must every mystic be a visionary? Is every visionary to be considered a mystic?" (326). McGinn's position is subtle and one that has met and will continue to meet resistance. He distinguishes three categories:

> mystics, in the sense of those who recount experiences of the im-
> mediate presence of God; mystical authors, who have not only
> had such experiences, but have written and taught about the
> process of attaining and living out lives based on mystical experi-
> ence of God's presence; and visionaries, whose visions may or
> may not be mystical in content, depending on whether or not they
> involve direct contact with the divine (327).

How to arrive at this later distinction is not clear. What McGinn almost seems to be saying is that visionaries with theological or transformative components are, in the final reckoning, the ones that are really to be counted as mystics. The true test of his choices and distinctions will likely emerge in the next volume as he navigates through the medieval period wherein visionary accounts become widespread and constitute a separate almost contagious literary genre. Arguing that "each case must be taken on its own merits" (327), here four twelfth-century visionaries are presented: Rupert of Deutz, who is "best not thought of as a mystical author" (328); Elisabeth of Schonau, "clearly not a mystic" (327); Joachim of Fiore and Hildegard of Bingen, who are likewise not to be ranked as mystics, although McGinn, along with Peter Dronke, will concede that Hildegard is of "mystical disposition" (33).

The final chapter of this volume concerns the Victorine authors Hugh and Richard of St. Victor, whose powerful contemplative systems also serve as transitions for the shift of theology to the university and the birth of scholasticism. As with the first volume, this second one abounds with footnotes, which include primary works quoted in the text appearing in their original language, followed by an extensive bibliography and indices (all told some two hundred pages). Throughout McGinn generously acknowledges other scholars who have assisted him in his research.

These two volumes, *Foundations* and *Growth* of mysticism, represent a stunning achievement. McGinn is a master craftsman in command of his field. His prose is steadily clear, but its conceptual richness does require slow reading. I have read part of the manuscript of the third volume, provisionally entitled *The Flowering of Mysticism*. It continues the quality work already initiated and should not be too long in coming. Still, many centuries of the complex mystical heritage lie ahead and one hopes that the wings of the Paraclete and the strong food that Bernard of Clairvaux says is needed for those who have a long journey to take will be provided for McGinn to complete his task. With the cumulative and "layering" effect of close attention to the historical record, McGinn, as promised, should be able in the final volume to shed important light on some of the crucial questions of mystical theology. For instance, if visions are not essential in determining whether one is a mystic or not, what role do these palpable bodily effects of divine presence play in the spiritual life? How can one theologically flesh out the interaction of the mystical with the other elements of the Christian vocation? How do concepts such as experience, presence, and consciousness relate to contemporary psychological theory? Can one successfully delineate stages in mystical growth? What is the distinctive place of Christian mysticism in the interreligious dialogue? These and so many other questions remain. For the time being, it is perhaps fitting to end this review by slightly paraphrasing the two towering figures of the period just covered: A note of gratitude is due to McGinn for so ably introducing us to those great witnesses of the direct presence of the One whose "beauty is so ancient and so new" (Augustine) and to follow up on the invitation "to read in the book of our hearts" (Bernard) the traces of the Beloved.

A Review Symposium

Run to the Mountain: The Story of a Vocation.
Vol. I of the Journals of Thomas Merton
Edited by Patrick Hart, O.C.S.O.
HarperSanFrancisco, 1995
xvii + 478 pages, with index

Participants:

Patrick O'Connell
William H. Shannon
David A. King

I

Patrick O'Connell

On April 18, 1941, back in New York after his Holy Week retreat at the Abbey of Gethsemani, Thomas Merton reflected on the disorientation he felt in moving from monastic quiet to urban bustle:

> There is a huge gap between the monastery and the world, and Louisville is a nice enough town but I wasn't happy to be thrown back into it. . . . There had been a big robbery on Fourth St., Louisville. . . . The sign "Clown Cigarettes," on, I think, Walnut Street, made me laugh wanly. There was a lot of sun. I didn't want to see any of the city, or any of the people.

The startling contrast between this entry and the much more famous "Fourth and Walnut" passage from *Conjectures of a Guilty Bystander* (1966), in which Merton talks of being "suddenly overwhelmed" by an awareness of his love for all the people passing by, in whom he recognized the divine image shining "like a pure diamond," might tempt the reader to conclude that these radically divergent responses at the same location epitomize a "huge gap" between a younger, world-denying Merton and the mature monk who was deeply engaged by the joys and the problems of all humanity.

While there can be no question of the remarkable spiritual development Merton experienced between April 1941 and March 1958, when he would again stand on this corner, a careful reading of *Run to the Mountain,* the first volume of Merton's complete journals, in which this entry appears (356), reveals that too stark a dichotomy between early and later Merton would be a considerable oversimplification. A good part of the new book's fascination is provided by the discovery of seeds and early growth of many of the concerns and convictions that characterize the better-known writings of Merton's later life. If he is disillusioned by the trivialities of everyday life after the transcendent experience of Easter at the monastery, he will later recognize Harlem as well as Gethsemani as "stables of Bethlehem where Christ is born among the outcast and the poor" (464). If he is skeptical of the agenda of a "Left wing" priest he meets in Washington, and other "half-baked liberals" (100–1), he is deeply inspired by the Gospel witness to the poor shown by Catherine de Hueck (382) and Léon Bloy (386). If he writes that the bombing of London "for the first time, made me want to fight" (245), he soon filed for noncombatant conscientious objector status "so as not to have to kill men made in the image of God" (316) and wrote passages on the inhumanity of war, on bombing of civilians and production of "humane" poison gas (264, 413), that, as Michael Mott has noted, could be inserted into *Conjectures* without changing a word. Though the pre-monastic journals sometimes express a recent convert's overly romanticized view of the Church and overly judgmental view of secular society, they also document both Merton's profound interest in and curiosity about the people and scenes and events he observes, and the seriousness and intensity of this early phase of his quest for God and for his own identity and vocation in God.

These journals cover the period from May 2, 1939, when Merton was living on Perry Street in New York's Greenwich Village, less than six months after being baptized a Catholic and ten weeks after receiving his master's degree in English from Columbia, through December 5, 1941, five days before leaving St. Bonaventure College for the Trappist monastery of Gethsemani. During this time of slightly more than two and a half years, Merton made plans to become a Franciscan priest, taught night classes in Columbia's Extension School, visited Cuba, spent two summers writing novels with his friends at an Olean, New York, cottage, was turned down by the Franciscans, taught English for three semesters (and a summer) at St. Bonaventure, and decided to enter the Cistercians. He also read much, thought much, talked much, drank much, laughed much, wrote much, prayed much, and attempted to make sense of his own life in the midst of a world which itself made less and less sense as it plunged into another war. While this is a period already well known from other writings by and about Merton, this volume provides a sense of concrete immediacy, and an abundance and richness of detail, not available in the retrospective account of *The Seven Storey Mountain,* nor in the much abbreviated version of the same material in *The Secular Journal,* nor in the quotation and interpretation of journal passages by Michael Mott in *The Seven Mountains of Thomas Merton* (though a comparison of the complete text with Mott's excerpts confirms the judiciousness with which he made his selection).

These pages record Merton's enthusiasms and his struggles, his firm commitment to the faith he had embraced and his restless uncertainty about where that faith was or should be leading, which gradually and then insistently gives way to the conviction that he belongs at Gethsemani. Not without its own omissions and reticences that must be supplemented from other sources, *Run to the Mountain* is clearly an indispensable document for encountering and understanding Merton during this momentous time of transition.

Perhaps the predominant initial impression created by these journals is one of sheer variety, the continually shifting focus of Merton's observations and reflections on people, books, places, ideas, projects, plans, personal and world events, which may receive passing or more developed comment, appreciative or critical. Nowhere else, for example, do we get so vivid an impression of the breadth of Merton's reading, both secular and sacred. Not only James Joyce, in general, and *Finnegan's Wake,* in particular, but William Saroyan and Aldous Huxley and Graham Greene, Wordsworth and Dylan Thomas, Valery Larbaud and Guillaume Apollinaire and Léon Bloy (in the original French), Dante (in Italian), Federico García Lorca (in Spanish), even Damon Runyon, among others, attract his attention and interest. His love of superlatives testifies to his enthusiasms, as when he calls *Sir Gawain and the Green Knight* "one of the best books in the world," only to add a few lines later that the biblical Book of Tobias is "even better" (243), or when he calls Lorca "easily the best religious poet of this century." Though he immediately appends the rueful comments—"I wish I could stop trying to make judgments—'best in the century' etc.," and "Never got over the sin of editing a college yearbook" (106)—this is a habit that will stay with him throughout his life, as new discoveries are elevated, at least for a time, to the status of "the best."

The focus of Merton's reading is noticeably more theological (though by no means exclusively so) after his arrival at St. Bonaventure, with extensive quotations from Kierkegaard, Anselm's *Proslogion,* Bonaventure's *Itinerarium* (as well as from his *De Septem Donis Spiritus Sancti,* inexplicably omitted from the present edition), and Gilson's study of Bonaventure, some of which, at least, reflects his studies with Fr. Philotheus Boehner (who will, of course, be a key figure in Merton's decision to seek admission to Gethsemani). *The Secular Journal* provides some excerpts from Merton's Holy Week meditations on self- knowledge, prefiguring later reflections on identity in *Seeds of Contemplation* and elsewhere, but only here are we made aware that these are part of a commentary based on a careful reading of the *De Diligendo Deo* of St. Bernard (misidentified as St. Benedict by Mott). There is a similar though less extensive use of the third book of *The Imitation of Christ* during the Labor Day 1941 retreat at Our Lady of the Valley Abbey, which also prompts reflections in which we may already detect accents that will characterize the later Merton:

> What we are—our identity—is only truly known to God— not to ourselves, not to other men. . . . The measure of our identity, of our being (the two are the same) is the amount of our love for God. The more we love earthly things, reputation, importance, pleasures, ease, and success, the less we love God. Our identity is dissipated among things that have no value, and we are drowned and *die* in trying to live in the material things we would like to possess, or in the projects we would like to complete to objectify the work of our own wills. Then, when we come to die, we find we have squandered all our love (that is, our being) on things of nothingness, and that we are nothing, we are death. . . . But tribulation detaches us from the things of nothingness in which we spend ourselves and die. Therefore tribulation gives us life, and we love it, not out of love for death, but love for life. . . . My life is measured by my love of God, and that in turn is measured by my love for the least of His children: and that love is not an abstract benevolence: it must mean sharing their tribulation (398–9).

Clearly words such as these, based on reading of original sources (in the original language), already signal that this is not the usual convert, not the average Catholic.

More typical of the journals than such extended meditative passages, and perhaps equally revealing, are series of briefer comments on an extraordinary range of facts and incidents that come under Merton's observation, with an equivalently wide variation of tone, in turn sardonic, ironic, humorous, exuberant, serious, passionate. For instance, in a single entry (November 12, 1940), loosely focused on the topic of violence, he moves from speculation that Hitler would fall down stairs or die from some inconsequential cause like the mumps, to a remark about one of his students, who "knocked out a freshman and then fell into a hedge and got a thorn so deep in his hand the doctor couldn't cut it out," to his assigning his class the task of modernizing a passage of Chaucer, which "will probably . . . do violence to their tempers," to Father Hubert's anger at the *New Yorker* for being anti-Catholic, while Merton himself is "mad at it for being anti-funny, and extremely dull," to human entrails as the only "meat" pigs will eat, to the decision not to hold the Bonaventure junior prom in Bradford, Pennsylvania, because no one could negotiate the twenty-mile return trip without "cracking up against a tree somewhere." After these comments and various other asides (such as mention of an invitation from Jinny Burton to spend Christmas in "Richmond, that drunken city"), he concludes, "This is a violent world, in which I am not doing nearly enough work, although I appear to be busy all the time" (255). Though there is nothing particularly profound in these comments or significant in the events that prompted them, the many entries of this sort typify the alert, inquisitive, often amused or bemused state of Merton's mind when it is "off duty," not struggling with any crises or major social or political or religious issues, yet not unmindful of serious implications not too far beneath the surface of even the trifling details of everyday existence.

In Merton's penchant for making lists there is an almost Whitmanesque conviction that virtually anything is at least potentially significant. His fascination with language is evident in the long catalogue of up-to-date terms (74–5) or *"Words culled like flowers from a page of George Eliot"* (364–5) or the roster of French adjectives for place names (23–4) or Spanish words taken from Lorca (104–5) or, in another vein, the fifty-five items in his list of "snatches of songs and jingles and stupid catches" (76–82) or on a somewhat higher level, "snatches of verse I can remember" (258–9). (Footnotes identifying the passages would have been helpful here and in similar places elsewhere in the volume.) He enumerates such mock-serious categories as *"Merton's political memories,"* including seeing the Chancellor of the Exchequer and President Roosevelt's mother (38–9), and "Modern Ceremonies" (e.g., the draft, opening the subway, pep rallies, etc.) (254–55), and even "Things I like about the story of Rudolf Hess' flight from Germany" (372). The lists can be of externals, like "List of Things in Boston" (259–61), or subjective, like things "I lately saw in my mind's eye or in a dream" (290–1) or the twenty-nine "Illuminating thoughts I have had lately" (312–4). Much of this, of course, is trivia, as Merton is well aware, and often list-making is part of an exercise in taking neither himself nor what he will later call "pseudo-events" too seriously. On June 28, 1940, he writes, "What (besides making lists of the vices of our age) are some of the greatest vices of our age?" (233). Occasionally, as with the May 14, 1941, synopsis of twenty-one regretted arguments (366–8), such lists do serve a purpose of self-examination (and provide nuggets of biographical information not otherwise available), but mainly they suggest the teeming abundance of phenomena that attracted and held Merton's attention and provide a rough analogue of the complex storage and retrieval system that must have been incessantly in operation in his mind.

But *Run to the Mountain* does not consist only, or mainly, in an accumulation of diverse and eclectic data, nor does it give the impression of a diffused, unfocused consciousness. The volume is aptly subtitled "The Story of a Vocation," though the reader might initially wonder if "A Tale of Two Vocations" would have been more evocative and more accurate. While the attraction to religious life grows in significance as the months pass, the intense desire to be a writer is evident from the very first page, when Merton mentions giving a talk on poetry at the Columbia Writers Club (3–4). While comments on his various writing projects are often brief, they are persistent. He summarizes his time on Perry Street with the words, "Most of the time wrote and wrote" (220), and despite his teaching duties, a similar statement would apply to his time at St. Bonaventure (and even more to the summers at the cottage, though apparently novel-writing left little time for journal-keeping, since these periods are the most sparsely documented in the volume). At least four novels, many poems, even abortive attempts to write short stories are mentioned in these pages. We are privy to Merton's disappointment at numerous rejection slips, to his dissatisfaction with past work and hopes for current projects. He records the use of "Joyce doubletalk" (149) in the early, lost "pastoral" of 1939–40, an influence that will reappear in the last of the pre-monastic novels, "Journal of My Escape from the Nazis" from the spring and summer of 1941. The example of Joyce is also evident in Merton's own predilection for autobiography, both factual and fictional; he is already quite aware of his own limitations and strengths as a writer:

> I have tremendous preoccupations of my own, personal preoccupations with whatever is going on inside my own heart, and I simply can't write about anything else. . . . I try to create some new, objective, separate person outside myself and it doesn't work. I make some stupid wooden guy. Give me a chance to write about the things I remember, things that are in one way or another piled up inside me and it is absolutely different. There are a whole lot of rich and fabulous and bright things in that store (118; see also 20–1, 37, 91, 138–9).

Given this focus, it is not surprising that the most frequent discussions of writing in the journals concern the journals themselves, a sort of running commentary on his running commentary. Though he declares at one point, "I am not going to try to justify what I am writing here" (133), he does return repeatedly to the subject of journals and their purpose, or rather the purpose of his own journals in particular. While early in the Perry Street Journal he insists that "this stuff is not written for anybody to read, yet it is practice and it is helpful and good, so long as I do not think of it in terms of its being published and read, and so a source of pride" (35), by the end of 1940 he has admitted that the journal is indeed

> written for publication. It is about time I realized that, and wrote it with some art. . . . If a journal is written for publication, then you can tear pages out of it, emend it, correct it, write with art. If it is a personal document, every emendation amounts to a crisis of conscience and a confession, not an artistic correction (271–2).

Yet a continued ambivalence is evident in the fact that he actually was keeping two versions of journal during much of 1940–41, one typewritten and more public, "the one I don't mind if people read over my shoulder in the subway," the other handwritten and "more private, more nondescript, and more religious—more personal, I guess" (375). (Most of the typewritten entries for the so-called "Brown Journal" of this period duplicate, in revised form, the handwritten entries; the handful of typewritten entries that do not correspond to passages in the handwritten journal are not included in the original edition of *Run to the Mountain,* but are published in an appendix to the paperback version.) This effort to delineate the purpose, and the limits, of self-revelation—an effort that will continue throughout Merton's life—indicates the importance Merton attaches to his journal-writing, a genre that many readers consider to be the most significant of his entire corpus, in large part precisely because of its balance of honesty and modesty, forthrightness and reticence. But his ultimate criterion is enunciated early on: "Confessions are only valid (in literature) if they confess God" (21).

The most important topic Merton is both forthright and reticent about in these journals is, of course, his vocational struggle. The reticence is more immediately apparent than the forthrightness. There is no mention, for example, of the scene recorded in *The Seven Storey Mountain* when Merton decides to become a priest after a late night out on the town with his friends. The first indication of his intention is the brief note on October 4, 1939 (the Feast of St. Francis), that "soon I will have all the necessary documents together and will write to the Father Provincial" (40), though on October 16 there is a long retrospective account, prompted by his visit to the diocesan vocation director, of the course of his efforts to that point, especially Father Ford's arguments in favor of the secular priesthood and Dan Walsh's encouragement of his interest in the Franciscans. The most evocative comment comes at the end of the entry: "But now, on top of this, the arguments in Saint Thomas: that the man who has repented of great sins should forsake even lawful things and give up even more than those who have always obeyed God, and sacrifice *everything.* Nothing was ever so near certain. *Deo Gratias!*" (60). Of course what was "so near certain" became far from certain as pertaining to the Franciscans, but Aquinas is speaking of religious life, not specifically of Franciscanism, and ultimately Merton's confidence proved to be well founded: there is an uncanny anticipation here of the phrasing that will recur (minus the explicitly penitential motivation) as his wrestling with the vocational issue nears its climax: "[G]oing to the Trappists is exciting and fills me with awe, and desire; and I return to the idea 'Give up *everything—everything!*'" (456; in a slightly revised form, this is the penultimate line of *The Secular Journal,* while there are six more very significant entries in this complete version).

After mid-October the Franciscan vocation seems to be largely taken for granted, or at least the matter seems settled in Merton's own mind. It certainly does not dominate his thoughts, at least those that he writes down; it does not seem to excite him or fill him with awe or engage his imagination in any profound way, perhaps because, as he later realizes, "there was much that was very imperfect about my motives" (461). He does mention Ed Rice's thoughts about priesthood (61), the Franciscans' devotion to St. Philomena (65), a Greenwich Village peasant wood-seller as a good model for Franciscans (70), and, eventually, on December 11, his disappointment that he will have to wait until August to be admitted to the novitiate (101). After this entry, the vocation question virtually disappears from the journals, first because he is set to join the Franciscans, then because he is not. The most significant reticence concerns Father Edmund's reversal, late in the summer of 1940, of his decision to admit Merton. It is only much later, on March 2, 1941, and then obliquely, that he writes, "I was very happy last year up to the time I learned I had no vocation for the priesthood and was not acceptable. After that the year complicated itself terribly" (315). It is impossible to determine whether Merton never confided his feelings about this rejection to his journal at all or did so at the time and later destroyed the pages, since no handwritten journal for the period from mid-February through mid-October 1940 remains (if indeed there was a handwritten journal for this period).

But as early as February 8, 1941, in one of the interior dialogues Merton occasionally invents, "Q" asks, "Incidentally, now that we have mentioned the plan you once entertained, this time last year, of you know what: How does it look now?" "A" responds, "The same. But I think I'd be a Trappist" (303). Already, two months before his visit to Gethsemani, at a time when he presumes that the priesthood is an impossibility for him, an attraction to the Cistercians is making itself felt. As late as the Fourth Sunday in Lent, March 27, he is still uncertain if he "will get to Gethsemani Monastery, near Louisville, for Holy Week" (327), but of course he does, and his life, and therefore his journal, are radically affected. His later comments on the retreat reveal that it was more complicated and conflicted than his immediate written reflections indicate, precisely because he was thrown into turmoil about whether he could possibly have a Trappist vocation himself, an idea that he is still calling an "irrelevant question" and a "futile argument" at Our Lady of the Valley nearly four months later (399). He entrusts none of this to the journal at the time, but the longing is not far beneath the surface of his awed admiration for this "earthly paradise" that is also "an earthly purgatory" (335—shades of Dante and seeds of *The Seven Storey Mountain!*), "one of the last good places in the universe" (341), "the most beautiful place in America" (347). (The old habit of superlatives is far from disappearing!) Little wonder that Louisville was a disappointment.

It is in the fall of 1941 that the vocational drama becomes central in Merton's own mind and in the journal. Though he claims during his second retreat that "[t]his time I have no perplexities about a vocation to be a Trappist—so far! I cannot be a priest" (396), if the perplexities have indeed disappeared they will soon return. On November 4 he writes, "I still think of the Trappists. And I still wonder if what was an obstacle to the Franciscans might not be one to the Trappists: and I still keep thinking: maybe I could write to them and find out. And still I do not" (449). The question is made more urgent by alternative possibilities, either freely chosen (work at Friendship House) or imposed (the army). This part of the story is, of course, very familiar to anyone even moderately acquainted with Merton's life, but the day-to-day account of the dilemma and its resolution provides a dramatic intensity not available elsewhere, even in the edited version of the same material in *The Secular Journal*. Whereas that volume ends with the portentous decision to "speak to one of the Friars," here the next entry traces the result of that resolution, the hesitations finally overcome, the consultation with Father Philotheus, the lifting of the cloud, the advice to go to Gethsemani over Christmas, the "prayers and prayers and prayers" of thanksgiving (458). And then, once the decision is made, the action suddenly accelerates as a new notice from the draft board arrives, two days later, prompting in Merton both a tremendous sense of relief that he had already confronted the issue and not given in to the temptation "to let the whole thing wait several days" (465), for a delay would have tainted the decision with doubts about his true motives, and a confidence "that, whether I am drafted or not, I may sometime be a Trappist" (466). Though in the final entry (two days before Pearl Harbor) he is still waiting for responses from the draft board to his request for a delay of his reexamination, and from the abbey to his request to move up his visit, in less than a week he will be at Gethsemani to begin the second half of his life. "The Story of a Vocation" has reached its superb climax.

And yet, as Merton himself writes in this final entry, this is still just "the real beginning of my conversion" (470), the beginning of a process of growth and transformation that will move in directions that would surprise the Thomas Merton of December 5, 1941. Two days earlier he had written, "No more concern with opinions about worldly ideas, politics, or books: they are knocked out of me: and if I may come to be a Trappist, I hope they are knocked out of me for good!" (469); they may have been, temporarily, but not, fortunately, "for good." Likewise, when Father Philotheus cautions him "to be very careful about deciding to be a Trappist" and asks, "What about my vocation to be a writer?" Merton's response is: "That one has absolutely no meaning any more, as soon as he has said what he has said" (458). But the word "vocation" here, whether quoted from Philotheus or inserted, unwittingly, by Merton himself, resonates more strongly than the author of the journal would have realized at the time.

For *Run to the Mountain* is ultimately a story not of two separate vocations, but of a single vocation with two major dimensions, coexisting in a fruitful (though not always harmonious) tension that would make Thomas Merton the most widely read Cistercian in history. It is immensely stimulating and satisfying finally to have the opportunity to observe so directly this early stage, complex in its details, luminously simple in its conclusion, in the development of a vocation that would enable Thomas Merton to recognize and to realize his full identity as monk, as writer, as image of God and, as he wrote so memorably in the (second) "Fourth and Walnut" passage, as "a member of the human race."

II

William H. Shannon

This first of a projected series of seven volumes of Merton journals actually comprises three journals that Merton kept: all of them prior to his entrance into the Abbey of Gethsemani. The first deals with his life while he lived on Perry Street in New York City, the second with his trip to Cuba (with a stopoff at Miami), the third with his life at St. Bonaventure University (where he taught for a year and a half). "The Cuban Interlude" (February 18, 1940–May 30, 1940) is the shortest of the three (76 pages) and contains some of the best descriptive writing in the book. The Perry Street journal (150 pages) covers the period from May 2, 1939 to February 13, 1940, and, among other things, his acceptance (later to be rescinded) into the Franciscan Order. The final journal in this volume, the St. Bonaventure years (1940–1941) is the longest (240 pages). It details the story of his life as a teacher at the university, reaches a high point in his Holy Week visit to the Trappist Abbey of Gethsemani, and brings the reader to the threshold of his entrance into the monastic life at Gethsemani.

Altogether these three groups of journals make up a remarkable book. In them we see a young unproved writer (he was in his mid-twenties and unpublished, save for articles in school papers and a few book reviews) flexing his literary muscles to his own obvious delight. There can be no question that Thomas Merton loved to write and was not sure from one day to the next what he might write about. At one point in the Perry Street journal he asks himself: "Why do I write so much about things about which I know so little?" (144). Setting aside the modesty implicit in the question (he often did know what he was talking about), the answer probably is: "Because you can't control your pen. Once it gets on a roll, you simply can not stop it. It is, as you yourself said 'a release for the things I am full of and must try to say'" (35).

The style of the Journal is not easy to describe: it varies considerably from one part to another. It is, I feel safe in saying, quite uniformly good writing. It can be clever, casual, breezy; witty, sprightly, dynamic, enthusiastic; frivolous, conceited, arrogant, dogmatic, overly erudite. But it is often serious, pensive, impressive, insightful, and profound. There are splendid passages of reflection that touch deeply into the human soul and there are passages of fun and humor when he plays with ideas and words and sentences and shows a sharp eye for the foibles in human nature, including his own. His penchant for superlatives is here, as it will be in his later writings. Thus, "Lorca is easily the best religious poet of this century" (106), and not many pages later: "[Joyce] happens to be the best writer in this century" (153); still later, "*Robinson Crusoe* may be one of the best books ever written" (317).

Were the journals, as we now have them, completely spontaneous, that is to say, just as he wrote them on the spur of the moment, without any emendations? Perhaps a good bit of the journals were. Yet considering the size of the ledger-type book in which he wrote, for instance, the Bonaventure journal, it seems clear that it must have been his custom to carry a notebook with him in which he jotted his reflections and then transferred them to the ledger book. Were changes made in the transfer?

This question is different from the one which the editor, Patrick Hart, O.C.S.O., asks in his introduction, namely, whether the Cuban journal (which exists only in typed form) was directly transferred from a written journal or if it was something reworked at a later date. Hart, in consultation with Robert Lax, concluded that the immediacy of the writing was sufficient to convince them that these entries were direct transfers from a journal and therefore had a rightful place in *Run to the Mountain.* I agree completely with that evaluation. The question I want to ask is a different one, namely, did Merton, when he transferred material from his shorter notebooks to the extant journals, make corrections, additions, and even do some (perhaps, at times, considerable) rewriting?

I believe the answer must be in the affirmative. My reason for saying this is that Merton had a passionate desire to publish. He tried to persuade himself that he did not. For example, he wonders whether the urge to write is vanity (35). His answer is no, as long as he doesn't think of it "in terms of its being published and read." He states very clearly: "This stuff is not written for anyone to read." These words were written on October 1, 1939. A little over a year later, on December 3, 1940, he admits, in effect, that when he wrote those words he was being less than honest with himself:

> Why would I write anything, if not to be read? *This journal is written for publication.* It's about time I realized that, and wrote it with some art. All that screaming last year, to convince myself a journal was worth writing but not to be read. If a journal is for publication, then you can tear pages out, emend it, correct it, write with art (271, italics added).

I suggest that he not only did this sort of polishing of his jottings after making this "confession," but probably had been doing it all along.

These journals present us with a writer who had a prodigious memory. In reading *Run to the Mountain,* I was fascinated by the many events of his past that he recalls, as something happening on the day he is writing reminds him of an event of yesteryear. On January 18, 1940, for instance, thinking of picnics, he recalls the afternoon at Oakham when Tom and Iris Bennett came to visit him and they went to tea, taking with them one of his schoolmates, Tabacovici, the Romanian (141). Again, he mentions a day in 1928 at St. Antonin "in which father and I ran a race up the middle of the street and I was astonished that he beat me so badly" (290). Recalling a sign he had seen on the Long Island Railroad, he asks: "What is this terrific importance that memory seems to have for me?" (58). In response we might quote back at him what he quotes about St. Augustine: "Walsh quotes Gilson or someone saying [that] what Augustine is interested in is his own religious experience: he narrates it over and over" (83).

By May 1939, when this Journal begins, Merton's reception into the Roman Catholic Church was a year and a half behind him. But the influence of it remained strong and colored so much of what he wrote. In a variety of ways he does, like Augustine, "narrate it over and over." He muses on the relationship of this wonderful power of recall to spirituality, and tells us, somewhat ruefully, that St. John of the Cross says the memory must be completely darkened (35). That would be no easy task for Thomas Merton.

The Journal is often wonderfully descriptive. He was always fond of guide books, he tells us. While he may have used a guide book for the details of his descriptions, his narrative picture of Havana, for instance, as he disembarked from the ship and entered the city, is a gem of descriptive writing. Similar descriptive passages abound. In fact, I think it can be said that Merton was better at describing places than people.

A good bit of the narrowness of Roman Catholic thought in the early forties is painfully evident in this Journal. There are the stereotypes of Jews and Protestants so typical of the Catholicism of that time. He tells us that purgatory burns with the same fires as those of hell, the one difference being that the souls in purgatory burn with love not with hate. Even the recent, quite conservative, *Catechism of the Catholic Church* has pretty much put out those fires. But Merton was writing in 1941.

I was intrigued by two unexpected omissions in the Journal. I remember so vividly from *Seven Storey Mountain* Merton's pilgrimage to the Basilica of Our Lady of Cobre during his visit to Cuba. At the basilica, he promised the *Caridad del Cobre* that, if she would enable him to be a priest, his first Mass would be in her honor. It was a promise that he kept. Yet strangely, there is no mention in the Journal of such a promise or even of a visit to Cobre. In the Journal he mentions getting only into the province of Camaguey, not to the more eastern one, Oriente, where Cobre is located.

The other omission is even more remarkable. The Bonaventure journal tells us nothing of the critical events that occurred in the summer of 1940. It was in August of that summer that Merton was scheduled to enter the Franciscan Order. Early in the summer he had gone to the cottage in Olean, and since it was crowded that June, he asked to be allowed to live at the monastery of St. Bonaventure. Permission was given and the summer was going well, until suddenly he was stricken with the fear that he had no right to enter the order or to become a priest. He had not come clean with Fr. Edmund Murphy when they had talked of his entering the Franciscans. He had not told him about his past. Father Edmund did not know him. In a fit of scruples he hastened back to New York, hoping Father Edmund would tell him that he had nothing to worry about. But Father Edmund did not. Eventually he advised Merton to withdraw his application. Merton went across Seventh Street to the Capuchin Church, where, almost hysterical, he entered the confessional. The priest was not helpful. He left the confessional in tears, all his dreams destroyed.

Yet, if he could not be a priest, he could at least say the office that priests said each day. He went to Benziger's book store and bought a set of breviaries. On the return to Olean on August 4, he said the office for the first time. It was the office for feast of St. John Vianney, the patron saint of diocesan priests.

Since there would be no novitiate for him, he had to look for work. He applied for a teaching position at St. Bonaventure and was accepted by the university president, Fr. Thomas Plassman, as an instructor in English literature.

These harrowing events of the summer of 1940 were certainly important events in Merton's life. Yet in the fairly brief entries for that summer in the Bonaventure journal nothing is said about any of them. A strange omission indeed. All I can venture is the conjecture that they cut wounds too deep for him to write about at the time, even though he wrote of them in some detail later in *The Seven Storey Mountain.*

The climactic event of the Journal is without doubt his visit to the Trappist monastery of Gethsemani during Holy Week of 1941. He was ecstatic. "This is the center of America. I had wondered what was holding the country together. . . . It is this monastery . . . the only real city in America—in a desert" (333). His journal entries are full of love for the monastic life and joy at being at Gethsemani. There are many quotations from St. Bernard's *De Diligendo Deo.* Little could he have realized then that one day his own writings would be compared favorably with St. Bernard's.

There still remained the fear that his past had created an impediment that would debar him from the priesthood. Back at St.

Bonaventure, he finally summoned up the courage to ask one of the friars, Father Philotheus, who promptly told him that no such impediment existed. He writes to Gethsemani and awaits the answer. It is on this note of expectancy, and with a prayer that he may renounce everything and belong entirely to the Lord, that this impressive Journal concludes.

One regret I must express. The footnotes are few, the index is skimpy. I presume this was an editorial policy (the publisher's perhaps?). More generous footnotes clarifying names, places, topics, and a more extensive index would have assisted the serious reader and enhanced the book's value. But, that being said, readers can approach this Journal with high expectations. They will not be disappointed.

III

David A. King

It is Saturday, September 30, 1939, a damp early autumn evening in New York City. The twenty-four-year-old Thomas Merton returns to his small room on Perry Street. He is cold, tired, perhaps a bit hungry, but he decides to write for a while in the new journal he started in the spring. "I don't really feel like writing anything much at all. Can't feel that anything I would write down would have any importance" (30). He remembers then, suddenly, that "there is one good thing to be thankful for to God: . . . found out about Saint Philomena" (30), and in recalling this "blessed little Saint, flower of martyrs" (30), Merton realizes "what excuse is there for misery and unhappiness then, when there is the intercession before the throne of God of such a saint as this" (31):

> Not only her, then, but all the Saints; not only the saints, but the angels, and above the angels, their Queen, Mary, the Mother of God and Queen of heaven sitting before the throne of God above the nine choirs and the seraphim, all filled with love and mercy and interceding for us before God himself who loves us most of all, because in Him is all love, and he gave his body and blood in sacrifice for us upon the cross. But that body and blood, that sacrifice is daily perpetuated in the churches, and the church herself is there, a great everlasting source of wisdom and consolation (31).

And at the close of his journal entry, what we might more properly call a meditation, Merton is able to write with complete joy and confidence: "And now I am glad to have written something" (31).

This episode is but one of many gifts offered in *Run to the Mountain: The Journals of Thomas Merton Volume I 1939–1941*, and it indicates several of the themes that appear in the journal, as well as throughout the more mature work of Merton's vocation. The journal is a wonderful example of the medieval mindset—live wholeheartedly in the physical world while remaining spiritually detached from it—that fascinated and delighted Merton. It is a vivid depiction, a valid historical document of life at one of the most exciting and terrifying moments of the twentieth century, a testament to the love of God, and a search for what that God wills. It becomes a kind of survival manual for the soul and for the imagination, and it affirms the presence of both, in a world that no longer attaches much significance to either. Above all, the journal demonstrates what Merton's life and vocation as a monk and artist would come to exemplify—that conversion is a process, a developing, continuous miracle.

Editor Patrick Hart divides this volume, the first of seven to be published, into three sections: Perry Street, which covers May 1939–February 1940; The Cuban Interlude, written between February 1940 and May 1940; and St. Bonaventure's, New York, the journal Merton kept between June 1940 and December 1941. In each section, the voice of the young Thomas Merton reveals itself as at times perceptive and curious, at other moments as slightly pretentious, even unsure. But throughout the journals of 1939–1941, one gets a sense of a sensitive, deeply thoughtful young man certain of one thing: the need to serve God by finding his vocation within the Church.

In reading Merton's private meditations, we, of course, have the benefit of knowing where he is headed; that is one of the pleasures of reading any journal. When Merton longs to enter the cloister and prays, "If God only would grant it! If it were only his will" (458), we know that far away in Kentucky, the monks at Gethsemani are praying for the same thing, and we know of the vocation Merton will have there. Yet one cannot help feeling that somehow Merton knows, too. "I know I want to be a Trappist. I remember the terrific sense of holiness and peace I got when I first stepped inside Gethsemani" (457). The entire journal is really a search for this; the desire was there all the time. On September 8, 1939, for example, Merton sits in his room, surrounded by the works of the saints, happy in the knowledge that "they are hearing confessions now at Saint Francis' church. Everywhere, tomorrow morning, Masses" (20). "Here is liberty," he writes. "All I have to do is to be quiet, sit still" (20). Silence. Solitude. Contemplation. Merton fulfilled all these desires within monasticism, an institution we sometimes ironically view as an escape into isolation. Yet the paradox of the monastic life in relation to the modern world is that in an ancient, separate way of life there is a greater sense of genuine community than any of us in the consumer culture will ever know. So while we often portray Merton as a quiet individual seeking total isolation from others, the journals show us a man who needed and wanted a sense of belonging, of community.

This desire to be part of the world, to experience fellowship with others, while at the same time having solitude, is a theme that runs throughout Merton's later work; indeed, it defines his work, for in writing Merton was able to communicate with the outside world, even while he was cloistered. This theme is present throughout the journals as well, and it makes for some of the most interesting and entertaining reading in the book. Merton has a gift for making wonderful stories out of the most ordinary, commonplace events, and all of these episodes in the journal—drinking wine with a peasant, attending a showing of *Gone With the Wind*, viewing the Picasso exhibit at the Museum of Modern Art—exhibit Merton's Whitmanesque fascination with people.

It is another kind of paradox. Even as he is making preparation to leave the world, Merton immerses himself in it. He has a writer's eye; he notices physical details, language, mannerisms. Though he is often critical of people, he ultimately has a great deal of love for them, and his observance of others always leads him toward a greater awareness of himself and his vocation. Consider for example the Italian peasant from whom Merton buys firewood:

> He is a very remarkable guy, to be a peasant in the middle of the city and still completely a peasant. . . . The kind of a guy that is the same as though he were still on his land with his wife and kids and his vines and his olives and his beasts . . . and is humble and poor in Spirit too and loves God and prays to Him like a child. . . . If I were to be a good Franciscan, that is, Christlike, I would first of all have to be in almost all points as this peasant appears to be . . . this peasant, obscure and dark, and silent, and not knowing much how to talk: of such were Christ's Apostles (70).

In this episode, and in others like them, Merton has a great sense of character. At the Picasso exhibit, Merton is irritated by an audience that includes an "old man, highly excited, running among the pictures like a dog with his tail between his legs," "a Harvard type, very pimply, who read out the names of the pictures very loudly and then laughed after each name," artists and intellectuals, "all the wiseguy fat people with their witty remarks," and "the 'cultured people,' the fops, the Yale fribbies and the hundreds and hundreds of bleak ugly wives of Park Avenue dentists, and the whole club of reviewers, and the Village boys" (89–91). Yet even after this diatribe, a rather mean-spirited categorization (with which we nevertheless find ourselves smiling and agreeing), Merton is capable of tenderness:

> There must have been dozens of quiet people saying nothing but loving the pictures. I am sure there were. You would not notice them . . . but I did see two girls go quietly across one of the rooms with very shining eyes and expressions of wonder and delight: they were as beautiful as anything, just because of that (91).

Another more personal episode exhibits a similar sensitivity. On January 5, 1940, Merton takes his novel to Macmillan. He imagines the man who will read his manuscript as "not any fierce expert fellow . . . not some dim-witted illiterate, with a rolling head full of teeth that snaggle and snarl at my book" (127). Instead, Merton decides:

> He is a guy who wants to be happy and wants to go to heaven and be blessed, and he wants to love people and he makes mistakes that confuse him and he gets embarrassed and he gets sick and has pains and wonders where his money is coming from next. And he sure wants to read a good book (127).

In other words, he is a lot like Merton. This kind of identification with others is crucial to the journal and may be interpreted in a variety of ways. Of course, Merton is using the journal as an artist's workbook. He's practicing characterizations, and he's working with dialogue and situations, but there is something else important about this observation. For one, Merton senses throughout this period that "there is nothing for [him] but to pray and do penance and belong to Christ in poverty, in my whole life and without compromise" (315); in a sense, then, his observation of people becomes like a subconscious kind of goodbye. For another, it exhibits one of the great paradoxes of the modern world, a world crowded with more people than ever before who have forgotten how to communicate with one another. The desire may exist, but the retreat into the self makes it impossible to communicate. Merton, however, begins to arrive at a more optimistic view of this alienation:

> The world is full of the terrible howling of engines of destruction, and I think those who preserve their sanity and do not go mad or become beasts will become Trappists, but not by joining an order, Trappists in secret and in private—Trappists so secretly that no one will suspect they have taken a vow of silence . . . we must seek silence (267).

This is a crucial realization for Merton to achieve. Essentially, in this journal he is watching a silent world, an enormous populace that, whether at the movies or at an art exhibit or in the publishing houses, has lost something. Merton criticizes and applauds the ways we've tried to improve upon this loss or ignore it all together. He attacks the futility of ceremony, saying, "All these modern ceremonies are rotten because their only reason for existing is a vague feeling 'that there ought to be some sort of ceremony'" (255). At the same time, he is fascinated by spaces, public and private, particularly churches, that reflect the modern desire for a simultaneous solitude and involvement. At the Church of La Reina in Cuba, for example, Merton is most moved by the building's ability to "communicate a terrific sense of the reality of God's power as something that moves with deep might in the most secret places of every person's self" (199).

What Merton is struggling toward in his examination of the modern psyche really seems to be a concept of prayer, a prayer as he writes on September 2, 1941, that "gives the spirit a sense of liberation and of freedom" (393). True prayer is, after all, concerned not only with the relationship between God and the self, but also with how the larger world experiences God. In this sense, Merton's journal is best seen as a kind of prayer, for it moves quite consciously through doubt and vanity and darkness into the light of the knowledge that it is only through communion with God that we "learn our own identity—truly; we finally see ourselves as we really are!" (398). Yet in the background, always, are other people. As Merton writes, "even the present contemplative orders . . . are societies where men live together" (425). It is therefore easy for Merton to arrive at the Abbey of Gethsemani and pronounce the monastery as "the center of America . . . the axle around which the whole country blindly turns" (333), for he understands that even in our desperate silence, even in our modern isolation from one another, it is the silence of contemplative prayer that unites us even when we are least aware. Yet still Merton wonders, "Why do I ask myself questions, all the time, about what I ought to be doing? Why am I always unsatisfied, and wanting to know what is my vocation if it is my vocation to stay here reading and praying and writing?" (445). This, too, is a prayer, and as Merton prays throughout this journal we are privileged to approach the same understanding he had at Gethsemani, for now we see his prayers being answered, even when he is unaware.

What Merton had to do as both a writer and as a young man searching for a vocation, indeed what he was already attempting to work out in this early journal, was complicated: he had to find a way to retreat into the silence of the cloister while somehow sharing that silence with the cacophony of the modern world. As a young man, Merton already knew that to understand the modern world and to communicate with it he could not live within it. A perfect metaphor for this realization, the same kind of device Merton would employ in the "Firewatch" sequence in *The Sign of Jonas*, is used when Merton describes his comical search in Cuba for a good Spanish edition of the works of St. John of the Cross. The episode is another fine example of Merton's talent for revealing an element of mystery within the familiar. Browsing through several different book stores becomes frustrating, in a humorous sense; Merton "laughs somewhat in a quiet scholarly way" (183) at a volume called *The Philosophy of Nudism*. Eventually Merton gives up, especially after what looks to be "a huge shiny big bookstore!" (183) turns out to be a department store. Later he learns that "there is also another department store in Havana called 'La Filosofia.' It would have been funnier if I had run into that one first" (184). The point is obvious and serious, even though it is rendered in a comical manner. Even in a Catholic country, the modern world cannot fully satisfy what the individual really needs.

Certainly, as Merton acknowledges, "The only happiness I have known in the last six years has had some connection with my conversion, and has been tied up with the increase in my belief and my desire to serve God" (137). This is an important observation, for it indicates an early understanding of what Merton would in a sense spend his life as a monk and writer defining. An essential link exists between conversion and vocation; one cannot last without remaining true to the spirit of the other. Conversion as Merton would come to understand it, and as any convert to the faith must also comprehend, becomes most rewarding when it is viewed as a miraculous journey. Any true conversion goes through some initial stages of development, however, and these stages are all in evidence here. They include a sense of astonished joy, a feeling of wonder, perhaps even disbelief, at being chosen. After the first excitement begins to decline and the conversion becomes part of routine existence, a convert may experience, as well, feelings of doubt or inadequacy. This marks the first real turning point in conversion, and it was an especially pivotal moment for Merton. At this time, a convert may reject the decision; it may become simply another interest, or even a diversion. For true conversion to continue, the convert must develop a vocation that serves, among other purposes, to preserve and further the initial joy felt upon conversion. Furthermore, true conversion seeks community; it can never be fully realized in isolation, though a foundation in solitude is beneficial. All of this, of course, applies to Merton, and it is all described within the journal.

Most readers of this essay are well aware of the background to Merton's own conversion to Catholicism in the fall of 1938, especially as it is recounted in *The Seven Storey Mountain*. There he describes his excitement following his conversion, but he also writes about the difficulty he had in making his new faith part of him. Merton was perhaps too hard on himself; all converts experience a strange kind of alienation from the faith that continues to excite them. Assimilating all the relevant theology and scholarship quickly is daunting if not impossible, and customs and traditions are difficult to absorb. A convert feels a certain degree of loneliness following the conversion, but it is a necessary solitude. And if the convert happens to be an artist, as Merton was, another kind of challenge is presented: how does the artist incorporate a new faith into a new art?

Merton began writing not long after the era of High Modernism, and not long before the new Beat aesthetic; caught between two artistic movements, and still under the spell of Blake, whose work best exemplifies the visionary nature of art, the young writer seems to sense here, even in the pages of his private journal, the need to balance form with content while at the same time attempting to incorporate aspects of his new faith into his writing. A fine example of what Merton wanted to do in his writing appears early in the journal, in an entry that deals with Merton's idea that "art is a virtue, nourished, and infused and entertained by God" (36):

> The craftsman who thinks he possesses his craft, and loses his patience and humility and love that are necessary to it, loses his art: the theory today is that artists by their own will and own supreme human understanding can be artists: so there is very little art and a lot of pride and bad pictures and quarrelling (36).

It was a difficult proposition; in prose, as Merton himself often admitted of his early work, he was not always up to the task. One notices here, in entry after entry, that often when Merton turns to a Catholic theme, he has a tendency to become overwrought and pious; he soars to angelic flights of fancy, and the end result is not unlike what one might find in religious tracts and pamphlets at the back of a church. This should not be viewed as a fault, however, for Merton does what any exceptional artist must do. The journal becomes a workshop, a place to experiment with new forms and new influences.

There are instances, however, where Merton is able to balance form, content, and faith, and the results are startling. Consider, for example, Merton's poem on pages 116–7, which comes at the end of his sketch for "a short story about a hermit" (114). Translated into English from the Latin, the poem relies upon repetition of the phrases "now let us go . . . let us bless," which lend it a meditative quality. Thematically, the poem is about the desire for silence:

> Let us walk in
> this beautiful stillness
> let us say "Ave Maria"
> let us say "Ave Maria"
> Walk in the precious stillness:
> Take up your own delicate flight (117).

It is a fine short poem, which lends validity to Patrick Hart's claim that "Perhaps [Merton's] best writing can be found in the journals, where he was expressing what was deepest in his heart" (xii). It also introduces a number of quintessential Merton themes: a desire for silence, a simultaneous need for solitude and community, the liberation afforded by prayer. All of these themes are, as well, concerns of a convert, especially when one views conversion as a journey.

Coming to the realization that one could have a dual vocation was a critical revelation for Merton, but it was also a difficult process, one plagued by doubt and anxiety. These misgivings about serving God as both monk and writer followed Merton into the monastery, where he finally became comfortable with reconciling the two, and he expresses similar worries here. In several instances in this journal, Merton is highly critical of himself not only as a writer, but as a Catholic as well. Early in the journal Merton already knows what he desires; he wants to be "a good poet, a good priest" (40), yet being both at once will prove arduous. "I am ashamed to start out talking about writing instead of writing about God. . . . I have also been ashamed to pray for my books and my poems to be published" (392–3, 396), writes Merton, yet he also acknowledges that:

> whatever writing I do is done by God's grace and only through Him: but it is a talent; He has given it to me for Himself, for use, for Him. . . . But I ask that I write in humility, knowing that I am nothing, that all my desire to write comes from God's grace. . . . Once I have written what I have written, what have I to ask, what is there left, except that the writings be disposed of according to God's will. . . . I would pray to be the best writer of a certain time and never to know it, and to be also the most obscure (397).

This is a beautiful example of the struggle Merton faced in being torn between the two things he loved the most, and it is typical of the journal in that even after writing what is essentially a prayer, even after reaching what seems to be a reconciliation, Merton thinks the very next day, "I am disgusted to read myself writing like an ascetic when I have never suffered anything or denied myself anything . . . what I have written is cheap and sloppy and, compared with what I want to say, phony" (401).

Of course, Merton is being unrealistic. He's comparing himself with Thomas á Kempis, and while such comparisons may be valuable for a young writer, in Merton's case they are often damaging. In praying that God strip away his pride and make him humble, Merton worries, "I wish I could write it better out of respect for God . . . it would be better to write about it in good words, not cheap words. . . . Holy Father, pray that I may write simply and straight anything I ever have to write, that no dishonor come to God through my writing rubbish about him" (406).

Almost a month later Merton writes, "The purest activity is contemplation" (425). It marks a tremendous step forward in his conversion, for he is beginning to sense how he might be a writer as well as a Trappist. Self knowledge has failed him:

> The one thing that most appals me is my own helplessness and stupidity: a helplessness and stupidity that come from a complete and total and uncompromising self reliance that, to the world,

appears to be a virtue in me, and a great source of strength! What a lie and what a crazy deception that is: to be self reliant is to be strong and smart: to be self reliant will get you through all your problems, without too much difficulty or anguish (456).

Merton comes, then, to the realization that only God can assist him: "In a question like that of a vocation the danger is met with faith and patience and humility and love and constant prayer, and in time the answer comes clear" (448).

It is a moment of recognition that all converts, indeed any person of faith, must come to repeatedly; Merton reaches it here for the first time. Yet as soon as he seems to have peace, he arrives at the next paradox. At Gethsemani Merton thinks:

> there will be no more future—not in the world, not in geography, not in travel, not in change, not in variety, conversations, new work, new problems in writing, new friends, none of that: but a far better progress, all interior and quiet!!! If God only would grant it! If it were only his will (458).

Isolation is valuable, especially for a convert. It affords time to think, to pray, to meditate. Yet, as Merton knows, "we reach contemplation, it seems, through acts of our own. But the strength to carry out those acts, and their success, depend on God's grace and His will. What are the acts His will drives us to do? . . . acts of love" (425).

Reading this early journal, we have the benefit of knowing what happens. We know that Merton's decision to enter the monastery was not an escape, but a new beginning, an entrance into a true community that understood more about love and sacrifice and commitment than the modern world will ever comprehend. We know that in his silence, he was able to speak volumes and that his life's work was always an act of love. It took time, of course, for Merton to achieve a true total resignation to the will of God, but at the end of *Run to the Mountain* it is clear he has made the right beginning: "Lord, how little I am! How little I know! . . . Lord! You have left the real beginning of my conversion until now!" (470).

Run to the Mountain, the first volume of a series for which we have waited over twenty-five years, is a gift that promises to be of permanent value to Merton scholars and readers. As a journal, it is of course unpolished. Yet while the entries here were meant as private meditations, the journal is not entirely personal. In these pages, one realizes that Merton was already beginning to formulate what he wanted to say to the world. The book is filled with "opinions, judgments, arguments" (365) that are often irritating, but we must be patient with Merton as he gradually comes to the understanding, "What does a man want with opinions, if he has beliefs? And if he has beliefs, what is there to argue about?" (365). *Run to the Mountain* should be read as Merton wrote it—as the chronicle of a conversion. Here are the first tentative steps of the journey of the greatest spiritual writer of our time; here too, then, are the pathways of our own individual journeys.

Editor's Response

First, I want to thank the three reviewers of *Run to the Mountain* for their careful reading and insightful critique of this first volume of the Merton Journals. All three are eminently qualified since they have steeped themselves in the writings of Thomas Merton and write from years of experience. It is clear to me that they have all read the book with serious attention and so I want to respond in like manner.

Patrick O'Connell's textual critique was wisely chosen to lead off the symposium since it sets the stage in depth for what follows. I agree with his conclusions for the most part. At one point he mentions in parenthesis that it would have been helpful to have more footnotes, especially in identifying passages like the poetic lines from Lorca or words from George Eliot or Merton's list of "snatches of verse I can remember." This is an understandable criticism, and ideally it should have been done. But in actual fact, the publisher, HarperSanFrancisco, made it clear to all the editors of the Merton Journals that in this trade edition there would be a minimum of footnotes allowed. What was asked of us was to provide a readable text much as Merton himself had done in publishing excerpts from the journals over the years, except in this case all the extant journals would be published in sequence.

It is pointed out in this review that several passages were omitted from the first edition, especially the four transcriptions from the so-called "Brown Journal." This was an unavoidable omission since I was unaware of the existence of these entries when I did my research at St. Bonaventure's Library. They only surfaced after the publication of *Run to the Mountain*. I am happy to say that they have been included in the paperback edition of the work, along with several more pages that were discovered by Patrick O'Connell during the year following publication. (See my article in this volume, "Editing the Journals of Thomas Merton.")

Fr. William Shannon brings up the question of the authenticity of some of the transcriptions of the Merton Journal, and he raises a valid point. Not having the actual holographic journal, it cannot be proven with absolute certainty that what we have is actually the original version Merton wrote. There is always a possibility that the transcriptions may have been rewritten or improved upon. That was the main reason for having Robert Lax go over the manuscript with me page by page. What we had left out among the transcriptions were passages that we considered a second or even third redaction of the original text included in *Run to the Mountain*.

Again, this reviewer would like to see more footnotes and a more comprehensive index, to which I must agree. As mentioned above, the publisher set down some rather strict guidelines about footnotes, saying we should keep footnotes to a bare minimum: "We don't want these journals to resemble a German doctoral dissertation with more footnotes than text." Likewise, the publisher provided the index, over which the individual editors had little control. This is an area that should be corrected in the paperback editions that are projected for the entire series.

Finally, a word of thanks to David King for his thoughtful comments with which I am in total agreement. I am grateful for his reflections on Merton as a young convert, and how his writings were significantly influenced by the conversion experience. I feel very fortunate that this first volume of the Merton Journals is reviewed by such distinguished and qualified Merton scholars.

Patrick Hart, O.C.S.O.

Contributors

Kimberly F. Baker, M.Div., is Dean of Students at St. Catherine College in Springfield, Kentucky.

Christopher C. Burnham, Professor of English at New Mexico State University, serves as Associate Head, Writing Program Director, and Essay Editor for the Literary magazine *Puerto del Sol*.

Thomas Collins is Principal of the St. Thomas More Parish School in Decatur, Georgia. He is active in educational matters at the local, regional, and national levels and holds a doctoral degree from the University of Iowa.

Roger Corless has academic degrees in and institutional affiliation with the Buddhist and Christian traditions and attempts to study them individually and in their interaction as a participant observer. The author of four books, including *The Vision of Buddhism*, and fifty articles, he is Professor of Religion at Duke University, Durham, North Carolina.

Thomas Del Prete, author of *Thomas Merton and the Education of the Whole Person*, is Associate Director of the Hiatt Center for Urban Education at Clark University in Worcester, Massachusetts, and President-Elect of The International Thomas Merton Society.

Michael Downey is Professor of Systematic Theology and Spirituality at Saint John's Seminary, Camarillo, California. His most recent book is *Understanding Christian Spirituality*.

Robert Faricy, a member of the Society of Jesus, is Professor of Theology at the Pontifical Gregorianum University in Rome.

Duane K. Friesen is Professor of Bible and Religion at Bethel College in Newton, Kansas.

Patrick Hart, O.C.S.O., a monk of the Abbey of Gethsemani since 1951, was Thomas Merton's last secretary and has edited numerous books by and about Merton. He is general editor of the seven-volume series of the Merton Journals and editor of *Run to the Mountain*.

George A. Kilcourse, Jr., is Professor of Theology at Bellarmine College and the author of *Ace of Freedoms: Thomas Merton's Christ*.

David King teaches at Kennesaw State College in Georgia and is working toward a Ph.D. in English at Georgia State University. His poetry appeared most recently in *Concepts* and *The Southern Poetry Review*.

Dewey Weiss Kramer teaches at DeKalb College in Atlanta. Currently she is serving as a board member of The International Thomas Merton Society (1996–1998). She writes on women's spirituality and monasticism.

Victor A. Kramer is Professor of English at Georgia State University and the editor of the fourth volume of the Merton Journals, *Turning Toward the World*.

Ross Labrie, Professor of English at the University of British Columbia, Vancouver, is the author of *The Art of Thomas Merton* and a member of the board of directors of The International Thomas Merton Society.

Paul Lachance, O.F.M., is involved in hospital ministry in Chicago and has written widely on Franciscan and Christian spirituality. His edition *Angela of Foligno: Complete Works* has been published as part of the Paulist Press Classics of Western Spirituality Series. He is the co-translator of a dozen books.

Patrick O'Connell is Professor of English at Gannon University in Erie, Pennsylvania. Presently he is President of The International Thomas Merton Society. He writes a column for *Living Prayer* and is the editor for the fifth volume of Henry David Thoreau's *Journal*.

Dennis Patrick O'Hara, a chiropractor and naturopath, is a Ph.D. candidate at the University of St. Michael's College in Toronto, where he is Assistant to the Director of the Elliott Allen Institute for Theology and Ecology. His Ph.D. dissertation is entitled "The Implications of Thomas Berry's Cosmology upon an Adequate Understanding of the Spiritual Dimension of Human Health."

Richard D. Parry is Fuller E. Callaway Professor of Philosophy at Agnes Scott College in Atlanta, Georgia. He is author of *Plato's Craft of Justice* and several articles on Plato's philosophy.

Paul M. Pearson, librarian at University College, London, completed his Ph.D. dissertation on the autobiographical metaphors of Thomas Merton at Heythrop College, London University. He is Secretary of the Thomas Merton Society of Great Britain and Ireland and a frequent contributor to Merton conferences in Europe and the United States.

Clare Ronzani is Co-Director of the Institute for Spirituality and Worship at the Jesuit School of Theology in Berkeley, California. In addition to teaching courses in spirituality and liberation, she conducts classes, retreats, and workshops on Thomas Merton.

William H. Shannon, Professor Emeritus at Nazareth College in Rochester, New York, is the author of *Seeds of Peace: Contemplation and Non-Violence* and *Something of a Rebel: The Life and Works of Thomas Merton: An Introduction.*

Glenn Stassen, Lewis B. Smedes Professor of Christian Ethics at Fuller Theological Seminary, is the author of *Just Peacemaking.*

Margaret O'Brien Steinfels is the Editor of *Commonweal* magazine.

Ronald Stone is John Witherspoon Professor of Christian Ethics at Pittsburgh Theological Seminary.

Raymond Wilkie is a native of Kentucky and Professor Emeritus of Psychology and Education at the University of Kentucky, Lexington. He is involved in Merton seminars at Gethsemani Abbey and in Lexington.

Paul Wise is a graduate student at Georgia State University in Atlanta.

John Wu, Jr., of Taipei, Taiwan, Republic of China, has been a regular speaker at Merton conferences and has published essays on Merton and the Asian spiritual traditions.

Index

THE MERTON ANNUAL

Studies in Culture, Spirituality, and Social Concerns

THE MERTON ANNUAL publishes articles about Thomas Merton and about related matters of major concern to his life and work. Its purpose is to enhance Merton's reputation as a writer and monk, to continue to develop his message for our times, and to provide a regular outlet for substantial Merton-related scholarship. *THE MERTON ANNUAL* includes as regular features reviews, review-essays, a bibliographic survey, interviews, and first appearances of unpublished, or obscurely published, Merton materials, photographs, and art. Essays about related literary and spiritual matters will also be considered. Manuscripts and books for review may be sent to any of the editors.

EDITORS

Michael Downey
Saint John's Seminary
Camarillo, CA 93012-2598

George A. Kilcourse
Theology Department
Bellarmine College
2001 Newburg Road
Louisville, KY 40205-0671

Victor A. Kramer
English Department
Georgia State University
University Plaza
Atlanta, GA 30303-3083

Volume editorship rotates on a yearly basis.

ADVISORY BOARD

1941-25

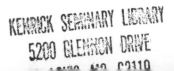